ON COMBAT

ON COMBAT

The Psychology and Physiology of Deadly Conflict in War and in Peace

by Lt. Col. Dave Grossman

with

Loren W. Christensen

Warrior Science Publications

Third Edition

Library of Congress Cataloging-in-Publication Data

Grossman, Dave.
On Combat: The Psychology and Physiology of Deadly Conflict in
War and in Peace / Dave Grossman.—3rd ed.

10   9   8   7   6   5   4

Printed on Recycled Paper

Published in the United States of America by Warrior Science Publications

A Dedication

To "The Fighting Man"

"Into Battle"

. . . And life is colour and warmth and light,
And a striving evermore for these;
And he is dead who will not fight;
And who dies fighting has increase.

The fighting man shall take from the sun
Take warmth, and life from the glowing earth;
Speed with the light-foot winds to run,
And with the trees to newer birth;
And find, when fighting shall be done,
Great rest, and fullness after dearth.

The blackbirds sing to him, "Brother, brother,
If this be the last song you shall sing,
Sing well, for you may not sing another;
Brother, sing."

. . . And when the burning moment breaks,
And all things else are out of mind,
And only joy of battle takes
Him by the throat, and makes him blind.

. . . The thundering line of battle stands,
And in the air death moans and sings;
But Day shall clasp him with strong hands,
And Night shall fold him in soft wings.

—Julian Grenfell

Contents

Contents

Acknowledgments

A Humble Shrine

> Your monument shall be my gentle verse,
> Which eyes not yet created shall o'er-read,
> And tongues to be your being shall rehearse
> When all the breathers of this world are dead.
>
> —Shakespeare
> *Sonnet lxxxi*

I am on the road nearly 300 days a year training military units, such as the Green Berets, Rangers, Marines, fighter pilots and many others, and law enforcement officers, including the FBI, ATF, SWAT, CHP, and RCMP, about the psychology and physiology of combat. It is a great job and I am honored and humbled to do it. I teach them and then they teach me, in an endless, ever refining feedback loop. I coined the term "The Bulletproof Mind" to describe the ever-evolving body of material that I teach these warriors. The audio tape/CD by the same title has become a top national best seller in the law enforcement community in the United States.

I cannot fully communicate my appreciation to all the law enforcement officers, soldiers and others who have been willing to share the intimate details of their combat experiences with me. They have given me the narratives and the data that forms the heart of this book.

We are truly pioneers in this new field of "Warrior Science™" (used with permission of Bruce Siddle) Like explorers on a vast new continent, we can identify the general outline of the coasts, some key rivers and a few major mountain ranges. Some of what we think we know will be subject to refinement and development in the years to come. Yet, for all our current limitations, I sincerely believe that future generations will look back on this as a renaissance. Men have been at war for millennia, but only today have we discovered, or been willing to talk about, the reality of combat. Now we are learning about auditory exclusion (for most people in combat, the shots get quiet), slow motion time, tunnel vision, loss of bowel and bladder control, and posttraumatic response.

Nietzsche said: "The value of many men and books rests . . . on their faculty for compelling all to speak out the most hidden and intimate things." The goal of this book is to seek out those hidden facts and intimate things, so that we can send warriors into battle who are forewarned and forearmed. As Shakespeare put it, "All things are ready, if our minds be so."

This book is different from my previous one, *On Killing*, in that it is more focused toward empowering warriors to participate in the toxic, corrosive, destructive environment of combat. Today, more than ever, we need virtuous, competent warriors to serve in our military, law enforcement and many other fields. It is my hope that this book can assist them.

Still, I hope that there is much in this book that will be of service to the gentle, decent and discerning spirits in the peace movement who have been able to use *On Killing* to study and understand the nature of the battlefield. As I said in *On Killing*, our objective must be: " . . . no judgment, no condemnation, just the remarkable power of understanding."

As Chaplain Fred LaMotte put it:

> Don't judge, just observe from a quiet witnessing awareness, and the illusions will dissolve. Just let the research and the warriors' words speak for themselves.

Loren Christensen and I are warriors, but we have struggled to craft the words that will communicate our respectful acknowledgment of the views of others. Our goal is to avoid bruising the spirit of the gentle warrior who seeks to understand combat, while still helping to steel the hearts of those who must go into combat. In the words of Alexander Pope:

> Cursed be the verse, how well so e'er it flow,
> That tends to make one worthy man my foe.

Knowing the truth about combat is of value to warriors, to citizens who rely upon warriors, and to those in power who send warriors into battle. Combat is not antiseptic or dry, it is just the opposite: a septic, toxic realm, wet with tears and blood. And the more we understand this, the more likely we will be to explore other options for resolving conflict. May these words be of some small service in such worthy endeavors.

None of this information would be available without the pioneering work of my fellow warrior scientists (many of whom I recognize in this book) and, most importantly, the constant, daily feedback given to me by literally thousands of warriors in the decade since the release of *On Killing*. Again, I cannot thank them enough, and throughout this book I have tried to prove myself worthy of their trust. This work does not belong to me. It belongs to them.

Many of the incidents I relate in this book involved the loss of lives: the lives of friends lost in combat and lives taken in the line of duty. One Vietnam veteran wrote a note and attached it to a tattered old photo that depicted a young

North Vietnamese soldier and a beautiful little girl. He had taken it from the wallet of a man he had killed in battle. Two decades later, the veteran laid the picture and this note at the base of Vietnam Veterans' Memorial in Washington, D.C.:

> For 22 years I have carried your picture in my wallet. I was only 18 years old that day that we faced one another on that trail in Chu Loi, Vietnam. Why you didn't take my life I'll never know. You stared at me for so long, armed with your AK-47, and yet you did not fire. Forgive me for taking your life, I was reacting the way I was trained to kill V.C . . . So many times over the years I stared at your picture, and your daughter, I suspect. Each time my heart and guts would burn with the pain and guilt. I have two daughters myself now . . . I perceive you as a brave soldier defending his homeland. Above all else, I can now respect the importance that life held for you. I suppose that is why I am able to be here today . . . It is time for me to continue the life process and release my pain and guilt. Forgive me, Sir.
>
> *Offerings at the Wall*

May this book be a humble shrine to all the young warriors across the centuries. We will never know those countless young men and women who went willingly into the heart of darkness, into the toxic, corrosive, destructive realm of combat. This is my humble shrine to them, and to all the young men and women who do so now, and to those who will go in the years to come. The least we owe them is to understand the nature of combat and to truly understand what we are asking them to do.

Dave Grossman
Lieutenant Colonel, U.S. Army (ret.)
www.warriorscience.com

with

Loren W. Christensen
www.lwcbooks.com

A Brief Note on Gender

The words of combat and most combat narratives lend themselves to male examples and male gender. There are significant exceptions to this rule—some magnificent female warriors are presented in this book—but in general the authors will use the male gender. This is in no way intended to exclude females from the uncertain honors of combat.

Gavin de Becker

Gavin de Becker is widely regarded as our nation's leading expert on the prediction and management of violence. He is a best-selling author whose first book, *The Gift of Fear*, spent four months on the *New York Times* bestseller list. His current book is *Fear Less: Real Truth About Risk, Safety, and Security in a Time of Terrorism*. His books have been published in 13 languages. Gavin is the designer of threat assessment systems used by the U.S. Supreme Court, the U.S. Marshals Service, and the CIA. He was twice appointed to the President's Advisory Board at the U.S. Department of Justice, and he served two terms on the Governor's Advisory Board at the California Department of Mental Health. He is co-founder and former Chair of Victory Over Violence, the Domestic Violence Council Advisory Board. He is a Senior Fellow at UCLA's School of Public Policy and Social Research, and an activist for families affected by violence, appearing several times as a guest on the *Oprah Winfrey Show*, *60 Minutes*, *Larry King Live*, *20/20*, and in the pages of *Time*, *Newsweek*, the *New York Times*, and many others. He is a Senior Advisor to the Rand Corporation on public safety and justice matters. (www.gavindebecker.com)

Foreword

by **Gavin de Becker**

Dave Grossman is the leading expert in a subject nearly all people recoil from. It is also a subject people run toward every day: killing.

Readers of Dave's classic book, *On Killing,* experienced something rare: an unobstructed glimpse into what we are and how we function—at our best and our worst. We are compassionate and violent; we are humane and animalistic; we are protectors and killers.

No other book had ever so completely set aside politics and judgment, and revealed so effectively—in precise scientific detail—what happens when one human being kills another.

For soldiers and police officers, Dave's work changed everything. *On Killing* became a central resource at the FBI Academy, at West Point, at hundreds of police departments and military organizations, and at universities like Berkeley. *On Killing* was also nominated for a Pulitzer Prize.

Now, how do you make West Point, the FBI Academy, and Berkeley all happy with the same book? Well, you just tell the truth.

And that's what Dave Grossman does.

Now, in *On Combat,* Dave Grossman and Loren Christensen pioneer beyond the old horizons of history, psychology, and physiology, and bring back critical new insight. This book will fascinate readers of all types, its insights perhaps most interesting to military leaders, psychologists, scholars, and statesmen—but for warriors, much more is at stake than mere information: Warriors will learn how to keep going even if shot, and how to prepare the mind and body for survival instead of defeat. Thus, the teachings in this book amount to modern armor.

Police officers and soldiers already know a lot about maintaining physical readiness, but it is the mind that must first be properly prepared, the mind that controls the hands, arms, eyes, and ears. *On Combat* shows us how the body responds to lethal combat, what happens to your blood flow, your muscles, your judgment, your memory, you vision and your hearing when someone is trying to kill you. And you'll learn what it's really like to kill another human being, what you'd feel right after you shoot someone, and what you'd feel an hour later, a day later, a year later.

Dave teaches police officers and soldiers that, "Just as a fireman has to know all about fire, you have to know all about violence." Indeed, warriors have gained great knowledge about violence, but many gained it while in danger. And far too many didn't survive the lethal academy of combat. This book makes all past warriors our teachers. One interesting lesson is that our bodies sometimes have more wisdom about combat than our minds.

We have a brain that was field-tested millions of years ago in the wild. I call it the wild brain to distinguish it from the logic brain so many people revere. The logic brain can't do much for you once the situation becomes critical. The logic brain is plodding and unoriginal. It is burdened with judgment, slow to accept reality, and spends valuable energy thinking about how things ought to be, used to be, or could be. The logic brain has strict boundaries and laws it wants to obey, but the wild brain obeys nothing, conforms to nothing, answers to nobody, and will do whatever it takes. It is unfettered by emotion, politics, politeness, and as illogical as the wild brain may sometimes seem, it is, in the natural order of things, completely logical. It just doesn't care to convince us of anything by using logic. In fact, during combat, the wild brain doesn't give a damn what we think.

Ideally, the wild brain helps us to receive the most powerful asset nature has given us: intuition. The root of the word intuition, *tuere*, means "to guard and to protect," and that's exactly what it can do for us—particularly if prepared with accurate and relevant information.

For example, courage is usually the star in war stories, but fear too does great things in combat. Fear readies the body for action by increasing blood flow in the arms and legs. Lactic acid is heated in the muscles, and our breathing and heartbeat become more determined. Most people know about adrenaline, but fear provides another amazing chemical to increase our chances of survival: cortisol. This one helps the blood clot more quickly, just in case we are cut.

The body can also react to combat in ways that are not at all helpful. Warriors might experience impairments to vision, judgment, and hearing, or they might experience reduced motor skills—and they likely will experience all this during violence—unless the mind and body are integrated. That's where *On Combat* makes its greatest contribution. By the act of teaching warriors what to expect, Dave and Loren have given a whole new resource to those we ask to fight on our behalf, and it isn't only enhanced fighting ability. Knowing how to tame and manage the sometimes counterproductive reactions of the body, many more warriors will have the presence of mind to avoid combat altogether. They'll be able to make choices rather than merely hold on to the physiological roller coaster during combat.

The concepts in this book will soon reach millions of police officers and soldiers around the world, and I am grateful for the opportunity to say what you'll want to say just a few pages from now: Thank you, Dave and Loren, for this profound gift.

—Gavin de Becker

Introduction

The New Warriors, the New Paladins

Until technology enables me to handcuff you from afar, I will need to arrest you, face-to-face, man-to-man. This means that, when we fight, when I call upon those elements of the warrior within, I will be close enough to smell you, to touch you, to strike you, to cut you, to hear you, to plead with you, to wrestle with you, to shoot you, to handcuff you, to bleed on you and you on me, to tend to your wounds, to hear your last words. Our meeting may be brief, but I will have had a more intense contact with you, my unwanted adversary, than with most of my loved ones.

—Scott Mattison, Chief Deputy
Swift County Sheriff's Dept, Benson, MN

If you are in a war, you are a warrior. Is there a war on drugs? Is there a war on crime? Is there a war against terrorism? Are you confronting and containing aggression as a peace officer at home, a peacekeeper in some distant land, or a warrior combating terrorism around the world? Or perhaps you have chosen to be a martial arts practitioner or an armed citizen, seeking to defend yourself or your loved ones in their hour of need? Are there people who wake up every morning determined to send you back to your family in a box?

Then you are in a war and you are a warrior.

There are only two kinds of people once the bullets start to fly: warriors and victims, those who fight and those who are unprepared, unable or unwilling to defend themselves. Since you chose to pick up this book, I assume that you walk the warrior's path.

Today the peacekeepers and the peace officers are moving toward each other. Around the world, warriors in blue (police and other peace officers) and warriors in green (soldiers, marines and other peacekeepers) find themselves facing the same kind of missions.

Increasingly, the police must face organized opponents armed with assault rifles and bombs. Indeed, they may very well face deliberate acts of war from international terrorists. In response, police have begun to carry assault rifles and call upon Special Weapons and Tactic (SWAT) teams.

Meanwhile, the military is finding that the use of artillery and air strikes in peacekeeping and counterterrorism missions can be counterproductive, and that it can be more effective to use small teams on a "beat" or checkpoint. In Bosnia and New York, Iraq and Los Angeles, and Afghanistan and Littleton, Colorado, the police are becoming more like the military in equipment, structure and tactics, while the military is becoming more like the police in equipment, missions and tactics.

A New War at Home: Record Crime and Terrorism

Despite our wonders and greatness, we are a society that has experienced so much social regression, so much decadence, in so short a period of time, that in many parts of America we have become the kind of place to which civilized countries used to send missionaries.

—William J. Bennett

In addition to the threat of domestic terrorism (such as the Oklahoma City bombing, which is the all-time record domestic terrorist act in U.S. history, and the slaughter at Columbine High School, which is the all-time record juvenile mass murder in human history) and international terrorism (such as the 9/11 attack on the World Trade Center, which is now in the *Guinness Book of World Records* as the all time record terrorist act), there has been an explosion of violent crime that has influenced this change for law enforcement agencies. Per capita aggravated assaults in the U.S. increased almost sevenfold between 1957 and 1993. During the 1990s there was a slight downturn in crime rates, due largely to aggressive policing, the longest sustained economic boom in American history, and a fivefold increase in per capita incarceration rates since 1970. Still, the violent crime rate today is five times greater than in 1957.

In Canada, per capita assaults increased almost fourfold since 1964. Since 1977 the per capita serious assault rate (as reported by each nation to InterPol) is up nearly fivefold in Norway and Greece and it has increased approximately fourfold in Australia and New Zealand. During the same period, the per capita serious assault rate tripled in Sweden, Austria, and France, and it approximately doubled in Belgium, Denmark, England-Wales, Germany, France, Hungary, Netherlands, Scotland, and Switzerland. It is not just happening in traditional "Western" nations. Brazil, Mexico, and all of Latin America are seeing an explosion of violent crime, while nations like Japan and Singapore are also experiencing unprecedented increases in juvenile violent crime.

To respond to this extraordinary rise in violence, law enforcement agencies of the free world have trained and organized the finest peace officers we have ever seen. In spite of ever better equipment, training, organization and tactics, American law enforcement fatalities in the line of duty went up 21 percent in 1997. We know that if it were not for all the body armor (bulletproof vests) worn by our officers, law enforcement fatalities in the United States would easily be double or even triple what they are today.

If this is not a war, then tell me what is.

Post-9/11: A New War Abroad and a New Mission for Our Military

> Methinks I see in my mind a noble and puissant nation rousing herself like a strong man after sleep, and shaking her invincible locks; methinks I see her as an eagle mewing her mighty youth, and kindling her undazzled eyes at the full midday beam.
>
> —John Milton
> "Areopagitica"

Meanwhile in the military, our soldiers and marines are called upon to stabilize nations around the world with peacekeeping operations in places many of us have never heard of prior to the deployment of American troops. This is a reality of the post-Cold War era.

The West has won the Cold War, and now for the first time in history the majority of the world's population elects their national leaders. It might just be that the world today is finally safe for democracies. (I use the word democracy in its broad, popular sense, since America is technically a "representative democracy" or a "republic.") One commonly accepted truism is that democratically elected governments generally do not go to war with other democracies. Historians love to pick around the edges of this concept, finding exceptions (primarily by bending the definition of "democratically elected governments") but even if we do accept some of the rare "exceptions," this is still a very valuable "heuristic" or "rule of thumb."

Writing in his syndicated newspaper column, political science professor Bradley R. Gitz flatly states that "there is no agreed-upon historical case of a democratically elected government going to war against another democratically elected government." He believes that one of the "axioms" of political science is that "democratic states don't fight democratic states or provide support for terrorist groups." He quotes political scientist John Mueller, who "has gone so far as to assert that war between such states has become 'subrationally unthinkable,' not even on the radar screen of options to be considered as a means of resolving disputes."

With the Soviet Union and the Warsaw pact gone, the goal of democracies around the world is to foster democracy. Once a nation has been made a democracy, it has effectively been inoculated against going to war with other like nations.

How do we help make a nation a democracy? We do it with peace keeping, stabilization and internal development operations around the world. We do it with peacekeepers whose job is very similar to that of peace officers.

xxii   On Combat

In the war against terrorism, warriors assault the remaining threat to democracy: global terrorism sanctioned and fostered by, and festering in, totalitarian nations. In Afghanistan, and around the world, warriors have been called to action to bring terrorists to justice for the murder of nearly 3,000 American citizens on September 11, 2001.

When they complete this formidable task, and have routed out terrorism, we will have to rebuild those nations, as we will not be truly safe until they are democracies. To accomplish this, we need peace officers and peacekeepers. Warriors. Warriors to attack. Warriors to defend. Warriors to build, preserve and protect.

A New Paladin

If we don't keep the warrior in the mix we become glorified social workers with guns. We will fail at our ultimate responsibility, saving innocent human lives.

—A police officer

Have you ever wondered why police officers wear a shield on their left side? This is a direct, intentional, overt reference to the knights of old. There really were knights. They woke up every day and donned armor. They hung a weapon on their hip and a shield on their left side. And they went forth and did good deeds and administered justice in the land.

Gunpowder defeated armor, and the knights went away.

Today, for the first time in centuries, in both the military and law enforcement communities, we have warriors who don armor every day, take up their shields, strap on their weapons, and go forth to do good deeds.

If that is not a knight, if that is not a paladin, a new order of chivalry, then you tell me what is.

The knights of old are somewhat mythical, but these new knights are real and are embodying the spirit of the ancient model of the knight paladin, the champion of the weak and the oppressed, dedicated to righteousness and justice.

One U.S. military leader (whom I have promised to keep anonymous) wrote these words as he witnessed his soldiers engage in great acts of valor:

Dear God, where do we get such men? What loving God has provided, that each generation, afresh, there should arise new giants in the land. Were we to go but a single generation without such men, we should surely be both damned and doomed.

Think about it. If we went but a single generation without men (and women) who are willing to go out every day and confront evil, then within the span of that generation we should surely be both damned and doomed.

We could go for a generation without the doctors, and it would get ugly if you were injured or sick, but civilization would continue. We could go for a generation without engineers and mechanics, and things would break down, but civilization would survive. We could even go for a generation without teachers. The next generation would have to play "catch up ball," and it would be hard, but civilization as we know it would still survive.

If, however, we went "but a single generation" without the warriors who are willing to confront human aggression every day, then within the span of that generation we would truly be "both damned and doomed."

So "where do we get such men" and, may I add, women? We build them. We train them. We nurture them. There can be no more important or noble endeavor for a civilization. They are the warrior clan, the fellowship of arms.

Do not limit, my brothers and sisters, the role of the warrior. I had the privilege of being the co-keynote speaker with a Nobel Peace Prize recipient at an international peace conference. There I proposed the term peace warrior to refer to those in every profession, with and without guns, who are dedicated to moving our world forward toward peace. This term has been in use for a long time, and today it is widely accepted. It includes the Red Cross, the non-governmental organizations in a war zone, the probation and parole officers, the doctors and EMTs, the firefighters, the social workers, and even the clergy. Whether it is the passengers of United Flight 93 battling terrorists with their bare hands over the skies of Pennsylvania, a Red Cross worker in Africa, a Green Beret in Afghanistan, or a police officer walking the streets of LA, they are all peace warriors. I hope that this book has something to say to each and every one of them.

On Killing introduced the concept of the scholarly study of killing, coining the new term "killology." Now let us conduct a scholarly study of the psychology and physiology of combat. Perhaps we can call it "combatology." George Washington warned us that, "He who would have peace, must prepare for war." This means that there must be warriors. Good warriors. Paladins. Peace warriors who must study and master combat, as the firefighter would study and master fire. That is the purpose of this book. May it be of some small service to those who serve.

> The bravest are surely those who have the clearest vision of what is before them, glory and danger alike, and yet notwithstanding, go out to meet it.
>
> —Thucydides

Section One

The Physiology of Combat:
The Anatomy of the Human Body in Battle

Too delicate is flesh to be
The Shield that nations interpose
'Twixt red ambition and his foes —
The baston of liberty.

—E.V. Lucas
"The Debt"

chapter **one**

Combat: *The Universal Human Phobia*

> Every battle in world history may be different from every other battle, but they must have something in common if we can group them under the term 'battle' at all . . . it is not something 'strategic,' nor 'tactical' nor technical. It is not something any quantity of colored maps will reveal, or any collection of comparative statistics of strengths and casualties or even any set of parallel readings from the military classics, though the classics brilliantly illuminate our understanding of battle once we have arrived at it. What battles have in common is the human: the behavior of men struggling to reconcile their instinct of self-preservation, their sense of honor and the achievement of some aim over which other men are ready to kill them. The study of battle is therefore always a study of fear and usually of courage, usually also of faith and sometimes vision.
>
> —Sir Herbert Butterfield
> *Man On His Past*

I introduced the concept of the "Universal Human Phobia" in papers presented to the annual conventions of the American Psychiatric Association, the American Psychological Association, and to the Internal Congress of Critical Incident Stress Management. This concept is not controversial, but it does attach a new name to something that is generally well known. Nor is it truly "universal" since it probably affects around 98 percent of the population. (But that is probably close enough for the behavioral sciences.)

Understand that a phobia is much more than just a fear. It is an irrational, overwhelming, uncontrollable fear of a specific object or event. Before I discuss the number one human phobia, let me first tell you what most experts consider to be the most common phobia, which I would say is the second most common. Snakes.

Research into phobias is not a hard science. Even the definitions of what exactly constitutes a "phobic scale response" can vary greatly, but many experts agree that the most common phobia (after the universal phobia) is snakes. Roughly 15 percent of the population has a phobic scale response to them. This means that if I dropped a bucket of snakes into a crowded room, approximately 15 percent of the individuals in that room would have a true, phobic scale response. Upon seeing the mass of squirming, wriggling snakes, a message would shoot directly from their eyes to their feet, bypassing the logical portion of their brains. These unfortunate individuals would run toward the doors without conscious thought, some leaving a trail of unnecessary body mass behind them.

What would the remaining 85 percent do? Some would get out of the way, some would fight the snakes, and some would sell tickets to the show.

Most people have some phobia that "pushes their button." If yours is not snakes, it might be spiders, heights or darkness. However, one phobia that pushes almost everyone's button is interpersonal human aggression. That is the Universal Human Phobia. If I walked into another crowded room and emptied a pistol into one of them, or hacked at one of them with a machete, up to 98 percent of the average audience would experience a true phobic-scale response.

Consider the case of John Muhammad, and his little buddy, Malvo, the serial "snipers" in the Washington D.C. area in the fall of 2002. Literally millions of citizens in a multi-state area modified their daily behavior because the "Beltway Sniper" was still on the loose. Many motorists stopped refueling at self-serve stations and opted for full-service gas stations to avoid having to get out of their cars. Shoppers literally ran from their cars to the entrance doors of stores, and after shopping, they ran back. Kid's sporting events were curtailed, as were a myriad of other everyday activities.

This is not rational behavior. It is an irrational, uncontrollable fear—a phobia.

We are arguably in the most violent times in peacetime history. The murder rate is being held down by medical technology, but the aggravated assault rate, the rate at which we are trying to kill or seriously injure each other, might be at the highest levels in peacetime history. This is true in almost every major industrialized nation in the world, and yet violence is still incredibly rare. The per capita aggravated assault rate in the U.S. is only four per thousand per year. This means that 996 out of 1,000 Americans will go a year without someone attempting to inflict serious bodily harm on them. Every day, nearly 300 million Americans bounce off each other, but the average American will go a lifetime and never have someone commit a felonious assault upon them.

When violence does happen to us, it devastates us. It shatters us. Most of us approach every strange dog we meet with an expectation that it might bite. Likewise, most of us expect snakes to strike. That's what they do! But we do not expect that one of the millions of Americans we interact with in an average lifetime will try to kill us. We simply cannot lead our lives expecting that every human we meet might try to kill us.

So when someone does try to kill us, it is simply not right and, if we are not careful, it can destroy us. The *Diagnostic and Statistical Manual of Mental*

Disorders (DSM), the "Bible" of psychiatry and psychology, specifically states that any time the causal factor of a stressor is human in nature, the degree of trauma is usually more severe and long lasting. Conversely, the *DSM* says that posttraumatic stress disorder is comparably rare and mild in response to natural disasters and traffic accidents. In other words, when it is another human being who causes our fear, pain and suffering, it shatters, destroys and devastates us.

Unchecked, extreme stress is an emotional and physical carnivore. It chews hungrily on so many of our law enforcement officers with its razor-sharp fangs, and does so quietly, silently in every corner of their lives. It affects their job performance, their relationships and ultimately their health. In World War I, World War II, and Korea, the number of soldiers who pulled out of the front lines because they were psychiatric casualties was greater than the number of those who died in combat.

The stress of combat debilitates far more warriors than are killed in direct, hostile action. It is in this toxic, corrosive, destructive domain of the Universal Human Phobia that we ask our soldiers and police officers to live, and to die. This is the realm of combat.

Moving to the Sound of the Guns

> Death must not be feared. Death, in time, comes to all of us. And every man is scared in his first action. If he says he's not, he's a goddamn liar. Some men are cowards, yes, but they fight just the same, or get the hell slammed out of them.
>
> The real hero is the man who fights even though he's scared. Some get over their fright in a minute, under fire; others take an hour; for some it takes days; but a real man will never let the fear of death overpower his honor, his sense of duty, to his country and to his manhood.
>
> —General George Patton

Since police officers and soldiers move toward the Universal Human Phobia, intentionally moving into this domain where other human beings will try to hurt or kill them, it is vital that they understand that realm and understand combat. As the firefighter understands fire, the warrior must understand combat.

Every other sane, rational creature on the face of the earth flees from the sounds of the guns. A few brave people crawl up to treat the wounded, and a few deranged individuals might crawl up to take pictures. But, in general, when shots are fired and bodies are falling, every other sane, rational creature gets the hell out of there. The bunny rabbits and the students, the teachers and the gazelles, and the lawyers and the cockroaches, they are all gone.

Now, the firefighter, the paramedic and even the press might move to the sound of the guns, but they have absolutely no intention of actually confronting the human being making all that big noise. There is only one individual who does that: the warrior. While every other creature flees, the warrior goes 100 miles per hour to get to a gunfight.

Loren Christensen tells of responding to an incident where a man, armed with a shotgun, was on the 12th floor of an office high rise. Dispatch said he had already killed one person and was now stalking the hallway. After getting jostled by the crowd that ran hysterically out of the building, Christensen, two other officers, and three medics boarded an elevator in the lobby. As they rose to the horror that awaited them, the officers made quick plans as to how they would exit the elevator and then proceed along the hall. The medics made no plans, but rather pressed themselves flat against the back wall with expressions that indicated they wished they had waited in the downstairs lobby. When the doors whisked open, the medics very wisely stayed behind, pressing themselves even harder against the elevator's back wall. The cops, on the other hand, immediately exited the elevator and moved toward the killer.

Is there something wrong with these people?

No. There is something gloriously right with them. Because if we did not have warriors, men and women willing to move toward the sounds of the guns and confront evil, within the span of a generation our civilization would no longer exist.

It's Personal!

All hell shall stir for this.

—Shakespeare
King Henry V

To understand why interpersonal human aggression is so toxic, let me first ask you to consider the difference between two scenarios. In the first scenario, a tornado rips through your house, sending you and your family to the hospital. In the second scenario, a gang comes in the middle of the night, beats you and your family into the hospital, and then burns your house to the ground. In both cases the end result is the same: your house is gone and your family is in the hospital. So what is the difference?

Every time I ask this at presentations anywhere in the world, the audience answers the same. The tornado is an act of nature. When the gang does it, it is personal. "It's personal! It's personal! I'm gonna hunt 'em down and kill 'em like dogs!" Have you ever seen anyone respond that way to a tornado?

The gang attack makes it personal, with emphasis on the word "person," as in human. We process interpersonal human aggression completely differently. It is not a fear of death. We all know that we are going to die, but we want to have some degree of control over how we will die. We can accept the fact that we will die of old age, or that an "act of nature" might take our lives or the lives of our loved ones. But we cannot accept the thought of someone "playing God" and choosing, without provocation or authority, to take away the most precious thing we have. Even worse is the idea of someone intentionally choosing to steal away our loved ones' lives.

The presence of just one serial killer in a city can change the behavior of that entire city. Detective Sergeant Joe Friday, on *Dragnet*, put it this way:

> Serial killers are like viruses, different strains destroy different cells. But they all ultimately run the same course. Unless they're stopped, the host dies. In this case the host is the city, and the toxin is fear.
>
> —Detective Sergeant Joe Friday
> *Dragnet*

One serial killer can change the behavior of a whole city, but over 400,000 Americans will die slow, hideous preventable deaths this year from smoking cigarettes and that does not change the behavior of most smokers. I'm not taking a "cheap shot" at smokers here. I like to smoke the occasional cigar, and if I ultimately pay the price for that, it was my choice. But if you want to come into my house and inflict a slow, hideous death on me and my family, that is a completely different matter.

Just the distant possibility of interpersonal confrontation influences our behavior more than the statistical certainty of a slow, horrible death from cancer. Statistically speaking, this is not rational.

One of the most common phobias is public speaking, which is really just a distant echo, a reflection of the Universal Phobia. We fear getting in front of large groups and taking an action that might result in making us a target for their aggression. Again, this is not rational. It is an irrational fear—a phobia.

In order to truly understand the magnitude of the toxic, corrosive realm of combat, and those who must function in it, we must begin by understanding the concept of this Universal Human Phobia.

Psychologist Abraham Maslow established the concept commonly known as Maslow's Hierarchy of Needs. He wrote that certain lower needs must be met before higher needs can be satisfied. Maslow said that a society exists upon a foundation and that foundation is an environment that is reasonably secure, safe, and out of danger. Basically, what Maslow is saying is that if a nation cannot create an environment in which its citizens are reasonably safe (especially from interpersonal aggression, whether it be violent criminals, terrorists, or invaders) then that nation has violated its social contract, and it may ultimately lose its justification for existing. Why should citizens pay taxes and obey the laws of a nation that cannot even keep its children safe from violent predators?

Our warriors are the ones who create this foundation of safety. They are the ones who face down the Universal Human Phobia, the most toxic, corrosive, destructive element that can impact our society. They are the foundation of the building, and if the foundation of the building crumbles, the building will fall.

When you begin to doubt the nobility of your mission or the sanctity of your profession because your heart is heavy, or you feel anger, disillusionment, disenfranchisement, betrayed or confused— Stop and listen to the voices . . . the voices that rise up from . . . a field in Pennsylvania, from a wall at the Pentagon and from the spot of earth the world has come to know as Ground Zero. Because if you listen, you will hear those souls tell you "Thank You" for what you do . . . hear them cheering you on. Let them carry you through this difficult moment, allow them to nourish you and encourage you-and doubt no more-for you are warriors and champions for those who have gone before and to those most vulnerable now. You are admired and respected, for you are the best at what you do. God bless you and God bless America.

—John R. Thomas, First Deputy Superintendent
Chicago Police Department

chapter **two**

The Harsh Reality of Combat:
What You Don't Hear at the VFW

> Despite the years of thought and the oceans of ink which have been devoted to the elucidation of war its secrets still remain shrouded in mystery.
>
> —General George Patton

Loss of Bowel and Bladder Control

> I have never seen such mud and of such depth, whose moisture came only from the blood and terror-piss of the men who fought upon it.
>
> —Steven Pressfield
> *The Gates of Fire*

A warrior must be a master of the realm of combat, and as such, he must understand its reality. Most of what you think you know about combat is a pile of baloney stacked six feet high. To illustrate the true magnitude of our ignorance about combat, let me tell you a true story about a little mouse in a kindergarten classroom. Don't get too attached to the mouse, he will soon meet an untimely demise.

I was in a southern state giving a presentation to school educators about the explosion of violence happening in our society and what they can do to help combat it. I also outlined what actions they should take in the event, God forbid, violence should touch their children's lives in school. One of the many things I talked about was the importance of conducting critical incident debriefings. When I finished, an elementary school principal stood up and told a story about one of his kindergarten teachers, who happened to be in the audience and had given him permission to tell this story.

"I was monitoring her class," the principal said, "as she stood up front teaching her kindergartners. All of a sudden a mouse came running across the floor, hit the inside of her shoe, and ran up the inside of her slacks. When it reached her upper thigh area, she latched onto it with her hand over her slacks and started rolling around on the ground, screaming, 'Help me! Help me!'"

The principal asked, "What was I supposed to do?! Was I supposed to pull her pants down in front of all those kids to get that mouse? All I knew was we had us one of those 'critical incidents' Colonel Grossman's talking about. So I got all the kids and we got the heck out of there. I sent some female teachers in to help her out, and then later on that afternoon we had one of those critical incident debriefings.

"You've got to do it," the principal continued. "It was nothing fancy. We just brought the counselor in, sat all the little Bubbas and Bubbalinas down, and said to the kids, 'Ya'll are fine. Here's the teacher, and she's fine. We sat there and talked our way through what happened. It was all going well until this one little Bubba stood up and said, with wide-eyed kindergarten innocence, 'Yah know, the most amazin' thang of all ta me, was how much water came out of that little mouse, when she squarshed it."

The moral of the story is that to wet your pants in a situation like this is a perfectly natural human response. Research shows that if you have a "load" in your lower intestines during a highly stressful survival situation, it's going to go. Your body says, "Bladder control? I don't think so. Sphincter control? We don't need no stinking sphincter control!" What do you do if that happens? You keep on fighting.

If you have dealt with injured people as a medic, police officer or firefighter, you know that a significant number urinate or defecate themselves. It even happens to criminals. Loren Christensen tells of helping the feds do a forced entry of a warehouse in which a powerful drug dealer stored huge quantities of drugs and property stolen in countless burglaries. The drug dealer was a large, boisterous man with a history of violence on his comrades and law enforcement officers. There was a high probability that he would greet them with a hail of bullets.

The raid was a big operation involving a score of officers wearing combat fatigues, listening devices and high-tech weapons, with a synchronized and explosive entry from all sides of the building. So how did the big bad drug dealer react when the officers crashed through the doors yelling and pointing their weapons? He froze, cupped his hands on the sides of face, and squealed like a little girl, as a wet spot spread rapidly across the front of his slacks. This is a normal stress response; let's call it a redirection of the assets.

The same thing happens to people in combat, but while a teacher can freely admit it and even joke about it (as in our mouse story), most warriors cannot. They are too macho, believing that such things just do not happen to them. When it does occur, they feel shame and think something is wrong with them—but they are wrong. *The American Soldier*, the official study of the performance of U.S. troops in World War II, tells of one survey in which a quarter of all U.S. soldiers in World War II admitted that they had lost control of their bladders, and an eighth of them admitted to defecating in their pants. If we look only at the individuals at the "tip of the spear" and factor out those who did not experience intense combat, we can estimate that approximately 50 percent of those who did see intense combat admitted they had wet their pants and nearly 25 percent admitted they had messed themselves.

Those are the ones who admitted it, so the actual number is probably higher, though we cannot know by how much. One veteran told me, "Hell Colonel, all that proves is that three out of four were damned liars!" That is probably unfair and inaccurate, but the reality is that the humiliation and social stigma associated with "crapping yourself" probably results in many individuals being unwilling to admit the truth.

"I will go see a war movie," said one Vietnam veteran, "when the main character is shown shitting his pants in the battle scene." Have you ever seen a movie that depicted a soldier defecating in his drawers in combat? Have you ever heard that bit of reality in all the war stories told at the VFW? Can you imagine an old vet saying, "Yeah, Billy Bob, I remember the night I messed my drawers!" Or, 30 years after the war when you are bouncing your grandbaby on your knee and the child looks adoringly into your eyes and asks, "Grandpa, what'd you do in the war?" The very last thing you are going to say is, "Well, grandpa crapped himself!" The reason you will not hear that at the VFW, and the reason you will not say that to your grandbaby, is because of an old axiom: All's fair in love and war. Meaning there are two things men will always lie about. It also means that everything you think you know about war is based on 5,000 years of lies.

No, you will never tell your grandbaby about the degrading, demeaning, debasing, humiliating things that happened to you in combat. Instead, you will fill him with popcorn and sunshine. The problem with this is that 20 years later when he is in combat and has just messed his drawers, he will ask himself, "What's wrong with me? This didn't happen to grandpa and it didn't happen to John Wayne. There must be something terribly wrong with me!"

My co-author wrote an article for a major police magazine about the effects of stress on police officers forced to defend themselves in deadly shootings. The editor accepted and loved the piece but deleted the section about the possibility that officers might soil themselves. The myth is perpetuated across the generations. Remember, the data indicates that most veterans of intense combat do not have this happen, but for that large minority who do experience this response it can be their deep, dark secret, and there is power in knowing that it might happen.

It is amazing how much this is covered up, in what has become almost a cultural conspiracy of silence. A few months after the September 11, 2001, attacks, I had the privilege of training a group of federal agents. One of them had been at the World Trade Center during the attack. He came up to me after I had taught about loss of bowel and bladder control, and said, "Thank you. Now I understand what happened to me." Then he told me his story.

He and the other agents in his office were able to evacuate the building after the hijacked airplane had hit it. They were wearing their tactical gear and assisting local police when the first building began to come down. At first they didn't know what to do, and then they realized that they had better, as he put it, "Run like hell." He said that a black cloud of smoke and dust enveloped them and darkened the sky. He couldn't breathe and was losing consciousness. Then the cloud passed and he turned around and went back in to help.

Then the second building began to collapse. I found myself admiring his ability to find humor in the situation as he said, "By now we'd gotten to be experts at falling buildings, and we knew exactly what to do. We turned and ran like hell." Again a black cloud enveloped him and darkened the sky, and again he thought he was dying as he began to lose consciousness. But when the cloud passed, he once again turned around and headed back in.

A few hours later, as he was climbing through the rubble, someone tapped him on the shoulder and said, "I'm your relief," and he was directed back to a cleanup point in a gym.

"The thing that I always wondered about," he said, "was why everyone there had crapped themselves, except me. Now I understand. You said, 'If there's a load in the lower intestines, its gonna go.' Just before those bastards hit our building, I had taken a really good morning visit to the bathroom."

Probably no event in human history has been reported and studied more than the 9/11 attacks, and yet almost no one knows that, apparently, most of the survivors lost bowel and bladder control. Does this diminish their courage? Not in the least. But if it ever happens to us, it would be good to know that it is perfectly normal.

It is time to cut through the baloney and learn what really happens in combat so that a generation of warriors is raised to be mentally and emotionally prepared to go into the toxic realm. As we shall see, loss of bowel and bladder control is only the tip of the iceberg when we examine what really happens in combat.

Mass Psychiatric Casualties

In every war in which American soldiers have fought in this [twentieth] century, the chances of becoming a psychiatric casualty— of being debilitated for some period of time as a consequence of the stresses of military life—were greater than the chances of being killed by enemy fire. The only exception was the Vietnam War, in which the chances were almost equal.

—Richard Gabriel
No More Heroes

Are the warriors of today any better than those who fought in the trenches of World War I? Are today's warriors tougher than those who landed on the beaches of Normandy or Iwo Jima in World War II? Are they better than the ones who fought their way out of the frozen Chosen or the Puson Perimeter in Korea? No. Today we are no better than those heroes. And we are no worse. We are the same warriors. We might be better equipped, better trained and better prepared, but we are the same basic, biological organisms as those who have gone before us.

Richard Gabriel, in his excellent book, *No More Heroes*, tells us that in the great battles of World War I, World War II and Korea, there were more men pulled off the front lines because of psychiatric wounds than were killed in combat. There was a study written on this phenomenon in World War II entitled, "Lost Divisions," which concluded that American forces lost 504,000 men from psychiatric collapse. A number sufficient to man 50 combat divisions!

On any given day in World War II, thousands of psychiatric casualties were in camps close to the front lines. A procedure called "Immediacy, Expectancy, and Proximity" was applied, meaning they were kept in proximity of the front lines with a sense of immediacy and expectancy that they would go back into battle. Even with that in place, as well as the normal cycles where men rotated out of combat after a reasonable time, more soldiers were lost from psychiatric casualties than all of the physical casualties combined.

Very few people know about this. While everyone knows about the valiant dead, most people, even professional warriors, do not know about the greater number of individuals who were quietly taken out of the front lines because they were psychiatric casualties. This is another aspect of combat that has been hidden from us, and it is something we must understand.

Worst of all were those rare situations in which soldiers were trapped in continuous combat for 60 to 90 days. In those cases, 98 percent became psychiatric casualties. Fighting all day and all night for months on end is a twentieth century phenomenon. The Battle of Gettysburg in 1863 lasted three days, and they took the nights off. This has been the case throughout history. When the sun went down, the fighting stopped, and the men gathered around the campfire to debrief the day's fight.

It was not until the twentieth century, beginning with World War I, that battles went day and night, for weeks and months without end. This resulted in a huge increase in psychiatric casualties and it got vastly worse when soldiers were unable to rotate out of the battle. On the beaches of Normandy in World War II, for example, there were no rear lines, and for two months there was no way to escape the horror of continuous fighting, of continuous death. It was learned then that after 60 days and nights of constant combat, 98 percent of all soldiers became psychiatric casualties.

What about the other two percent? They were aggressive sociopaths. They were apparently having a good time. (At least that is the conclusion of two World War II researchers, Swank and Marchand. But recent research shows that that two percent breaks down into wolves and sheepdogs, which we will discuss later in the book.)

Consider the six-month-long Battle of Stalingrad, the decisive World War II Soviet victory that stopped the German southern advance and turned the tide of the war. Some Russian reports say that their veterans of that great battle died around age 40, while other Russian males not involved lived into their 60s and 70s. The difference? The war veterans had been exposed to continual stress 24 hours a day for six, long, grueling months.

To fully comprehend the intensity of mental stress from combat, we must keep other environmental stressors in mind, while at the same time understanding the body's physiological response as the sympathetic nervous system is mobilized. In addition, we must understand the impact of the parasympathetic nervous system's "backlash" that occurs as a result of overwhelming demands placed upon it.

If we agree that we are basically no different creatures than the warriors of World War I, World War II and Korea, then we must admit that the same thing could happen to us. The goal of this book, and the new body of "Warrior Science™" research that this book is based upon, is to be better trained and prepared, in order to prevent that from happening to us.

three

Sympathetic and Parasympathetic Nervous System: *The Body's Combat and Maintenance Troops*

> The study of war should concentrate almost entirely on the actualities of war – the effects of tiredness, hunger, fear, lack of sleep, weather...The principles of strategy and tactics, and the logistics of war are really absurdly simple: It is the actualities that make war so complicated and so difficult.
>
> —Field-Marshal Lord Wavell
> In a letter to B.H. Liddell Hart

Sympathetic Nervous System: Mobilizing the Body for Survival

> But when the blast of war blows in our ears,
> Then imitate the action of the tiger:
> Stiffen the sinews, summon up the blood.
>
> —Shakespeare
> *King Henry V*

Your autonomic nervous system (ANS) consists of the sympathetic nervous system (SNS) and the parasympathetic nervous system (PNS). Most of your organs receive impulses from both the SNS and the PNS, though they generally work opposite each other. For example, the SNS increases your heart rate and the PNS decreases it. The SNS is also associated with stress response—the "fight or flight" response—as it prepares your body and mind for perceived danger. The SNS is generally concerned with the expenditure of energy from reserves that are stored in your body, inhibiting digestion, increasing secretion of epinephrine and norepinephrine, dilating the bronchial tubes in the lungs, dilating heart vessels, and tensing muscles.

The SNS mobilizes and directs the body's energy resources for action. Think of it as the physiological equivalent of the body's front-line soldiers, the ones who do the fighting in a military unit. The PNS is associated with relaxation and is often concerned with activities that increase your body's supply of stored energy (such as salivation and digestion). It is the physiological equivalent of the body's cooks, mechanics and clerks who sustain a military unit over an extended period of time.

When you are asleep at night, the PNS processes are totally ascendant; you do not even have a guard at the front gate. Your military unit is on stand down, your ship is in port, and you are completely helpless. Then you wake up in the morning, get a cup of coffee, take a shower, and you hit what is called homeostasis: a balance between the sympathetic and parasympathetic processes. You have some troops in the front lines and some troops doing maintenance, which allows you to conduct sustained operations. But all units must stand down sooner or later, so that night you go to sleep, and once again your PNS processes take over. This is a normal, routine, maintenance cycle. Tomorrow, however there is a surprise waiting.

You get up and begin your routine. Homeostasis is established, and then suddenly someone tries to kill you. Your body's response is total SNS arousal. PNS processes like digestion shut down: We don't need no stinking digestion. You guys blow the ballast and get down to the legs where I need you. The cooks, mechanics, and clerks drop what they are doing, grab a rifle, and rush to the front lines. Meanwhile, salivation may shut down, resulting in what is known as dry mouth or cotton mouth.

If we can believe the data at face value, 75 percent of combat veterans did not lose control of bowel and bladder, but almost everyone gets what is called "stress diarrhea." The Greeks say: "Your bowels turned to water." The medical term for it is "spastic colon," which is rather . . . evocative. One of the last things many police SWAT teams do before they make a high-risk entry is to take what they call a "battle crap." The body blows the ballast so that no resources are wasted on unnecessary functions. There is a total mobilization of all assets toward one thing and one thing only—survival.

As soon as the danger is over there is a crash, a parasympathetic backlash of enormous magnitude.

Parasympathetic Backlash: The Body Shuts Down for Maintenance

I was part of an arrest team of seven veteran drug agents…we were doing hotel buy busts where our informant inside a hotel room would order up several pounds of drugs, and when the bad guys showed up we would watch the deal go down via video camera from an adjoining room. To watch the actions go down in front of you and just watching and waiting for the bust signals, all the time looking and listening to your target, raised our stress to the point of almost being able to touch it.

[After the first deal was made and the arrest signal was given] we made entry from the adjacent room and arrested four suspects and seized two pounds of methamphetamine. As we were taking the suspects out into the parking lot, a car pulled up, driven by an associate of our bad guys. When he backed up and headed for the exit, some of the officers ran after him, and I ran to cut him off. The car changed paths and headed straight at me. I noticed the backdrop for my shot, thinking I was going to have to kill the driver, but my teammates were in direct line. I jumped out of the way and the car passed right where I had been standing.

I jumped into a car and we began a chase, eventually finding the car at a church lot. As I drove to it, I began getting the shakes. No problem, as I knew that would happen. By the time we searched the church, I figure I had experienced three or four adrenaline rushes. On the way back to the hotel, I felt very car sick, dizzy and I had a terrible headache. I knew it was a backlash from the activities, so I began tactical breathing. That helped for a while with the headache and dizziness, but I was still very tired and had a hard time staying awake. What bothered me the most was I knew what was going on, and why, but I couldn't stop it.

—Correspondence to Colonel Grossman

During the Korean War, a team of psychiatrists accompanied a unit of veteran soldiers into battle. The unit got a night of good sleep and then launched an attack at dawn. By noon they had secured an enemy hilltop position and the immediate danger was over. While they waited for the inevitable counterattack, the psychiatrists were astounded to see that the officers and NCOs had to go from position to position, waking up the troops. The parasympathetic backlash after the battle had been so powerful that the men had fallen into an exhausted sleep, though they knew they would soon be attacked.

Napoleon said, "The moment of greatest vulnerability is the instant immediately after victory." As soon as the troops relaxed, there was a parasympathetic backlash of enormous magnitude. It is more than just letting down your guard; it is a powerful physiological collapse. This process is not unlike sex in the male body: You are up, you are rocking, you are down, and you are not getting back up again. There has been a physical, hormonal discharge and your body needs time to recharge itself. This is why the military always holds back a reserve. When the troops are suffering from the burden of exhaustion, and a fresh enemy unit attacks, the exhausted troops collapse like a house of cards.

Burning Off the Adrenaline Dump

I had been in Vietnam as a military policeman for only a couple of weeks, when I was assigned to go on a raid of several Vietnamese shops for stolen American merchandise. The owners of the first two shops resisted and we had to wrestle them to the floor so other MPs could recover the goods. At the third shop, things got ugly fast when South Vietnamese soldiers, armed with M-16s, came to the merchants' aid. Before it was over, we had about 25 MPs there and 30 or 40 enraged Vietnamese. Shots were fired in the air, everyone was screaming racial epithets, and several fistfights broke out. We were just a hairbreadth away from shooting a couple of Vietnamese before we got order.

Two hours later I was in the mess hall, still so wired that I had trouble picking up food with my fork. When I did spear something, my hand shook so hard the food would flip off. I finally gave up and ate with my hands, like an animal. There were other times like this, some worse, but this was the first.

—A Vietnam veteran

It can be a different story for police officers and other warriors who are not in sustained combat. When the average law enforcement officer gets into a gunfight, he often has trouble sleeping that night. Why did those infantry soldiers in Korea have trouble staying awake at noon, but the average law enforcement officer after a gunfight cannot get to sleep? The difference is what has happened to the adrenaline dump in the combatants. The soldiers went through six hours of grueling combat where they burned up every drop of adrenaline in their bodies. The police officer had the same adrenaline dump flooding through his body, but his combat event took only a few trigger pulls to resolve, leaving him with adrenaline still surging through his body. For the officer to sleep, he must first come down from his adrenaline rush.

Have you ever sat on the edge of your bed at night with your mind spinning, your heart pounding and your body raring to go? That is what residual adrenaline does to you. To burn it off you need to conduct calisthenics, go for a long run or lift weights. Afterward, take a shower and go back to bed. Often that is all you need to fall fast asleep. My co-author, Loren Christensen, said that his partners often drank several beers after a high-risk situation, but he preferred to punch and kick a heavy bag until he had burned every last drop of remaining adrenaline. When he hit the pillow, he fell asleep quickly, and awoke the next morning feeling good from the exercise, while his partners slept poorly and awoke with hangovers.

Pacing Yourself for a Four-Quarter Game

The race is not to the swift, nor the battle to the strong.

—Ecclesiastes 9:11
The Bible

Dr. Kevin Gilmartin, a retired police supervisor and a psychologist, trains police officers on what he calls "emotional survival." He talks about how the parasympathetic backlash can impact warriors every day. While they are at work, their sympathetic nervous system is ascendant and they are alive, alert, energetic, and involved. When they go home, the parasympathetic backlash hits and they become tired, detached, isolated and apathetic. The greater the excitement and demand at work, the greater the potential for a backlash that can debilitate them in their home life and destroy their family. The purpose of this book is to prepare warriors for the reality of combat and we will focus on the parasympathetic backlash from a specific combat experience, but Gilmartin's book, *Emotional Survival*, is mandatory reading for all warriors to help them understand how to manage this daily "biological roller coaster."

Managing daily stress is vitally important because we are continuosly bombarded with it. Life-and-death, combat incidents are comparatively rare, but when they do occur, managing the emotional, physiological crisis after the event can be even more important.

In the immediate days after a combat situation, a warrior can be at his most vulnerable. He may be so sleep deprived, confused, uncertain, and physiologically out of balance that he might respond to a subsequent combat situation with an inappropriate level of aggression. Think of a warrior as a finely calibrated machine. His job is to decide in a fraction of a second exactly how much force to use. If he should use a little too much, he gets into trouble, and if he uses too little, he can die. In the first few days after a shooting, the calibration on this finely tuned individual may be out of whack.

Artwohl and Christensen's book, *Deadly Force Encounters* contains copies of the International Association of Chiefs of Police (IACP) protocols, which state that after a law enforcement officer has been in a gunfight, he should be given three or four days off so that he can recover from the extraordinary event. If he does not get this time to recuperate and he is thrust into another stressful event, he is vulnerable to severe psychological damage as a result of additional stress stacked on top of the original stress. (More on this later when I talk about the "Bathtub Model" of stress.) Consider this example of a veteran warrior who intuitively understood this concept.

> I've been involved in three shootings over my 14-year career. After the first one, I went right back to work because that's what everyone did. No debriefings, no talking, just get back out there and prove to yourself and others that it didn't bother you. After my second shooting, I had come to realize that that approach was a mistake. I decided to take care of myself regardless of what my agency or any of my fellow officers had to say.

I didn't go right back out but instead took two weeks off. Afterwards, I was getting restless and eager to return to the work I love so much. So I went back. I walked into the locker room and put on my uniform and my gun belt. But it felt wrong. I knew I wasn't ready to be on the street and I definitely wasn't ready to go out there and make life or death decisions. So I took off my uniform and told—not asked—my sergeant that I was going home. I didn't care what he thought. It was my life and I knew that I cared about it more than anyone else. I was going to protect it.

So I took another week off and this time when I went back it felt right. I walked out of the locker room with my uniform and gun belt on and I knew I was ready. Then on my second shift back I got into my third shooting. Since I had allowed time to recover from the second shooting, I was ready to survive physically and psychologically. And I did. Today I'm doing fine with all three shootings and I'm still on full, active duty."

—A police officer
From Deadly Force Encounters

In past wars we tended to wait until a soldier was mentally or emotionally "broken" before we would pull them out of the front lines. In the 2003 invasion of Iraq, when combatants began to show signs of stress the policy was to rotate them back to where they could get a shower and a brief rest, and then put them right back with their units. One *USA Today* report stated that, "Usually they snap back," and would begin to demonstrate "The subtle swagger that communicates the unconscious confidence of a combat veteran."

The loss of one man for a day or so is not such a big price to pay, if you realize that the alternative may be to lose that warrior permanently. Warriors in combat don't always have the luxury of being able to pull out, but think of it this way: If you were a football coach and one of your players took a hard hit in the head, you would take him out of the game for awhile so he could recuperate. While he might want to go back in, you would tell him to sit on the bench for a couple of plays, because it is a four-quarter game and you need him for the whole game. A warrior is in the game for all four quarters, too, so he must pace himself. Shoving him back into the breach too soon just might cut short his career, or cause him to fail at a critical moment when others are depending upon him.

The Moment of Greatest Vulnerability

Oh, moment of sweet peril . . .

—Edward Robert, Earl of Lytton

Look at the "Officer vs. Suspect Stress" graph and note the difference between the officer and the suspect during and after a violent arrest. This was first introduced by the U.S. Marshals in reference to escapes during prisoner transports, but it has far wider and broader application to military and law enforcement.

The officer went into the arrest when he was in "Condition Red," a heightened state of alertness and awareness. He managed to catch the suspect when the man was completely off guard in "Condition White." There was a scuffle and the officer got the man "cuffed and stuffed" into the back seat of the patrol vehicle. Now, if the officer is not careful on the way back to the station, he might think that the danger is over and allow himself to relax. Meanwhile, the suspect is still high on adrenaline and growing increasingly unhappy over the loss of his freedom.

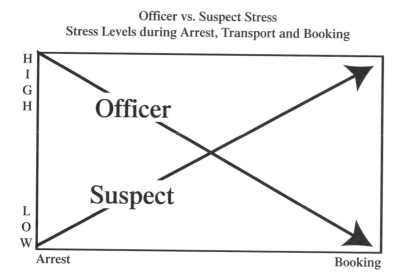

Officer vs. Suspect Stress
Stress Levels during Arrest, Transport and Booking

Consider what happened in one tragic incident in Florida. Two trained, competent detectives arrested and handcuffed a man after a short chase. They put the man's rifle in the trunk of their police car and sat him in their back seat, unaware that the career criminal carried a handcuff key around his neck. While being transported to jail, the suspect used the key to get out of the handcuffs, and then lunged at the detectives, disarming one of them. He emptied the gun into both detectives, killing them both, and then kicked their bodies out of the car. He retrieved his rifle from the trunk, and after a high-speed chase, killed a state trooper, and then took a hostage in a gas station. The standoff ended when the suspect took his own life. So, how is it possible for an unarmed, handcuffed man to overwhelm and kill two armed and trained detectives? The answer lies in the minds and bodies of the officers' and the suspect. The officers had probably relaxed after the chase and the arrest, and were experiencing a parasympathetic backlash, while the suspect had not yet begun to fight.

We know that a cooperative person can have a violent, psychological response to hearing the clicking sound made when a pair of handcuffs open. Similarly, we know that many times as a police car nears the jail, and the officers have relaxed their guard after the arrest, the sight of the structure can spark a violent reaction in the officers' prisoner.

> Before our shiny new glass and plastic high-rise jail was built, we housed prisoners in an ancient, three-story stone structure. It was an ugly place, dark, medieval and dungeon-like with towers and barbwire. The problem was that prisoners in the back seat could see the dungeon as we neared the place, and many times they would go completely berserk when we opened the backdoor to get them out. Their violent reaction often took us by surprise because we had mellowed out after the arrest and long drive.
>
> —A police officer

Both military personnel and law enforcement officers need to understand that they can be vulnerable when a prisoner sees their final destination. Just as there is a psychological impact on some prisoners to seeing the jail out the back seat window of a police car, there are also prisoners who react violently upon seeing a jail cell. Law enforcement officers, and military personnel handling POWs, must have careful processes in place to make sure that prisoners are treated appropriately, weapons have been removed and secured, and every step is done properly. This should include ensuring that officers and guards are alert and ready in the booking facility or POW handling area. Many police departments require that a fresh officer take over because they understand that there might be a dangerous vulnerability.

"Consolidation and reorganization on the objective" is a standard military term for what occurs after victory. The enemy has fled and the hilltop has been secured. The battle is over. Or is it? Remember Napoleon's words that "the moment of greatest vulnerability is immediately after victory." This is why a smart military leader will counterattack immediately after the enemy has pushed his troops off of a position. It's preferable for the leader to counter with fresh reserves, soldiers not depleted from the physical and psychological roller coaster ride of the fight. Since the enemy might relax and become vulnerable in their victory, it is possible that even a small force could overpower them and recapture the objective.

In order to prevent warriors from becoming vulnerable after they have secured an objective, they should be trained to automatically begin a series of tasks to keep them occupied. They should establish 360-degree security and prepare defensive positions and fields-of-fire in the event of an enemy counterattack. They should redistribute ammo, drink lots of fluids, provide first aid, evacuate casualties and prisoners, and account for all equipment. Leaders should supervise and report the situation to a higher authority. In the military and on SWAT teams the acronym L.A.C.E. is often used to define this swirl of activity: liquids, ammunition, casualties, and equipment. By rehearsing this continuation of operations during training, warriors in real combat will not relax during this vulnerable moment but stay busy performing the vital duties required to survive and thrive on the battlefield.

This is sometimes referred to as "follow-through considerations" in the law enforcement community. As Gary Klugiewicz says to his students, "It's not Miller time now! There's still a lot to be done before the mission is complete."

Military, police officers, firefighters, paramedics, and others working in stressful occupations need to develop this mindset by practicing consolidation and reorganization so they are ready to take on the next mission. For those in such professions, the next high-risk call can come at anytime and lives depend on their ability to drive on to the next objective. An old Japanese saying communicates this concept succinctly: "After the battle, tighten your helmet cords." In other words, just because you have won, don't let down your guard.

No Man Knows But a Soldier, How Sweet Sleep Is

With a sand bag for a pillow
I chase a distant memory of a thing called sleep,
I whisper in the dark and pray God my soul to keep.

—James Adam Holland
"The Freedom Of A Soldier"

Throughout early history, man almost always got enough sleep, because when the sun went down there was nothing else to do. You could only have so much sex and do so much talking, and then you rolled over and went to sleep. So the human body never had to develop the powerful signals needed to make you get enough sleep. Then with the arrival of cheap, artificial lighting, man was physically able to go nonstop for days on end, but psychologically and physiologically the human body is not designed to go for long periods without sleep.

We are not even sure why we need sleep. When *U.S. News and World Report* magazine did a special on the "Great Mysteries of Science" a few years ago, one of the mysteries discussed was "Why do we need sleep?" We do not understand why we dream and we do not even understand why, for example, males get an erection (and females experience clitoral engorgement) during rapid eye movement (REM) sleep stage. (In the psychology curriculum at West Point, we teach that this is why males sometimes awake with an erection. Urinating is a non-sexual act which apparently sends a message to the body that makes the erection go away. But the erection does not occur just because your bladder is full.)

Everything about sleep is a mystery, but one thing is certain: our body needs four things to survive: air, water, food, and sleep. You can die from lack of sleep faster than you can die from lack of food. Your body sends powerful signals that make you breathe, drink and eat, but over the millennia there has been little need for the body to send strong sleep signals. Those that are sent can be pushed aside and ignored far more easily than the signals for other essential requirements for survival.

All of us know that missed sleep makes us feel drowsy and lousy, but most people are unaware of the profound negative impact on health and performance associated with a lack of sleep.

Stress is a major destroyer and disabler of a warrior. More soldiers were pulled out of combat in World War I, World War II and Korea because of psychiatric casualties than were killed by the enemy. Without argument, stress is a primary concern for our warriors and their leaders, and one of the best ways to heal and recover from psychological stress is to sleep. "Sleep that knits up the ravell'd sleave of care," as Shakespeare put it.

Sleep deprivation is the best way to physically predispose yourself to become a stress casualty. It has been linked to mental health problems, cancer, common colds, depression, diabetes, obesity and strokes. As it relates to job performance, sleep deprivation impairs: reaction time, judgment, vision, information processing, short-term memory, performance, motivation, vigilance and patience.

On the other hand, research shows that sufficient sleep, combined with a nutritious diet, lots of fluids and exercise are critical for a long and healthy life. Unfortunately, our society is full of sincerely deluded people who honestly believe that they can get by forever on four hours of sleep.

When you take a Mr. I-can-go-forever-on-four-hours-of-sleep and put him in the timeless environment of a sleep lab, he immediately begins to catch-up on his "sleep debt." He might sleep up to 12 hours a day until he has recuperated, and then he sleeps seven, eight and nine hours a day on a normal healthy sleep cycle. Scientists used to say that you could not catch-up on lost sleep, but now we know they were wrong. Dead wrong--as in killing people wrong. Your body builds up a sleep debt, and just as you can catch-up on dehydration and malnutrition, you can catch-up on sleep. So, if you got only three hours sleep last night, you can use caffeine to get yourself through the day. But as soon as you get a chance, sleep in late or take some major naps to catch up on your sleep debt.

There was a study conducted by the United States Army on an artillery battalion. The troops suffered terribly for us to get this data, so perhaps we should pay attention. The battalion was divided into four batteries, and then conducted fire missions (artillery exercises) for 20 days straight, every waking hour of every day. The first battery, Group One, got seven hours of sleep a day, Group Two got six hours, Group Three got five, and Group Four really suffered with only four hours sleep a day. At the end of 20 days, Group One, which got seven hours of sleep fired at 98 percent of peak efficiency. Group Two fired at 50 percent, Group Three at 28 percent, and the poor guys who got only four hours sleep fired at 15 percent of peak efficiency. The four-hour group was not only useless, they were dangerous!

When you get about seven hours sleep a night, you can go a long time, though eight is probably better. Any less and you start building up a sleep debt that can take a profound psychological and physiological toll. If you spend your life severely malnourished, it will probably take years off of your life. Likewise, if you lead your life severely sleep deprived, it will probably take years off of your life. Few healthy individuals will voluntarily lead a malnourished life, but many individuals do voluntarily lead a sleep-deprived life.

Throughout history sleep has always been the soldier's best medicine. In World War I and World War II, troops would rotate out of the trenches or out of the front lines and the first thing they would do is sleep. But in Iraq and Afghanistan, U.S. troops coming off combat patrols would often return to their barracks and play video games, watch DVDs and television, and surf the Internet.

This form of escapism and the false sense of control given by video games seem to be incredibly alluring as well as addictive to men and women in combat. In reality, this can be a self-inflicted wound that greatly increases their vulnerability to PTSD, and to illness since the immune system diminishes with sleep deprivation.

Every pro ball team on the planet has "lights out" by at least 10 or 11 o'clock the night before a game. If a pro ball player stays up the night before a game, playing video games or watching TV, the other players would kick his tail, the coach would fine him, and that nonsense would stop immediately. Well, our military and our cops are their city's and their nation's pro team! But in this game, in the merciless, unforgiving, high-stakes game of combat, if you lose people die!

We are warriors. We are willing to walk out the door and suck up bullets if we have to. But it ought to seriously tick you off to suck up bullets when it could have been avoided. Similarly, way we are willing to be sleep deprived if the mission absolutely demands it. But it ought to seriously tick you off to be sleep deprived if it could have been avoided. And if you do it to yourself, it is a self-inflicted wound!

Thus, the U.S. military has learned that sleep management can be a major war-winning, war-losing issue. And if a large number of PTSD cases have come out of the war in Iraq and Afghanistan, this could be a major reason why. So our senior NCOs and officers have accepted the responsibility to be "mommy" and make the troops get the sleep they need. I tell this to the police officers I teach, and then I ask them, "Who's going to be your mommy? You have to do it yourself. You have to make it happen." It is a matter of professionalism and self-discipline. A matter of life and death . . . as are so many things for those who walk the razor's edge, in the merciless, unforgiving realm of combat.

The Equivalent of Legally Drunk

. . . like a drunken sailor on a mast,
Ready with every nod to tumble down.

—Shakespeare
King Richard III

A person deprived of sleep for 24 hours is virtually the physiological and psychological equivalent of being legally drunk. Dr. Jacques Gouws, a retired military psychologist, makes the point that this can be even "more so in the combat zone where you are pumping adrenaline like mad, and not just infrequently as the cops do. The soldier in combat is physically and emotionally significantly more fatigued because of the duration of the sustained military combat operations." *Tired Cops: The Importance of Managing Police Fatigue*, by Dr. Bryan Vila, is a superb book that should be mandatory reading for everyone in the warrior community. In this book, Dr. Vila tells about one study which showed that sleep-deprived people scored as badly or worse on reaction-time tests as those with a blood-alcohol level of .10 percent, a percentage deemed legally drunk in all states. After alcohol intoxication, lack of sleep is the next major cause of accidents. The National Highway Traffic Safety Administration links nearly 100,000 crashes a year to drowsiness.

Over a century ago, railroad engineers were required by federal law to get enough sleep. Today, airline pilots, truckers, nuclear plant operators, air traffic controllers, and many others are also mandated to get sufficient sleep for their jobs. In the summer of 2002, the medical community established regulations requiring that doctors and interns get enough sleep because the legal liability of having zombie-like medical personnel making life and death decisions was simply too great.

Sleep deprivation inflicted upon students in a controlled training environment can be a useful form of stress inoculation. But every effort must be made to avoid sleep deprivation if those students have to make real decisions that might result in the loss of lives, such as doctors in a hospital and military leaders in combat.

When I was in Ranger school, the U.S. Army used weeks of extensive food and sleep deprivation to provide stress inoculation designed to prepare me for the stress of combat leadership. This training is highly effective and it works in controlled environments where lives are not on the line and dangerous situations are closely monitored. Also, sleep deprivation in leadership schools teach you how to work with and lead sleep deprived people. Sleep deprived warriors will have great difficulty understanding what you tell them, so you learn to speak in simple sentences, avoid giving them complex tasks, break tasks into simple intermediate objectives, repeat the essential points, have them repeat your instructions back to you, and closely supervise their performance. These are all valuable lessons to learn in training, but in situations where lives are on the line, we must do everything humanly possible to make sure that the individuals who are responsible for human lives get enough sleep.

We must not deprive students of sleep or food for so long that it does physical harm. Indeed, in recent years the use of food deprivation in Ranger school has been reduced after long-term studies determined that just those few months of food and sleep deprivation were causing serious, long-term health effects on the students. As Dr. Clete DiGiovanni put it, "You cannot condition yourself to get by with significantly less sleep." The lesson that Rangers should take from Ranger school is not that they are immortal and don't need sleep or food. The lesson a wise man takes from such experiences is to remember just how poorly you performed when you were sleep deprived, and to remember to always sleep and eat whenever you get the chance.

Today, the medical community must adhere to strict regulations that require them to get enough sleep so that they can perform their life-and-death duties. Police officers, peacekeepers and combat soldiers, however, have no such requirements. Today's understaffed and overworked warriors carry guns, drive vehicles and make life and death decisions, all the while suffering from sleep deprivation.

I guarantee that a sleepy police officer (or maybe even a sleepy peacekeeper) will one day soon make a questionable decision that negligently hurts or kills someone. When the case goes to court, the lawyer will ask, "Officer, how much sleep did you get the night before the incident? How much sleep the night before that? And the night before that?" They will subpoena the officer's work logs to show the volume of overtime he worked, and they will show that he, like so many other officers today, had no more than four hours sleep each night for the last 20 days. Or, better yet (from the accusing lawyer's standpoint) he will prove that the officer had not slept for 24 hours, and was therefore the equivalent of being legally drunk. Then the lawyer will ask the jury what they think the officer would do if he caught them legally drunk behind the wheel of a vehicle. The result of such a lawsuit, to the officer and to the department, would be devastating.

When a warrior is sleep deprived, he is grouchy, his IQ seems to go down, his hand and eye coordination is poor and he nods off at inappropriate times. My co-author tells of an officer in his department who worked two weeks of double shifts and a couple of triple shifts, meaning 24 solid hours. Officers working in neighboring patrol districts complained of his poor performance and incoherent speech. The sleep-deprived officer told Christensen that he was so fatigued that he had stopped taking a shotgun out with him because he was unable to handle it safely. Clearly this was an injury and a lawsuit waiting to happen. Fortunately, the two weeks passed without officers or citizens getting hurt, or the department getting sued. When sleep deprivation and its dangerous side-effects happen on overtime, the only good thing is that the officer is making one-and-a-half times more money than one on regular time. But the risk is too great.

Let's look at this from another angle. Say you are a police chief or a combat unit commander and, like most organizations, you are short on manpower. I come to you from, say, Brand X academy and offer to let you hire my Brand X officers. I tell you that they have an IQ five or 10 points less than the average cop or soldier, their hand and eye coordination is poor, they are incredibly grouchy, their decision-making skills are virtually nonexistent, and they tend to nod off. Oh, and I might ask you to pay one and a half times as much (overtime pay) for these warriors. You want them? I can hazard a guess as to where you would tell me to put my Brand X police officers or soldiers.

The frightening reality is that my Brand Xers have the same negative characteristics as real sleep-deprived warriors working multiple shifts or overtime. Some people might think this is helping the organization, but, with the possible exception of some extreme combat circumstances, they are wrong. As Colonel Gregory Belenky, the lead sleep researcher at the Walter Reed Army Institute of Research, puts it, "There's nothing heroic about staying up."

Sleep and PTSD

O sleep, O gentle sleep,
Nature's soft nurse!

—Shakespeare
King Henry IV

Insufficient sleep and physical exhaustion is a key factor in predisposing you to be a stress casualty. As Patton said, "Fatigue makes cowards of us all." If we know that stress is a key disabler of warriors and that lack of sleep is a key factor that predisposes warriors toward stress casualties, physical illness and PTSD, then proper sleep management should be a "no brainer."

Many law enforcement agencies have told me that they have a serious stress problem and want me to teach them how to deal with it. When I tell them that they must first ensure that everyone gets enough sleep, they argue that it is impossible. "Okay," I say. "Then die." I am kidding, of course, but I say it to make the point that if they want to draw overtime, enjoy a full career and watch their grandbabies grow, then one of the most important things they can do is manage their sleep.

Exxon Valdese, Chernobyl and Three Mile Island had one thing in common: They were all industrial accidents that occurred in the middle of the night involving people with sleep management problems. Insufficient sleep is responsible for billions of dollars of industrial accidents. Similar problems have been happening to our warriors for decades and we are just now beginning to be held accountable for them. Yes, police agencies and military units are often in desperate need of manpower, but grinding the warriors they have into the dirt is not the answer. If we were to do to our airline pilots what we do to our cops and soldiers, 747s would be falling out of the sky like hailstones.

During the Vietnam War and the Gulf War, soldiers went for days on end without rest or sleep. My co-author can recall many days of sleep deprivation in Vietnam. Christensen said that once he went so long without sleep that when he finally did get some, he slept through a rocket attack. If you have not been in one of those, believe it when I say that they are really noisy.

Due to a better understanding of a soldier's requirement for sleep, this type of deprivation is now considerably less common. Since the early 1970s, the United States military has tried to initiate a revolution in sleep management. Ideally, when the military goes long and hard, it is done intentionally, but then they immediately get themselves back on a sleep cycle, because they know that sleep is as vital as air, water and food.

Steven Brust, one of my favorite authors, had a veteran military commander proclaim after reviewing the troops that, "I can always tell who has never seen battle before." A subordinate asks if that was because they seemed nervous? "No," the commander replies, "anyone in his right mind is nervous before a battle."

Well, the subordinate asks, is it because they seem more eager than those with more experience? No, that's not it either. Finally the subordinate asks directly, then how can you tell?

"Because they look more tired than the rest," the commander answered.

Many old warriors have told me during my interviews with them that a soldier never misses the chance to sleep. As John Mosby said in his Civil War memoirs, "No man knows but a soldier, how sweet sleep is."

Caffeine Can Be Our Friend; Nicotine is Not

Good coffee is like friendship: rich and warm and strong.
—Pan-American Coffee Bureau

Caffeine is a powerful and useful drug to temporarily combat the effects of sleep deprivation, but only if you have not abused it. If you need a "three-bagger" to get you kick-started first thing in the morning, a 64-ounce "Big-Gulp Cola" to keep you going throughout the morning, two or three big, strong cups to keep you moving after lunch, and a big cup to face the family at the end of the day, you are addicted and abusing a powerful drug that will not be there for you when you need it the most. It is best to use caffeine only when necessary, such as first thing in the morning and right after lunch, two times when most of us need a little help. Never use caffeine within five or six hours of bedtime.

If caffeine does not bother your sleep, that is proof that you have already built up a powerful tolerance, and it will be ineffective when you need it. Cut back, but do not go cold turkey. Starting tomorrow, drink half of what you normally consume, cut it in half the next day, and so on, until you are taking caffeine only two or three times a day. Then when you really need it for that extended operation, it will be of use to you.

Nicotine does not help sleep deprivation. There is always a troop out on the perimeter, who says, "If I could just have a smoke I could stay awake." Wrong. After he completes the busy work of retrieving a cigarette and lighting it, he returns to being just as sleepy as he was before, but now he has a fire starter in his mouth.

There is, however, one way that nicotine can help you with sleep deprivation. I was in Texas once giving a law enforcement presentation when an old Texas Ranger came up during a break, and said, "Colonel, you're wrong. Nicotine can keep you awake."

I said, "Sir, who am I to argue with you?"

He said, "No, listen to me. You've got to chew it."

"Well," I said, "maybe if you have something in your mouth, I guess I can see that."

"No, listen to me. You have to chew your tobaccy, spit it in your hand, then you rub it into your eyes."

Actually, this is an old technique. The son of a World War II veteran told me about his father, a man who had been besieged in Bastogne in the Battle of the Bulge with the 101st Airborne Division. He said that the enemy kept attacking relentlessly, day after day, making it impossible for him and his fellow troops to sleep because they did not know when they would be hit again. To stay awake and alert, they would get a cigarette, remove a little flake of tobacco and drop it underneath the eyelid of their non-firing eye (the one not used to sight your rifle). It burned and stung so badly that it was impossible for them to drift asleep. Pain will keep you awake, and that's the only way that nicotine will do you any good.

four

Fear, Physiological Arousal and Performance: *Conditions White, Yellow, Red, Gray and Black*

On the battlefield, the real enemy is fear, not the bayonet or bullet.

—Robert Jackson

Conditions White, Yellow, and Red

We boil at different degrees.

—Ralph Waldo Emerson
"Eloquence"

When you are asleep or just going about your day unfocused and unprepared for anything bad to happen, you are at your lowest level of readiness. Call it, "Condition White," a place where you are helpless, vulnerable and in denial. White is for sheep.

When you move up to a level of basic alertness and readiness, a place where you are psychologically prepared for combat, you have entered the realm of "Condition Yellow." Dogs, who are predators by nature, seldom leave Condition Yellow. They are always ready to play, fight, frolic, mate, or run. They are survivors. Warriors, too, must strive to exist in Condition Yellow. A warrior always tries to sit with his back to a wall.

There is no specific heart rate associated with Condition White and Condition Yellow; the difference is more psychological than physiological. However, as the level of arousal increases, we can begin to associate the "Condition" levels with specific heart rate levels.

There is a zone that exists, generally between 115 and 145 beats per minute (bpm), where you are at your optimal survival and combat performance level. Let us call this, "Condition Red." Your complex motor skills, visual reaction time and cognitive reaction time are all at their peak, but you begin to pay a price. Starting at about 115 bpm, your fine-motor skills begin to deteriorate.

We should be cautious about fixing specific heart rate numbers (or any other precise measures of physiological arousal) on Condition Yellow, Red, or Black. The impact of these Conditions can vary greatly depending upon

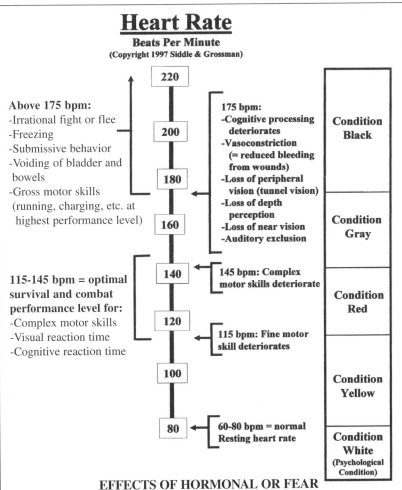

Heart Rate

Beats Per Minute
(Copyright 1997 Siddle & Grossman)

220

Above 175 bpm:
-Irrational fight or flee
-Freezing
-Submissive behavior
-Voiding of bladder and
  bowels
-Gross motor skills
  (running, charging, etc. at
  highest performance level)

175 bpm:
-Cognitive processing
  deteriorates
-Vasoconstriction
  (= reduced bleeding
  from wounds)
-Loss of peripheral
  vision (tunnel vision)
-Loss of depth
  perception
-Loss of near vision
-Auditory exclusion

Condition Black

200

180

160

Condition Gray

**115-145 bpm = optimal
survival and combat
performance level for:**
-Complex motor skills
-Visual reaction time
-Cognitive reaction time

140

**145 bpm: Complex
motor skills deteriorate**

Condition Red

120

**115 bpm: Fine motor
skill deteriorates**

100

Condition Yellow

80

**60-80 bpm = normal
Resting heart rate**

Condition White
(Psychological Condition)

EFFECTS OF HORMONAL OR FEAR INDUCED HEART RATE INCREASE

Notes:
1. This data is for hormonal or fear induced heart rate increases resulting from sympathetic nervous system arousal. Exercise induced increases will not have the same effect.
2. Hormonal induced performance and strength increases can achieve 100% of potential max within 10 seconds, but drop 55% after 30 seconds, 35% after 60 seconds, and 31% after 90 seconds. It takes a minimum of 3 minutes of rest to "recharge" the system.
3. Any extended period of relaxation after intense sympathetic nervous system arousal can result in a parasympathetic backlash, with significant drops in energy level, heart rate and blood pressure. This can manifest itself as normal shock symptoms (dizziness, nausea and/or vomiting, clammy skin) and/or profound exhaustion.

training, physical fitness and other factors. Also, it must be understood that these heart rates apply only to survival stress or fear induced heart rate increases. You can do a set of wind sprints and get your heart rate to 200 bpm, but the effect of this exercise induced heart rate increase will not be the same as when fear or survival stress causes the increase. Furthermore, when you combine the vasoconstriction of fear induced heart rate increase with physical exertion or exercise demands, the result seems to be an "amplifying" effect, which can result in some extraordinarily high heart rates. So we must note that physiological factors are poor indicators of combat performance, since so much depends upon individual characteristics. Still, everyone has a Condition Yellow, Red, and Black, and it is important to understand how physiological arousal can interact with combat performance.

Thus 115 bpm is not an absolute with every person, but for most it is a starting point. Police officers often see a symptom of this when they stop a motorist for a traffic violation and the driver's hands shake so badly that he can barely sign the ticket. The same is true of people involved in a traffic accident, when afterwards they have difficulty scrawling down their telephone number. Such symptoms are a result of early stages of vasoconstriction, a condition that restricts the flow of blood to the extremities.

I frequently train special operations warriors. When you think about special ops you envision Rangers, Green Berets, or SEALS, but a large portion of our special ops community also consists of the superb pilots and flight crews who support these elite warriors. Some U.S. Air Force pilots I have worked with told me about one pilot trainer who gives them small, yellow dots with adhesive on the back. The pilots stick these dots on their watches and on their cockpits as a reminder to stay in Condition Yellow—alert, but not over aroused. If a pilot becomes too aroused and begins to enter Condition Red, the price he pays is loss of fine-motor skills. Having your helicopter pilot lose his fine-motor control as he makes a close approach on a hot landing zone is not a good thing. Pilots try to exist in a zen-like state of constant, mellow Yellow.

Other warriors must also maintain a state of Condition Yellow. For example, when I train hostage negotiators, I stress the importance of functioning in Condition Yellow. I am proud to be a member of the Board of Technical Advisors to the American Sniper Association, which is probably the world's leading private, law enforcement and military sniper training organization. Snipers must maintain precision fine-motor skills, so when I train them I emphasize the need to remain in Condition Yellow. I had the privilege of training an international bomb technicians' conference. Now that is a group of individuals who must remain calm and in Condition Yellow when they are doing their job.

It's an entirely different situation for the point man on a SWAT team going through a door to confront a barricaded gunman. He needs to have his cognitive reaction time, visual reaction time and complex-motor skills all functioning at the highest levels. He needs to be in Condition Red. Yes, he loses some of his fine-motor skills, but in his case that is an acceptable price to pay. Through intense, high-repetition training, he will turn the skills that he needs to perform into "muscle memory." Magazine changes, misfeed drills, weapons handling, and handcuffing are just a few of the many skills he must rehearse until he can perform these intricate tasks flawlessly, without conscious thought, even though he is in Condition Red. He might be in trouble if he is required to perform a fine-motor skill that he has not rehearsed, but this is an acceptable risk.

The Optimal Level of Arousal

Screw your courage to the sticking place . . .

—Shakespeare
Macbeth

The linking of specific heart rate with task performance was pioneered by Bruce K. Siddle, author of the excellent book, *Sharpening the Warrior's Edge*, and one of the great pioneers in the field of "Warrior Science™." In 1997, I was asked to write the entry on "Psychological Effects of Combat" in the *Academic Press Encyclopedia of Violence Peace and Conflict*. I asked Bruce Siddle to co-author the article with me because of the research he had conducted on the physiology of combat. We included the "Heart Rate and Performance" chart with its thermometer scale in the article. World-class experts were asked to conduct a peer review of this encyclopedia entry. The reviews were very supportive, and one even stated that, "This is brilliant!"

Due to the nature of the double-blind peer review process, I'll probably never know the identity of this kind and generous reviewer, but the truth is that this research is not really "brilliant." It is only an old soldier and an old cop asking questions that no one has asked before.

These initial findings will continue to be updated and modified as new information becomes available. Today we can take this model a step further by integrating the color codes and the "Inverted-U" model (a classic, universally accepted model of stress and performance) with Bruce Siddle's heart rate data, to form a "Unified Model of Stress & Performance."

It should be noted here that the color code system (which was popularized by Colonel Jeff Cooper, one of the greatest of the early pioneers in the field of warrior science) has always been a mental state, rather than a physiological level. It is applied here with due apologies and full credit to its original developers.

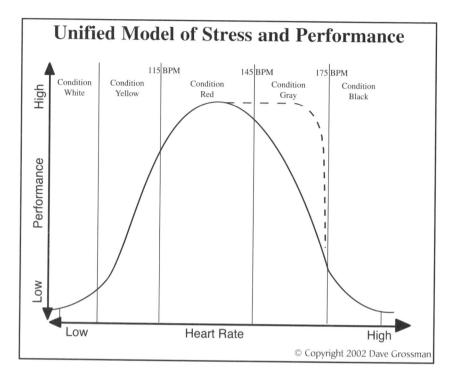

The Gray Zone, Autopilot and Stress Inoculation

> I tell my men it's okay to be afraid. If I didn't think you had fear, I'd think twice about you. But it's learning how to operate with that fear, and break through it, and do your job as a professional.
> —Command Sergeant Major Bob Gallagher
> U.S. Army, Veteran of Somalia
> On preparing his soldiers for the invasion of Iraq

Pete Pomerleau and Don Lazzarini are law enforcement instructors associated with the BAHR Training Group, an organization that provides law enforcement training on a large scale. They have been replicating some of Bruce Siddle's research in which heart rate monitors were attached to law enforcement officers engaged in highly stressful, combat simulation training using "paint bullets." These bullets hurt when they hit, which is desirable because pain and the possibility of pain makes this training a form of "stress inoculation."

We need more systematic research in this area, but the BAHR research got the same results as Bruce Siddle. Pomerleau and Lazzarini found that when the average police officer experiences a stress induced (i.e., adrenaline-induced) heart rate increase in the area of 145 bpm, there is a significant breakdown in performance. But this is not true for everyone. Apparently, if you have practiced the required skills extensively, you can "push the envelope" of Condition Red, enabling extraordinary performance at accelerated heart rate levels. Let us call this zone, roughly between 145 and 175 bpm, "Condition Gray." (Beyond Condition Gray is "Condition Black," an area marked by catastrophic breakdown of mental and physical performance, which will be covered shortly.)

All of this research is still in its inception, an embryonic realm of fascinating new inquiry. Bruce Siddle writes in *Warrior Science*™ that,

> The study of man's behavior in combat is a study of paradoxes, enigmas and extremes. The combat experience is an intangible, and hides in the deep recesses of the human psyche. Therefore, the combat experience is difficult to chart with scientific measurements – and even more difficult for the world of scholars and historians to enter.

Condition Gray in particular is a truly "gray area" about which we need to do considerably more research.

Ron Avery is a law enforcement trainer and a world-class competitive combat pistol shooter starring in three highly successful instructional videos called *Secrets of a Professional Shooter*. Ron says that he functions on two levels during competitions. When he is "running and gunning," his heartbeat is around 145 bpm. For the individuals in the law enforcement research conducted by Bruce Siddle, and in the BAHR research, 145 bpm represents a level at which performance begins to break down, but for Ron this is his optimal level of arousal. He has pushed the envelope. He has rehearsed and trained, turning each action into "muscle memory," permitting himself to function at an expert level in Condition Gray. This concept of muscle memory is also referred to as "autopilot," which will be addressed in greater detail later.

Ron Avery calls this process "stress acclimatization," which is a good, descriptive term. The fundamental concept is that prior success under stressful conditions acclimatizes you to similar situations and promotes future success. I use the psychological term "inoculation" to describe this process. Whatever we call it, there can be no doubt that it works. Ron puts it this way:

> With the proper training and requisite conditioning and practice, we can achieve skills that others think impossible. I think there is a whole realm of possibilities that we can teach and train [warriors] to do. Stress acclimatization is about measuring precise doses of stress followed by waves of recovery and then repeating these cycles very specifically. There must be time for adaptation to take place and there must be enough training, repeated over time, to help it stick as well as reinforcing the conditioning.

My old boss at West Point, Colonel Jack Beach, Ph.D., always makes the point that emotions have at least three components: cognitive, physiological and behavioral. An important part of what we achieve through stress inoculation is cognitive. The student's experience in training helps to take some of the surprise out of it when the real situation arises. Effective training also elevates the student's sense of confidence, which is another cognitive aspect of stress inoculation. The sense of personal effectiveness and self-confidence created by realistic training is as much a stress reducer as when the muscles go on autopilot. As the Duke of Wellington put it, "No man fears to do that which he knows he does well."

Taking the surprise out of combat, raising the sense of confidence, and cognitively preparing the warrior for battle is one of the primary objectives of this book. Thus, this book can be seen as a form of stress inoculation, and the reduction in surprise and the increase in confidence provided within these pages will hopefully reduce the stress of combat. Throughout this book I will focus on the physiological and behavioral aspects of preparing for combat, but we should always keep in mind these cognitive aspects.

There is evidence to indicate that world class experts in top physical condition, under specific, controlled situations, can use autopilot and stress inoculation to push the envelope of Condition Red high into the Gray zone. For example, one report in *Popular Science Magazine* says that top NASCAR and formula one drivers generally maintain a heart rate of around 175 bpm for hours on end. Using what we know from other realms of research involving performance under stress, we can hypothesize that these race car drivers have a limited set of skills (turn left, turn right, accelerate, brake) that has been extensively rehearsed, and needs to be performed with extraordinary speed. Thus, the best-of-the-best among these drivers appear to be pushing themselves, pushing the envelope of their personal Condition Red, up to the outer edge of the Gray zone.

In 2001, as part of a comprehensive two-week combatives instructor course, a U.S. Army Special Forces (Green Beret) officer (in conjunction with Dr. C.A. Morgan of the Yale Center for PTSD and Gary Hazlett, a U.S. Army special operations psychologist) conducted "heart rate variability research" on some of our nation's most elite warriors. Due to the rigorous and demanding course of instruction, this select group of Special Forces soldiers was already at an exceptionally high level of physical fitness. Thanks to many years of hard physical training and extensive combat skills development, they essentially have become world-class combat "athletes." The primary instructor designed and conducted a force-on-force close quarter battle (CQB) "stress-test." Having to rely upon a combination of urban warfare and hand-to-hand combat skills, each Green Beret individually engaged trained role-players who wore Blauer High Gear impact reduction suits and acted out varying levels of compliance. While wearing full combat equipment and using simunition "paint bullet" equipped firearms for "lethal force" as well as full-contact empty-hand skills for "non-lethal" situations, the Green Berets were assaulted with an overwhelming noise stimulus and a poorly lit macabre environment. At one point in the event, and completely without warning, a controller produced a significant pain stimulus with an electric shock to the upper body of each participant replicating hits from enemy gunfire.

Despite these extraordinarily challenging circumstances, all of these warriors performed superbly. Looking only at maximum heart rates is a gross oversimplification of the complex subject of "heart rate variability," but it is interesting to note that those who performed best had maximum heart rates near 175 bpm, while those who were marginally less proficient had maximum heart rates around 180 bpm. Like our NASCAR drivers, 175 bpm seems to be the optimal level of performance, and even at that level their physical condition and their extensive training provided the stress inoculation and the autopilot responses that permitted them to push the "Condition Red" envelope to the outer extent of "Condition Gray."

There were however, exceptions. After every engagement, the Green Berets were required to restrain each role player, whether "dead" or subdued in hand-to-hand combat, with "flex-cuffs"—a type of flexible handcuff consisting of a narrow plastic strip with a small one-way hole on one end. The opposite (running) end is inserted into the hole and can then be tightened. (Smaller versions are sometimes used to tie off plastic garbage bags.) Inserting the end of the restraint into that little hole takes a relatively high level of fine-motor control, a process that had not been rehearsed extensively by the Green Berets. The result was that the individuals who had not "pre-threaded" their flex-cuffs as they had been taught, had significantly more difficulty when it came to performing cuffing procedures under extremely high stress. Some were, at times, visibly unable to thread the cuffs and subsequently did not adequately restrain the subjects. The soldiers who properly prepared their cuffs performed the skill on "autopilot" and were able to simultaneously cuff and scan their environment.

When learning skills and ingraining them as muscle memory or autopilot responses, it is important that only one way be taught. W.E. Hicks' 1952 study found that as the possible responses increased from one to two, reaction time increased by 58 percent. In other words, having to choose between options takes time, and the more options you have, the greater the reaction time. This is often referred to as "Hicks' Law," but Sun Tzu said the same thing many centuries ago: "The more possibilities you present to the enemy, the more diffuse he is forced to become. The more diffuse he becomes, the more difficult it is for him to concentrate sufficiently to make a successful attack." We want to confuse the enemy with a variety of possibilities, but we do not want to do that to ourselves. Thus, a simple set of skills, combined with an emphasis on actions requiring complex and gross motor muscle operations (as opposed to fine-motor control), all extensively rehearsed, allows for extraordinary performance levels under stress.

Leo Frankowski is a brilliant engineer with several patents and many successful science fiction books to his name. He and I have collaborated on several military science fiction novels. He says, "On the walls of most engineering outfits, you will find a sign that reads 'KISS!' When a rookie asks what it is all about, he is told, 'Keep It Simple Stupid.'" This fundamental law of engineering also applies to training and preparing warriors for combat.

There are many forms of stress inoculation. Firefighters are inoculated against fire. Sailors are inoculated against sinking ships by placing them in compartments that flood with water as they fight to repair simulated damage. Many individuals are inoculated against heights through rappelling and rock climbing experiences.

Every warrior organization should coordinate with the local police K-9 unit or a patrol dog company, to see if the organization's members can put on the appropriate protective equipment, and experience what it is like to be bit repeatedly by numerous attack dogs. Preferably one at a time, as opposed to all at once. (My personal thanks to the Arizona K-9 Association for permitting me to be bit by every dog in the state of Arizona . . . in the prescribed manner.) Gavin de Becker's organization is the first warrior group I know of to incorporate this training for all of their personnel. They call it "Combat Fear Inoculation," in which each member of their team of elite bodyguards is required to participate. A true, deranged, killing rage can only be experienced and inoculated against in this manner, since trainees always know that a rational trainer will not intentionally commit an act that will seriously injure them. But an attack dog will, quite happily.

Reacting calmly and rationally to fire, taking necessary and appropriate actions in situations involving heights, and dealing effectively with an attacking dog are examples of skills that save lives, but they are not the hardest thing that warriors are called upon to do. These are bad enough, but warriors must also move toward the sound of the guns, toward the most cunning, ingenious, destructive creature on the face of the earth: one of their own species trying to kill them. As we have demonstrated, for most human beings this is the universal human phobia.

So how do you inoculate someone against a gunfight? As we will see later, warriors can (and must) be inoculated against this stressor by experiencing force-on-force scenarios in which they shoot and are shot at by paint-filled, gunpowder propelled, plastic bullets. When I trained the Singapore special operations forces, they referred to these as "pain bullets"— an appropriate name.

Stress inoculation is not perfect, and to get a useful degree of protection it has to be precisely applied. Last year's flu vaccine is of limited value this year. A smallpox inoculation provides little protection against yellow fever, and a firefighter's inoculation against fire is of little value if people shoot at him. Yet, there does appear to be a transfer or "seepage" in the area of stress inoculation. Just as learning one language makes it easier to learn others, stress inoculation in one area makes it easier to quickly adapt to a new stressor. Paratroopers are stress inoculated against parachuting out of an aircraft, thus making them elite troops who were better able to adapt quickly and fully to the demands of ground combat.

There are many case studies that support the theory that the value of stress inoculation is not just inoculation against a specific stressor. There seems to be a kind of "stress immune system," which permits you to get better and better at adapting to new stresses.

A training officer in one major U.S. police department told me that they used a full-contact fighting champion to train their police. He was deeply respected, and an extraordinarily competent hand-to-hand combat fighter. His level of stress inoculation in unarmed combat was off the scale. However, when they invited him to join them in a force-on-force, paint bullet scenario, his skills in unarmed combat were of no use to him. In his first engagement, his heart rate shot up to over 200 bpm and he dropped his gun. However, his previous stress inoculation allowed him to quickly adapt, and by the end of the day he was performing superbly. (This warrior must be respected and admired for his willingness to subject himself to the embarrassment of learning a new skill in front of others. There is no shame in failure. For a warrior the only shame is in not trying.)

Using Tactical Breathing to Stay in the Zone

I will not fear. Fear is the mind-killer. Fear is the little-death that brings total obliteration. I will face my fear. I will permit it to pass over me and through me. And when it has gone past I will turn the inner eye to see its path. Where the fear has gone there will be nothing. Only I will remain.

—Frank Herbert
Dune

Autopilot responses developed through repetitive practice, and stress inoculation through realistic, stressful training are two powerful and effective tools to push the envelope and stay in the zone. One additional tool to control physiological response is the tactical breathing exercise.

Let us go back to Ron Avery and his performance as a professional shooter. When running and gunning in a pistol competition, his heart rate peaks around 145 bpm, but when he is standing and shooting, his heartbeat stays around 90 bpm. He pulls himself down to Condition Yellow, like a sniper taking calm, precision shots. A good professional shooter functions at two levels, bouncing back and forth between Condition Yellow and Condition Red (or, sometimes, in a Condition Red that extends into the realm of Condition Gray).

Something similar happens with professional basketball players. They are running up and down the court, functioning in high Condition Red, often pushing the envelope well into the Gray zone, which is fine for that phase of the game. However, should a player stop and attempt to make a free throw while his heart is pounding in his chest, he is going to "throw a brick"—a miss. Typically, a professional basketball player pauses for a moment before making a free throw and intuitively knows to take a few deep breaths. He uses all the time available to him to bring his heart rate down. He rolls his large shoulder muscles, consciously relaxes his body and avoids looking at the crowd as he concentrates on his task. He intentionally pulls himself down into Condition Yellow, becoming a "sniper" in order to make the shot. Every basketball player intuitively understands that if he wants to make that free throw, he must switch back and forth between Condition Yellow and Condition Red.

For those who don't push the envelope through physical fitness and repetitive training, Condition Gray is generally a realm in which complex motor skills begin to break down. One of the things that appears to be happening here is that bilateral symmetry begins to set in, meaning that what you do with one hand you are likely to do with your other. For example, startle a baby and both of its little arms and legs jerk in what is known as the startle response, doing the exact same thing on both sides of the body. Bilateral symmetry can have grave consequences for a police officer in a tense situation where he is holding a pistol on a suspect. Say the suspect attempts to flee and the police officer grabs him with his free hand. Now, this is never a good tactical technique, and it is especially bad when the officer's heart rate is racing past 145 bpm. His accelerated heartbeat causes bilateral symmetry, so that as the officer grabs a fistful of the suspect's shirt with one hand, he has a convulsive clutch response in his gun hand, which causes an unintentional discharge of the weapon. That is my definition of a bad day for our police officer, and a very bad day for the suspect.

Bilateral symmetry can also happen when you are startled. In an article titled, "The Impact of the Sympathetic Nervous System on Use of Force Investigations," Bruce Siddle writes,

Being startled while otherwise physically and/or mentally preoccupied will result in four involuntary actions occurring within

150 milliseconds. First, the eyes blink; second, the head and upper torso move forward; third, the arms bend at the elbow; and lastly, the hands begin to tighten into fists. If a person is under extreme stress and adrenaline has been introduced into the system, the resulting startle response contraction [of the hands] can generate as much as 25 pounds of pressure. That amount of force is approximately twice the amount needed to discharge a double action revolver.

Now, there are many safeguards to prevent this convulsive clutch response. One is to keep the finger off the trigger until it is time to destroy the target, a technique that has become the standard for military and law enforcement training. Even that is not a guarantee, since the clutch response can sometimes be so intense that the finger will slip back into the trigger guard causing an unintentional discharge.

My co-author told of being involved in a large brawl as a military policeman (MP) in Saigon.

> There were six enraged American soldiers and five or six MPs, and we were going at it hot and heavy all over the sidewalk, out into the street, and back onto the sidewalk again. At one point, one of the soldiers started to disarm one of the MPs, so I pulled my .45, pumped the slide to chamber a round, and stuck it into the man's face. When he obeyed my commands to lie on his stomach, I pointed my .45 into the air and inadvertently squeezed the trigger, discharging a round into the sky. It startled everyone and stopped the fighting so that we were able to get the suspects into handcuffs. By the way, I got a verbal commendation from the provost officer for my quick thinking. Since I had not received any commendation up to that point, I accepted his with grace and humility, never mentioning that it had been a mistake.

Another standard safeguard is to hold the gun at a low port position, angled downward. Should there be an unintentional discharge, the round will hopefully strike the floor, or at least hit the lower portion of any individual unfortunate enough to be in front of the weapon.

The greatest safeguard, however, is to not allow your heart rate to get too high. Calm people are much less likely to make these kinds of mistakes. Once your heart rate rises above Condition Red (generally beginning around 145 bpm) there is nothing there that you want.

Most people have experienced anxiety before taking an important test. There are two components to test anxiety: the psychological and the physiological. The latter is characterized by an accelerated heart rate and a loss of fine-motor control. When I was teaching at West Point and Arkansas State University, I found that football players generally suffered the worst from test anxiety. Now, on most campuses the football players have an unfortunate reputation of being "dumber than a box of rocks," as one of my fellow professors put it, which is generally unfair. The truth is that they are generally no less smart than any other athlete, but their sport can work against them.

With the exception of the quarterback and the kicker, no one on the football team needs fine-motor control. The blockers and the backers certainly do not need it, and most of the time the receiver (catching with two hands) only needs bilateral symmetry. When a football player is in the game, functioning in what is often referred to as his "sweet spot," his performance level, his Condition Red (which may be pushed very high up into the Gray zone), is somewhere between 140 and 175 bpm.

An unfortunate by-product of this is that because he performed in his sweet spot so often in middle school and in high school, and now in college, his performance-level bpm can overlap to the classroom. He might have studied all night for a test, he knows the material and he is raring to go, but when he sits down to take it, his heart pounds in his chest just as it does on the field. He suddenly cannot get his fingers to operate his pen, and the harder he tries, the worse his condition gets. So, he blanks. He cannot get even the first question, and he goes downhill from there. When he fails the test, everyone is convinced he is stupid and, sadly, he may even believe it himself. But he is not stupid; it is just his body working against him.

During my time as a professor at Arkansas State, most of the coaches tried to send their students through my Introduction to Psychology class. It was not because I am an easy professor, but rather because I taught them a powerful breathing technique, the same one that I will give you later in the book. I would watch the students as they took their test, keeping an eye out for cheating, but mostly I watched for signs of test anxiety. Often I would see them hunch their shoulders and hyperventilate. If they were light complexioned, their faces would turn white around the nose and lips, and their knuckles would turn white. When this happened I knew I had someone suffering from test anxiety. So periodically during the test, I would have them all stop and put their pencils down, and I say my mantra: "It's a free throw. It's a free throw." Then I would make the whole class do exactly what a basketball player does to prepare for a free throw: breathe to lower the heart rate. More specifically, I would have them do the four-count tactical breathing exercise used by elite SWAT teams and special ops soldiers world-wide. And it worked.

Tactical breathing is truly a revolution in warrior training and I am just one of many individuals teaching this technique. The Calibre Press Street Survival Seminar is a world-class program that has trained hundreds of thousands of law enforcement officers in this method, and they have received extensive feedback confirming that tactical breathing has undoubtedly saved many lives. If this technique can be useful for college basketball players in the heat of a game, and for football players contending with test anxiety, how infinitely more important is it for warriors making life and death decisions and taking life and death shots in the middle of the toxic, corrosive, destructive environment of the universal human phobia?

Condition Black

> O judgment! Thou art fled to brutish beasts, and men have lost their reason.
>
> —Shakespeare
> *Julius Caesar*

Bruce Siddle's heart rate research, *Popular Science's* reports of NASCAR drivers, and the Green Beret "stress test" research, all indicate that 175 bpm is about as high as Condition Red can be pushed into this mysterious Gray zone. Again, we must be cautious about putting specific numbers on these Conditions, but it would appear that even under the most ideal circumstances, above 175 bpm a catastrophic set of events begins to happen.

Cardiologists tell us that at a certain point an increased heart rate becomes counterproductive because the heart is pumping so fast that it cannot draw in a full load of blood before pumping it back out. As the heart rate increases beyond this point, the effectiveness of the heart, and the level of oxygen provided to the brain, steadily decreases. One cardiologist suggested to me that this might be what is happening when SNS arousal induces a heart rate above 175 bpm.

Whatever the cause, something remarkable appears to be happening when the SNS accelerates the heart rate above 175 bpm. For our purposes here, let us call this Condition Black, and let's examine what is going on inside the mind of a person trying to function at that level.

The "Triune Brain Model" was developed by Dr. Paul MacLean, chief of the Laboratory of Brain Evolution and Behavior at the National Institute of Mental Health in Bethesda, Maryland. He suggests that we think of the human brain as consisting of three parts—the forebrain, the part that makes you a human being; the midbrain, or mammalian brain, the part that all mammals have in common; and the hindbrain, or the brain stem. The forebrain performs basic thought processes, the midbrain performs extensive reflexive processes, and the hindbrain takes care of the heart rate and respiration.

If you were to get shot in the forebrain, you might survive the wound since you can survive a lot of damage in that portion of the brain. In fact, until you were a young teenager, doctors could perform a hemispherectomy and remove half your brain, and you could still have a fully functional life. Severe damage occurs, however, when a bullet hits your midbrain and, should even a small caliber bullet enter your hindbrain, the intrusion would probably shut down your breathing and your heartbeat.

As you enter into Condition Black, your cognitive processing deteriorates, which is a fancy way of saying that you stop thinking. About 2,500 years ago, Brasidas of Sparta said that, "Fear makes men forget, and skill that cannot fight is useless." In Condition Black you can run and you can fight like a big, hairless, clawless bear, but that is about all you are capable of doing. Your forebrain shuts down and the midbrain, the "puppy" inside, that part that is the same as your dog's brain, reaches up and "hijacks" the forebrain.

It is important to note that there is a tremendous difference between the performance impact of a heart rate increase caused by fear (i.e., the sympathetic nervous system flooding stress hormones into your body), and a heart rate increase caused by physical exercise. When your heart is pounding due to physical exertion, your face will usually be beet red, as every vessel dilates wide open to get blood to the muscles. But with a fear-induced heart rate increase, your face will usually turn white, due to vasoconstriction. If there are extreme physical demands placed upon the body at the same time that the vasoconstriction is occurring, then these two processes apparently work against each other to cause a skyrocketing heart rate. We are not sure why this happens, but the current, dominant theory is that the physical demands cause the body to scream for oxygen while the vasoconstriction shuts down the blood flow that provides the oxygen, causing the heart to beat ever faster while achieving very little.

I mentioned this earlier but it bears repeating here in order to understand that using physical exercise to increase your heart rate is an excellent technique to simulate the effects of combat stress. But we must remember that the powerful physiological effects of someone trying to kill you are not something we can replicate in training, although force-on-force paint bullet training (someone trying to hurt you) can come fairly close.

Have you ever tried to have an argument or a discussion with a truly frightened or angry person? It cannot be done, because the more frightened and angry the person is, the less rational he is. This is because his forebrain has shut down and his midbrain, the one like a dog's, is in control. In fact, you might as well try to argue with your dog; he might be intrigued by the experience but it will not accomplish much. Nor will you accomplish much when trying to talk to a human being in this heightened condition. To connect with him, you must first calm him down.

Artwohl and Christensen, in *Deadly Force Encounters*, give a classic example of this irrational behavior.

> Officer Peterson didn't hear the other officer's shotgun explode or his partner's handgun fire or even his own fire, but every shot fired hit the suspect.

"I went up on the guy, who slid down the side of his car into a seated position, and kicked his Beretta away. Another officer picked up the gun as two others pulled the guy onto his stomach and handcuffed him."

Peterson was hit with a rush of adrenaline, greater than any synthetic pill could create. "I went to the car phone and punched in my home number. I got the recorder, but I knew my boys were home, probably still sleeping. I screamed for someone to pick it up and I kept screaming until it awoke my boys downstairs. When they answered, I screamed at them what had just happened and that I wanted to see them. I just needed to hold them. When they asked how they would get to me, I told them that my partner would come and get them."

Peterson says the rush was so intense, so extraordinary, that it was almost like an out-of-body experience. The boys were not brought to the scene.

Vasoconstriction: White with Fear

I ain't got time to bleed.

—Jesse Ventura

Think of those cold mornings when your fingers are white and not working for you. That is an example of vasoconstriction caused by the cold. It also happens as a result of stress. At its earliest stage, as you enter into "Condition Red" (starting around 115 bpm), you begin to experience a loss of fine-motor control. In "Condition Gray" (beginning around 145 bpm) the average individual begins to lose complex motor control. But when your heart roars up into the realm of "Condition Black" (around 175 bpm), the effects of vasoconstriction become catastrophic. It is easy to detect this in a light-complexioned person (though it happens to everyone of every race), because you can see the skin turn white when the blood flow to the outer layer of his body is constricted. Specifically, the blood pumps from the heart through the arteries and then, at the pre-capillary stage (just before entering the capillaries), the blood flow constricts.

At low levels of vasoconstriction (from cold or stress), only the little capillaries shut down, causing some loss of fine-motor control. It happens to your fingers on those cold mornings and it happens when you are under stress. As the vasoconstriction becomes more intense, the blood flow to the complex motor muscles begins to shut down. The blood pools into the body core and large muscle groups, and your blood pressure skyrockets. (This increase in blood pressure is an important aspect of what is happening to your body; research at the Federal Law Enforcement Training Center suggests that systolic blood pressure is a much better indicator of stress than heart rate.) The outer layer of your body becomes almost a layer of armor, and as long as an artery is not hit, you can take extensive damage without much blood loss. (This is why surface wounds on the face and scalp tend to bleed more. In this region the intake and output vessels are both close to the surface, so the ability of vasoconstriction to limit bleeding is less effective here.)

This appears to be a survival mechanism intended to limit blood loss in a combat situation. The price you pay, however, is a loss of motor control because when the muscles stop getting blood, they stop working. Eventually, there is going to be a backlash called vasodilatation, which is the opposite of vasoconstriction. When vasodilatation occurs, your veins go wide open, and (if you are light-complexioned) your face turns red. Police officers sometimes refer to this as a "tomato face," and they have learned that it generally represents significantly less danger than the white face of vasoconstriction.

Bruce Siddle gives a classic example of vasoconstriction. As three police officers checked each other for injury after a shooting, one of them found a small pucker in the front of his upper sleeve and another pucker on the other side. "The bullet must have missed me," he said, visibly relieved. But as soon as he uttered those words, the wound in his arm opened and the hole gushed blood. When he thought he was okay he relaxed, which caused the vasoconstriction to stop and the vasodilatation to begin.

Dial 9-1-1!

The midbrain has no philosophy, no hesitation, and no regret. It knows only death, and life, and nothing in between! The midbrain is never confused and never dithers. Its job is to get us out of this mess alive! It is poor at multitasking. It acts decisively and only does one thing at a time. It never apologizes, never looks back, and sheds no tears.

Unfortunately, the midbrain is ignored in the training philosophy of many institutions. We do too much training "in the abstract." "In the abstract" is where all training must begin, because the front brain is the entry point for all information. Unhappily, that is where much of what passes for training also ends. As the student is gradually immersed in the training environment, stress levels must be increased so that important psychomotor skills begin to filter into the midbrain. The midbrain will only "know what to do" if the student has been "stress inoculated."

—John Farnam
Correspondence to Colonel Grossman

As you grow increasingly stressed and move into Condition Black, it is common to lose your peripheral vision, a condition commonly referred to as tunnel vision. The more stressed you become, the more narrow the tunnel. There will also be a loss of depth perception, meaning that a threat looks closer than it really is, and a loss of near vision, meaning that you have trouble seeing close things. You literally become "so scared you can't see straight."

People facing a threat, such as a man with a knife, often back away to see more of the situation. It is a terrible irony in some stressful situations, that at a time when you need your eyes the most, you may lose your near vision. So what does this loss mean?

Consider the simple act of dialing 9-1-1 on your telephone. Allow me to give you an easy homework assignment, one that I implore you to do. Some night while you and your family are watching television, disconnect your telephone and have everyone in your family practice dialing 9-1-1. Do it at least 20 times each and do it several times a year. Why practice such a simple act?

Say your child has never practiced dialing 9-1-1, and she is home alone in the back bedroom while someone is breaking down the bedroom door. Her terrified heart rate will probably be hammering at 220 bpm. Remember, her fine-motor control began deteriorating at 115 beats, and her near vision began diminishing around 175 bpm. Now, at 220 beats, your child's life depends on her ability to dial three numbers she has never dialed before. If she has rehearsed it, her fingers will know what to do even at the accelerated heart rate. But if she has not rehearsed it...

One police officer gave me an excellent example. "I'm kind of a lazy guy," he said. "I've never looked up a phone number in my life. I just dial 4-1-1." One day while he was home alone, he accidentally shot himself in the leg. "I dialed and dialed and dialed 9-1-1, but I kept getting 4-1-1." Since that is what he normally dialed, under stress his fingers were on autopilot. "I finally gave up," he said, "and I told the Information operator, 'I'm a cop. I've shot myself. Contact emergency for me.'" Whatever you rehearse is what you will do under stress. If you spend years and years dialing 4-1-1 and never practice 9-1-1, then under stress you are likely to dial 4-1-1.

In another case an officer had to apply CPR on his infant daughter. He handed the phone to his wife and told her to dial 9-1-1, but she could not do it. Without prior practice, she could not see the numbers and she could not use her fingers, even to save her own child's life. Another officer told me that his wife was home alone with the kids when the dogs started barking, and someone began smashing down the kitchen door. She fumbled desperately with the telephone but she could not see the numbers. She did manage to press the "zero" button, which ultimately saved their lives.

An officer at a law enforcement training center suffered a heart attack and as he lay dying, the administrative assistant tried in vain to dial 9-1-1. She dialed over and over but could not get an emergency operator. Finally, in anger and frustration, she threw the phone across the room, ripping the cord from the wall. Later, when she was calm and collected, she realized she had not been dialing nine to first get an outside line.

Whatever skill you require under stress must be rehearsed ahead of time. For example, if you are going to dial 9-1-1 on a cell phone, you must remember to hit "send" at the end. You know that now when you are calm and collected, but what about when your heart is racing at 220 bpm? Rehearse it now a few times so that it is there for you when you need it. Be sure the phone is turned off first.

Police officers know that they have to rehearse changing magazines in their weapons. While it is easy to put a magazine in the well of a gun and slam it in tight, experienced officers know that if they have not drilled on this simple action, they might not be able to do it in a stressful situation. There is particular value in practicing skills under stressful training situations, such as during force-on-force paint bullet engagements. If warriors perform an action under survival stress, then they will truly own the skill in the midbrain.

Loss of Near Vision and Pistol Marksmanship

As difficult as it may seem during the heat of the battle it is important to shift your focus from the weapon itself to the living, breathing, human being wielding the weapon—the same human being who eats, sleeps, urinates and also puts his pants on one leg at a time like you did this morning.

—Steve Tarani and Damon Fay
Contact Weapons: Lethality and Defense

In a heart-pounding situation, the loss of your fine-motor control and near vision makes it mandatory that you drill on those things that seem simple when you are calm and collected. In *Sharpening the Warrior's Edge*, Bruce Siddle notes that fine-motor skill decreases as heart rate increases, but you can limit the impact by preparing mentally and physically ahead of time.

With a loss of near vision, you may not be able to see your pistol sights. (On a rifle, it appears that the front sight is far enough away that the ability to see it clearly is not affected by loss of near vision, and on a military peep sight the rear sight is supposed to be out of focus. That may help explain why virtually all armies in all nations converted to the peep sight on their military weapons throughout the 20th century.) There is no debate about the fact that this inability to focus on the pistol sight can occur, although there is an ongoing debate as to how to deal with the problem. Some say that if you are taught to see the front sight long enough and hard enough, you will see it at the moment of truth. Others say that should you suck up two slugs and your heart races to 220 bpm, you cannot be expected to see your sights and you need to learn instinctive shooting (sometimes called target-focused shooting or point shooting).

I don't want to get involved in this point-shooting vs. aimed-shooting debate. I have good friends (men I admire and respect greatly) on both sides of this issue, and I think we are probably evolving to a solution that uses a combination of the two methods: When you have time and distance, use those sights, but when you do not, at extreme close ranges there may be value in reverting to point shooting.

Just know that under extreme stress you might not be able to see your pistol sights. There are several case studies of police officers reporting after their gunfights that because they could not see their sights, they did not fire. Know ahead of time that this phenomenon might happen and don't let it paralyze you.

If you find yourself in a desperate, life-and-death, point-blank confrontation, and you have a clear shot, trust your instincts, point and fire. But, if you are having difficulty focusing on your sights and you have just a few seconds, breathe. Most of us were taught to breathe during our first day on the firing range, using the acronym BRASS, Breathe, Relax, Aim, Sight, and Squeeze. Breathe in, hold it, let it out, hold it and squeeze. This is perfect opportunity to use the tactical breathing method.

If you have the time, breathe and pull yourself down to Condition Red so you can get those sights into focus. Or, take it a step further and pull yourself down into Condition Yellow and make a rock-solid, precision shot. The breathing technique will be covered in greater detail later, but let me give you just one example of an individual who consciously used this technique to bring himself down into Condition Yellow. One officer told me of an experience he had while hunting. "I had this magnificent buck in my sights," he said.

> I'm up in my deer stand and my heart is pounding in my chest. It's a long shot at an awkward angle and all I can see is the back of his head and neck. I had the time, so I took four, deep, belly breaths, just like you taught us. The breathing brought my heart rate down and I made the shot.

If a little breathing exercise can work in competition, on the range and while hunting, know that it will have enormous power to control your stress response during combat.

Section Two

Perceptual Distortions in Combat:
An Altered State of Consciousness

A friend asked me an impossible task: Describe pitched close combat in words. Impossible! Because it is all encompassing, six dimensional, from the front, the left, the right, ricochets from the back, exploding shells from above and shaking ground from below. One actually "feels" the combat in the body.

It involves blurred vision from sweaty eyes, the acrid choking smell of layers of gunpowder smoke, ear bursting horrific noises, the kinetic nerve vibrations from exploding mortars, hand grenades and shells, the screams of humans, the cries of the wounded, the piercing whine of ricochets of bullets and shrapnel, hiding behind or stepping over bodies of perhaps someone you know. All at one time. No media can ever duplicate it. No mere words can ever convey it.

Thank God, it only happened to me a few times!

But, once exposed to the heat of it, it welds you into a bonding, not only with friend, but foe, that no one else, no matter how close to you, will ever be able to share.

Hmm. Maybe I did describe it.

—Keith Kreitman

World War II veteran as told to Colonel Grossman

Like Keith Kreitman, most of the individuals who have been in combat will tell you that it is simply indescribable. There are no words to depict it. It is like trying to describe a vivid painting without having words for colors and hues. Now, with the research outlined in this section, we have begun to collect descriptive terms to create a rough "palette" of basic, primary "colors" to paint a crude picture that will help us understand each individual's diverse experience in the realm of combat.

In painting our picture we must never forget that combat is 99 percent sheer boredom and one percent pure terror. But it is within that realm of one percent pure terror that we have the most to learn and it is where pioneers like Dr. Artwohl and Dr. Klinger, whose research is outlined in this section, have blazed a trail for others to follow.

one

chapter
The Eyes and the Ears: *Auditory Exclusion, Intensified Sound, and Tunnel Vision*

> Who is so deafe or so blinde as is hee
> That wilfully will neither heare nor see?
>
> —John Heywood (circa 1565)
> *Proverbs*

A bizarre set of perceptual distortions can occur in combat that alter the way the warrior views the world and perceives reality. It truly can be an altered state of consciousness, similar to what occurs in a drug-induced state or when sleeping. It is amazing that we never knew about this before. All we had to do was ask. Now that we are asking combat veterans the right questions, we have learned more in the last few decades than in the previous 5,000 years, and we are learning more every day.

Police psychologist Dr. Alexis Artwohl has conducted what I believe to be some of the best research on perceptual distortions in combat. Dr. Artwohl and Loren Christensen collected this data in their book, *Deadly Force Encounters*, which I highly recommend to my military and law enforcement audiences.

Note that the perceptual distortions of hearing and vision that are addressed in this chapter are significantly different from normal, day-to-day experiences in which you don't notice certain sights and sounds simply because you are not paying attention to them. Not seeing or hearing something because you are concentrating on something else is a psychological manifestation. Whereas "tunnel vision" and "auditory exclusion" appear to involve both psychological "concentration" influences and powerful physiological effects caused by biomechanical changes to the eye and ear. We need much more research on this topic, but the dominant theory at this time is that these biomechanical changes to the sensory organs are a side effect of vasoconstriction and the other stress responses that were addressed earlier.

Auditory Exclusion: "Our Guns Just Went 'Pop!'"

> In rage deaf as the sea, hasty as fire.
>
> —Shakespeare
> *King Richard II*

Perceptual Distortions in Combat

From *Deadly Force Encounters*
by Dr. Alexis Artwohl & Loren Christensen
Based on Survey of 141 Officers

- 85% Diminished Sound (auditory exclusion)
- 16% Intensified Sounds

- 80% Tunnel Vision

- 74% Automatic Pilot ("Scared Speechless")

- 72% Heightened Visual Clarity

- 65% Slow Motion Time
- 7%   Temporary Paralysis

- 51% Memory Loss for Parts of the Event
- 47% Memory Loss for Some of Your Actions
  ("Perseveration")

- 40% Dissociation (detachment)
- 26% Intrusive Distracting Thoughts
- 22% Memory Distortions ("Perceptual Set?")
  (Role of fear and past associations)
  (Role of videotaping)
- 16% Fast Motion Time

For additional info on perceptual distortions in combat, refer to,
Into The Kill Zone by Dr. David A. Klinger is highly recommended.
www.warriorscience.com

Dr. Artwohl surveyed 141 police officers who had been in what law enforcement agencies sometimes call "deadly force encounters." We would call them gunfights. She found that more than eight out of ten officers experienced diminished sound, that is, the gunshots "got quiet."

Hunters know that they will be temporarily deafened and their ears will ring for the rest of the day if they do not wear hearing protection when they zero in their deer rifles. Yet they do not wear hearing protection when they actually shoot a deer, and they often do not hear their shots, or the sound is muted, and their ears do not ring afterward. If this is a common stress response to shooting a deer, how much greater would that stress response be if the deer were shooting back?

Consider this classic example of auditory exclusion from *Deadly Force Encounters*:

> My partner and I were pursuing a stolen vehicle. The suspect was driving erratically, stopping only when the vehicle spun out of control and crashed into a ditch. My partner had the shotgun and I had my semi-auto drawn as we cautiously approached. When a bullet exploded out one of the windows, I opened fire.
>
> I faintly heard one round go off, then nothing. I could feel the recoil of my own gun so I knew I was firing but I didn't hear the shotgun and I was afraid my partner had been shot. When it was all over, it turns out I had fired nine rounds, and my partner, who was five feet away, had fired four shotgun rounds. The suspect also got off two more rounds before we killed him. Neither of us was injured.
>
> I had no idea how many rounds we had fired until I was told later. To this day, I still have no memory of hearing any gunfire except that first round.

The vast majority of officers reporting diminished sound upon firing indicated that it was their gunshot(s) that were muted, or at the most, their shots sounded like a "cap gun" or "pop gun." Others said their shots were not as loud as they "should" have been, while a small number said they did not hear them at all. One SWAT sniper reported that he and another team member fired their weapons simultaneously in a small room, yet the twin gunshots, even in a confined space, sounded quiet.

Massad Ayoob is a national champion competitive shooter, a law enforcement trainer, a leading researcher, and one of the most prolific police writers today. He put it this way during our personal correspondence on this subject:

> Everything I've seen tells me that most of auditory exclusion (like most of tunnel vision) is a matter of cortical perception. The ears still

hear and the eyes still see, but as it focuses on the survival mission, the cortex of the brain is screening out awareness of what it deems insignificant to the goal.

This process of tuning out sensory input happens all the time. As you read this, you are probably not conscious of the feel of your shoes or the waistband of your pants. You are also probably tuning out all kinds of background noises such as the hum of your refrigerator or distant traffic. Our brains must constantly tune out sensory data or we would be overwhelmed.

In extreme stress situations, this screening process can be even more intense, as we tune out all senses except the one we need for survival. Usually that one sense is vision, but in low-light conditions the ears can turn "on" and the eyes turn "off," as the combatants hear the gunshot but tune out the less salient muzzle flashes.

Massad Ayoob is quite correct, there is definitely a mental, cognitive component to this. The brain is screening out awareness of what it deems insignificant to the goal, and the goal is survival. But if your ears don't ring after shots are fired, that would indicate that there might also be a physical shutdown of some kind in the inner ear. Reports from the audiology research community indicate that the ear can physically, mechanically shut out loud sounds, just as the eyelid can shut out bright lights. It would appear that this biomechanical shutdown in the ear can occur in a millisecond in response to sudden, loud noises.

Two things are happening here. First there is a form of aural or auditory "tunnel vision" in which specific sounds, such as sirens, are tuned out under high stress. We tune out unnecessary sounds and focus on one sound all the time. When I was a young private sleeping in the barracks, I learned how to tune out the grating snores coming from a fellow soldier by listening intently to the steady, droning sounds of air whistling out of a heating vent. Something very similar, but much more intense, is happening in combat as we mentally shut down unneeded sensory stimuli and focus on the one thing that is critically needed.

Then there is a form of aural or auditory "blink" in which loud noises are physically and mechanically muted or silenced for a brief moment. There is not even the usual ringing in the ears afterward. This auditory blink can be roughly broken down into three types.

-One response, which appears to happen at lower levels of arousal (perhaps in Condition Yellow) is to soften or shut down the sounds of your own shots (which, at some level, you are anticipating), while the sounds of someone shooting next to you can be deafening. This happens often when two hunters fire together at a game animal, and I know of several cases where an officer has reported that his own shots sounded quiet, while shots fired by another officer standing next to him were deafening. All such cases that I know of involved moderate levels of stress.

-Another response, which seems to occur under extreme stress situations (perhaps in Condition Black), is to shut out all sounds so that you do not remember hearing anything afterward. Apparently, the greater the stress, the more powerful this effect. This is not an aural blink, but rather the auditory equivalent of squeezing your eyes shut until the bad man goes away. This appears to be associated with exceptional stress, extreme heart rates and intense physiological arousal.

-A third response, which is probably the most common, occurs when you shut out all gunshots, but you hear everything else, including the shouts of those around you and the tinkle of your expended brass hitting the floor. This appears to be a classic Condition Red response, in which your body is capable of bio-mechanically shutting down your ear in a millisecond in response to the leading edge of the shock wave of a gunshot, and then reopening immediately so you hear everything else around you. In Dr. Dave Klinger's superb book, *Voices from the Kill Zone*, he tells of,

A SWAT officer who fired a . . . burst from a fully automatic submachine gun . . . reported that while he did not hear his gunshots, he did hear the "clack-clack" sound of the weapon cycling as the slide moved forward and backward, ejecting spent casings and delivering fresh rounds to the breech.

It is simply astounding that the body is apparently capable of this, and even more astounding that we never knew about it until recently. I was teaching on this subject in Ohio, and a state trooper said,

Now I understand what happened! It was so embarrassing I never told anybody about it. My partner and I were on a one-car roadblock. A guy blows the roadblock at 100 mph, and we both fire one shot as we leap out of the way. I called the sarge, and I say, 'Sarge he's blown the roadblock!' and the sarge tells us to pursue him. I said, 'Sarge, we can't pursue! Honest, our guns just went "pop"!' We thought there was something wrong with our ammo. We actually took a pencil and ran it down the barrel of our weapons because we were afraid there might be a bullet lodged there.

How many warriors, across the generations, have fired their weapons and failed to continue fighting because they thought there was something wrong with their weapons when they could not hear their shots? In this case there was nothing wrong with their ammunition or their weapons, but there was definitely something wrong with their training. We have gone through centuries of the gunpowder era and we are just now informing our warriors that their shots might get quiet in combat.

As I collect data from literally thousands of warriors about their combat experiences, this auditory exclusion effect is the single most common occurrence. Consider this example of a police sniper taking a shot at an armed assailant:

> The rifle fires, but I don't hear it. That's not quite true: I hear it but it sounds very far away. There is no recoil. The sight picture is not lost. I see the small white hole form in the glass, and behind it I see her head explode…The sight picture has turned murky. Something doesn't look right. It's then that I realize the reason my sight picture is murky is that her skull and brain have been blown all over the inside of the car and are now dripping down from the headliner and sliding down the windows.
>
> —Russ Clagett
> *After the Echo*

There is reason to believe that the biomechanical aspects of this auditory exclusion effect can occur in a millisecond, given only the briefest intuition of warning. Author Gavin de Becker tells of an unintentional discharge of his weapon that occurred early in his career of managing protective assignments. At the end of a work shift, he pointed his semiautomatic pistol in a safe direction and began easing the hammer down so as to clear it, but something happened and the weapon accidentally discharged. No one was hit, but the noise of the pistol firing in that small room was so painfully loud that all the individuals who were present complained afterwards of their ears ringing—except Gavin. Gavin de Becker is the world's leading expert in the realm of intuition and danger, and author of the best-selling book, *The Gift of Fear*, which is a true classic on the topic. Discussing this incident with me years later, he realized that at some intuitive level he must have had a brief millisecond of warning that the hammer was not going down properly, and that was all his body needed to shut down the sound.

It is not just gunshots that can go unheard. Many police officers tell me that they did not hear their vehicle's sirens or the sirens of other emergency vehicles during their deadly force encounters. One California park officer told me how he tuned out the sounds of a helicopter hovering overhead during his gunfight. This is probably happening in the brain, rather than as a mechanical mechanism in the ear, and is the equivalent of aural tunnel vision as opposed to an aural blink.

Warriors often do not hear the shouted communications that occur in combat. Small unit leaders have always understood that in order to get the attention of their troops and be heard and be seen in combat, they have to be in front of them. Infantry fire team leaders do not get in front of their men, in the most dangerous position on the battlefield, because they want to; they do it because they have to if they are going to be seen and their commands are going to be heard.

Even then you cannot be certain that a command will be heard in combat. This narrative from a police training officer is an example of a very common occurrence.

Many times I have seen students with auditory exclusion in some of our training scenarios. We have a person enter a scenario playing an armed off-duty officer or an armed citizen and announce their presence. But the good guys only see the gun and many times the person gets shot, so to speak. It is for this reason that we recommend that whether you mean well or not, you need to announce your presence from behind cover and expose minimally when arriving on a scene that is already hot. There have been some recent, real-life shootings that emphasize the need for this.

If this is happening in the limited stress of training scenarios, you can bet that it is also happening in combat.

A Second Type Of Auditory Exclusion: "You Don't Hear The One That Gets You"

An old adage (which apparently dates back to World War I and refers to incoming artillery) states, "You don't hear the one that gets you." In my interviews with numerous combat veterans since the publication of the first edition of On Combat, I have confirmed that this appears to be literally true in most cases. Consider these incidents:

- A Canadian accidentally bombed by the US Air Force in Afghanistan.
- A Navy SEAL hit by a rocket propelled grenade (RPG).
- A US Army officer hit by multiple improvised explosive devices (IEDs) during several tours in Iraq.
- A US Army Special Forces officer under enemy mortar fire in Operation Anaconda in Afghanistan.
- A booby-trapped police car explodes in the officer's face when he opens the driver's side door.

All of these individuals told me the same thing: when an explosion is close enough to slam your body with a powerful concussion, you do not hear the sound and your ears do not ring afterward. For example, the police officer with a booby-trapped car says that although the bomb blew him off his feet he was able to call the dispatcher on his cell phone and speak without ringing in his ears or problems communicating. Explosions farther away can be extremely loud and cause ear ringing and loss of hearing, but it would appear that many people do not hear the ones that are close enough to create a powerful physical impact on your body. Thus, it would seem that the old veterans were telling us the truth when they said, "You don't hear the one that gets you."

This is apparently a form of auditory exclusion, similar to what we have already discussed, which many people experience when shooting a rifle in combat or while hunting. In these cases, which I term Type-1 Auditory Exclusion, the individuals firing the weapons report that they did not hear the sound or that the sound was muffled, and that their ears did not ring afterward. The auditory system appears to "blink" creating a biomechanical shutdown that protects the ears from ringing afterwards. However, as we have observed so far in this book, Type-I Auditory Exclusion, for example, does not happen when you are under the stress of competitive shooting. It only happens in the actual killing circumstances of recreational hunting and combat.

Type-II Auditory Exclusion can happen when you are completely relaxed (i.e., not in an excited state) and appears to be a result of the body receiving two simultaneous and overwhelming sensory stimuli. In a conversation with Gavin de Becker (author of The Gift of Fear), he pointed out that when a creature in nature lands on your back and roars at the same time, your dominant survival information would be the sensation of something on your back. Under stress, the body tends to tune out all senses but one to avoid sensory overload and confusion. In this case, it is the impact of the creature that the human body interprets as vital survival data.

Tom Davis, a retired U.S. Army colonel and a Vietnam veteran gave me a classic example of this phenomenon.

> I was wounded in Vietnam by an RPG [rocket propelled grenade]. It hit no more than three to five yards from me. I saw the fireball but did not feel the concussion, nor did I hear the sound. My ears had closed automatically. My ears became functional again immediately. I lay under the front of a jeep and I thought another RPG was coming. However, I was hearing the air coming out of all four tires! The concussion should have burst my eardrums but did not. We should thank God for building these automatic shut downs into our body.
>
> Later in the year, the compound I was in came under attack. The incoming [bombardment] was so loud that my captain was screaming

into the radio that we were under attack. I was screaming at him to get back under cover. I could not hear myself screaming, and he could not hear himself for the sounds of the incoming.

In the second incident, Col. Davis believed that his ears were working - that auditory exclusion wasn't happening - because the incoming rounds were outside the bunker and he was somewhat protected from the concussion.

This phenomenon might also explain why some individuals who have accidentally shot themselves often report that they did not hear the shot and their ears did not ring afterward. Again, in this situation, the body experiences two simultaneous and overwhelming stimuli: the sound of the gun and the feel of the bullet hitting. Although there might not be pain initially, we can hypothesize that the body is immediately aware of physical trauma and the sound has been tuned out.

Thus we now begin to understand that when the old veterans told us, "You don't hear the one that gets you," they were telling us the truth, and this old saying now joins the ranks of these other adages:

- scared out of your wits (shutdown of forebrain processing),
- so scared you can't see straight (loss of near vision,
  loss of depth perception, and loss of peripheral vision),
- and scared shitless (loss of bowel and bladder control),

as being accurate representations of what is actually happening in combat.

Intensified Sounds: You Hunker Down and Die, Blind and Afraid.

Sight was gone and fears possessed me . . .

—Francis Rowley
"I Will Sing the Wondrous Story"

In Dr. Artwohl's research, 85 percent of the individuals she interviewed experienced diminished sound, but for 16 percent, the sound of gunshots was intensified. Under what circumstance would the brain choose to shut down the eyes and turn on the ears? In low-light conditions. This is because, again, the brain focuses on the salient stimulus, and in the dark the salient stimulus is sound.

Modern police and military train to fire at man-shaped silhouettes and photorealistic images of humans. While this is fine, the problem is that in the dark it is difficult if not impossible to see the threat. Often, the muzzle flash is the only visual stimulus in a gunfight under low-light conditions. The eyes turn off, the ears turn on and, as one law enforcement trainer put it, "You hunker down and die, blind and afraid."

John Peterson, an Army Green Beret and innovative firearms instructor, conducted extensive research on this matter while serving as a trainer at the SigArms Academy in New Hampshire. John and his people would take a trainee into a dark room for a force-on-force, gunpowder projectile, paint bullet exercise, where they would fire one or two rounds into the trainee's bulletproof vest the moment he stepped into the room. In almost every instance, the trainee returned fire—at the sound.

Only a bat can precisely triangulate the location of an attacker based on sound. To accurately zero in on an attacker in low-light conditions, it is best to aim at the muzzle flash. To teach this, Peterson brought his students into a darkened room and fired multiple rounds of paint bullet ammunition to show what the flash looked like. (Gunpowder propelled, paint bullet ammunition emits a muzzle flash, making it particularly effective for this kind of training.) Once the students were mentally "cocked and primed" to look for this stimulus, the next time they walked into the darkened room and were shot with a paint bullet, they zeroed in on the muzzle flash with accurate shots. From that point on, they performed in night combat situations with a much higher degree of proficiency.

Sometimes a warrior transitions back and forth from the visual to the audio and back again, depending on which sense he needs the most at the moment. This explains Dr. Artwohl's findings that 85 percent of officers in gunfights experienced auditory exclusion and 16 percent diminished sound—which adds up to 101 percent—since some individuals experienced both in the same gunfight.

One officer told me that on one occasion he was at the bottom of a stairwell with a suspect above shooting down at him. He said the sound of the gunshots was overwhelming. "I had a shotgun in my hand," he said, "I raised it, drew a bead on this guy, and all of a sudden the shots got quiet." When the officer got a visual lock-on with the suspect, his eyes turned on and his ears turned off—a phenomenon that happens frequently when warriors are caught in an ambush. The sounds of the incoming shots are initially overwhelming: *Boom! Boom! Boom!* Since he is taken by surprise, he has limited visual ability, but after he quickly scans the environment and gets a visual lock on the attacker, the shots become quiet.

Sometimes there is an opposite effect, in which you go from auditory exclusion to intensified sound. I had the privilege of talking to a law enforcement officer in Florida about his gunfight. He told me that he and his partner had conducted a traffic stop and had reason to arrest the driver and the passenger. They first handcuffed the passenger and put him in their police car, but when he placed the first cuff on the driver, the man suddenly grabbed a gun, spun, and fired a bullet into the second officer's brain, killing him instantly. The shooter then spun and fired rounds into the first officer. The officer told me:

I saw that gun and that's all there was in all the world [tunnel vision]. I didn't hear the shots; I heard nothing [auditory exclusion].

> One of the rounds went beneath my vest and severed my spine. I tried to turn and run, but my legs weren't working. I couldn't understand why.

When the officer fell to the ground he could no longer see his assailant. His vision shut down so that he would have no visual memory of what followed, though he did hear the suspect's footsteps approaching (intensified sound). The footsteps stopped. Then he heard bullets being fired into the back of his vest. Then the suspect fired one more bullet into the back of the officer's head. Fortunately, the angle was such that it did not penetrate his skull, although it did scalp him. The officer lay there bleeding and listening as the footsteps moved away. (When I met this magnificent young warrior, he had built himself up to where he could walk with two canes and was dedicating his life to training others how to live with and overcome spinal injuries.)

Many people who have been in a gunfight talk about having significant gaps in their memory of the incident. When interviewed further, it turns out sometimes that they lost visual input during the gunfight, but they do have auditory memories of the event. In one case, a tactical team member was making entry into the front door of a house and ran straight into an ambush. The suspect had made a kind of foxhole by crouching down in the basement stairs and as the officer rushed through the door, the man opened fire.

> I leaped to the right, off the well-lit porch and over this wall, and hit the ground in total darkness. I used to think I had no memory of the event until I heard you teaching about this. Now when I think back, I had sound, but once I got out of the light and out into the dark night, there wasn't anything for me to see.

The officer's arm was horribly broken. He said:

> I was trying to get my arm up; I was sort of flipping it up to try to hold my shotgun, but it wouldn't work. When I got back into the light [he was firing the shotgun one-handed], my eyes suddenly came back on, and I have memory of what happened after that.

Sensory Exclusion: "I Haven't Got Time for the Pain"

> Pain is no evil,
> Unless it conquer us.
>
> —Charles Kingsley
> *St. Maura*

You have probably experienced sensory exclusion when you received scrapes, scratches and bruises in a wrestling match, fight or a football game, and later you wondered how you got them. You were not aware of these injuries because during your stressful event your sense of pain shut down. Other senses probably shut down, too, but you were not aware of them since you did not bring home "souvenirs," such as your bruises and scrapes.

My co-author experienced a classic example of this when he arrested a man on a warrant in the lobby of a precinct. "The instant I grabbed the weight-trained ex-con" Christensen said, "he started thrashing violently, slamming the two of us into walls, against a counter and over the top of a long, wooden bench." The suspect was oblivious to Christensen's wristlock, because the man's pumping adrenaline blocked his sense of pain. When Christensen finally managed to maneuver him into a position to really slam home an arm lock, the suspect yelped and leaped completely off the floor like a cat on a hot plate. Although this reaction is what Christensen wanted, the suspect unintentionally kneed him in the groin as he went airborne.

"I realized I'd been struck," Christensen said, "but I didn't feel anything as I continued to wrestle him down onto the floor and subsequently into my handcuffs. I then half drug and half walked him to a holding cell."

It was not until Christensen locked the door and leaned against a table to catch his breath, that a wave of nausea came calling. Nearly 10 minutes had passed since he had been struck, but it was not until his adrenaline began to subside that the pain and nausea hit. When the suspect's adrenaline subsided about 20 minutes later, he began shouting that his wrist was broken.

Sensory Overload: "Tilt. Game Over. Reboot."

. . . stuns with thundering sound.

—Oliver Goldsmith
"The Traveller"

A flashbang is a device used by police tactical teams, such as SWAT, in situations where distraction, disorientation or diversion is needed. According to the National Tactical Officers Association (NTOA), the technically correct term for a flashbang is a "noise/flash diversionary device," or "NFDD." When one is rolled into a room where a suspect is hiding, it explodes with a deafening bang and a blinding flash, causing a sensory overload so the officers can storm the room and overwhelm the stunned suspect. Artwohl and Christensen give this example from a SWAT officer's personal experience:

The suspect opened the small door and stepped out with the hostage in front of him. Although our sniper could only see a small portion of the suspect's forehead, a counter and a series of inner-office mail slots made the shot difficult, he fired, but a box deflected the round. Still a bullet fragment struck the suspect, causing only a minor wound.

The guy pulled the hostage back into the room, shouting for us to get back, and that he was going to kill her. This was it; we had to move. We ran along the wall until we got to the open door and I threw the flash bang into the room. A second later we rushed in and saw the guy standing in sort of an alcove where the ᵔᵔʳⁱloyees hung their coats. The flash bang startled him because the woman was beside him now, and he was holding her with just one arm.

We had our MP5s [submachine guns] on semi-auto; I fired into his face and Miller fired into his chest. Blood and brain chips sprayed across the walls. The suspect crumpled to the floor.

The flash stuns the suspect's eyes and the bang stuns his ears. His skin feels the concussion, and his nose and mouth suck in some of the smoke. All five senses simultaneously send an emergency message to the brain, and the overloaded brain says, "Tilt. Game over. Reboot."

The idea is to stun the suspect so that officers can apprehend him without having to use deadly force. Problems arise, however, when a suspect is inadvertently inoculated to the flash bang. Occasionally, SWAT officers tell me that their flash bangs failed to work on a suspect. When I ask how many were used, they say something like, "Well, we used a dozen as we searched room to room before we finally found the suspect." While circumstances might have necessitated them to use flash bangs in every room, by the time they got to where the suspect was really hiding, he had been warned, emotionally prepared, and inoculated against the effect.

We live in incredibly violent times. The domestic terrorism rate, international terrorism acts and violent crime rates are at historical highs. When a police situation gets exceptionally violent, a tactical team is called in. If there is going to be a shooting, it is usually done by them, although in the vast majority of cases they do not have to shoot. When they do, there is a tendency to blame the killing on the tactical team, though blaming them for having to use deadly force is like blaming a headache on the aspirin. The tactical team is the solution, not the problem. The NTOA has powerful data demonstrating that if not for these highly trained teams, the number of people killed in the line of duty would be vastly higher than it is.

Remember Barney Fife and Andy Griffith in the old *Andy Griffith Show*? In a real situation where a Barney and an Andy have to go in after a dangerous suspect, Barney would die and Andy would have to kill the bad guy. In the real world, however, when a tactical team goes in with their shields, CS gas, flash bangs, negotiators, and overwhelming force, the majority of the time they do not have to kill the dangerous suspect, and the officers go home safely to their families that night.

Flash bangs are a great tool that saves lives in these tragic, violent times, but most police officers and soldiers do not carry them on a daily basis. If you carry a weapon, however, you have a "flash bang." You pull the trigger, it flashes and it bangs. We know that a firearm is a psychologically daunting instrument. If you are a police officer, you must understand that in a large percentage of combat situations, the perpetrator is going to fire the first shot—meaning that you begin the engagement on the receiving end of a flash bang. Proper mindset and realistic training to develop autopilot responses can help warriors to overcome this problem.

The Bigger Bang Theory: "Doink, Doink." vs "Bang! Bang!"

Some certain of your brethren roar'd and ran
From the noise of our own drums.

—Shakespeare
Coriolanus

Napoleon said that in war, "The moral is to the physical as three is to one." That is, the psychological factors are three times more important than the physical factors. In combat, one of the most important of these 'moral' factors—or morale or psychological factors, as we would call it today—is noise.

In nature, whoever makes the biggest bark or the biggest roar is most likely to win the battle. Bagpipes, bugles and rebel yells have been used throughout history to daunt an enemy with noise. Gunpowder was the ultimate 'roar,' since it had both a bark and a bite. First used as fireworks by the ancient Chinese and later in cannon and muskets, gunpowder was a noisemaker that provided sound and concussion. The concussion was felt and heard, and gunpowder provided the visual effects of flash and smoke. Since a gunpowder explosion and its drifting smoke could be tasted and smelled, it provided a powerful sensory stimulus that could potentially assault all five senses.

This is one of the primary reasons why the early, clumsy, smoothbore, muzzleloading muskets replaced the longbow and the crossbow. The longbow and the crossbow had many times the rate of fire, more accuracy and far greater accurate range when compared to the early smoothbore muskets. Yet these superior military weapons were replaced, almost overnight (historically speaking) by vastly inferior muskets. While they were inferior at killing, they were not inferior at psychologically stunning and daunting an opponent.

Once when I asked a room of officers why incredibly superior killing instruments like the crossbow and the longbow were replaced with the comparatively useless musket, a police officer stood up and answered, "Administrators!" That got a great laugh, but the truth is that very little happens on the battlefield without a good reason. In this case, if you are in a battle going *doink, doink* with a crossbow and the other guy is going *Boom! Boom!* with a musket, all things being equal, the doinker will lose every time.

Some observers, not fully understanding the all-important psychological aspect of combat, have assumed that the longbow disappeared because of the lifetime of training required to master it. However, this logic does not apply nearly as well to the crossbow. If training and expense were the real issues, then the tremendous expense and lifetime of training needed to create a mounted knight or cavalry trooper (and his mount) would have been sufficient to doom those instruments of war. If a weapon system provides military dominance (be it the knight, the frigate, the aircraft carrier, the fighter jet, or the nuclear missile), then a society will devote the resources needed to get that weapon system. But if a more effective weapon is found, then the merciless Darwinian evolution of the battlefield will doom the older weapon and embrace the new. Thus, with the invention of the first crude muskets, the longbow and the crossbow were doomed, and the psychological reasons for this are, in Napoleon's words, "three times more important than the physical."

The concept of psychologically daunting and defeating your enemy is as old as Sun Tzu, writing 2,500 years ago. Clausewitz in his classic, nineteenth century book, *On War*, said that "Shock and awe are necessary effects arising from an application of military power and are aimed at destroying the will of an adversary to resist." Of course, the "shock and awe," campaign used by the coalition forces in the U.S. led invasion of Iraq in 2003 was a large scale application of this concept, but for our purposes here we are applying it to small arms and close combat.

You have probably heard of the Big Bang Theory. I call this the Bigger Bang Theory, which states that, "all other things being equal, in combat whoever makes the bigger bang wins." The psychological effects of gunpowder can be thought of as a continuum. At the top of the continuum are the flash bang, the hand grenade, the aerial bomb and the artillery barrage. At the bottom is the pistol and in between is the rifle.

If you have been down range and heard a rifle fire, you know that the concussion and the supersonic "crack" of a rifle bullet can be far more impressive than a pistol shot. Taking a rifle to a gunfight is the equivalent of taking a chain saw to a knife fight. In both cases, you have a range advantage, a damage advantage and a powerful psychological advantage.

A classic example of this occurred in North Hollywood, California, on February 28, 1997, where two determined bank robbers, heavily armed and wearing body armor, fired hundreds of rounds from automatic weapons before police finally stopped them. When it was over, 17 people lay wounded and the suspects were dead. What happened was that there were two idiots with assault rifles going *Boom! Boom! Boom! Boom! Boom!* while L.A.P.D. officers (more than 200 were at the siege) shot back with 9 millimeter pistols going *ding, ding, ding, ding, ding*. All other things being equal, who wins this kind of gunfight? The answer is *Boom! Boom! Boom!* That is the reality of combat. Now, it is not impossible for a man with a pistol to beat a man with a rifle; it happens all the time. It is just difficult.

If you are a police officer and a suspect brings a rifle to a gunfight, it would be good if you had a rifle, too. Rifles are slowly but surely replacing shotguns in the law enforcement community, and the time has probably come when every officer should be trained to use a rifle and carry it in his vehicle. Do you think the international terrorist threat is going to limit themselves to pistols? No. They will bring rifles and body armor to the gunfight. The terrorists' rifle will punch right through our officers' body armor, while the cops' pistols will be physically and psychologically ineffective.

Consider the 1999 massacre at Columbine High School in Littleton, Colorado. Two kids, wearing long trench coats and armed with a variety of firearms, including a 10-shot, Hi-Point model 995-carbine rifle and two Savage 12-gauge shotguns, came to school to bring death to their fellow classmates. When it was over, 14 students, including the shooters, and one teacher lay dead and 23 other students and faculty were seriously injured.

The shooters began their carnage in the front of the school where a school resource officer pulled up and engaged them in a gunfight. He started out well (one report said he hit the magazine of one killer's carbine) however, he quickly ran out of ammunition and had to pull out, leaving the school to the two most horrendous juvenile mass-murderers we have ever seen. If he had had a rifle in his vehicle and had been trained to use it, do you think the situation at that school might have turned out differently?

Sergeant Major Daniel Hendrex (a US Army veteran with two years combat duty in Iraq, and author of the book A Soldiers Promise) wrote to me after I taught a class on the Bulletproof Mind at the U.S. Army Sergeant Major's Academy. He gives an excellent example of the Bigger Bang Theory when the 120mm main gun of the Abrams Tank was used in city fighting in Iraq. (Remember, a 120mm gun is huge compared to anything used in the past. By comparison, the dreaded German "Tiger" tank, used late in World War II, carried an 88mm main gun.)

I wanted to thank you for shedding light on the science that is behind what I have already known to be true. The Bigger Bang Theory holds a lot of merit for me. Being a First Sergeant in the 3rd ACR [Armored Cav Regiment] during OIF 1 [the invasion of Iraq], in Al Anbar led me to understand the importance of that concept. Here is part of a report that I wrote following our first deployment:

Use of the 120mm tank main gun in military operations in urban terrain (MOUT): No ambush or battle lasted longer than a couple of minutes when 120mm main gun was fired.

Of the forty rounds fired, none were further than 500 meters and some were as close as 25 meters. The effect of a HEAT [high explosive antitank] 120mm main gun round, fired in MOUT is devastating on the enemies 'will' to continue the fight. It is not devastating to the infrastructure of the city! Average engagement was two HEAT rounds. The most fired during enemy contact was four HEAT rounds.

I was witness to 'muj' [enemy troops] continuing (very unsuccessfully) a fight against Bradleys (25mm main gun). Here is a weapon that is just as deadly as tanks, but the insurgents would continue to fight. I think the psychological effect of a 120mm tank main gun round going off and echoing throughout the tight confines of a city had an enormous effect on the enemies will to fight. I can't remember one battle lasting over 5 minutes when we had the luxury of tanks. Even when I didn't have tanks, my HMMWVs [wheeled tactical vehicles] were loaded with at least two AT-4s [anti-armor rockets]. A similar effect was produced by the AT4s.

Sergeant Major Daniel Hendrex went on to say, "I think the Bigger Bang Theory is what defines my thoughts on 'escalation of force' in my after action report:

Escalation of Force: The hardest concept to get soldiers to understand was teaching them not to be at a disadvantage during an attack or ambush. If soldiers are being attacked with AK-47s (7.62mm rifles) and only returning fire with an M-4/M-16 (5.56mm rifles) then they are at a distinct disadvantage. The US Army is touted as the most technologically advanced force and brings heavy fire power to the table, but on a daily basis I would hear about and see our soldiers put themselves at a disadvantage.

If attacked with RPGs [rocket propelled grenades] and only returning fire with machine-guns, you are at a disadvantage. It takes a command decision to ensure your soldiers are given the best opportunity to survive and win every engagement. If you're attacked with small arms, priority is to maximize crew serve weapons (7.62mm M240B, .50 cal M2, 40mm MK19) immediately.   If RPGs are fired then return fire with 120mm HEAT or appropriate weapon system (AT-4 or 25mm). An RPG, a high explosive round, demands the most hostile response you can give. Most RPGs were fired from behind concrete walls, or from within buildings, firing only machine-guns does not give you a high likelihood of immediately ending the engagement or defeating the ambush.

Sgt. Major Hendrex concluded, "After our year was up, we were replaced by a USMC [marine corps] unit and got word of battles lasting up to 14 hours. We were confused by these reports until we realized they didn't have the luxury of tanks! Thanks again for the insight."

In the end, winning the battle in the enemy's mind is the key to victory. And the Bigger Bang theory is a core concept that makes it possible to stun, daunt, and defeat your enemy, whether you are a police office using a rifle to defeat a felon armed with a pistol, or a soldier using a 120mm tank round to defeat enemy troops on the modern battlefield.

Tunnel Vision: "Like Looking Through a Toilet Paper Tube"

For now we see, as through a glass darkly.

—I Corinthians, Chapter 13
The Bible

Dr. Artwohl found that eight out of ten of the officers she surveyed experienced tunnel vision during their shootings. This is sometimes referred to as perceptual narrowing, and as the name implies, under extreme stress, such as occurs in a shooting, the area of visual focus narrows as if the officer were viewing the situation through a tube. Christensen and Artwohl tell of one police sergeant who says that as a suspect ᴍed rounds at him from his handgun, his eyes focused totally on a ring the shooter wore on a finger of his gun hand.

One law enforcement trainer and SWAT team member in South Florida tells how tunnel vision combined with auditory exclusion as he wrestled with a suspect armed with a sawed-off shotgun.

Both of us had a hand on the muzzle and both of us had a hand on the trigger of the shotgun. Most people talk about tunnel vision saying that it is like looking through a toilet paper tube. For me it was like a soda straw.

(This is one of many case studies indicating that, as your heart rate goes up, your tunnel vision can get narrower and your auditory exclusion can increase.) Then, he said,

We're wrestling with this shotgun and—*Boom*! The 12-gauge goes off between our faces. Can you think of anything much louder than a 12-gauge in your face? The thing that absolutely astounded me was that I didn't hear a sound, and afterwards my ears didn't ring.

An interesting example that gives us insight into how tunnel vision can affect shooting accuracy. A SWAT team in Portland, Oregon, streamed through the doors of a drug house, barking orders to two men sitting on a sofa and a third man sitting in a chair. The man in the chair leaped to his feet, pulled a small pistol from his pocket, and pointed it at the closest officer. The officer was faster, though, and fired a burst from his MP5 submachine gun, killing the man instantly.

After all the rooms had been secured without further incident, the officers rolled the dead man over to retrieve his weapon. It was not there.

As the officers searched every inch of the room, the SWAT officer who fired swore that the man held a pistol. Just as they were about to give up, a crime scene photographer noticed a paper bag under a table (an officer later said he had kicked it aside to get it out of the way during the commotion). Inside the bag were several nuts and bolts – and the pistol.

A subsequent investigation showed that the officer had seen the man pull the pistol from his pants and raise it quickly in his direction. At that moment, the pistol was all that mattered to the officer, it was all that he saw as he poured a stream of hot lead into the suspect's gun hand. The officer's concentrated fire ripped the weapon from the man's hand and launched it through the air, before it landed neatly inside the open bag of bolts.

Of course the press tried to make a case that the gun had been planted in the bag, but there was one piece of evidence the media did not know about until the police revealed it during the grand jury.

Inside the trigger guard of the pistol was the man's severed trigger finger.

Tunnel vision, along with auditory exclusion and a host of other perceptual distortions, are commonly associated with the high levels of anxiety normally present in everyone involved in a potentially lethal situation.

In most cases the same thing happens to your adversary. He may very well be looking at you through that toilet paper tube or, what others have called "a hole in a doughnut." To take advantage of his visual distortion, sidestep quickly to your right or left so that you, in effect, disappear or "go off his radar screen." In order to visually reacquire you, he has to blink, draw back and move his head in your direction. In the critical second it takes for him to do that, you have a brief moment of advantage. This sidestep technique is now widely taught, and has been found to be extremely valuable in paint bullet scenarios. Understanding the effect of tunnel vision helps us to design such techniques and to understand how they work.

There is cause to believe that we can train warriors to break out of tunnel vision by having them scan and breathe after taking a shot. Physically turning the head and scanning the battlefield after an engagement seems to cause tunnel vision to diminish. Even if the warrior stayed in tunnel vision, turning his head permits him to see additional threats, like scanning with a flashlight beam. Tactical breathing (which will be covered in detail later) also helps the individual to be calm and regain his composure. By having individuals scan and breathe on the range every time after every engagement, the procedure soon becomes a valuable and automatic conditioned response.

There is enormous value in warning our warriors ahead of time that such phenomena might occur. One police officer in Artwohl and Christensen's book, gave a classic example of the tremendous advantages of knowing about these things.

> I've been involved in three shootings. Before the first two, I had no training in what to expect. I performed well, but felt shocked, disoriented, confused, and at times out of control by all the weird stuff that I experienced during and after the shooting. I didn't know what to think and that made it harder to cope during and after the event. After the second shooting, I sought counseling and learned about all that weird stuff I'd been experiencing. The doctor also taught me the principles of Stress Inoculation Training and I started using it to prepare myself for the future. Then when I got into another situation, the training made all the difference in the world. This time I knew what to expect and I was even able to control and compensate somewhat for the tunnel vision, sound distortions, and other strange things my mind and emotions were going through. I also bounced back a lot quicker because I knew I wasn't crazy and I knew what to do to take care of myself.

Our goal is to create warriors like this, preferably before they go into combat for the first time. "Forewarned is forearmed," and we must send our warriors into combat as well armed and well informed as humanly possible.

two
chapter

Autopilot: *"You Honestly Don't Know You're Doing It"*

In life's small things be resolute and great
To keep thy muscle trained: know'st thou when Fate
Thy measure takes, or when she'll say to thee,
"I find thee worthy; do this deed for me?"

—James Russell Lowell
"Epigram"

Dr. Artwohl's research found that 74 percent of the officers involved in a deadly force encounter acted on automatic pilot. In other words, the actions of three out of four officers in combat were done without conscious thought.

My co-author, Loren Christensen, is a career police officer and world-class martial arts instructor, with many best-selling books and video tapes on the fighting arts. He says that many veteran martial artists, highly motivated individuals who have spent 30 or 40 years of their lives ingraining fighting techniques through hundreds of thousands of repetitions, often find after an explosive self-defense situation that they have no recall of what they did. Although the attacker has been reduced to a whimpering bloody pile, the martial artists cannot recall what they did because their responses were purely automatic.

One police officer told me of his powerful autopilot experience:

Let me tell you how powerful this autopilot business is. I came around the corner of this guy's van; I'm just going to tell him to move it. I didn't know that he'd already killed one person. You honestly don't know you're doing it. All of a sudden a gun appears in his hand. Then a hole appears in his chest and the guy drops. My first thought was, "Whoa, somebody shot him for me!" I actually looked over my shoulder to see who shot this guy. Then I realized I had my gun in my hand and it was me who had shot him.

Is it possible to see a gun pointed at you, draw your own weapon and shoot without conscious thought? Not only is it possible, in this case it is highly desirable. Of course, his training must be state-of-the-art so that he knows instantly that the threat is indeed a gun, and not a wallet or a cell phone.

If, however, our warriors are still using blank, man-shaped silhouettes, they are being conditioned to shoot anyone who jumps up in front of them. Or they may hesitate when a real armed opponent—complete with clothing, a face and a gun—pops up in front of them, because the target they trained with did not have these features. A far superior training tool is the photorealistic target. When one of these pops up, revealing a life-size photo of a man holding his wallet, the trainee does not shoot. When the next one pops up with a picture of a man holding a gun, the trainee reacts to the deadly threat by instantly firing. On the range, it looks like this: gun!-shoot, gun!-shoot, cell phone-don't shoot, gun!-shoot, gun!-shoot, wallet-don't shoot.

Warriors don't shoot bull's-eyes. Warriors don't shoot silhouettes. Warriors shoot lawful, legitimate, deadly force threats. With this preferred method, warriors develop conditioned reflexes using superior, dynamic, realistic training to ingrain the proper response.

Whatever is Drilled in During Training Comes Out the Other End in Combat–No More, No Less

> Whatever you would make habitual, practise it; and if you would not make a thing habitual, do not practise it, but habituate yourself to something else.
>
> —Epictetus (first century A.D.)
> *How the Semblances of Things are to be Combated*

In January 2003, I went to Camp Lejeune, North Carolina, to train the 2d Marine Division. We filled up the base theater twice, each time giving a four-hour block of instruction to Marines about to deploy to Iraq. As usual, I taught them, and they taught me. One marine told me, "Colonel, my old Gunny taught me that in combat you do not rise to the occasion, you sink to the level of your training."

We can teach warriors to perform a specific action required for survival without conscious thought but, if we are not careful, we can also teach them to do the wrong thing. Some trainers call these "bad muscle memory" or "training scars." They are "scar tissue" in the midbrain that is counterproductive to survival. One example of this can be observed in the way police officers conducted range training with revolvers for almost a century. Because they wanted to avoid having to pick up all the spent brass afterwards, the officers would fire six shots, stop, dump their empty brass from their revolvers into their hands, place the brass in their pockets, reload, and then continue shooting. Everyone assumed that officers would never do that in a real gunfight. Can you imagine this in a real situation? "Kings X! Time out! Stop shooting so I can save my brass." Well, it happened. After the smoke had settled in many real gunfights, officers were shocked to discover empty brass in their pockets with no memory of how it got there. On several occasions, dead cops were found with brass in their hands, dying in the middle of an administrative procedure that had been drilled into them.

Stories like this would be hard to believe if you heard them in a bar. It is "passing strange," indeed, but after hearing about this repeatedly in personal interviews and seeing it in scholarly research, we know that it is actually happening. In biomechanics and kinesiology this is called the "Law of Specificity." In other words, you cannot get stronger legs by doing push-ups, you must train your specific leg muscles to get stronger legs.

One police officer gave another example of learning to do the wrong thing. He took it upon himself to practice disarming an attacker. At every opportunity, he would have his wife, a friend or a partner hold a pistol on him so he could practice snatching it away. He would snatch the gun, hand it back and repeat several more times. One day he and his partner responded to an unwanted man in a convenience store. He went down one isle, while his partner went down another. At the end of the first aisle, he was taken by surprise when the suspect stepped around the corner and pointed a revolver at him. In the blink of an eye, the officer snatched the gun away, shocking the gunman with his speed and finesse. No doubt this criminal was surprised and confused even more when the officer handed the gun right back to him, just as he had practiced hundreds of times before. Fortunately for this officer, his partner came around the corner and shot the subject.

Whatever is drilled in during training comes out the other end in combat. In one West Coast city, officers training in defensive tactics used to practice an exercise in such a manner that it could have eventually been disastrous in a real life-and-death situation. The trainee playing the arresting officer would simulate a gun by pointing his finger at the trainee playing the suspect, and give him verbal commands to turn around, place his hands on top of his head, and so on. This came to a screeching halt when officers began reporting to the training unit that they had pointed with their fingers in real arrest situations. They must have pantomimed their firearms with convincing authority because every suspect had obeyed their commands. Not wanting to push their luck, the training unit immediately ceased having officers simulate weapons with their fingers and ordered red-handled dummy guns to be used in training.

Consider a shooting exercise introduced by the FBI and taught in police agencies for years. Officers were drilled on the firing range to draw, fire two shots, and then reholster. While it was considered good training, it was subsequently discovered in real shootings that officers were firing two shots and reholstering— even when the bad guy was still standing and presenting a deadly threat! Not surprisingly, this caused not just a few officers to panic and, in at least one case, it is believed to have resulted in an officer's death.

Today, in most police agencies, officers are taught to draw, fire, scan and assess. Ideally, the warrior should train to shoot until the deadly threat goes away, so it is best to fire at targets that fall after they have been hit with a variable number of shots. Today, there are pneumatically controlled steel targets on which photo realistic images are attached. The shooter might fire two rounds and the target falls, or the exercise can be designed so the target is supposedly wearing body armor and remains standing even after it is shot multiple times. To knock it down, the shooter must hit it in the head. Even better, in paintball or paint bullet training, the role players are instructed not to fall until they have been hit a specific number of times.

You do not rise to the occasion in combat, you sink to the level of your training. Do not expect the combat fairy to come bonk you with the combat wand and suddenly make you capable of doing things that you never rehearsed before. It will not happen.

There must be a continual effort to develop realistic simulations training so the warrior develops a set of skills that will transfer to reality. One two-tour Vietnam veteran put it this way.

> In Vietnam, I was always surprised to find I had done the right thing in tight situations. I sort of went into automatic and didn't think about what I was doing, or even remember it later. I'm a firm believer in training, that dull, boring "If I have to do this one more time I'll scream" training that every GI hates. It lets people like me perform in combat when common sense was telling me to run like hell.

Killing on Autopilot: S.L.A. Marshall Was Right

> There's hope a great man's memory may outlive his life half a year.
> —Shakespeare
> *Hamlet*

Again, whatever you train to do comes out the other end. Self-preservation can become secondary to training. Any natural or learned resistance to killing, any sense of the sanctity of human life, any human emotions, any remorse or compassion at the moment of truth, can all be overcome and overwhelmed with training.

The subject of training to kill on autopilot, without conscious thought, was addressed extensively in *On Killing*. Therefore, I will only recap and update the information here.

You may think that it is easy to kill, that a person only has to walk onto the battlefield and he will become a killer simply because he has been ordered to. The truth is that it is hard to get people to kill. Consider the murder rate, which is only six per 100,000 per year. Millions of people bump against each other every day, many of them depressed, angry, hostile and full of hate, but only six out of 100,000 will kill. Only four per thousand even attempt to inflict serious bodily harm and suffering (aggravated assault) in the average year. How is that?

We learned in World War II that only 15 to 20 percent of the individual riflemen fired their weapons at an exposed enemy soldier. If there was a leader present ordering soldiers to fire, then almost everyone would do so. Likewise, a crew-served weapon, with a gunner and assistant gunner fighting together, almost always fired. But when soldiers were left to their own devices, the vast majority of them, on all sides, could not kill.

There was concern about the scholarship of these findings a few decades ago, shortly after the death of the key researcher in the field, Brigadier General S.L.A. Marshall. But his research has since been extensively replicated and validated. I wrote an entry to the *Oxford Companion to American Military History* and three encyclopedia entries on this topic, all peer reviewed by leading international experts in the field.

At the end of World War II, our military leaders knew that Marshall's findings were true and they understood that this was not a good thing. After all, a 15 percent firing rate among our riflemen is like a 15 percent literacy rate among our librarians. These veteran leaders understood that the low firing rate was a problem that had to be fixed, which is exactly what they did. Twenty years later in Vietnam the firing rate had increased to around 95 percent. There was still a lot of "spraying-and-praying" going on, but among the individuals who saw an exposed enemy soldier, the firing rate was up to 95 percent.

Some would argue that this dramatic increase in the firing rate in Vietnam was a result of the M-16 weapon and the jungle environment, but this theory does not hold up to careful evaluation, since M-1 carbines and Thompson submachine guns in the South Pacific jungles in World War II were not more likely to be fired than other individual weapons of that era. One of the most dramatic examples of the value and power of this modern, psychological revolution in training can be seen in Richard Holmes' observations of the 1982 Falklands War. The superbly trained British forces were without air or artillery superiority and were consistently outnumbered three-to-one while attacking the poorly trained but well-equipped and carefully dug-in Argentine defenders. Both sides fought with similar weapons (mostly 7.62mm NATO standard rifles) in open terrain. Superior British firing rates (which Holmes estimated to be well over 90 percent), a result of modern training techniques, has been credited as a key factor in the series of British victories in that brief but bloody war.

The definitive U.S. military source, The United States Training and Doctrine Command (TRADOC) Historical Monograph titled, "SLAM, the Influence of S.L.A. Marshall on the United States Army" strongly defends Marshall's observations. His work was widely accepted at the end of World War

II when our Army consisted of a high ratio of veteran leaders who had led us through one of the greatest wars in history. In Korea and Vietnam, Marshall was treated with the deepest respect by men in war, and he was asked repeatedly to visit, train and study.

Were all of these military leaders wrong? Did Marshall fool all of them, and then, somehow, a few people discovered the "truth"? Marshall may have padded his resume in a few small areas as to his World War I experience. He claimed that he had received a battlefield commission while he was actually an OCS graduate after the war, although he may have been assigned to an officer's position prior to the training. He also claimed to be in an infantry unit while he was really in an engineer unit, but his unit may well have been attached to a line infantry unit. Admittedly, Marshall's methodology does not meet rigorous modern standards, but that does not mean that he lied. Let us hope that our life's work gets better treatment after we are dead and gone, than to have a few people question our work, and everyone thereafter simply assume that we had intentionally lied.

Basically, all that S.L.A. Marshall was saying was that some of our warriors do not shoot in combat, and more realistic targets will raise the firing rate. Marshall was the pioneer whose research and writing spurred warrior trainers to change from bull's-eye targets to realistic combat simulations, and who can argue with that? We can disagree about how much of an advantage it gives us, or exactly how much of an increase in the firing rate this kind or realistic training has created, but today no one wants to go back to shooting at bull's-eye targets. And every time you shoot at a silhouette, or a photo realistic target, or a video training simulator, you should take a moment to remember and thank S.L.A. Marshall.

Today the body of scientific data supporting realistic training is so powerful that there is a federal circuit court decision which states that, for law enforcement firearms training to be legally sufficient, it must incorporate realistic training, to include stress, decision making, and shoot-don't-shoot training. This is the *Oklahoma v. Tuttle* decision (1984, 10th Federal Circuit Court), and today many law enforcement trainers teach that a law enforcement agency is probably not in compliance with federal circuit court guidance if they are still shooting at anything other than a clear, realistic depiction of a deadly force threat. And, again, we have S.L.A. Marshall to thank for that.

Bull's-eye Targets Don't Shoot Back

> Every habit and faculty is preserved and increased by correspondent actions,—as the habit of walking, by walking; of running, by running.
>
> —Epictetus (first century A.D.)
> *How the Semblances of Things are to be Combated*

The men who fought in World War II were superb soldiers armed with excellent weapons, but they had poor combat training. The problem is that most of the time they were taught to fire at bull's-eye targets, as were police officers just a few decades ago. The fundamental flaw in training for combat this way is that there are no known instances of any bull's-eye targets ever attacking our warriors.

If we expect our warriors to be capable of using the weapons they have been issued, they must practice on realistic simulators that replicate what they are going to face. Men and women who served in the U.S. military since the Vietnam era were universally taught to shoot at man-shaped silhouettes that popped up in their field of view, thus ingraining in them a conditioned response. The stimulus appeared and they had a split second to respond. Stimulus-response, stimulus-response, stimulus-response. Hundreds of repetitions. When an enemy soldier popped up in front of our troops in Vietnam, the enemy was shot and killed, reflexively, without conscious thought. Stimulus-response. It was a revolution on the battlefield, and any military or law enforcement organization that does not train this way today will get their tails seriously kicked by those who do.

If you have served in the military since 1990, you have seen a transition in training. It took only the implementation of a plain, man-shaped "E-type" silhouette during the Vietnam era to dramatically improve the firing rate of our troops. But now we use a pop-up target that is a three-dimensional image of an enemy soldier. The target has a face, it wears a helmet and it is depicted holding a rifle. It is many times more realistic than the old green silhouettes, making it much easier for soldiers to transfer what they learn to reality.

This is an example of a principle called "simulator fidelity". A simulator's fidelity refers to the degree of realism provided by a training simulator. The higher the fidelity, the greater the transfer to reality. The realistic images on the new shooting targets depict a face, a body and hands that grip a weapon, all designed to train our soldiers and law enforcement officers to react instantly to any deadly threat that pops up in front of them. It is the same training concept used by our pilots who train extensively on state-of-the art, highly realistic flight simulators.

Today our young warriors are performing peacekeeping operations all over the world, and in that capacity they have precise rules of engagement, just like law enforcement officers. With the right training and realistic simulators, killing can become a conditioned, response that will save the lives of fighting men and women. It is paramount, however, that they be taught to do so only under the rules of engagement.

Violent Video Games and Automatic Pilot

Small habits well pursued betimes
May reach the dignity of crimes.

—Hannah More
Florio

Violent video games have been in existence for several decades now, and many kids who played them years ago are now in their mid- to upper- teens and even into their 20s—the exact age group of the average perpetrator our law enforcement officers are confronting every day out on the streets. When talking about conditioned reflexes, we must also talk about violent video games, because to understand how we can make killing a conditioned reflex—stimulus-response, stimulus-response, stimulus-response—it is important to understand how the average opponent has been trained. This topic was outlined briefly in *On Killing*, and more extensively in *Stop Teaching Our Kids to Kill*, co-authored with Gloria DeGaetano. Once again, I will only recap and slightly update this information here.

Does a kid playing a violent video game shoot at blank, man-shaped silhouettes? How about bull's-eye targets? No, he shoots at people—that is, vivid, realistic depictions of people. The holy grail of the video game industry is realism, and every year they get ever more realistic. The incredibly lifelike characters bleed, twitch, sweat, beg, fall, and die, all before the eyes of the very impressionable young players.

Today's video games offer a completely different type of play than my generation engaged in as kids. When I was little and playing cops and robbers, I said, "*Bang, bang*, I got you, Jimmy." Jimmy said, "No you didn't." So I said, "Well, *bang, bang*. Now I got you." Again he argued that I didn't. So, I smacked him with my cap gun, and after he went crying to his mother I got in big trouble. Along the way I learned one of life's important lessons, a lesson that usually had to be taught over and over again: Jimmy is real, Sally is real, and Fido is real, and if I hurt them, I'm going to get into big trouble.

For thousands of years kids have whacked each other with wooden swords, or played *"Bang, bang*, I got you." This was healthy play because as soon as someone got hurt the play stopped, and all the kids gathered around and tried to convince him not to tell momma. Today, kids are immersed in a virtual reality environment where they repeatedly blow their virtual, hyperrealistic, playmates' heads off in explosions of blood and gore. Do they get into trouble? No. They get awarded points! This is pathological and dysfunctional play.

When kittens or puppies play they gnaw at each other's throats. When one of them gets hurt, though, the play stops and mama walks over to see what is going on. When a player gets hurt in a basketball or a football game, the play stops and the ref hurries over to deal with the injured and the one who caused it. The purpose of healthy play is to teach the young how not to inflict serious harm upon their fellow species.

The video game industry says that the images on the screen are not real people. This is true, but puppies and kittens are not real human beings either, and we know that the way a child treats a puppy or a kitten predicts how they will treat real people. Think of a puppy as a virtual human that is used to teach kids how to interact with real people. What if you awarded a child with a cookie every time he made that puppy cry in pain? Would you consider that sick?

Our kids today have virtual playmates in the form of realistic characters that populate the video games. Many kids live in a dark, gray and depressing world, and for them the video games are more real than reality. Dr. Marshall Soules, at Malaspina University in Canada, calls this the "hyperreality effect," meaning that some kids "begin to think of the hyperreal as more meaningful than the thing or event it relates to." Kids playing these games make the puppy cry, that is, they make virtual human beings die in what the child deems to be a vivid and intense reality. Then they are given a cookie, a reward. This is pathological play.

In July 2000, the American Medical Association (AMA), American Psychological Association (APA), American Academy of Pediatrics (AAP), and the American Academy of Child and Adolescent Psychiatry (AACAP)—all of our doctors, all of our pediatricians, all of our psychologists, and all of our child psychiatrists—made a joint statement to both Houses of Congress. They said that, "Well over 1,000 studies point overwhelmingly to a causal connection between media violence and aggressive behavior in some children." Words such as "cause" or "causal" are powerful scientific terms that are not used lightly. In this statement they also concluded that, "Preliminary studies indicate that the negative impact of interactive electronic media [violent video games] may be significantly more severe than that wrought by television, movies or music."

That statement by our medical community was reinforced in 2001, when the National Institute for Media and the Family released their research involving a database of over 600 8th and 9th grade students from four schools. They concluded that:

> . . . children who are least aggressive in nature but are exposed to violent video games, are more likely to get into fights than children who are very aggressive but do not play violent video games.

The study found that children who play violent video games:

-See the world as a more hostile place.
-Argue with teachers more frequently.
-Are more likely to be involved in physical fights.
-Don't perform as well in school.

Video Games As "Mass Murder Simulators" and "Marksmanship Trainers"

I see before me the gladiator lie.
There were his young barbarians all at play,
Butchered to make a Roman holiday.

—Lord Byron
Childe Harold's Pilgrimage

The American Sniper Association's training periodical published the following "Training Tip" from a law enforcement sniper in the April 2000 edition.

> After the incident in Littleton, Colorado, much was made of the fact that teens are using graphic video and computer games to train and condition themselves to kill. There is some truth to this. However, we do not and should not, allow them to have a monopoly on this training "tool." Video games can be used as a unique and inexpensive method for honing your skills as well.
>
> A new video game, *Silent Scope*, is the latest rage in the local arcades. This game puts you, the sniper, behind a scoped rifle, interacting in an unfolding scenario in which your talents are needed to help rescue the President's daughter from terrorists. The game will help you work on observations skills, tracking and identifying targets, snap shooting, and moves. It will never replace real range time, but it is a nice variation, and it's fun.

Violent media games are murder simulators, except when police officers and soldiers use them for training, in which case they are combat simulators. Remember that old point-and-shoot Nintendo video game called *Duck Hunt*? It was such a good marksmanship trainer that the United States Army bought several thousand of them. They replaced the plastic pistol with a plastic M-16, and instead of ducks popping up on the screen, the Army changed them to man-shaped silhouettes. The game was renamed the Multipurpose Arcade Combat Simulator (MACS). Of course, the troops were not fooled by the name; they just called it "the Nintendo game" since it has a big Nintendo stamp on it. By whatever name, it was a powerful and effective combat simulator for our men and women preparing for battle.

(It is interesting to note here; When I testified before committee hearings held by both the U.S. Senate and the U.S. House of Representatives after the Columbine school massacre. When I said that a modified version of the *Duck Hunt* game was used by the U.S. Army, the lobbyist representing the Nintendo

Corporation stood up and said that Nintendo has never sold anything to the U.S. military. No, they sold these games to a subcontractor, who then sold them to the Army.)

For the first time in human history we are dealing with a large scale epidemic of preteen and teenage mass murderers. The autopilot impact of the mass murder simulators was particularly obvious in the earliest of the school massacres. (These occurred before the frenzied national media coverage of the Jonesboro massacre established a national game in which the goal was racking up the "high score" in school massacres, with the "winner" getting his picture on the cover of *Time* magazine.) In the school massacres in Moses Lake, Pearl, Paducah and Jonesboro, the kids appear to have set out to kill just one person— usually a teacher or a girlfriend. But once they began, they shot every living creature in front of them until they ran out of bullets or were interrupted. Afterwards the police would ask something like, "Okay, you shot the person you were mad at, but why did you kill everyone else? Why did you kill the rest of them? Some of them were your friends."

One kid is reported to have said: "It just felt like I had momentum."

Why do these kids keep on shooting after they have gunned down the initial person they went after? Could it be their "training?"

When kids use these games they are not just murder simulators, but mass murder simulators. Is there a kid anywhere in the world who puts his coins into a video game machine, picks up a realistic-looking gun, shoots only one virtual person, puts it back down and then walks away? No. They are trained to kill all the virtual people, to rack up a high score.

In these school massacres, the kids kept shooting for the same reason that police officers, under the old training regimen, put their spent brass into their pockets in the middle of real gunfights without conscious thought. The kids kept on killing for the same reason that police officers fired two shots and then reholster in the middle of a gunfight when the deadly threat was still in front of them. These officers responded the way they had been trained on the firing range, and the same holds true for kids trained on violent, video game, mass murder simulators.

Once a kid makes the decision to cross that tragic invisible line and shoots his girlfriend, he earns one point. That is how the video games trained him. If his girlfriend is one point, then another kid is a second point, another garners him a third point, and then he gets a fourth, fifth, sixth, seventh, eighth, and on and on. Once that line is crossed, they all become points and the kid wants to earn a high score, just as he does in training. The mother of the 13-year-old killer in the Jonesboro school shooting sat across our coffee table and told my wife and I, several months after the killings, that she finally told her son who he had killed that day. She said her boy laid his head on the table, and sobbed, saying, "Those were my friends."

There are no friends in violent video games; there are only targets. Points.

Thus, by understanding how a conditioned reflex is developed in our professional warriors, we can understand what is going on in the minds of some of these killers.

We saw the killing-enabling effects of video games being intentionally applied by criminals in the "Beltway Sniper" attacks that terrorized the Washington, D.C. area in the fall of 2002. Soon after the suspects were apprehended, sources close to the investigation told reporters that the killers had used video game sniper simulators to desensitize and mentally prepare themselves for their crimes. This effect is not limited to the U.S. The German media reported extensively on the influence of video games on the boy who committed a school massacre in Erfurt, Germany, resulting in 17 tragic deaths.

As video game technology gets distributed to third world nations, our military forces that are fighting terrorists and serving as peacekeepers around the world, will also face opponents who are trained with mass murder simulators provided by the video game industry. In 1999, the International Committee of the Red Cross (ICRC) invited me to Switzerland to be a member of a team of international experts studying the effects of media violence and violent video games on atrocities and war crimes around the globe. One Red Cross official told of a gang operating in one war-torn, Central African nation, in a city without electricity. The only electricity was provided by a generator, which the gang used to keep their beer cold and to operate the violent video arcade game that they used extensively as a training device to psychologically prepare them to kill and to enhance their marksmanship skills.

Many competitive shooters practice by using "dry firing" to improve the necessary body mechanics required to shoot accurately. To dry fire, you simply point an unloaded firearm at a target, cock the hammer, and pull the trigger, keeping the sight picture as steady as possible. By concentrating on the technical elements of shooting—sight picture, grip, trigger pull, arm position—you get a better idea of what you are doing right and wrong without having to go to the range. There is also a highly effective way to dry fire with laser feedback, an innovation that requires a laser to be placed into your weapon so that each time you pull the trigger, it emits a bright, visible beam. When a realistic, human target is hit, it falls. It is a dynamic and effective simulation system used in the military and law enforcement communities. It is considered state of the art training. Frighteningly, our kids have it too when they play violent video games. The marksmanship training these games provide our police officers, soldiers—and our kids—is stunning.

In Paducah, Kentucky, Michael Carneal, a 14-year-old boy, fired eight shots into a prayer circle in the large foyer in front of his school achieving a hit ratio of 8 out of 8 head shot or upper torso hits. Conversely, in the Amadou Diallo shooting, four NYPD officers fired 41 shots at an unarmed man at pointblank range, hitting him with only 19 rounds. These NYPD officers achieved less than a 50 percent hit ratio with bullets distributed from Diallo's feet to his head. That is normal accuracy resulting from a fear induced, spray and pray response. In the summer of 1999 Buford Furrow went into a Jewish daycare center in Los Angeles and fired over 70 shots at a group of helpless children. He hit five of them. But in the Paducah school shooting Michael Carneal fired eight shots and got eight hits on eight different kids. Five of his hits were headshots, the other three were upper torso. We know that his video game training was a key factor in attaining this kind of marksmanship skills.

A student pilot can train on a flight simulator forever, but he needs at least one real flight with a copilot to help make that transition to a real aircraft. All the time the trainee spent on the simulator makes for fast learning during his transition period. The Army calls the transition from a simulator to a real weapon, "transition fire." Michael Carneal conducted his transition fire with two clips of ammo a few days before the Paducah school slaughter.

When I train elite military and law enforcement organizations such as the FBI, Green Berets, LAPD SWAT and Texas Rangers—warriors highly trained in firearms—they are stunned when I tell them of this 14-year-old boy's deadly accuracy in the Paducah case. Nowhere in the annals of law enforcement, military, or criminal history can we find an equivalent achievement. This unprecedented marksmanship was not done by some deranged Army Ranger (like me), it was done by a 14-year-old boy who had never fired a real pistol before stealing one and firing two clips of ammunition on a previous night. But he had been on the simulator every night for years on end.

After I testified before the U.S. Senate and the U.S. House of Representatives about this, the video game industry's lobbyists circulated a bizarre "confidential" document to legislators and reporters, attacking my work but forbidding anyone to quote them. This document was full of the kind of things you would expect lobbyists to say in defense of their industry—just like the tobacco lobbyists told us tobacco didn't cause cancer. Their most absurd claim was that "police reports indicate that Carneal [the Paducah killer] had his eyes closed during the shooting and fired blindly."

The police reports said no such thing. It was Carneal who said in a statement to his psychiatrist: "I don't know, it was all, like blurry and foggy, I just didn't know what was going on. *I think I closed my eyes for a minute.*" (Emphasis added.) All of the witness statements refute this. The psychiatric and psychological evaluation of Michael Carneal, by Dr. Bebedek, Dr. Weitzel, and Dr. Clark conclude that: "Certainly his claims . . . to have closed his eyes when he shot . . . are scarcely to be believed." But the video game industry's lobbyists told legislators and reporters that this self-serving statement by a juvenile mass murderer was a "fact" from a "police report."

Witness statements say that Carneal had a strange, calm look on his face as he held his gun up in a two-handed stance. He never fired far to his left or right. His first bullet went between his girlfriend's eyes, and then he proceeded to put one bullet in every target that popped up on his "screen." His own sister wrote in her statement that she started to move toward her brother to tell him to stop, but then she says that she recalled thinking to herself, "He doesn't know who I am. He's going to kill me," so she started to run.

What was Carneal doing? I believe that there can be little doubt that he was playing a video game. He was in Condition Yellow, calmly putting a bullet in every target that popped up on his screen. It is not natural to put just one bullet in every target. What is natural is to shoot at a target until it drops and then, maybe, move on to another. Many video games, however, train kids to make a one-shot kill, and then before that target drops, move on to the next one, and the one after that, because the goal is to earn lots of points. Shoot them all and kill as many as you can as fast as you can. By the way, many video games give bonus points for headshots. Carneal was doing exactly what he was trained to do. Whatever we are trained to do is going to come out the other end.

Across the decades, millions of police officers put their brass in their pockets on the firing range so they would not have to pick them up when the training was over. Only a few of them got into real combat situations in which they did this, but those were enough for us to know that it was stupid to train cops this way.

Although hundreds of thousands of police officers were trained to fire two shots and automatically reholster, only a handful got into real gunfights and did that as their adversaries were still shooting at them. But that was enough for us to understand that we were teaching them to do something stupid.

Millions of kids train on violent video games every day, and only a few will go on to use the skills and conditioned reflexes that they learned in the video games to commit an unprecedented juvenile mass murder. But that should be enough for us to understand that we are doing something very foolish indeed.

In the military and in law enforcement communities, people qualify at the firing range every six months. More is better, but every six months appears to be the minimum since conditioned reflexes have a kind of "half-life" and begin to decay after just a few months. It is truly like a radioactive half-life: there is a steady decay, but there is always a little residual available to tap into. However, as long as warriors can refresh their skill at least every six months, it will be there when needed. Again, more training is better, but every six months is minimum. Kids, on the other hand, qualify on these murder simulators every day.

John Foy, the head firearms instructor and range master for the Ohio Peace Officer's Training Academy, has developed a powerful model that helped me understand exactly what video games were doing to kids. For many decades John has tapped into some of Abraham Maslow's work, teaching that there are four levels of mastery.

Unconscious incompetence. This is the lowest level of mastery. Most American male teenagers are at a level of unconscious incompetence when it comes to driving. They are bad drivers. They don't know it and usually they refuse to admit it. The first step in making them better drivers is to get them to admit that they need experience and practice before they can be entrusted with human lives at high speeds.

Conscious incompetence. Most young men coming into military firearms training are convinced that they are experts with a weapon. The drill sergeant's first job is to convince them of their ignorance. Many firearms instructors will tell you that women are easier to train because they know they need to learn, they know that they are ignorant, and they are willing to listen. They are easier to train because they are already at the level of conscious incompetence.

Conscious competence. You can do the right thing, but you have to think about it. That is fine for many tasks, but for life-and-death skills to be performed under stress, it is not good enough.

Unconscious competence. This is the highest level of mastery. As martial artist Bruce Lee put it, you, "Learn it until you forget it." *This* is what autopilot is all about. *This* is the goal of warrior training

Many firearms instructors tell me that there are some officers in today's new generation of young recruits who walk onto their pistol ranges, hold a real pistol in their hands for the first time and, after firing a few shots to adjust themselves to the weapon, are supernatural marksmen. When asked, almost all of them say that they are avid players of the point-and-shoot arcade video games. Their video game play has permitted them to reach a level of unconscious competence, just like Michael Carneal in Paducah, Kentucky, when he hit eight-for-eight, with five head shots.

There can be no doubt that video games can teach marksmanship skills. A controlled experiment conducted by the Center for Successful Parenting, written by Tom Stoughton and published in 2002 in the *Newsletter of The UNESCO International Clearinghouse On Children, Youth and Media*, demonstrated that those kids who were proficient at point-and-shoot video games are significantly better shots when they pick up a real gun for the first time.

Ray Blinn, a police officer in East Providence, Rhode Island, wrote, telling me about a 15-year-old police cadet who went through the qualification program on their Firearms Training Simulator (FATS)—a highly realistic, state-of-the-art video simulator used by military and law enforcement agencies worldwide.

> He went through five scenarios, with only one miss (just barely missing a headshot). He had multiple double taps to the heads and center mass of the suspects. Of the 100 officers that went through the training, this cadet shot in the top five percent.

At the end I questioned him about his shooting ability. He stated that he had never shot a real gun in his life. I then asked him if he played a lot of video games and with a big smile he said, "All the time, especially the shooting ones. They're the most fun."

Good thing he wants to be a good guy.

The tobacco industry was able to hire doctors to appear on national TV and lie for them, saying: "I'm a doctor, and I don't believe that tobacco causes cancer." But to the best of my knowledge the TV, movie and video game industry cannot find one single medical doctor or psychiatrist to take their money and say that their violent products are not harmful to kids. Any medical practitioner who did so might very well lose their license. However, they have found one psychology professor in Canada, Jonathan Freedman, who freely admits that his research is funded by Hollywood. Yet even he does not try to claim that video games do not teach skills.

In an interview in the on-line video game magazine, *The Adrenaline Vault*, Freedman is referred to as "the anti-Grossman." (I've always wanted to ask them if that is anything like being the Antichrist.) He is one of those "scholars" who uses the murder rate to claim that violent crime is down to 1960's levels, when we know that it is medical technology that is holding down the murder rate. Yet even he says,

> If you go into a video arcade: it's a gun you hold, and you aim it. Gun clubs teach you to shoot more accurately, presumably. Why shouldn't this? So I think that's a silly argument. Grossman's right: of course they get better at shooting.

The "Game Over" Effect: What Made Them Stop

How use doth breed a habit in a man!

—Shakespeare
The Two Gentleman of Verona

Let us examine one final aspect of what warrior science can teach us about the influence of video games on an up-and-coming new generation of mass murderers. What was it that made these juvenile mass murders stop shooting their classmates; what was it that turned off their autopilot?

Dr. James McGee wrote the brilliant "Classroom Avenger" profile of 19 school shooters, which is used by the FBI and many other law enforcement agencies. McGee studied all aspects of these young kids, and he identified the fact that all of them had an infatuation with media violence.

Not every kid who plays a violent video game becomes a mass murderer, and not every kid with an unbuckled seatbelt is going to smash through the windshield. The vast majority of kids who ride with unbuckled seatbelts will be just fine, though not fastening it is a risk factor. Likewise, most kids who play the mass murder simulators will not commit mass murder.

But some will. Consider these case studies (which as Dr. McGee notes, are all kids infatuated with media violence), and note what made them stop.

-**Pearl, Mississippi.** A 17-year-old kid walks along a hallway in Pearl High School gunning down other students. The vice-principal has a .45 automatic in his car (a federal offense, though no one has ever pressed charges) and runs out to the parking lot to retrieve it. A moment later, this educator stands face-to-face with the kid, pointing his gun at the young man, and says, "Stop!" Amazingly, the kid stops. A 17-year-old crazed mass murderer with a loaded gun in his hand is ordered to stop shooting people, and he does.

-**Paducah, Kentucky**. A 14-year-old stands in a perfect shooting stance in the middle of a hallway shooting other students, one after the other with seemingly supernatural accuracy. He still has one round left and there are still lots of targets running and screaming all around him. But before he can shoot one more time, the principal runs up to him and demands, "Stop!" He stops. "Put the gun down," the principal says, "You've done enough." And the kid put the gun down. So, right in the middle of committing a mass murder, with the capability of killing at least one more, a simple verbal command stops the killer.

-**Jonesboro, Arkansas.** Two young killers empty their weapons into 15 people, reload and begin running over a hill toward their stolen van. The boys are 11 and 13 years old. As they approach the van, a police officer yells, "Police! Down on the ground. Drop the weapon. Down on the ground." These two boys have just committed a bloody mass murder and they still have loaded weapons in their hands, but what do they do? They obey the officer and drop their weapons.

-**Taber, Canada.** A 15-year-old is gunning down kids in a high school when an unarmed educator approaches shouting, "Stop!" and the killer stops.

-**Fort Gibson, Oklahoma.** An armed 13-year-old boy walks up to a crowd of classmates waiting for the morning bell and opens fire, wounding four. A science teacher runs up to the shooter, right in the middle of his spree, and commands, "Stop," and the kid stops.

What is going on here? We have never before seen mass murderers stop just because someone tells them to. Could it be because these killers are still kids, and their training teaches them to accept interruptions? When a kid plays a video game and his mom tells him to stop, the kid puts the game on "pause," and then looks up to see what she wants. Kids are used to the "game over" feature, and they are used to a verbal command telling them when it is time to pause. In these cases, the dynamics of their training—and it really is training that we are talking about—is clear. The killers are reacting as they have been conditioned to react: They stop when told to.

It is important that we do not assume that all shooters will stop just because you tell them to. I believe the two killers in Littleton, Colorado, would never have stopped just because someone told them to. The killer in Springfield, Oregon, gunned down 24 kids. It was not a verbal command that stopped him, but a high school senior, an Eagle Scout and wrestler, who sucked up the killer's bullets but still tackled the shooter and wrestled the gun away. This juvenile mass murderer, a high school freshman, curled into a ball and began sobbing, "Kill me, kill me, kill me. I wanna die." His gun had to be wrestled out of his hand. Incidentally, he was not thoroughly searched and as soon as he was alone in the jail, he retrieved a buck knife that was strapped to his leg. He called a deputy to him, and then lunged at the man in an attempt to add one last body to his count. Never assume that all will stop on command.

Under the proper circumstances, Plan A is a verbal command. If Plan A doesn't work, you need a Plan B. Plan B is to shoot them before they can hurt anyone else.

Never before in history have we had juveniles capable of committing mass murders like we have today. In Vietnam and in World War II, most 18-year-old kids responded with nausea and trembling after the first time they had to kill in combat. They pulled the trigger, and then watched as another human being fell at close range, gurgling and dying. Though many of these young warriors vomited after their first kill, they found that the next one was easier because they knew what to expect.

Many kids have also made their first kill—and their 101st and their 1001st—playing realistic, state-of-the-art violent video games. They have watched over and over as their "victims" bled, gurgled, twitched and begged for mercy, all the while earning points for inflicting brutal death and suffering upon their virtual playmates. Those of us whose job it is to make killing a conditioned reflex can understand the training dynamic that is at play. Never before have we seen juvenile killers like Pearl, Paducah, Jonesboro, Springfield, Columbine, and Erfurt, and all of us—adults, parents, and the video game industry—are enabling these mass murders.

Scared Speechless: "All That Came Out of My Mouth Was This Weird, Inarticulate Garbling Sound."

I understand a fury in your words,
But not the words.

—Shakespeare
Othello

Let us set aside the subject of video games to examine one last aspect of the autopilot effect in combat: the tendency to be literally "scared speechless" in combat.

Speech is a fine-motor skill, and the voice is one of the first places that you can observe stress in most people. This appears to happen as a result of the vasoconstriction effects of Condition Red shutting down the fine-motor control of the larynx. Remember on the *Andy Griffith Show* when Deputy Barney Fife got excited? Remember how his voice sounded? That could be you!

Unless you have been properly trained, it is quite easy for you to experience a profound breakdown of speaking ability, and in Condition Black you may literally be scared speechless when operating at extreme levels of stress. One veteran police training officer put it this way:

> I have heard the dispatch operator tell more than one overly excited officer in a pursuit to calm down because she could not understand what he was saying. When I was coaching rookies, I told them to take a calming breath before they spoke into the police radio. Whether they were about to call a car chase or were chasing someone on foot, that breath almost always gave them a sense of calm or at least a degree of control so that the pitch of their voice wouldn't go through the ceiling and they could be understood. I also taught my young charges to use the siren as little as possible, because the sound of it elevates the heart rate, and ultimately the pitch and pace of the voice.

However, you can partially transcend these limitations through training. Like most fine-motor skills, if you rehearse what to say ahead of time there is an increased likelihood that the skill will be there for you at the moment of truth when you are operating in Condition Red. Police officers, for example, are taught to call out, "Police! Drop the weapon. Get down. Get down." They train for this repetitively in a variety of training scenarios typical of what officers encounter on the street. It is because they train to use verbal commands in high-stress situations that they are able to employ them when needed.

Officers did not always train this way. One veteran detective gave me this example.

> We didn't train giving verbal commands, so they weren't available to us during high stress situations. One time, 20 years ago, a guy shoved a gun in my face. So I shoved my gun in his face and told him, 'Arrr-arrr-arggggh!' All that came out of my mouth was this weird, inarticulate garbling sound. I was literally scared speechless.

I asked him what he did then, and he said, "What could I do? I blew his stinking head off!"

Several officers have told me that they did not remember giving verbal commands during their fights or deadly force incidents, but were told afterwards that they did. One officer told me about a time when he was wrestling with a suspect armed with a knife.

> Afterwards I told the other officers who were with me as we wrestled this guy down, that I should have given him some verbal orders, but I guess I was just too busy staying alive. They laughed and said, "You never stopped shouting at him to 'Drop the weapon' throughout the fight. You never shut your mouth." Funny, I honestly don't remember doing it.

Ken Murray, in his book, *Training At The Speed Of Life*, makes an excellent observation about training warriors to give verbal commands. He notes that we must program police officers to say "Drop the weapon" rather than "Drop the gun" since officers will often order role players to "Drop the gun" during simulations, when the role player is holding a knife or other type of non-firearm. If this kind of mistake happens in a real, life-and-death situation it can confuse the suspect and it may result in the officer's judgment being called into question in court. By thinking through exactly what we want a warrior to do in combat, and training him say or do exactly the right thing in training, we can insure that the right words and actions will be there when lives are on the line.

Whatever you drill for ahead of time will be there for you in combat. No more, no less. If you drill for specific verbal commands, then you dramatically increase the likelihood that at the moment of truth those commands will be available to you under stress. And if we drill our children on mass murder simulators, that too will be a reflexive, autopilot skill that is available to them at some tragic moment of truth.

three

chapter

A Grab Bag of Effects: *Visual Clarity, Slow Motion Time, Temporary Paralysis, Dissociation and Intrusive Thoughts*

Trials dark on every hand and we cannot understand

—Charles Tindley
"By and By"

Visual Clarity: "A Perfect Image"

You may see a muzzle flash, as if in stop action, or even see a bullet in the air. You may have a vivid image of the gun, or even a ring on the suspect's hand, but not remember his face.

—Artwohl and Christensen
Deadly Force Encounters

Scientific research and volumes of anecdotal evidence indicate that in many shooting situations there is a sudden visual clarity, an incredible moment when the body dedicates all its resources to get maximum value out of the eyes. You might get a clear picture of details you ordinarily would not notice or remember. Dr. Artwohl found that 72 percent of her survey group reported heightened visual clarity during their deadly force incident.

My co-author, Loren Christensen, tells of sleeping at home and being awakened suddenly at 2 a.m. to a terrible racket. He said it took a second for the fog in his head to clear, and when it did, he looked up into a man's face about a foot above his, a burglar climbing through the bedroom window, apparently too high or drunk to realize anyone was home. The man let out a small squeal when his eyes finally focused on Christensen's face peering up at him, and he quickly scooted back out the window.

Christensen leapt from his bed, grabbed his gun off the dresser, ran through the living room, and jerked open the backdoor. There was the burglar, a huge man, preparing to kick in the door. Christensen said, "The big ape was nuts or dumb, maybe both." When Christensen raised his gun, the burglar did have enough smarts to leap off the porch and bound through the shrubs like a spooked rhino.

Christensen said that as he waited for 9-1-1 to answer, he remembers thinking that he had no description to give since he had not made a conscious effort to note the man's hair color, age, height and what he was wearing. When the operator answered, he first told her what had happened. Then she asked the dreaded question: "Could you describe him?"

To his amazement, he could. "It just poured out of me," he said.

> It was as if the creep were standing right there and I was looking him up and down. I gave a complete, ultradetailed description, none of which I consciously noted when I was about to shoot him. It was as if a perfect image had been ingrained in my mind's eye. Officers apprehended him about 10 minutes later.

In their book, *Deadly Force Encounters*, Artwohl and Christensen give another classic example:

> I focused on the weapon pointed at my face from 12 feet away and I could see the bullets in the cylinder of the revolver. I saw the suspect's forearm muscles and tendons tense as he squeezed the gun. I looked down the barrel and knew I was going to get shot somewhere between my nose and neck, probably my teeth. I fired one shot and it struck the suspect.
>
> I couldn't believe I got off a shot before he did.

Like many combat stress responses, the visual clarity effect can make it possible for the human body to do things that we previously would not have believed possible. This narrative from a sniper who has to shoot an armed suspect in a low-light situation pretty much says it all.

> I have heard of things like auditory exclusion and other dramatic things that happen to our senses under stress, but I experienced something I had no idea could occur. At the very instant I picked my aiming point on her head that night, a light turned on inside my scope. I'm not even sure how to properly explain this, but here goes. It was like a light actually came on, not an illuminate reticule, more like an actual light. It simply got brighter in the scope, just like somebody flipped on a switch. I have never seen the reticule more clearly and beautifully focused . . . it's my subconscious mind taking over control of my senses in order to put the emphasis exactly where it needs to be for this shot . . . my subconscious knew I didn't need particularly good hearing or taste to accomplish what was necessary, but I did need my

eyes working at top form . . . So the subconscious mind takes over and does what is necessary for you to succeed. If this ever happens to you, you'll probably recognize it right away. Be glad for it. It was a big help.

—Russ Clagett
After the Echo

Slow-motion Time: "Time Ambles"

Time travels in divers paces with divers persons. I'll tell you who Time ambles withal, who Time trots withal, who Time gallops withal, and who he stands still withal.

—Shakespeare
As You Like It

Perceiving the action in slow motion can definitely be a survival mechanism. Over the years, many people have talked about slow-motion time, but until Dr. Artwohl collected data showing that 65 percent of officers engaged in a gunfight experienced it, no one really understood that it was so prevalent. I have collected numerous case studies of officers who found slow-motion time so powerful that they were able to see bullets pass by them. On several occasions, they were able to validate what they perceived by pointing to where the rounds had hit. They were not implying that bullets moved by them at a crawling pace, as when special effects are used in movies. What they meant was that the rounds passed by the same way that low velocity paintballs or paint bullet rounds can be seen going past.

Every case study gives us a little more information, a little better insight into what is happening. Notice in this case study from Loren Christensen's files, how slow-motion time combines with auditory exclusion to create a powerful effect:

Officer Anderson stood over them, less than four feet away, pleading with the suspect to drop the knife. But the suspect had another plan. "You got three seconds or I will kill this guy," he said, holding the hostage tightly against him.

"I tried to grab the knife," Anderson says, "but he raised it in an arc above the hostage's head." When it reached its highest point, the hostage moved, just enough to expose the suspect's chest. "All I could see was his chest and the knife, and then everything got quiet and all movement slowed. I felt like I could stand back and consider options: What would happen if the hostage were slaughtered in front of me? What if the killer then dropped the knife and laughed at me? Did the hostage trust that I knew what to do?

"I knew I had to shoot or the hostage would die. For just a second, it seemed as if my whole life had been for this moment, a moment that was now and would never happen again. It was mine to decide."

When the knife paused ever so briefly before its descent, Anderson fired. His first round demolished the suspect's wrist, and one of the other five rounds that followed punched through the center of the man's heart. His partner blasted the man with a shotgun.

"I remember the smell of the gunpowder, but not the sound of my shots," he says. "I remember the face of the hostage, but not his words. I remember the wail of sirens but not who came. I remember my decision, but I don't remember pulling the trigger. Later, I told detectives I thought I had fired only twice. If I'd had 20 more rounds, I would have fired those, too."

While slow-motion time can be a survival mechanism, it frequently comes with too much baggage. It often happens in Condition Black and is accompanied by an extremely elevated heart rate and loss of fine and complex motor control. Perhaps someday we will be able to train elite warriors to make slow-motion time kick in when they need it, without the additional complications. If there was a pill that caused slow-motion time without the baggage, we could give it to baseball players so the batters could watch the ball creep toward them. Now, that would be something.

Until that day arrives, all we can say is that the slow-motion time effect seems to be a random, unpredictable and sometimes useful response to combat. For now it is sufficient to warn our warriors that it might happen.

Temporary Paralysis: "I Couldn't Move My Legs"

Anything you do can get you shot; including doing nothing.
—Clint Smith

Seven percent of the officers in Dr. Artwohl's study experienced temporary paralysis in their gunfights. If this paralysis, sometimes referred to as freezing, were actually occurring, then we could say that it is a phenomenon that is clearly not a survival mechanism. Freezing does happen sometimes in combat, but in some cases we know that those who think they are experiencing temporary paralysis are actually experiencing slow-motion time.

A SWAT team member and law enforcement trainer in Wisconsin told me of an experience he had during one of his early entries. After they had tossed flashbangs into the house, they rushed in and began a search. As he moved around a corner, he abruptly came face to face with several armed men. "All of a sudden, I couldn't move my legs," he said. "I couldn't move my legs, and I didn't understand what was wrong with me. Why couldn't I move them?" After a moment, he realized he could move his legs. "Just v-e-r-y slowly," he said. "I realized that this is that slow-motion time everybody has told me about. I've got all the time in the world." Is that a survival mechanism? In general, yes.

The problem is that there are soldiers and police officers experiencing temporary paralysis and slow-motion time during deadly encounters but no one has warned them that it might happen. Suddenly they cannot move their legs, and they panic. They think they are paralyzed. Dr. Artwohl talks about an interview she had with a police officer after he had been in a gunfight. The officer said: "The suspect shot at me and I froze. It took an eternity for me to finally return fire at him." Well, it only seemed that long to the officer. There was an audio tape of the gunfight and we know that the officer returned fire only a fraction of a second later. For him, though, it felt like forever.

Dissociation and Intrusive Distracting Thoughts

Chaos of thought and passion, all confused . . .

—Alexander Pope
Essay on Man

The following two narratives from *Deadly Force Encounters* are good examples of the dissociation effect.

During high-threat situations you may experience a strange sense of detachment, as if the event were a dream, or you were looking at yourself from outside your body. You may go from that "oh-shit" moment with an intense awareness of fear, to feeling almost nothing as you focus only on staying alive. Afterward, when you snap back to reality, it will seem as if the event took place in the Twilight Zone. Even hours later you may have difficulty accepting that it happened, as if some part of you is still in denial that it could really happen to you.

I made a traffic stop on a man who turned out to be under the influence of cocaine. Everything moved in slow motion when I fired three shots (only two of which I remember). I was clearly "out of body" as I watched the shooting from above and ahead of my actual position. There was no sound from my .45 either, or any recoil.

We are still at a very early stage in our understanding of these effects, and there can be no certainty as to precisely what they mean or imply about the individual who experiences any specific perceptual distortion. However, the initial conclusions from the 2001 stress studies of Green Berets, conducted by Morgan and Hazlett indicate that dissociation may be associated with less effective performance in combat and a predisposition to PTSD after combat. I believe that dissociation may well represent a powerful Condition Black response, indicative of extreme high levels of arousal that could indeed predispose someone toward a posttraumatic response. There is also data to indicate that dissociation and slow-motion time often occur together in combat situations, which would indicate that slow-motion time is also a Condition Black response that may predispose someone toward a posttraumatic response. (The link between Condition Black and PTSD will be addressed in detail later in the book.)

The final perceptual distortion effect to be addressed in this chapter is the phenomenon of intrusive distracting thoughts. Dr. Artwohl found that 26 percent of the officers in her survey, roughly one out of four, had thoughts that were truly intrusive and distracting during their shootings. Often the intrusive thoughts were bizarre, such as one officer who said that when a man shoved a gun in his face, his first thought was, "Wow, that is just like my partner's gun. I wonder where he got it."

In the heat of battle, many warriors think of their family. One police officer said that during a gunfight, he had a vision of his three-year-old boy toddling around in front of him in his pajamas. These intrusive thoughts are not always distracting, sometimes they can serve as an inspiration or motivation, as in the case of one police officer in Arkansas who was shot in the face. He says that a sudden thought about his young son motivated him to get up and return fire, killing his assailant.

Thoughts of a higher power are also common. This was exemplified by Bruce Siddle in his combat experience as related in his book, *Sharpening the Warrior's Edge*, and echoed by many warriors across the centuries: "God, get me out of this one, and I'll be there every Sunday from now on. I promise."

Charles Remsberg in his excellent book, *The Tactical Edge*, trains warriors to develop "positive self-talk," the most important of which is, "I will survive and keep going, no matter what." Often, wounded police officers report that this was all they heard in their minds after they were shot, and it was essential to their survival. These are the kind of intrusive thoughts that we must program into our minds if we are to survive in combat.

chapter four

Memory Loss, Memory Distortions, and the Role of Videotaping:

You Are Absolutely Convinced it Happened

> . . . few of us can hold on to our real selves long enough to discover the real truths about ourselves and this whirling earth to which we cling. This is especially true of men in war. The great god Mars tries to blind us when we enter his realm, and when we leave he gives us a generous cup of the waters of Lethe to drink."
>
> —Glenn Gray
> *The Warriors*

Memory Loss: "I Had No Memory at All of Making That Call"

We have already learned of the blindness that the war god Mars can inflict upon men in combat, now let us examine the effects of the "waters of Lethe," the waters of forgetfulness. Consider these two examples of memory loss from Dr. Artwohl's files.

> An officer was involved in a shooting in which over 20 rounds were fired. Immediately afterwards, [the officer] couldn't remember for sure if she had fired at all. She remained unsure until an hour later when she and her lieutenant checked her weapon and counted the rounds.
>
> An officer shot a suspect twice with a shotgun to prevent him from entering a residence and taking a hostage. It was a righteous shooting, but the officer could only remember firing one of two rounds. The shooting review board found one round "in policy" and one round "out of policy." Their reasoning was that both rounds were justified, but since [the officer] couldn't remember one of them, it must have been out of policy.

Nearly half of all law enforcement officers involved in deadly force encounters experienced "missing frames," that is, significant chunks of memory lost from their event. Artwohl found that 47 percent of officers in a gunfight experienced memory loss of at least part of their actions. Interestingly, Dr. Dave Klinger's groundbreaking research, which will be covered later in this section, found that if you fire only one or two shots, you usually remember the number. But as you fire more rounds, there is an increasing tendency to forget how many you shot, or you underestimate the number.

It is common for an officer to believe that he fired only a couple of rounds into the suspect, but then discover that he actually emptied his high-capacity magazine. Dr. Artwohl says that memories of high-risk situations are often like a series of snapshots, some vivid, some blurry and some even missing.

It is common for there to be some degree of memory loss in a deadly encounter, especially when the heart rate reaches the realm of Condition Black. This is a phenomenon that Bruce Siddle and I termed "critical incident amnesia" in an article published in the *Journal of the International Association of Law Enforcement Firearms Instructors*, in August 2001. (This article is posted on my web site, www.warriorscience.com, for those who would like more detail on the subject.)

It is common within the first 24 hours to recall roughly 30 percent of the occurrence, 50 percent of it after 48 hours and 75 to 95 percent after 72 to 100 hours. This is why it is so important for investigators to interview participants of a critical incident again after they have gotten one or more nights of quality sleep.

Artwohl and Christensen give this classic example:

> I was in a high-speed pursuit with a bunch of other officers, chasing a known felon with a long history of violent behavior. When he started firing a gun at us out the window, I had the disturbing thought that I may not live through this. In spite of the fear, my training kicked in and I performed well, and we killed the suspect before he killed us.
>
> When I finally got home, my wife made a comment about listening to the pursuit over the phone. I had no idea what she was talking about. It turns out that during the pursuit, I had called her on the cellular phone in my patrol car to tell her I loved her in case I didn't make it. My wife said she told me to hang up and concentrate on my driving.
>
> I had no memory at all of making that call.

Perseveration: Trapped in an Endless Do-loop

Insanity is repeating the same behavior expecting different results.

—Anonymous

Why would shooters lose track of how many rounds they fired? Why would they underestimate the number? Let's take a look at perseveration, a phenomenon we first learned about from studying fires in crowded theaters and nightclubs in the early and mid-1900s. In many of these tragic incidents, people rushed to the door and hit the crash bar, but the door was locked. Now, after a couple of tries on the bar, a rational human being would go to another door, but these individuals were not rational. The midbrain had taken over, the one that operates like a puppy's. Now the puppy was in charge, barking at these terrified people to hit the bar again. So they did, trapped in an endless do-loop, over and over, until they died. Gary Klugiewicz calls this "tactical fixation." We fixate on the tactic we are doing and do not consider other possibilities.

One police officer told me of a case in which he responded to a family fight call where a bare-chested man was running about the house in a rage, clutching a knife. When he saw the officer, he screamed, "You might as well shoot me because I'm going to kill you," and he began advancing. The officer fired two rounds into his chest, but the man only hesitated for a moment to look down at the holes, then he began moving toward the officer again. Back peddling, the officer rapidly fired round after round with his 9mm pistol, but like in a bad dream, the man kept advancing. "At one point," the officer said, "I was against a wall trying to push this guy off me. I fired one more time." That round punched through the top of the man's head and exited out his neck. Finally, after being struck multiple times, he collapsed.

This is probably a survival mechanism left over from our prehistoric ancestors. In those days, if a wolf was gnawing on your arm and you were smacking him with a rock, your best option was to keep hitting him as fast, as long, and as hard as you could, until either you or the wolf got some relief. Even as you were wilting under the fangs of the beast, your last conscious act would be to smack that wolf one more time, because that might be the blow that saved your life. In such a situation, it was easy to enter into a repetitive do-loop, with no sense of how many blows you had delivered.

The problem is that we are not fighting wolves anymore. Today we use precision instruments in life-and-death engagements. At a distance of just a few feet, an eighth of an inch variance in the barrel of a weapon can make the difference between a hit and a miss. We need precision control. The rule is that you do not fire any faster than you can hit the target. Is there a tendency upon occasion for police officers to fire faster than they can hit? You better believe it. When in a life-and-death struggle, it is not uncommon for a police officer, soldier or civilian to fire as fast as they can and as long as they can until the target goes away. Sometimes this is called "the spray and pray" response.

Earlier, I mentioned the tragic Amadou Diallo shooting where four N.Y.P.D. officers fired 41 shots at point-blank range into an unarmed man. It was shown after that shooting that the average officer could empty a high-capacity, 15-round 9mm magazine in four seconds. So does such a magazine give you the ability to blaze more ammo down range? Upon occasion, sure, and you can empty that magazine in four seconds. The problem is that unless you are firing at point-blank range the average shooter cannot hit a barn door at that rate of fire, and even if you hit the bad guy with all 15 rounds in four seconds, it is highly unlikely that he can die that fast. Imagine him saying, "I'm going to fall, but you got to give me a second here." The problem is that we now have a capacity to achieve incredible overkill in a spray-and-pray of vast numbers of bullets fired. Then, of course, the next day the press screams, "Alleged suspect killed in hail of police bullets." It is a problem nationwide in law enforcement.

Later in this section, an entire chapter will be dedicated to Dr. Dave Klinger's superb National Institute of Justice (NIJ) study of 113 police shootings. At this point, however, I want to pull out a portion of his study that provides a powerful insight into this perseveration effect. In this table drawn from Dr. Klinger's NIJ report, we see that as the number of shots fired goes up, the ability to recall how many were fired goes down.

# of Shots Actually Fired	# of Cases in Which this # of Shots Fired	# of Cases w/# Shots Recalled Correctly
1	33	32
2	16	14
3	14	12
4	18	11
5	7	2
6	8	3
7	3	1
8	3	0
9	3	1
13	1	0
14	1	0
15	1	0
16	1	0
18	1	0
28	2	0
41	1	0

You could conclude from this simply that the more shots fired the harder it is to remember (with equal chance of over or under estimating), but Dr. Klinger also recorded the fact that in 21 cases, the officers thought they had fired fewer rounds while nine officers had no idea how many shots they fired. The more rounds fired the more likely this was to occur. Only four individuals thought they had fired more rounds than they actually did.

A training sergeant from one major western city told me that his city had been having a significant problem with officers firing far too many shots with drastically low hit ratios. He said that on the firing range his officers could get around 90 percent hits, but on the street they were lucky to hit with 20 percent of the bullets fired. When the sergeant was ordered to call major police departments around the country to see if others were having the same problem, he found that the vast majority of departments were. One agency called it the "metro spray."

He also found that a small minority of departments had fixed the problem and were getting over a 90 percent hit ratio in real, life-and-death shooting events. The California Highway Patrol, Salt Lake City P.D., Toledo P.D. and other pioneers across America are now reporting extraordinary hit rates, while firing very few rounds. One of the key distinguishing characteristics that differentiates these departments from others is their training. In particular, in-service training that provides stress inoculation with paint bullets or some other kind of force-on-force training with marking capsules. There is solid evidence to believe that the problem of multiple shots with few hits is partly the result of a fear-induced stress response. The solution, therefore, is to inoculate against the stressor to prevent or reduce the fear. Force-on-force training with paint bullets or paintballs does exactly that.

Sam Faulkner, at the Ohio Peace Officers' Training Academy has an extensive program using simulated gunfights with paintball guns and "water ball" capsules that he calls his "Shot Avoidance" course. After training one major Ohio police department, their hit ratios were so high and their fire was so deadly that, in Faulkner's words:

> The [police department's] training sergeant was called in after a complaint was made to the chief by some departmental captains. They said in previous years their officers involved in gun fights had either missed or wounded the perpetrators. That year there were six gun battles; each was within departmental policy and in compliance with *Tennessee v. Garner* [case law standards on legal shooting].
>
> Your question then is what is their problem? Their problem is that in all of the six gunfights that year the officers had killed the subjects, and the captains were afraid that the training sergeant was turning the troops into "trained killers."
>
> The sergeant was upset by this and gave me a call. I explained my take on the situation this way. Can we teach our officers to shoot too well? I don't think so. If we trained our officers in first aid, and everyone they treated survived, did we train them too well? If we trained our officers in driving, and they never had anymore accidents, did we train them too well? If someone must die in an armed

encounter, let it be the subject who is initiating the hostile action, and not another officer.

Paint Bullet Training and Stress Inoculation: It is to the Warrior What the Flame House is to the Firefighter

Awareness is good, but without skills and ability tied to that awareness, all you have is anxiety.

—Tony Blauer
Extreme close-quarters combat trainer

I should make it clear that the most common brand of paint bullets is the "Simunition™" brand, which has become commonly used to refer to any gunpowder propelled, paint bullet marking capsules, just as Kleenex or Xerox are brand names which have become generic terms for a product. Ken Murray, in *Training At The Speed Of Life*, his definitive book on force-on-force simulations training, warns against referring to paint bullet training as "Simunition training," since the Simunition brand name also makes frangible ammunition and other types of ammo that is quite deadly if accidentally used in force-on-force training. Murray points out that this is like, "Tylenol making their product, but also making rat poison with the Tylenol brand name on it."

I am not endorsing the Simunition brand, but I am endorsing the training concept, which has been pioneered by this one corporation. Other useful tools for force-on-force training included very realistic, purpose built military and law enforcement trainers which fire paintballs and water balls, such as the line of products manufactured by Gun F/X Tactical Development. Because of the vast array of excellent products and systems available, this book could not possibly list them all. There is, however, a thorough discussion of the various training systems, products, protective equipment and the essential training philosophies necessary to extract the optimal training value in a safe manner in Ken Murray's, *Training At The Speed Of Life*.

Many elite military and law enforcement organizations have applied this type of training with remarkable success. Sometimes we see SWAT teams and special ops units whose members think they are good, but they get a rude surprise during their first force-on-force scenario using paint bullets. But then they get better. Much better.

One of Gavin de Becker's trainers clearly articulated the value of this training when de Becker's elite team of world-class bodyguards trained with Simunition brand paint bullets.

Prior to each student going through the scenario . . . I noticed that they were very calm. However, once the training began, we could tell that the stress level was higher either due to anticipation of what was about to take place or because of the realism of the scenario. Realism meaning, most people in my opinion, military or not, rarely point or get a real weapon pointed at them where they know something is going to come out and hurt them or the individual. In the military most soldiers use blanks where they know no one will get hurt. In simunition, we use our personal weapon, the same exact weapon we are going to use to protect our principal, our family, and even ourselves. We know it will kill an individual and we know it will kill us. So when one of the students actually picks it up, points it at someone, I notice how much they hesitate to pull the trigger when their stress level is heightened and their muscle memory tells them that this is a real gun, that something is going to come out, and someone is going to get hurt. I mention this because, I think it is one of our beginner class benefits. I believe it will save them if a situation ever arises and they have to use their weapon to defend their principal or themselves . . .

What I believe to be the most important lesson is that you are not dead until you are dead. During training, a few agents would die after being shot or after feeling the pain from the round. We would tell them that they are not dead until they are dead. Simunition training allows us to train them to continue on after they are shot and after feeling the pain from the round. I believe the pain from the simunition round instills a muscle memory that is beneficial because if they are ever in a situation where they are shot at, and they feel some pain, they will continue on to safety, instead of stopping to see if the pain they feel is indeed a gunshot wound.

There is a powerful obligation to participate in this type of realistic training. There are many officers who do not want to participate in paint bullet training for fear of having to lay their training skills on the line in front of their peers, fear of feeling the sting of a round impact their skin, and a general fear of having to function outside of their comfort zone. Yes, these factors do exist in this valuable, realistic training—but they also exist in a real gun battle.

Let's say there is a group of firefighters who have been going into dangerous fires and responding inappropriately. We discover by looking at their training records that these firefighters have never practiced in a real, "flame house" training environment. Firefighters who have never been in a real burning building! Whose fault is it that these individuals are performing poorly? Clearly, the culpability would lie with the trainers and the administrators who had not given them that important, state-of-the-art training resource.

Likewise, if there are law enforcement officers confronting life and death shooting situations and responding inappropriately, whose fault is that? Whose fault is it, when there are readily available state-of-the-art resources that prepare and inoculate officers for deadly force encounters, but the resources have not been provided? Again, it is clearly the trainers and administrators who failed to provide them with the resources to do their jobs as best they can. It appears that force-on-force paint bullet training is exactly such a resource. It is to the police officer and the soldier exactly what the flame house is to the firefighter.

What should be done with officers who do not want to participate in paint bullet training for fear of looking bad or simply because the rounds hurt a little? Say you are an administrator in a fire bureau and you have a firefighter who refuses to go into a burning house in a training exercise. You have trained him well up to that point, you have counseled him about his refusal, you have worked with him, but still he refuses to go in. As the administrator, what would you do with him? You would fire him. The firefighter has given you *prima facie*, *de facto* evidence that he is not qualified to carry a hose into a burning building. Such a person is not an inferior human being. He may in fact be a superior human being. He is just not qualified to carry a hose into a burning building, and you would be morally and legally liable if you permitted him to continue in that job.

If a law enforcement officer refuses to engage in paint bullet training after you have counseled him, trained him and worked with him in every way, what would you do if you were his captain? Again, he has given you *prima facie*, *de facto* evidence that he is not qualified to go into a real gunfight. He is not even qualified to carry a weapon. Should he run into a deadly force situation and fail to perform appropriately, you as the administrator, your agency and your city will go down hard in court.

Warriors have a moral obligation to protect society and it's citizens. Individuals who refuse to participate in realistic training should not be in the business.

Memory Distortions

A thousand fantasies
Begin to throng into my memory,

—John Milton
Comus

According to Dr. Artwohl's research, 21 percent of police officers involved in shootings experienced memory distortions. In other words, more than one in five officers in a gunfight remembered something that did not happen. Here is a classic example told by Dr. Artwohl.

Two police officers are in a gunfight, blazing away at the suspect. One said later that he saw his partner get shot. "I see the bullets rip through my partner's body," he said. "I see the blood gush out. I drop [kill] the suspect, holster my weapon, and turn to my partner. But he's fine; he's not hit." The officer clearly saw his partner shot. He saw the bullet holes and he saw the blood. When the battle is over, he goes to his partner's aid, but discovers he is not hurt at all. The officer believes what he saw with such intensity that he begins pulling at his partner's clothes . . . which understandably distresses the unharmed man.

When under great stress you may envision your worst fear—"My God, my partner is hit!"—and you see it so clearly in your mind that you are absolutely convinced it really happened. Sometimes people remember what actually happened, and what they envisioned as happening, creating what one combat veteran referred to as a "parallel worlds" effect.

Children are not usually good witnesses, so great caution must be exercised when there is no other choice but to use them. Until a child is about nine years old, he is incredibly malleable and suggestible; there is only a small difference between his fantasy world and his real world. Is it so hard to believe that the mind of a frightened adult might, under great stress, be just as malleable as a child's?

I had the opportunity to train Canadian soldiers shortly after they returned from a peacekeeping operation. One of the medics asked me: "Colonel, why do the wounded usually hallucinate, and why do they always hallucinate the most horrible things? They say things like, 'I let my buddies down. I failed.' 'My legs are gone. I'm paralyzed.' 'I'm never going to have babies.' 'All my buddies are dead.' 'I'm a coward.' Why do they always hallucinate such bad things?"

In life-and-death combat situations, people often envision possibilities, and sometimes those possibilities become reality in their minds. And seldom do they envision positive things occurring when people are trying to kill them and friends are dying.

Jill Watt is a remarkably perceptive observer who conducted extensive investigations among the survivors of a small battle to capture Villa Punta, just days before the end of World War II. In her research she found that,

> . . . it soon became apparent that very often a whole incident, a place would be blanked from someone's memory, if they believed themselves guilty of causing a comrade's death or letting their unit down. Most often, they proved not to be at fault at all. But the effect was so powerful that, out of a small unit, two had even taken up lifetime "whodunnit" careers—one becoming a judge, another a

senior police officer—without ever running their own seminal events to ground.

I was allowed to examine debriefing reports of the battle, and found that only one man had been alert enough to say, "At this point my memory of the action went blank. I do not remember anything that happened next until about an hour later." But all the others believed they had remembered every detail, even though blanking a whole floor of the villa, whole rooms from their accounts.

In one particularly striking case, a tough, reliable old Scottish batman [a personal servant/orderly to an officer] who had faithfully served the young officer whose death I was investigating, said that the boy had been pinned under falling masonry, his stomach completely torn away. "We couldn't tell his mother that," he said, "it was too terrible. But we couldn't move him—we'd never have left him behind otherwise." But the German doctor who cared for [the injured officer] till his eventual death said there wasn't a mark on him—he had died as a result of concussion, from the explosion that brought the ceiling down. The batman obviously sincerely believed he had seen the terrible mortal wounds. I felt he desperately needed a powerful reason to explain to himself how he could ever have left the young officer and run for the boats.

—Jill Watt
Personal correspondence with Colonel Grossman

If hardened soldiers and highly trained police officers are walking away from combat situations believing something happened that did not, might citizens and suspects also believe with all their heart that something happened that really did not? You bet.

I was training and assisting mental health professionals during the aftermath of one major school shooting. One of the psychologists told me about a teacher who was upset because he had not used towels to pack a gunshot victim's wounds. "I failed," he said in the debriefing the day after the event. One of the other teachers said to him, "But you did use the towels. Don't you remember?" Then he mentioned something else that he felt he should have done, and again his fellow teachers reassured him, "But you did, don't you remember?"

What happened in this case, and has happened to so many others, is that his memory loss linked with his guilt, and convinced him that he had failed. Now, if he had not had a debriefing, if he had not been provided with the opportunity to talk with other individuals who had experienced the same event, he would have spent the rest of his life guilt ridden and convinced that he had failed and was responsible for the death of an innocent person.

After a situation like this, who can convince you of what really happened? Certainly not you, since you are already convinced of the delusion. It is up to others who were there with you. In these horrific situations, we all hold each other's lives in our hands after the event. That is what a debriefing is all about, which we will discuss in detail later.

The Role of Videotaping: The Truth Is Not Your Enemy

But O the truth, the truth! the many eyes
That look on it! the diverse things they see!

—George Meredith
A Ballad of Fair Ladies in Revolt

Videotaping is the future and soon every official act by every warrior profession will be recorded through a lens. There are untold thousands of camcorders sold every year and there are ever more security cameras and media cameras. We are told that in just a few years we will all be videotaped wherever we go. Even now when you walk out the door, you must assume you are being videotaped. At public protests, for example, there are now as many video cameras being operated by protesters as there are media people with cameras. The protesters hope to capture the police using excessive force, or they deliberately tape just part of an incident to make the protesters look victimized and the police guilty. Sometimes these videographers do creative editing to make the police look bad and then take the doctored videotape to the media. If you are a soldier, police officer, firefighter, emergency medical technician, educator or any other modern warrior, know that your duties are performed in the public eye. While this may bother you, you shouldn't worry too much about it. If you are doing what you are supposed to be doing, the truth is not your enemy.

That said, there could be a problem: Videotape cannot record the perceptual distortions addressed in this section.

-Videotapes don't capture diminished sound. "What do you mean you didn't hear the shots?" the critics and investigators ask. "There it is on the videotape. You must be lying."

-The videotape cannot capture tunnel vision. "What do you mean you didn't see him? He's right there in your field of view. You must be lying."

-The videotape cannot capture autopilot affect. "Why did you do that?" they ask, and you tell them to study your training because you did exactly what had been drilled into you. Will they understand the procedure?

-The videotape does not capture the perseveration effect that is a normal, fear-induced response to a deadly threat.

-Nor can videotape capture memory distortions that are products of perceptual sets and past associations. "Wait a minute. First you said this happened, but now you say that it didn't. Why did you lie the first time?"

Since we can expect critics, investigators, juries and judges to use videotapes to play Monday morning quarterback and second guess the actions of warriors in the heat of battle, it is vital that they be informed about what happens to warriors under such incredible stress, and to understand the limitations of videotaping. This is why Dr. Artwohl and Loren Christensen's book, *Deadly Force Encounters*, is so important, and why Dr. Dave Klinger's research, which will be addressed next, is so important. This kind of cutting edge, warrior science research serves as a primer to help us understand what is really happening to the poor guys and gals who live in the heart of darkness, immersed in the universal human phobia: combat.

five

The Klinger Study: *A Parallel Study in Perceptual Distortions*

> Centuries have not changed human nature. Passions, instincts—particularly the most powerful instinct of self-preservation—these things are expressed differently in accordance with the times, the circumstances, the character and temperament of races . . . But, beneath it all, the same man is to be found.
>
> —Ardant du Picq
> *Battle Studies*

Having examined and expanded upon Dr. Artwohl's research, let us now look at another major study of sensory distortions in combat. This research was conducted by world-class criminologist Dr. Dave Klinger, in a project funded by the National Institute of Justice.

Dr. Klinger interviewed 113 police officers from 19 law enforcement agencies in four states, each of them a survivor of a gunfight. As you will see, he got data similar to Dr. Artwohl's, but in greater depth. This study was extraordinarily well crafted and conducted, and it has established a model for more work in this area. Dr. Klinger has compiled the results of his study and the powerful personal narratives of the individuals he interviewed, into a book titled *Voices from the Kill Zone*, which I highly recommend.

A Sample of Combat Memories: A Snowball's Slice of Hell

> Remembrance fallen from heaven,
> And Madness risen from hell.
>
> —Algernon Charles Swinburne
> *Atalanta in Calydon*

The Klinger study involved a survey and interviews with law enforcement officers (referred to as "subjects") who were in gunfights and hit their targets. In a process known as "snowballing," Dr. Klinger had his initial subjects ask other officers who had shot people in gunfights to contact him, and these individuals were to ask others, and so on. Therefore, all of his interviews were with officers currently working, who had shot someone in combat and had volunteered to be interviewed.

While this study sets the standard for such research, it is important to identify a few limitations, which Dr. Klinger freely admits.

The subjects were officers who hit their targets in a gunfight (with four possible exceptions), leaving out officers (the majority) whose shots missed, thus raising these questions:

-how is the data affected by the absence of those who missed?
-did they miss due to higher levels of stress?
-are they feeling a higher degree of stress because of perceived failure?

Subjects were generally police officers who stayed in law enforcement, leaving out those who left, thus raising these questions:

-how is the data affected by the absence of those who left the profession?
-did they leave due to poor adjustment after their deadly force incidents?
-did they leave because of "bad" shoots? Has the study systematically left out unlawful and inappropriate shots?
-did those who left the supportive environment of the law enforcement community have greater trouble adjusting, as is generally the case with Vietnam vets who left the military versus those who stayed in.
-the subjects were willing to be surveyed and interviewed, which may have caused some self-selection bias, as opposed to, say, Dr. Artwohl's study which obtained information from every officer who shot, immediately after the event and regardless of whether the officer had hit. Dr. Klinger's study may have left out those unwilling to discuss their shootings.
-how is the data affected by the absence of those who were not willing to discuss their shootings?
-assuming some individuals intentionally opted not to be interviewed, did they do so due to poor adjustment after their deadly force incidents?

In many cases, the subjects were reporting about events that occurred several years earlier, some nearly 30 years earlier. Only seven of the 113 cases had occurred within 90 days of the interview. The deterioration, decay and confabulation of memory across that time can be significant. Would the information have been different if it had been obtained sooner?

-Dr. Klinger says, "Several officers . . . reported that they lied to the mental health professionals who interviewed them after their shootings, because they did not wish to divulge their thoughts, feelings, and experiences to a stranger." We have to take into consideration that there are always people who will lie in a study, including this one. Consequently, the "BS meter" must always be on.

As a prior service street cop, Dr. Klinger has tremendous credibility, with a body of knowledge, experience and a well-calibrated "BS meter" which I believe greatly reduced the number of lies told to him. In addition, he was acting under statutory protection, as per 42 U.S.C. §3789(g) (a United States code that mandates that research data or statistics collected by the U. S. Department of Justice or by its grantees and contractors may be used only for the purpose of statistical reporting and analysis, may not be used to identify private individuals, and is immune from use in legal proceedings). Clearly, this is a powerful and useful tool to get research subjects to talk openly.

When we investigate such sensitive matters, we must accept the possibility that there will be a certain "lie factor" biased toward making the subject appear in a positive light. Therefore—and this is a key point—any negative reactions/data might be an indicator that there was more, but the subject was not willing to share. As a general rule, we can expect that events and responses that put a subject in a negative light (such as reporting fear responses) are less likely to be remembered and reported, while those putting the subject in a positive light tend to be "over" remembered and reported. Therefore, when we see negative data, it might be just the tip of the iceberg. As the saying goes: "All's fair in love and war." Sex researchers know that their field, like the field of warrior science, is ripe with the potential for twisting the truth, exaggerating or all-out lying.

Again, these are observations of unavoidable limitations. The thoroughness and depth of detail in Dr. Klinger's study makes most other studies into this subject pale in comparison.

Variance from Other Studies

The most beautiful thing we can experience is the mysterious. It is the source of all true art and science.

—Albert Einstein

The main reason I have outlined the possible limitations of Dr. Klinger's study is so you can see one possible explanation for variances between his study and others in the field. In the first nine pages of his NIJ report, Dr. Klinger does an excellent job of establishing a foundation of what past studies have found. (This alone makes the report worth the price of admission.) Then he goes on to present his findings. It is important to understand that variances between this study and others do not necessarily mean that another study is wrong or right, or that this one is wrong or right. I believe that each one gives us another piece of the puzzle, another feel of the elephant. In *On Killing*, I said that combat experience is like blind men feeling different parts of an elephant: One says that he felt a tree, another reports a wall, and the third says he felt a big snake. In the end, each person comes away with different impressions of the experience, and only by gathering them all together can we hope to get a complete impression.

Dr. Klinger's study not only gives us a feel of the elephant's right front leg (officers who have shot and hit in combat, stayed in the profession, and were willing to talk about it), but for the first time ever, it provides us with a biopsy straight through the hide, muscle, bone and marrow. When Dr. Klinger looks at a piece of the elephant, he really looks.

Thoughts/Feelings: Before and During

> Experience is the child of Thought, and Thought is the child of Action.
>
> —Vivian Grey
> *Disraeli*

One of the most important new findings in Dr. Klinger's study, an area that no one had previously explored, are his revelations as to what officers thought and felt before, during and after their shootings. Dr. Klinger reported the percentages who had particular thoughts and feelings (1) at any time during the shooting, (2) prior to it, and (3) upon shooting. Here is what he found:

	At any time	Prior to shooting	Upon shooting
Disbelief	42%	32%	34%
Fear for self	41%	35%	30%
For others	60%	54%	49%
To survive	30%	27%	23%
Rush	55%	44%	46%
Thoughts	14%	10%	9%

Thoughts/Feelings Experienced in 113 Gunfight Case Studies

Dr. Klinger makes several excellent points in his discussion on the role of "fear for self" and "fear for others" that occurred in the majority of cases. He talks about how some subjects were "concerned" about others, while having a negative response to the word "fear," claiming that they did not feel any "emotional trepidation."

One particularly telling example concerned an officer at a bank robbery who was fearful for himself and others. Dr. Klinger says, "Once he started shooting, however, the fear he felt for himself evaporated, as the sense that he had to protect the bank customers and employees took over. Thus, though the officer was engaged in a furious gun battle where all the shots fired by the robbers were directed at him, the only fear he felt was for others." This is an excellent example of the protective, warrior thought processes that occur in what I call the "sheepdog" response, which will be discussed later in the book.

Distortions of Vision, Sound and Time

With curious art the brain, too finely wrought,
Preys on herself, and is destroyed by thought.

—Charles Churchill
Epistle to William Hogarth

The perceptual distortions data is one of the real gems in this study. Drawing from his 113 cases, Dr. Klinger has given us another fix on the phenomenon, as can be seen in the following table.

	At any time	Prior to shooting	Upon shooting
Tunnel vision	51%	31%	27%
Visual clarity	56%	37%	35%
Both	**%	10%	11%
Intensified Sound	82%	42%	70%
Diminished Sound	20%	10%	5%
Both	**%	0%	9%
Slow Motion Time	56%	43%	40%
Fast Motion Time	23%	12%	17%
Both	**%	0%	2%

(** = not reported.)
Distortions of Vision, Time and Sound Experienced in 113
Gunfight Case Studies

It is useful to recap these figures, and note that in the "prior to shooting" phase, at least one distortion was experienced by 88 percent of the officers. In the "upon shooting" phase, the percentage went up to 94 percent. This implies that when the shooting begins, stress increases, as does the occurrence of distortions. (However, there is cause to believe that firing can be a sort of relief for some people that in some cases lowers the stress levels.)

Dr. Klinger observed that: "The rates for auditory distortions changed substantially across the two time frames . . . as the rate of auditory blunting [diminished sound] increased from 42 percent to 70 percent, the figure for increased loudness [intensified sound] was halved from 10 percent to 5 percent." This concurs with many others who have noted that diminished sound is most likely to occur when the officer is shooting. Many combatants (as was noted earlier in the chapter on auditory exclusion) reported that their shots were quiet, although they heard the subsequent echo of the shots and/or the rattle of their ejected shell casings hitting the ground.

My co-author experienced this when his partner was shot in the face, while Christensen stood just a few feet away and around a corner. "I heard the shot," Christensen says,

> . . . but I didn't think it was a gunshot because it was so quiet. Then when I came face to face with the bad guy and saw his gun pointed at my nose, I fired before he shot me. The sound of my shot was so muted that I have no recall of the sound, but I still have a clear memory of how he looked over my barrel.

Dr. Klinger says that some officers in his sample had similar experiences.

> In one case, the officer shot a man armed with a shotgun. When the officer's shot was muted, he thought his gun had misfired, but then realized that it was working just fine when the bad guy reacted to the impact of the bullet that hit him.

In Loren Christensen's book, *Crazy Crooks* he tells of one documented case in which,

> One dumb crook became confused when he did not hear his pistol fire. He turned the gun around and peered down the barrel to see if there was an obstruction; it was clear. Dumbfounded as to why it did not go bang, he squinted down the barrel even harder and pulled the trigger again.

At first glance this story seems so bizarre that our BS meter goes off the chart. But with an understanding of the effects of auditory exclusion in combat, perhaps we can see where it just might be possible.

Distorted Sense of Distance and Awareness of Distortions

The palpable obscure.

—Milton
Paradise Lost

Bruce Siddle's research identified that one of the responses to elevated heart rate and sympathetic nervous system arousal was a loss of depth perception, or a distorted sense of distance. In an article in the prestigious *FBI Law Enforcement Bulletin*, Dr. Artwohl gave an example of a law enforcement officer in a gunfight who experienced this distorted sense of distance, along with slow motion time.

During a violent shoot-out I looked over, drawn to the sudden mayhem, and was puzzled to see beer cans slowly floating through the air past my face. What was even more puzzling was that they had the word 'Federal' printed on the bottom. They turned out to be the shell casings ejected by the officer who was firing next to me.

Several law enforcement officers in Dr. Klinger's study reported that they experienced a distorted sense of distance,

. . . where the actual distance between themselves, suspects, other officers, citizen bystanders, and inanimate objects (e.g., vehicles) were either far greater or less than they had perceived at the time of the shooting . . . Only by viewing photographs of the shooting scene, reviewing investigators' sketches of the scene (including measurements), participating in a post-shooting 'walk-through' with investigators, or doing something else after the shooting to develop an understanding of the actual distance involved in their shooting, did officers come to know the accuracy of their understanding of the distances. Since many of the officers in the study did not later do anything that would inform them of the actual distances involved in their shootings, it is possible that their sense of distances is altered far more frequently than the current research suggests.

Dr. Klinger infers from this that "Officers may not always be aware of the sensory distortions they experience." I agree, and furthermore I believe that the incidence of these perceptual distortions may actually be higher than the percentages gathered in surveys such as this. In other words, they may be occurring, but we simply are not aware of them.

This is similar to the exclusion of pain, which was discussed earlier, where under moderate to high stress, such as when playing sports, you are unaware of your scratches and scrapes until afterwards when you see the physical "evidence" on your body. How many times do similar shutdowns occur in other senses but you are unaware of them because there is no telltale evidence or souvenir afterward?

Clusters of Distortions

> Though this be madness, yet there is method in't.
>
> —Shakespeare
> *Hamlet*

One of the most valuable aspects of Dr. Klinger's research is how he brings all the data together for an indepth understanding of how these distortions "cluster" immediately before and during combat. Prior to firing, 70 percent of the officers reported at least two distortions, 37 percent reported three or more, six percent experienced four or more, and one person said he had five distortions. No one experienced all six. The average (mean) was 2.02 distortions immediately prior to firing.

The incidence of distortions was greater during firing, with an average of 2.45. Officers experienced at least two distortions in 76 percent of the shootings, three or more in 57 percent, four or five in 15 percent and five distortions were experienced in four percent of the cases. To me, this implies that as stress levels go up—usually when the officer is firing—there is an increased incidence of perceptual distortions.

Combining the "prior to shooting" and "upon shooting" data, 89 percent of the officers experienced more than one distortion. In 82 percent of them, officers reported at least three distortions. Dr. Klinger notes that:

> [This] means that the vast majority of the observed multiple distortions in the overall [before and during] scale are not due to the continuation of a single type of distortion across [the] two time points . . . in most shootings, officers experience multiple perceptual anomalies during the course of the event.

The most common type of clusters occur when the same distortion happens both immediately before and during combat. A correlation, or "relationship" is commonly abbreviated as "r" with r = 1.0 being a perfect correlation (an extraordinarily rare event in nature), and r = 0.0 indicating absolutely no relationship (which is also an extremely rare event in the real world). The relationship between each sensory distortion, immediately, before and after firing a weapon in combat, is as follows:

r = .61 for visual clarity
r = .50 for tunnel vision
r = .46 for slow motion time
r = .44 for fast motion time
r = .23 for diminished sound
r = .14 for intensified sound

This means that if the subject had heightened visual detail during one period, before or after, he is likely to have heightened visual detail during the other period (r = .61). If he experienced intensified sound during one period, he is not particularly likely to have intensified sound during the other period (r=.14).

Of particular interest are the other relationships Dr. Klinger has identified. For example, fast motion time prior to firing is associated with intensified sound prior (r = .24) and while firing (r = .25). Those who experienced fast motion time while firing, were somewhat more likely to experience intensified sound prior to (r = .30) and while (r = .28) firing.

I believe these might be panic responses: Time flashes past at an accelerated speed and sounds are frighteningly loud and overwhelming. However, since all the officers in this study successfully fired upon and hit their opponents, the term "panic" may be inappropriate. Those officers who experienced diminished sound prior to firing were more likely to experience slow motion time both during (r = .28) and while (r = .24) firing. Other relationships included: tunnel vision and diminished sound while firing (r = .29), and slow motion time and diminished sound prior to firing (r = .28).

This may imply some kind of a predator response, where the hunter focuses so exclusively on the prey (tunnel vision) that other sounds diminish and time slows, so that the bellowing of the prey or the sounds and motions of the rest of the herd do not distract it.

Interestingly, there were some negative correlations or relationships, in which one element went up, or was more likely to occur, while another went down, or was less likely to occur (this is usually expressed with a negative number). Thus, some excluded each other to some degree. For example, tunnel vision prior to firing is somewhat less likely to occur in concert with heightened visual detail (r = -.38); this negative relationship is also true while firing (r = -.27). Thus we see tunnel vision as something that is less likely to occur with increased visual acuity. In the hypothetical prey model, increased visual acuity would be useful, since the fleeing prey needs to see every possible option and avenue of escape, while staying alert to any ambushing or intercepting predators. Meanwhile, the pursuing predator fears nothing except losing the prey. So for it, tunnel vision is potentially a survival trait.

The Wolf Pack Predator Model?

The Assyrian came down like the wolf on the fold,
And his cohorts were gleaming in purple and gold . . .

—Lord Byron
"Hebrew Melodies"

I could very well be reading too much into this, but there may be value in this concept of a predator and a prey response. While the correlations here are weak, our instruments (i.e., human memory under stress) are also flawed. We are truly looking "through a glass darkly," and where we do see the dim outline of a shape, I believe that most likely there is something there.

There is one other possible model that keeps coming up in my interviews with military and law enforcement personnel: I call it the "wolf pack predator model." When we looked at the predator previously, we thought only in terms of a charging lion that is oblivious to everything except the prey (tunnel vision, auditory exclusion and slow-motion time). But there is another rare model that keeps showing up, usually in highly trained-warriors with a great deal of combat experience. These individuals experience slow motion time, but they also experience an acute awareness of the sights and sounds of everything and everyone around them (visual clarity and intensified sound). For these individuals only the sounds of the gunshots are muted, enough so that their ears did not ring afterwards. I think that a wolf pack, full of mature, experienced, deadly wolves might very well work this way. They are aware of their fellow pack members, they listen to each other's signals and they experience slow-motion time.

One excellent example of this wolf pack predator can be seen in the action of one law enforcement officer in a major Midwestern police department. He is: a graduate of the U.S. Army Ranger School, which emphasizes the development of teamwork under stressful combat situations; a U.S. Army combat veteran, with extensive combat experience as a small unit leader; and a veteran of several law enforcement gunfights.

In his most recent gunfight, this officer reported hearing and comprehending everything with remarkable clarity, including reports coming over his radio, the actions and sounds of his fellow officers and the suspect, the movement of civilians and traffic in the line of fire, and slow-motion time, all of which gave him ample time to calmly and competently make decisions and take action.

It is interesting to note that all of the sensory distortions outlined in this book are extremely rare in normal life . . . *except* among hunters, where (for example) auditory exclusion is almost universal, and slow-motion time is very common. There may be something about the nature of hunting which taps into our ancient survival instincts. I believe that hunting is the only peacetime experience which will allow us to consistently tap into a "primal toolbox" of skills and experiences that is completely unknown to anyone else.

Among hunters and combatants, different circumstances call for different responses. "To everything there is a season, and a time for every purpose under the heaven." There is a time to run, and there is a time to be the charging lion.

But it may be that the highest and most difficult achievement of the human warrior is to be a dedicated and professional member of a "pack" of sheepdogs: predators, under authority, working together as team players, to protect innocent lives in the life-and-death "game" of combat.

Section Three

The Call to Combat:
Where Do We Get Such Men?

I am Pallas Athene, and I know the thoughts of all men's hearts and discern their manhood or their baseness.

From the souls of clay I turn away, and they are blessed but not by me. They fatten at ease like sheep in the pasture and eat what they did not sow like oxen in the stall. They grow and spread like the gourd along the ground, but like the gourd they give no shade to the traveler. When they are ripe death gathers them and they go down unloved into Hell and their name vanishes out of the land.

But to the souls of fire I give more fire, and to those who are manful I give a might more than man. These are the heroes, the sons of the immortals who are blessed, but not like the souls of clay, for I drive them forth by strange paths that they may fight the titans and the monsters and the enemies of Gods and men . . .

Tell me now, Perseus, which of these two sorts of men seem to you more blessed?

—Charles Kingsley
Canon of Westminster and Chaplain to Queen Victoria

one

Killing Machines: *The Impact of a Handful of True Warriors*

> The paradox of courage is that a man must be a little careless of his life even in order to keep it.
>
> —G.K. Chesterton (1908)
> "The Methuselahite"

Many people have a vision of combat based on thousands of hours of viewing television and movies. In our minds we see every soldier fighting desperately, contributing all out to the effort to kill the enemy. Maybe a few bad examples cower in the background, but they serve as the exception that proves the rule. Deep in our gut we believe, based on countless Hollywood "experiences," that most men in combat are shooting and killing. Well, that belief is simply wrong.

The reality is that only a handful of individuals actually participate fully and whole heartedly in combat—rare individuals who are true warriors. Charles "Commando" Kelly, a recipient of the Medal of Honor for his extraordinary actions in Italy during World War II, gives us an excellent example of what really happens in combat. The following narrative is a true account from his superb book, *One Man's War*. As you read, notice not just what Kelly was doing (he was virtually a one-man killing machine fighting Germans from his position inside a building), but notice also the lack of action by most of the other soldiers around him. This is an example of S.L.A. Marshall's findings that 85 percent of individual riflemen in World War II did not fire. Most of them were not curled into a ball and cowering, but they were definitely not interested in firing. While there were many American soldiers in that building with "Commando" Kelly that day, only one received the Medal of Honor.

> The Germans were behind a lot of bushes now; I pulled some tracers into my BAR [Browning Automatic Rifle], got those bushes right on the button and kept on shooting. Tracers look like white-hot beads flashing along an invisible string, with the far end of the string tied to the target. When I let up, the dust behind the bushes was gone and we had no trouble with that area after that . . . I seemed to be official sniper for the room. Somebody would yell, "Hey, Kelly, come here,"

and then he would show me some Germans. I'd give them a basting, come back to my cocoa, let a little of it slide down my throat, and somebody else would call, "Hey, Kelly, come on over here." It kept me running from window to window.

I had worked my BAR so steadily that when I put the magazine load of cartridges into it, it wouldn't work any more. I laid it against a bed and went back to get another BAR, but when I came back the bed was on fire. That first gun was so hot that it touched off the sheets and blankets. I worked the new BAR until the steel of the barrel turned reddish-purple with heat and it became warped. I couldn't find another BAR, so I went upstairs and scouted around until I found a Tommy gun with a full magazine. Then I went to the window and gunned for some more Germans. But that Thompson was too fast for me. It spat out thirty rounds almost as fast as I could pull the trigger, and it kept riding up and I had to bear down on it to hold it on the target. After I had used up the Tommy gun's magazine, I remembered I had seen a bazooka somewhere, but in order to fetch shells for it, I had to go to the third floor, and to get to the third floor I had to crawl over our dead and wounded.

Those bazooka shells weighed several pounds each. When I found them, I brought down six of them and put one of them in the gun, but it wouldn't go off. I worked on it for a while, then poked it out of the window again and pulled the trigger. The men in the house with me thought a German 88mm. shell had hit the place. All the pressure came out of the back end of that tin pipe along with a lot of red flame, and the house trembled and shook. I had shot it four times, when my eye lit on a box of dynamite sitting on the floor. I asked Sergeant Robertson if we couldn't use it for something, but it was no soap—we had dynamite caps but no fuses.

Lying beside the dynamite was an incendiary grenade. Picking it up, I threw it on the roof of a nearby building the Germans were holding. It exploded there and the house burst into flames.

What with all the equipment and ammo we had brought inside with us, the place was like an army ordnance showroom. Now I picked up a 60mm mortar shell and pulled out the pin or safety lock that controlled the cap, which set off the propulsion charge. There was still another pin or secondary safety lock inside of it, which I didn't know how to get out. I started to tap it on the window ledge and the safety dropped out, making it a live shell, or the way I planned to use it, a live bomb. For if I tossed it out of the window and it landed on its nose the weight of its fall would give it the twelve pounds of percussion needed to explode it.

As I looked out of the window a handful of Germans came up a small ravine in the rear of the house, so I whirled that shell around and let it drop among them. I did the same thing with another shell. When I let go of each one of them, there was a cracking roar and the next time I looked out, five of the Germans were dead. In all, I threw out nine or ten of those shells and seven or eight of them went off.

Next I found a carbine. But there were only a few clips of cartridges for it, and every time I fired fifteen rounds I had to reload the clips. I didn't know much about the proper care and feeding of carbines, and presently it got too hot. Your mind gets single tracked in a fight like that, and all I could think of was the problem of finding another weapon as fast as I used one up so I could keep on blazing away. Propped in a corner was an '03 Springfield like the ones the A.E.F. used in the last war. There were a few rounds of ammunition for it lying on the floor and I picked them up and shoved them into the gun. It was a very accurate gun. My target was the men coming down over a little hill trying to keep under cover and work their way closer to us.

Looking out of the window and down into the courtyard, I saw a 37mm antitank gun, and seeing it there gave me an idea. I ran down, opened its breech and threw in a shell. A church steeple, which the enemy was using as a fortress, had been giving us trouble, and we hadn't been able to cool off the Germans in it with our small arms. I set the sights of that antitank gun right on the building.

Then I ran into a snag. I didn't know how to fire it, but I kept on fumbling around, pulling this and jerking that until I got hold of a handle and it went off. Not knowing anything about it, I had my chin too close to it and the recoil knocked me kicking.

Both high explosive and armor-piercing shells were piled up around me and I couldn't tell them apart. My first shell knocked the top off the intervening wall only a few feet away from me. Later I found out that through sheer dumb luck I had fired an armor-piercing shell instead of a high explosive one. A HE shell would have gone off when it hit that wall and would have killed me.

As I kept on firing, holes sprang into sight all over the church, and I could see pieces of its bell tower slowly sliding out of sight. By this time I had begun to feel like a real artilleryman. Down near the bottom of the pile of ammo were some funny-looking shells with tin cans over their tops, like stocking caps. I found out later that they were canisters loaded with balls that scattered when they exploded.

In that courtyard I was fairly safe from the fire of nearby Germans, for the wall protected me and their bullets went over my head. When I saw some Germans coming down a hillside, I threw in one of the shells with a tin hat over its ears, and fired point-blank. It hit one of them squarely and put holes in the others. The Krauts who hadn't gotten it turned and ran.

Shells began dropping right into the courtyard, and I had to leave. I hated to do it; I was having a lot of fun and that antitank gun made me feel I had power to burn. But Captain Laughlin yelled at me to save some of the gun's ammunition and I went back into the house.

Once inside, I found a third BAR in the hands of a dead man on the third floor. He had been killed firing it. His ammunition was lying in a belt beside him, but there wasn't much of it left. So I collected machine gun bullets of the same caliber and put them in the BAR magazines. Then I took it down in the front room and fired away . . .

I worked that BAR until it began to smoke as if somebody had baked it in a too hot oven. A Heinie shell hit the side of the building and made a big hole in it, burying two men under the rubble. Snipers were touching them up down in the kitchen and someone sent for me to go down there and help.

I started down the hallway, but when I got there a group of dizzy G.I.s were cooking spaghetti just as if they were chefs in a ravioli joint back home and all they had to think about was food. They had spread tablecloths, laid out knives and forks, sliced bread, opened watermelon and honeydews, and put grapes and tomatoes on the table. I don't mind people doing screwy things—it helps to let off steam when things are so tight that otherwise you'd go off your rocker—but to see them readying the meal made me mad, and I got off a few overheated cracks . . .

I went over to the window through which the snipers' bullets had been coming. Nobody had had time to give those snipers much attention; they had been having things pretty much their own way and had grown careless about concealment. I saw one of them in a tree and drew a bead on him. His rifle dropped from the tree first, then after a few seconds he toppled to the ground after it.

For the moment I was out of targets, but presently two Germans ran out to pull in a dead pal and I took care of them. The other Germans out there must have thought the ones who had been knocked off were just wounded, for three others came out to pull those two in. All I had to do was to watch the dead ones and other targets showed up.

While I was squatting there working my gun, a man from upstairs came down with about fifty BAR clips, lay down beside me and began feeding me ammo. After working the BAR awhile, it began to heat up. I went back to that 37mm antitank in the courtyard once more. The men in the house were slipping away six at a time and there was nobody to tell me to stop firing the gun this time. So I started throwing shells into it and shooting at anybody that moved or anything I felt like shooting at. My principal targets were buildings, which might hold Germans.

When I went back to the house, most of the men were gone. I found a few more bazooka shells, grabbed two of them and made a dash across the courtyard and into the downstairs cellar. I figured I might as well get rid of those shells, so I loaded the tube of metal and pointed it at the buildings across the way where two roads met in a fork. There was a building at those crossroads from which our men were making little scuttling runs to get water, had been picked off. When the smoke cleared away there was a big hole in that building.

I went back to my upstairs window and Smiley Griggs, who had been wounded in the shoulder and foot, and Captain Harold D. Craft, whose foot had been shattered by a German slug, began to load weapons and slide them along the floor to Swayze and myself. Presently all the wounded men left who had been [loading weapons]. Before long I ran completely out of ammunition, and with Swayze I went down into the cellar and made ready to go.

My next worry was to get hold of a gun to take with me when I tried my break. I spotted a dead man with an M-1, two bandoliers of ammunition and two hand grenades. Armed with those, I crawled out of the house . . .

The tenacity and ferocity of a man like "Commando" Kelly is truly amazing, but the impact of men like him can be found in all fields and aspects of combat. Our goal is to create an environment that nurtures bold, brave, men (and women!) of action. Clausewitz said:

> . . . a bold act may prove to be a blunder. Nonetheless, it is a laudable error, not to be regarded on the same footing as others. Happy is the army where ill-timed boldness occurs frequently; it is a luxuriant weed, but indicates richness in the soil. Even foolhardiness is not always to be despised, for it stems from daring.

Another amazing example of the impact of a few true warriors can be found in aerial combat in World War II. In his excellent book, *Me-10*, author Martin Caidin writes that the Germans had 34 fighter pilots credited with over 150 kills in air-to-air combat. Erich Hartmann set the record with 352. Like "Commando" Kelly, these men were literally "killing machines." Caidin writes:

> Those 34 men, according to the official German figures, shot down in aerial combat no less that 6,902 enemy aircraft. There were another

60 aces who the Germans say shot down between 100 and 150 aircraft each. Those 60 men accounted for another 7,095 machines. Thus, according to the official German records, 94 aces of the Luftwaffe accounted for 13,997 enemy machines shot down in aerial combat.

Caidin makes it clear that the Germans did have some advantages that helped make this possible.

Erich Rudorffer on 6th November, 1943, is credited with 13 kills in a single battle engagement that lasted 17 minutes. This is by no means an impossibility since on 24th October, 1944, Dave McCampbell in a Hellcat shot down nine confirmed (plus two probables) when he roared into a flight of Japanese single-engine bombers obviously flown by green pilots who 'just sat there' while he flew, aimed, and fired to his heart's content.

Another point to consider is that the German pilots sometimes flew from two to five or even more sorties in a single day, their home fields being 'only a stone's throw' from the combat area. They flew almost constantly.

Nevertheless, even with these advantages, Caidin says, "Nearly fourteen thousand planes shot down by less than one hundred men . . . Such statistics make one stop and think."

My co-author, Loren Christensen, knows of a Medal of Honor recipient named Gino Merli, who single-handedly stopped an advance of 1,500 German troops in Bruyere, Belgium, during one long September night in World War II. On that horrific night in 1944, he and a buddy were assigned to cover an American retreat. The German attack was intense, and his buddy was soon killed.

When the Germans approached again, Merli feigned death, easily convincing the enemy since he was covered with his buddy's blood. When the Germans walked away, he slowly inched over to his machine gun and opened fire, mowing them all down. All through the night, the Germans sent out patrols as Merli continued to feign death, even when the Germans used their razor sharp bayonets to roll him over. Each time they believed he was dead, and each time they walked away he gunned them down. In the end, 52 German soldiers died that night. (Gino Merli's story was included here two days after his death. He died on his property, as he tended a pear tree he had planted 35 years earlier.)

Here is one more powerful example. Have you seen that old war movie "To Hell and Back" that depicts the heroic actions of Audie Murphy in World War II? After the war, Murphy went on to be an actor and starred in 44 movies, including *To Hell and Back,* in which he played himself.

The son of poor Texas sharecroppers, Murphy began his service as an army private. He quickly rose to staff sergeant and then was given a "battlefield" commission to 2nd Lieutenant. He was wounded three times, fought in nine major campaigns across the European Theater and rose to national prominence when he became the most decorated American combat soldier of World War II. He won 33 awards and ribbons, including every decoration for valor that existed then, some of them more than once, including five decorations by France and Belgium. He received the military's highest award for bravery, the Medal of Honor, for actions in which he was credited with killing over 240 of the enemy while wounding and capturing many others. At the end of the war, at the ripe old age of 21, he left the army.

The purpose of these examples is to demonstrate the tremendous impact that a tiny percentage of true warriors can have in combat. Their boldness, valor, initiative, and courage are vital to success and survival. The goal is to have many more of them, but where do we get such men? Some may occur naturally, but there can be no doubt that they can also be made, constructed, crafted, nurtured and trained.

Their role is not just in battle. We need warriors in peacetime as well. Justin Smith, a newspaper production manager in Pocatello, Idaho, demonstrated remarkable leadership and initiative in getting a special edition of his newspaper out while other people on his staff were still stunned into passivity in the immediate aftermath of the shock and horror of the 9/11 terrorist attacks. "It wasn't callousness," he said in a letter to me,

> . . . it was the necessity. I knew that people needed that newspaper in their hands to link them to other people and to help them deal with the horror . . .
>
> I have begun to learn that a warrior is not proven only in combat, but also in life. He lives by a code, not because codes are "honorable" or a fad, but because that is how a warrior thinks and so it is how he lives. Combat is an extension of that code, not the source. The rigidity of military discipline reflects his mindset and the two feed off each other, the man strengthened by the military and the military strengthened by the man.
>
> His code in peacetime is the same as that in the military: do your duty, protect the weak, protect the community, face the bully, stand tall, stay aware, think ahead, be ready, be loyal, avoid aggression if possible and, if not, win and win fully. Respect and honor are earned by actions, not granted by birth. There are a thousand military codes spread throughout history, but I believe they all say the same thing at heart: Live with honor, and let not your death be born by the pallbearers of disgrace, cruelty, weakness, and fear.

chapter two

Stress Inoculation and Fear:
Practicing to be miserable

> First class training is the best form of welfare for the troops . . . The more you sweat in training, the less you bleed in battle.
>
> —Irwin Rommel

There is an old Army adage that says, "You don't have to practice being miserable." There is some truth in these words, but sometimes they are used as an excuse to avoid hard, rigorous training. Sometimes there is value in practicing to be miserable.

Army Ranger school consisted of months of sleep and food deprivation in grueling environments of jungle, swamps, mountains and desert. After Ranger school, almost everything else in life seemed easy by comparison.

General Barry McCaffrey (best known as our nation's Drug Czar during the Clinton administration) told a story to a group of West Point cadets about his experiences in Vietnam that exemplifies what stress inoculation is all about. One day he and a friend (a classmate from West Point and Ranger school) were in Vietnam lying behind a rice paddy dike as bullets screamed over their heads. At the peak of the battle, the General's friend turned to him, and said, "Well hell, at least we're not in Ranger school."

One of these days, scientists will probably have to pay for what they have done to all those poor little rats that were standing in the wrong line and got chosen for laboratory duty. Dr. Paul Whitesell tells about one such experiment (conducted in the days before PETA), where scientists divided rats into three groups. Rats from the first group were dropped into a tub of water to see how long it took them to drown. According to this study, it took about 60 hours.

The second group was first held upside down to give them a dose of stress, and when they eventually stopped kicking and squirming (i.e., they gave up and went into parasympathetic backlash), the scientists dropped them in a tub of water. That group lasted about 20 minutes before they drowned.

The third group was also held upside down until they stopped kicking and fighting, but instead of being dropped into the water, they were placed back into their cages. Several times that day, the same group (actually, there was only this one group left by now) was again picked up, held upside down until they quit kicking, and again put back into their cages. Later that day when the same rats were held upside down, they had figured out that this was just how the white coats got their kicks and that it was no big deal. However, instead of being placed back in the comfort of their cages, they were dropped into the tub of water, where they swam—for 60 hours.

Unlike the second group of rats, the third group had been inoculated to the stressor. They had encountered it on two previous occasions and had always come out of the experience alive and triumphant. Being held upside down a third time was not a big deal to them and they were able to perform as if they had never even encountered the stressor.

One report says that over a third of all police officers killed in combat did not defend themselves. The solution to this lies in training, hard training that includes preparation for the possibility of being shot at and preparation for the possibility of being hit. Like our third group of rats, it is about being prepared ahead of time for the stress of combat. Let's look at three training principles that are critical for preparing the warrior for the harsh realty of life and death combat.

Principle 1: Never "Kill" A Warrior in Training.

Many training exercises involve trainees getting "killed" when they err in the exercise. "You shouldn't have done that. You're dead now!" This type of training only trains you to die. "I'm dead," you think when another trainee or a trainer shoots you with a paint bullet or pretends to stab you. This is wrong. A trainer should never declare his students to be dead, and if a student ever states that he is dead, the right answer is, "No, you aren't dead! I don't give you permission to die. I don't train people to die. I train them to live!"

I know of gangbangers who have sucked up a dozen 9mm rounds and drove on to survive. If they can do it, you can too. When a training scenario does not go the way you wanted it to, then do it again, but do not ever think you are dead in an exercise. If you are practicing knife defenses and your training partner "stabs" you, do not think you failed and that you are finished. I know of a little old lady who was stabbed 20 times and then crawled to the phone, dialed 9-1-1, and lived to tell about it. Never, ever give up after being shot or stabbed. Do not train yourself to die and do not train other warriors to die.

Ken Murray, author of *Training at the Speed of Life* and cofounder of Simunition, the company that developed the most widely used brand of paint ammunition, says to his officers who have been "shot" in training, "Yeah, you're hit, but you're sure as hell not done . . . now finish this bastard." His officers hear this so often in his training program that they "take him into battle" with them. In the event they are really hit, he wants them to hear his words—"Yeah, you're hit, but you're sure as hell not done"—and then do what needs to be done. Ken says that stress inducing simulation training places an obvious fork in a person's survival psychology pathway at the point of projectile impact. If the trainee is conditioned to stop when he is hit (as if the scenario is over), he programs an undesirable and potentially self-destructive action into his mind.

Ken Murray points out that it is a much more complex dynamic than simply demotivating trainees when they are told they are dead or allow themselves to believe they are dead. Ken points to the research done by Mike Spick in, *The Ace Factor*, a book that studies the salient differences between "Aces" and "Turkeys" in air combat. Spick's research clearly demonstrates that the survivability in air combat increases dramatically after a pilot's first five successful air combat engagements. These pilots become nearly undefeatable, except when faced with a pilot of a higher level of experience. This jibes well with Martin Caidin's book, *Me-10* that tracked the exploits of 34 pilots credited with 6,902 enemy aircraft being shot down.

Murray states that in law enforcement, most officers will never get to their decisive five engagements. As recognized by Russ Claggett, many officers leave law enforcement after their first live fire engagement, and the political winds of today would certainly breathe foul on patrol officers that would get into five shootings unless they were on a specialty unit. In the military world there may be warriors who get five engagements, but what of the price that is paid by all those who do not pass those first five tests? Today we have the tools to create what I have termed "pre-battle veterans," individuals with the survival skills of a veteran warrior but without the tragic cost of real combat.

Murray believes that when properly structured, reality based training can provide warriors with those essential five experiences necessary to ensure a high level of survivability, but he cautions that things can take a horrible turn if students are given the experience of losing, even in these simulated encounters—it can literally take the student in the wrong direction, creating "turkeys" rather than "eagles." It also creates a neurological deficiency that can be extremely difficult to overcome. Murray quotes Kosslyn and Koenig in their groundbreaking book, *Wet Mind—New Cognitive Neuroscience*.

> Conditioned fear can be extremely difficult to extinguish. It cannot be eliminated through passive deterioration or even active attempts to do so. Even if it seems that it has been extinguished, stress may cause it to reappear.

What this means is that giving warriors the experience of losing in a simulation actually begins to condition a risk aversion pathway in the brain to which they may turn during similar experiences in the future—they may actually stop fighting and give up as they were programmed to do in training. This is why Murray will never let a student out of the training arena without ensuring they are the decisive winner, not through the role player giving anything away that is not earned, but rather by forcing, if necessary, the student to engage once they have been engaged, even if they argue that they have been hit in a manner that is unsurvivable. Murray says that there are only three logical conclusions to a scenario: everyone makes "nice" and goes home, someone surrenders, or the bad guy chooses a lethal force encounter. Whether or not the student is shot, a lethal force scenario is not over until the student successfully engages the suspect, has sought a position of advantage (cover), has called for assistance, and is waiting while covering the suspect. No other conclusion is acceptable, since no other conclusion will provide a warrior with a survival experience they can take with them into future battles. "Shot ain't dead," says Murray, and we have a moral obligation to our warriors to give them the "survival five" experiences to provide them every possible physical and psychological advantage during a lethal force encounter. Anything less is unacceptable.

Principle 2: Try to Never Send a Loser Off Your Training Site.

Yes, there will be a certain percentage of people who never grasp the training, but your goal as a professional is to keep that percentage to a bare minimum. It is easy to design a force-on-force paint bullet scenario that makes every trainee look like an idiot, but all that proves is that the trainers are jerks. Ken Murray calls this "masterbation" – its only purpose is to act as a form of self-gratification for the trainer. But, suppose you are a trainer and you put a warrior through a scenario where he fails, and then you put him through it again and he succeeds. First you revealed a flaw in his armor and then you taught him how to shore up that weakness. In so doing, you brought him out the other end of the exercise as a superior warrior.

If there is not sufficient time and resources to run the exercise again, then just toss him a softball, and let him knock it out of the park. Your goal is to send winners out the door.

Principle 3: As a Trainer, Never Talk Trash About Your Students.

A warrior trainer is a sensei—a professional—who has confidentiality standards like a priest or a doctor. Say a doctor conducts a physical examination where he checks a police officer from top to bottom. Do you think at night over a beer he tells other doctors about the officer and laughs about the poor man's droopy butt? No, because he is a professional.

If you are a trainer and you laugh about Smith's failures when having a beer with other warriors, how do you think the others are going to take that? They might laugh at your story, but inside they think you are a jerk and that it will be a cold day in hell before they let you see them fail.

Friends tease each other. SWAT teams tease each other; it comes with the territory. If you are a leader, however, you are not permitted to play the teasing game. You never joke about your trainees' failures, but you do brag about their achievements. Your entire repertoire is to talk about what went right, and when you say these things over a beer with your peers, they will want you to brag about them next time. When word gets out that this is the type of trainer you are, people will no longer avoid training but will want to be there because of the environment you have created.

The fundamental rule of warrior leadership is to punish in private and praise in public. Report all failures and problems up the chain of command, but report successes to everyone. Maybe you were publicly punished and embarrassed at one time and now you despise the person who did it to you. Perhaps there was a time when a leader called you into his office and told you in private that you did a great job yesterday. While you appreciated the nice comments, you wish he had said them in front of everyone. (It's only fair, if you had messed up everyone would know!)

Create an environment in which your people want to train and be inoculated. Do not kill your warriors. Do not send losers off the training site. Do not talk trash about your students. Punish in private, praise in public. This is the way that a warrior-trainer, a sensei, creates a training environment in which the warrior spirit is nurtured and his warriors want to train.

A Word on Fear: Vacillating Between Four Stages

> Herein lies the problem—fear is unpredictable and inconsistent from one person to the next, or even the same person in a second but similar circumstance. Fear is like a ghost in the night—you can feel it's presence, but you cannot grab it and beat it into submission.
>
> —Bruce Siddle
> *Warrior Science*™

Dr. Paul Whitesell is a brilliant psychologist, counselor, Vietnam veteran and law enforcement officer who trains police officers in leadership and warrior spirit. He draws from the works of Lord Moran to teach his students that there are four kinds of fear.

> -There are those who know no fear and they do the job. These are rare people because most know fear. Usually, they are caught by surprise and the situation is over so quickly they did not have time to be afraid.

-There are those who know fear and no one knows it, and they do the job.

-There are those who know fear and everyone sees it and smells it, but it does not matter because the job gets done.

-There are those who know fear and everyone knows it because they failed to do the job.

Human beings usually vacillate between all four stages, with a propensity towards one or another. We all have bad days and good days. Allow yourself the flux. Do not destroy yourself because of a bad day, and do not destroy others because they had one.

Name your favorite baseball pitcher or football quarterback. Do they ever have bad days? Would you judge them for the rest of their lives on one bad day, one bad game? Instead, do as most professional ball players do when they throw a bad game or have a bad season: they learn from it. And, when the next season rolls around, they are usually all the better because of it.

My co-author won 50 trophies during his competitive years in the martial arts. Today, when Christensen's students ask him about those wins, he is quick to tell them that while he did indeed win 50 karate competitions, he entered well over 100. It was always fun to win, he tells them, and bring home big gaudy trophies for his den, but it is those empty places on the shelves where there are no trophies, places that represent his losses, that were the most valuable to him. When he won, he would bask in the glory, but when he had a bad day and lost, he always analyzed why, and tried to learn from his mistakes so that the next time he competed, he competed stronger and wiser.

As Dr. Whitesell puts it: "Do not destroy yourself over the bad days. Take pride in your good ones and strive to constantly improve." While it is acceptable to have a bad day, it is unacceptable not to train, not to try to get better, not to use the resources available to make sure that what caused that bad day never happens to you again.

It is all about prior preparation—preparation for warriorhood.

chapter

three
Sucking Up Bullets and Continuing to Fight: *You've Never Lived Until You've Almost Died*

In my mind, I'm never going to die in no ghetto. Absolutely never. If a man tries to punch me in the head, the fight is on. If he cuts me, the fight is on. If I'm shot, the fight is on. I'm not losing no fight to no scumbag out there in no ghetto. Period. That's it. No son-of-a-bitch out there is going to get me. The only way he gets me is to cut my head off, and I mean that. I'll fight you while I got a breath left in me. I don't think any of those animals in that street can beat me. I've gone that way for 18 years of street service, street duty, and that's the way I'm going to keep on going. You don't lose the fight.

—Jim Phillips
Calibre Press video, *Surviving Edged Weapons*, 1988

Warrior Attitudes Before Combat: Looking Forward to It, and Getting It Over With

To some, [combat] was an empowering event and a learning experience that made them stronger in uncountable ways. To others, it became a debilitating and life-altering event that sent them into an unrecoverable psychological tailspin.

—Steve Tarani and Damon Fay
Contact Weapons: Lethality and Defense

If you are in a war, you are a warrior. There are only two types on the battlefield: warriors and victims. Sheep avoid the battle, or refuse to participate, but warriors seem to have two basic attitudes as they go into combat. One group appears to honestly look forward to it. The second group doesn't really want to do it, but since it has to be done, their attitude is, "Let's get it over with." Both are perfectly healthy and appropriate responses.

Drew Brown is a reporter for *Knight Rider* newspapers who served in combat with the 1st Ranger Battalion in the invasion of Panama in 1989. He was with the U.S. forces preparing to invade Iraq in 2003 when he sent me an e-mail with this astute observation.

> I know that a lot of what I'm hearing is bravado. You often hear things, like "I just want to get in there, get it over with and get the job done" or "It's just part of the job," both of which indicate a more detached view. How does one explain these two attitudes from a psychological point of view? Do you really buy it when you read about soldiers who say they want to go to war? What is driving these men? And also, how does one account for the more detached attitude?

I told him that I sincerely believe that a sizable number of warriors really do want to see combat. Some of this might be mindless bravado, but some of it is not. Many of these individuals are mature, levelheaded warriors. They are like good football players who scrimmage and practice endlessly, but never get to play a game. Well, there is a "game" now and these warriors want to be in it.

I think these individuals must be thinking like Oliver Wendell Holmes, Jr., when he said:

> I think that, as life is passion and action, it is required of a man that he should share the passion and action of his time at peril of being judged not to have lived.

As I train warriors around the world, traveling on my endless odyssey, I often get to spend time in police cars with law enforcement officers who drive me from the airport to the city where our training session is to take place. One very senior state trooper told me once, as he was driving me across a vast Midwestern state in the middle of the night at 120 mph, that there were two things he wanted before he retired. One was to have a car fast enough to hit a crow (troopers do a lot of high-speed driving and have an interesting sense of humor about it) and the other was to get into a gunfight. He was not embarrassed or full of false bravado about it, he just simply stated the fact that he had trained for a lifetime and wanted to see how he would do. I train many members of the special operations community (SWAT, SEALS, Rangers, Green Berets, etc.), and I have found this attitude to be common with them.

In ages past it was quite common in popular poetry to speak of finding a degree of pleasure or satisfaction in battle. The poem, "Into Battle" by Julian Grenfell, which I placed as the dedication to this book, is an example of poetic writing seldom seen today: A poem that speaks of the "joy of battle." Here is another one with a similar theme:

I shall not die alone, alone,
    but kin to all the powers,
As merry as the ancient sun
    and fighting like the flowers.
How white their steel, how bright their eyes!
    I love each laughing knave,
Cry high and bid him welcome to
    the banquet of the brave.
Yea, I will bless them as they bend
    and love them where they lie,
When on their skulls the sword I swing
    falls shattering from the sky.
The hour when death is like a light
    and blood is like a rose—
You have never loved your friends, my friends,
    as I shall love my foes.

—G.K. Chesterton
"The Last Hero"

All this might be dismissed as mindless romanticizing by those who have never been in combat, but those who have been there often express their desire to go back into harm's way. It is politically correct to say that there is nothing good about war and no one who has seen it would want to do it again. This is the obligatory nod that everyone must give when talking about the possibility of going to war and, from one perspective, it is completely true. But I know many veterans who disagree. Some Vietnam veterans, for example, stayed for two, three, four, five and, in one case that I know of, six tours, and every one of these individuals who I have information about is a perfectly healthy, functional human being who does not appear to have paid any significant psychological cost for his years of combat. They are the sheepdogs that we examine in greater detail later. They liked it.

It is not uncommon for police officers who have been in gunfights to compete for a position on their SWAT teams where they have the greatest chance to see even more action, and it is common for SWAT team members to spend decades in those dangerous positions. Many of the SWAT and military special operations forces (SOF) I have worked with are sincere and open when communicating the pleasure they derive from combat.

These elite SWAT and SOF operators have dedicated themselves to a lifetime of combat because they like it and they are good at it. Few sane people would want to be in the trenches of World War I (to name just one example), but many individuals wanted very much to go to Afghanistan with the Special Forces to get some payback for the terrorist attacks on September 11. As Bob Posey, a veteran police officer and trainer in Washington state, said, "They are looking for a just, good fight. Sniffing the breeze, pissing on the trees: being the sheepdog." Or, as Sir Walter Scott put it, they are seeking:

> . . . the stern joy which warriors feel
> In foemen worthy of their steel.

I received an e-mail from Monte Gould, a career cop, a SWAT operator and trainer, who is also a sergeant in the U.S. Army Reserves. (We met when we were both training Finnish law enforcement officers in Helsinki.) He had this to say when he learned that he was "too old" to be accepted into the U.S. Army Special Forces.

> Damn the bad luck, I wanted time on target. Trust me I'm like a goddamn peacemaker. Every time I show up in the [theater of operations] peace breaks out and I get sent home. I feel like Mother Teresa instead of some kind of action hero. I'm going to start carrying a Bible and Jehovah Witness handouts. They need me in the Middle East, all hostilities would cease overnight, the Arabs and the Jews would be friends and I would get an express ticket home.

This was my response to him.

> There are people who say that no one wants to go to war, and that "A soldier hates war more than anyone." And I'm sure they are sincere. But I know a lot of people who would beg to differ. And best I can tell, there ain't nothin' wrong with them.

Sir John Keegan, in his superb, classic book, *The Face of Battle,* wrote: "We must take account of the undoubted willingness of some men at all times to risk, even apparently to enjoy, extreme danger." Keegan used as an example Corporal Lofty King, a British commando in World War II. King's commander said this about him: "He genuinely enjoyed fighting and looked happiest, indeed inspired, in battle." Keegan said "Lofty King is a significant figure whose outline can be discerned in the thick of the fighting on many battlefields," comparing him to the French Lieutenant, Legros, who was nicknamed "The Enforcer" at the great gate of Hougoumont during the Battle of Waterloo:

> . . . whose power to impose his superior will on his comrades lends support to one's suspicion that, after all, battle is to the strong; that without the presence of the Lofty Kings and the Legros most battlefields would empty of soldiers at the firing of the first salvos.

Keegan goes on to say that there are:

> . . . moral consolations with which battle compensates the soldier—it would be foolish to deny that there are compensations-for its cruelties: the thrill of comradeship, the excitements of the chase, the exhilarations of surprise, deception and *ruse de guerre*, the exaltations of success, the sheer fun of prankish irresponsibility.

Colonel Jack Beach, a combat veteran who was the head of the psychology program at West Point, calls this "postcombat malaise" and he puts it this way:

> Whether you are in the heat of battle or just in the theater of combat, I believe for most people just being there is the most intense (at least prolonged intense) experience they ever have. In many ways it's a very simple existence. Many of the cares of the ordinary life do not intrude. However, you are completely focused on a mission that you feel is vital and that you are contributing to—you feel very alive and form deep bonds of intimacy with those about you. Unless when you return you come back to very meaningful work, you hunger for a return to that.

This is not intended in any way to speak ill of the veterans who would strongly disagree with these warriors who have found a degree of pleasure in battle. Indeed, those who were willing to point out that "War is hell," in General William Tecumseh Sherman's words, were once the individuals who were being politically incorrect in their time. As Henry Van Dyke put it in a poem about Sherman:

> This is the soldier brave enough to tell
> The glory-dazzled world that "war is hell."

The point here is that there are conflicting opinions on this matter.

As to the lets-get-it-over-with attitude, I would submit that this is also a mature, level-headed and healthy response. Most people faced with a dirty, unpleasant job that has to be done would have a similar attitude. John Keegan, in *Fields of Battle*, put it this way:

> The United States continues to elude me. If I understand it at all, it is through the strange profession that has shaped my life, the study of war. War is repugnant to the people of the United States; yet it is war that has made their nation, and it is through their power to wage war that they dominate the world. Americans are proficient at war in the same way that they are proficient at work. It is a task, sometimes a duty.

Americans have worked at war since the seventeenth century, to protect themselves from the Indians, to win their independence from George III, to make themselves one country, to win the whole of their continent, to extinguish autocracy and dictatorship in the world outside. It is not their favoured form of work. Left to themselves, Americans build, cultivate, bridge, dam, canalise, invent, teach, manufacture, think, write, lock themselves in struggle with the eternal challenges that man has chosen to confront, and with an intensity not known elsewhere on the globe. Bidden to make war their work, Americans shoulder the burden with intimidating purpose. There is, I have said, an American mystery, the nature of which I only begin to perceive. If I were obliged to define it, I would say it is the ethos of work as an end in itself. War is a form of work, and America makes war, however reluctantly, however unwillingly, in a particularly workmanlike way. I do not love war; but I love America.

Keegan gives credit and honor to the American fighting man, but as a graduate of the British Army Staff College, and after a lifetime of working with warriors of many nations and cultures, I would say that this applies to the British soldier, and to many other professional warriors around the world and throughout history.

I think that either response—wanting to go, or a workmanlike desire to do it well and get it over with—is fine and it is not for us to judge those who feel either way. These are warriors who are willing to answer the summons of the trumpet and enter into the realm of combat; their response, I believe, is quite healthy. Those who do not face combat with eagerness or steely determination are probably the ones who, as Steve Tarani and Damon Fay put it in *Contact Weapons*, will have "a debilitating and life-altering event" that will send them "into an unrecoverable psychological tailspin."

Taking Hits and Driving On: Do They Make Them Like That Anymore?

Heroism is the brilliant triumph of the soul over the flesh.
—Henri Frédéric Amiel
From his journal

Once you have made the decision to enter into combat, the thought of getting injured becomes one of your worst fears. Let us confront this fear.

I want to share with you one of my favorite stories of survival, a true tale about a mountain man named Hugh Glass from back in the early days of mountain expeditions.

Glass was badly mauled by a bear, and it looked like he was not going to make it. The others there that day decided to leave young Jim Bridger with Hugh to wait for him to die. But the old cuss was just too mean to die, and it was a long time before he slipped into a coma. Bridger figured then that Glass was dead, so he dug a shallow grave, piled a few rocks on him, and left.

Hugh Glass was still alive, though, so you can imagine that being buried angered him a bit. After he managed to crawl out of his grave, he worked his way downstream, eventually making it to the Missouri River, where he floated along clinging to chunks of wood and living off the land. Finally, months later, he made it to St. Louis, where he told stories about wolves coming up to him and licking maggots off his wounds.

The first thing old Hugh did after he was rested and recovered was to buy a gun (one version of this story says he bought a knife), then he sat back to recover from his ordeal, and to wait. When Jim Bridger and the other men showed up, Hugh caught up with Bridger and held his gun on him. Hugh thought for a while about the situation, eventually coming to the conclusion that Jim Bridger was too young to die. So he let him go.

Do they make warriors like Hugh Glass anymore? Here is a man mauled by a bear, left to die and buried alive. He climbed out of his grave, crawled from Montana to St. Louis, and when he finally got the person in his gun sights who had made his life so miserable, he decided the man was too young to die.

Do they make them like that anymore? Yes, they do. Every day.

Consider a gunman in Florida who shot a law enforcement officer in the eye. The eye popped like a grape, and the officer fell to the ground. Though he had powder burns in his good eye and a bullet in the other, he drew his sidearm and emptied his magazine into the perpetrator. Later at the inquiry, the officer was asked why he fired all the bullets in his gun into the man. He replied, "Because that's all I had!"

The officer may have had a bullet in one eye and powder burns in his other, and he may have been down, but he was definitely not out. Do they make them like that any more?

Consider also Officer Stacy Lim from the Los Angeles Police Department, whose story is legendary among professional police warriors. It began when she pulled into her driveway after an enjoyable evening of softball practice. When Lim got out of her personal car, she was immediately confronted by a group of gangbangers who had followed her with the intent of carjacking her vehicle.

Her first response was to call out that she was a police officer. They responded by firing a .357 magnum round into her chest, which penetrated her heart, and blew a tennis ball-size exit wound out her back. Stacy Lim stayed in the fight. She not only returned fire, but she also became the aggressor as she pursued the man, shooting him repeatedly. The remaining gangbangers suddenly remembered previous, pressing engagements and very wisely fled for their lives.

After she dealt with her attackers she turned around and headed up her driveway toward her house to call for help. She does not recall doing it, but as she was losing consciousness, she stripped the magazine from her pistol and threw it 20 feet away where it was found the next day. She did this because in the academy she had been taught, "Don't let them use your weapon against you."

Her attacker died and Stacy Lim died twice on the operating table. She required 101 pints of blood, but she survived, returning to duty eight months later. Today, she still works uniform patrol on the streets of Los Angeles, and her training philosophy is, "You need to prepare your mind, for where your body may have to go." Do they make them like that any more?

Although Lim was the victim of a surprise attack by deadly predators, she not only stayed in the fight, she took the fight to them. She was victorious because she was both physically and mentally prepared. Lim had a competitive attitude that refused to lose, and she had a plan, a visualized determination to win. Always to win.

Some of the greatest heroes that our nation has seen in years, our law enforcement officers, patrol our streets on a daily basis doing things that make the Old West pale by comparison, heroic deeds that never even make the five o'clock news. Such is the case of a decorated Detroit police officer named Jessica Wilson who was shot in the chest and neck with a shotgun at a neighborhood disturbance call. With only seconds of life left, she was able to shoot the assailant with a single shot at 40 feet before she fell. A firefighter was on the scene within minutes, but she was already dead.

Warriors like these do not just happen: They are built; they are crafted; they are nurtured every day. Common among so many of them is their ability to suck up gunshot wounds and drive on to accomplish their mission. Read the Medal of Honor citations, and you find that the one commonality in almost all of them is that though the recipients were physically damaged, they drove on. They drove on.

If you are shot, step one is, do not panic. The fact you are alive to know you are shot is a good sign. Think of it as a very emphatic warning shot. Say to yourself: "I've been better, but I could be worse." Know that a mission, a goal, can keep you going. Okay, you have been hit, so now your immediate goal is to prevent getting hit with another bullet.

Let's say the person who shot you no longer represents a legitimate lawful threat because he has fled, surrendered, or been shot, or there are plenty of other people present who can take care of him. Your mission now is to crawl, walk, wiggle, run, writhe or drive to medical support. Get yourself back to medical support so that your friends don't have to expose themselves getting you back to safety. They have better things to do at this time. As Samuel Butler put it over 300 years ago:

For those that fly may fight again,
Which he can never do that's slain.

Understand that your heart can be stopped by a bullet and you still can have five to seven seconds left. What are you going to do with them?

Loren Christensen worked a case when he was assigned to Portland's Gang Enforcement Team where a gangbanger broke into a gun store. As the man exited out the broken front window, he confronted a police officer and raised his newly acquired rifle, but the officer fired first and hit him in the heart. To the officer's amazement, the banger did not die, but ran along the front of the store, around the corner and continued for another 150 feet before his ripped-open heart terminated its host's life force.

In another case, an officer was wrestling with the husband at a domestic violence call when the man managed to take the officer's police baton and commenced beating him with it. Seriously injured from the multiple blows, the officer pulled his firearm and shot the assailant through his heart. The man dropped the baton and ran across the large living room, yanked open the door, and fell dead a few steps out into the hall.

Stacey Lim (the LAPD officer with the bullet through her heart) is living proof that it is entirely possible to survive after being shot in the heart. Some people assume that a headshot will stop them, but we have seen that you can even take a bullet in the eye and keep fighting.

Let's say the person who shot you continues to represent a lawful, legitimate threat to your life, and there is no one there to help you deal with him. What are you going to do? Getting back to medical support is not the answer now. Your immediate mission is to stop him from shooting you again. There is nothing you can do about the bullet in you, but you can stop the next bullet, by shooting him back! It's only fair.

Understand deep in your being that though you are shot, even in the heart or the eye, you can still function: You can call for help, shoot the perpetrator and/or get yourself to safety. Know that with today's incredible medical technology you have a greater chance of surviving than at any other time in history. The key is to stop him from putting any more bullets in you. In most cases that means killing the SOB who just shot you. And, in the end, as Longfellow put it:

Ye are better than all the ballads
    That ever were sung or said;
For ye are living poems
    And all the rest are dead.

The Will to Kill: Daunting and Deterring Your Opponent

You are the weapon, everything else is just a tool.

—Anonymous

As a cop or a peacekeeper, your job is not to kill, it is to serve and protect. To do that, you may have to kill.

First you want to deter and then stop the threat. The most effective way to stop someone is to fire a bullet into his central nervous system. It is up to God and the paramedics as to whether the man dies. Your job is to stop the deadly threat and the most effective way to do that is to make the threat die. Whether you are a warrior hunting terrorists in a distant land, a peacekeeper in Bosnia or a law enforcement officer patrolling our mean streets, there are rules of engagement in which deadly force can be used under authority. When you do it right, as you have been trained, the threat may die, a possibility you must accept as a warrior.

As a soldier or a marine in active combat, there is far less ambiguity. Your job is to kill the enemy. If he surrenders first, that is fine, because that is what we want. And you will play by the rules, and accept his surrender. However, one of the best ways to convince him to surrender is to kill sufficient numbers of his friends and leaders. You must accept the fact that you might have to kill.

As a cop, a peacekeeper or a combat soldier, what will you gain by accepting this dirty, nasty, four-letter word: kill? First, you will not respond with panic to a deadly threat. The worst thing in the world is Barney Fife with a bullet in his gun. "Oh God! I might have to kill him!" The correct response is this: "I think I'm going to have to kill this guy. I knew it might come to this some day." By completely accepting the possibility, you maintain control of yourself and are better able to deter your opponent. Deterrence is something that law enforcement officers do over and over as peacekeepers in the streets of America, and it is something that soldiers do in the volatile streets of foreign lands. When people know that warriors are present, they slow their cars, they do not rob convenience stores, and they are less likely to commit deadly acts in the name of politics and religion. Warriors daunt and deter. Their very presence can save lives and stop killing.

Here are two case studies in deterrence: One is a tragedy and the other is a famous success story. First the tragedy:

One summer day in August 2000, I volunteered my time to train a major city police department that was experiencing a crisis of confidence as a result of a recent, violent incident. A man had fired a rifle at his girlfriend and then fled with officers in close pursuit. The suspect screeched to a stop in a driveway, with one police car pulling up behind him and the other stopping farther away. The officers in both cars got out and took cover behind their vehicles.

The suspect, armed with a 30-caliber M-1 carbine rifle, began advancing on the closest officers. As he got near their car, the officers shouted, "Police, drop the gun. Police drop the gun. Stop. Stop." The officers in the car that was farthest away shouted to the closer officers, "Shoot him! Shoot him! Shoot him!" But no one shot, and the suspect continued to advance until he moved around the police car and came upon one of the exposed officers. "Don't hurt me," the officer said, setting the weapon on the ground.

What do wolves do to sheep? They rip their throats out. That is what happened in this case. The suspect fired, and the .30-caliber round blew out the officer's spinal cord, leaving the officer paralyzed from the neck down. Sadly, this officer died from this wound two years later. Only after the officer fell, did the officer's partner open fire and drop the suspect.

As a warrior, you might one day face the single most difficult task any person will ever have to face: to decide whether to use deadly force and take a life. Most likely, you will have to make that decision in a split second, in the most toxic, corrosive environment known to man: combat, the realm of the universal human phobia. If you chose to take a life when you should not, or if you fail to take a human life when you should, a world of hurt will come down on you.

This is not an impossible task; it is a hero's task, a warrior's task. It is immensely difficult, but if we did not have men and women willing to walk out the door and face that challenge every day, within the span of a generation our civilization would no longer exist.

The time to decide whether you can kill another human being is not in the middle of combat. The time to decide, to the utmost of your ability, is right now. Dr. Ignatius Piazza puts it very clearly and succinctly to every student at his Front Sight Firearms Training Institute:

> These are terrible decisions to make and we would like to avoid them at all costs. However, if you do not make the decisions in advance, I guarantee you that you will hesitate to make them later and that hesitation may make the difference between you living and dying.

Understand that no one can ever be 100 percent certain. We all exist in a state of uncertainty, even those who have been there before do not know for sure whether they can do a good job the next time. But to the utmost of your ability, you must resolve now, in your heart and mind, that you can kill.

In 2002 I received the following e-mail from a law enforcement officer.

> A young man set fire to his ex-wife's house . . . and ran on foot. The officers arriving in the area heard gunshots and reported them on

the radio. As I arrived on the scene, the suspect ran out in front of my car, no more than three feet away, shooting at the other officers. For some reason he ignored me, though I was the closest to him. He charged the officers, shooting multiple times; I received two rounds of friendly fire through my front windshield, missing my head by less than a foot.

I drew my weapon and fired four rounds through my windshield, evidently hitting him at least two times, because he fell to the ground 25 feet from me. He realized I was the one hitting him and he turned and fired approximately eight rounds into my car. Still sitting, I fired eight more rounds at him until he stopped firing at me. He was hit nine times.

After the shooting, I found out that he had shot [a deputy who had been pursuing him] eight times, killing him. He had also entered a residence and killed an 85-year-old man by shooting him 12 times.

There was absolutely no hesitation in my firing, though I had difficulty drawing my weapon as it was tangled in the seatbelt. But once out and on target, I did my job well. Your lecture "The Bullet Proof Mind" and your book, *On Killing* had assisted me in removing all doubt from my mind that I could take a life in defense of myself and others. My lack of hesitation and no second thoughts proved that to me. I have served as a police officer 27 years and although I have come close many times this was my first shooting.

In considering your lecture and book, I had already dealt with the religious aspects of taking a life, and I knew what emotions to expect after the shooting. Your insight into these areas was most helpful to me.

As I attended the deputy's funeral, I found it difficult to grieve for him because I was so glad the funeral was not for me. Because I had considered all this prior to the shooting and because I knew to expect it . . . it was much easier to deal with.

There is a growing trend in this country of "active shooters" attempting to take multiple lives quickly. It is important that we train our officers to understand and be prepared for these people, because the only way to survive these incidents is to act without hesitation. They have to be prepared in advance to accomplish this.

It is truly an honor to be of service to warriors such as this, and the greatest service I can provide is to help them prepare ahead of time to kill, if need be.

Every human on earth is insecure. Those who can admit it are a little more secure than those who cannot. The finest baseball pitcher in the world and the greatest football quarterback on the planet wake up in the morning, and are not sure if they are going to play a good game. They are determined to do their very best, but they know from experience that they will have good days and bad days. They learn from the bad days and rejoice in the good days, but always they know that they can never be sure. This is simply being human, and it is why we have superstitions. It is why there are baseball players who insist on wearing their lucky socks, actors who never whistle backstage, and why in Vietnam our soldiers would leave the death card on their fallen foes, a symbol feared by the superstitious North Vietnamese. To the utmost of your ability, you must face your insecurity and resolve the issue of using deadly force in your mind. Look deep into your self and ask, "Can I do what my society calls upon me to do?"

Who decides how much force the warrior has to use? Who ultimately makes the decision that deadly force is needed? The suspect does. The enemy does. The threat does. He fights, you fight. When he uses deadly force, you use deadly force. He makes that decision for you. He has the option to surrender, and your job is to respond with what society says is your right and responsibility to do. This is why it is paramount that you resolve in your mind whether you can do it ahead of time. Only when you know you can respond will you have the ability to truly deter people. That is the great paradox of combat: If you are truly prepared to kill someone, you are less likely to have to do it. That person will look into your eyes and see the steely determination to kill him, and be less eager to attack and more likely to surrender. Having that steely determination in your eyes is not about practicing your "evil eye" in the mirror—although there is nothing wrong with that—it is about having made the decision in your heart ahead of time.

There is a statue of a Texas Ranger in the main lobby of the airport in Houston, Texas. He wears a hat, boots, a gun on each hip, and a little tin star. The statue commemorates the Texas Rangers, and it commemorates the warrior spirit.

The story began when the mayor notified the Rangers of a riot in his city and that he desperately needed their help. A couple of hours later, one lonely ranger stepped off the train, the man whose image is now depicted in the airport. Shocked, the mayor asked, "They only sent one ranger?"

The ranger shrugged and replied, "You only got one riot."

The big Texas Ranger walked into the middle of the mob wearing his hat, boots, little tin star, the hog legs strapped on each hip, and carrying a shotgun. All it took was one look at this man, and every one of those rioters went home. They left because they had looked into the eyes of a man who was playing the game for real. His posture, his bearing, his demeanor, his voice, his reputation, and his organization all said one thing: He was fully prepared to kill them if that's what the job called for. The rioters knew that the stakes were too high, and they took their marbles and went home.

Engraved at the base of that statue in Houston's Hobby Airport are these words: "One riot, one ranger."

Someday I would like to make a statue to the American law enforcement officer, and at its base it would read: "One crime, one cop." Now, an officer, or any warrior, doesn't want to be the lone ranger; he wants all the backup he can get. However, if the situation is one in which there is only one lone warrior at the scene, then that can be enough if that warrior is armed mentally, emotionally and spiritually. If he has prepared himself and invested himself as a warrior, he will be ready. Here again is the great paradox of combat: When you are truly prepared to kill someone, you are less likely to have to do it.

The Will to Live: "Get Up! Get Up! If He Can Do It, I Can Too!"

The smallest worm will turn, being trodden on.

—Shakespeare
King Henry VI

One of your primary goals as a warrior is to train and mentally condition yourself to keep going when you have been shot. You must understand and accept that you might get wounded, and understand deeply and intensely that you will keep fighting until the threat is no longer present. You can do it and you must do it. You must control and direct the power of your adrenaline.

One law enforcement officer shot a perpetrator five times with his .45-caliber handgun. He was an undercover narcotics officer and had just made a buy from a drug dealer. The back-up officers swooped in to make the arrest, only to be met with a hail of gunfire from the drug dealer. What would you do if you were this warrior and suddenly the perpetrator was shooting your friends? You would shoot him, and as a result of that action, you would probably kill him. Remember, it is really up to God and the medics whether he lives or dies. In this case, the undercover officer shot the perp with multiple .45 rounds, killing him. Later, the officer expressed his amazement that it had taken so many bullets. "I always thought when you hit someone with a .45 they just kind of flew away like on TV. I shot the guy five times before he dropped."

Later, the same officer got into another gunfight. This time the officer got hit and he went down. As he lay there, he says that he thought back on his first shooting where it took five big rounds to drop the perp. The officer said to himself, "Get up! Get up! If he can do it, I can too!"

That is exactly what you need to tell yourself. Every time you hear about a gangbanger sucking up rounds and driving on, every time you hear about some Medal of Honor recipient sucking up damage and driving on, every time you hear about a cop taking a bullet through the heart and driving on, say to yourself, "If that person can do it, I can too."

On Getting Shot: Bone Hits, Blood Loss, and Blistering Incoming Fire

Who, doomed to go in company with Pain
And Fear and Bloodshed,—miserable train!—
Turns his necessity to glorious gain.

—Wordsworth
"Character of the Happy Warrior"

Should a bullet slam into you, what can you expect? Sometimes in the heat of battle warriors are not aware that they have been shot until later. But those who are aware of it usually experience the normal stress responses: dry mouth, sweaty palms and a racing heart rate. We know that sometimes our sense of pain can shut down so that tissue wounds do not hurt, but those who have been shot say that bone hits can be extremely painful. While that is important to know, it is also important to understand that no one dies of broken bones.

A law enforcement officer lay on the floor in the back of a bus after being shot twice. One round hit a leg bone and a second went in his chest. From where he lay, he could look under the seats and see the feet of the shooter coming to finish him off. He said that he was bleeding his life out in this dirty bus and all he could think of was, "Why does the bullet in my leg hurt so bad and this one doesn't hurt at all?" After a moment, the officer realized, as he watched the suspect's feet get closer and closer, that maybe he had something more important to worry about right then. He had become distracted at this critical moment because no one had told him how different types of wounds could hurt. It is all about prior preparation.

You must also be prepared for blood loss. If you get holes punched in your body, blood will come out. On rare occasions, the contents of your intestines may come out, too, but do not worry about that because someone will clean it up. But most of the time blood is going to come out. How much? Well, your body holds approximately one and a half gallons of blood, and you can lose 30 percent, approximately a half gallon, without losing your hydraulics. To see what that much blood looks like, take a half gallon of strawberry milk and pour it on the ground. Yes, it is a large puddle, but tell yourself that that is the volume of blood you can lose and still fight. Erase all doubt that you can keep going and keep fighting. Know that if you stop before you lose that much blood, it is your will that failed, not your body.

Sucking up damage and driving on. That is what great warriors do. Consider this narrative of special operations soldiers in Afghanistan, from the online column of that great warrior-author, Colonel David Hackworth:

Earlier, the platoon [1st Platoon of Alpha Company, 1/75th Rangers] had been spread across the battlefield on separate missions.

When word came down to find MIA Navy Seal Neil Roberts, the lead element air-assaulted, its chopper shot to smithereens upon landing, and the Rangers and aircrew were stuck on a rocky ridge surrounded by a large, well-dug-in Al-Qaida force.

Because of blistering enemy incoming fire, a 1st Platoon reinforcing element landed by chopper at the base of the mountain, about a mile from the besieged warriors. The 10 men began clawing their way toward the top—loaded down with 100 pounds of kit—on what would prove to be a 5,000-foot, almost-vertical three-hour climb. And throughout this near mission-impossible feat, they were battered by enemy rifle and mortar fire that wounded several of these elite warriors.

When the Rangers got to the top, they busted through the enemy's bunker line and linked up with their surrounded mates. But they soon found themselves waist-high in snow, the thermometer hovering around zero, in an increasingly hotter frying pan—with incoming RPGs, recoilless rifle fire, mortars thumping in and bullets snapping like angry bees across the open plain at 12,000 feet.

An SAS commando who watched the fight said, "These blokes, along with their tactical aircraft and chopper air support, killed a bloody lot of them."

Apart from their own incredible guts, the air support—virtually on top of them—is what kept them alive. If USAF air controller Kevin Vance wasn't on the ground bravely directing the fire, it would have been taps for all these good men.

Ranger Marc Anderson said, "This is where all the training pays off" before catching one with his name on it while bounding toward the enemy.

Ranger Bradley Crose was hit in the head by a round that smashed under his helmet and out the back of his head, and Ranger Matthew Commons went down for the count as well.

Air Force warrior Jason Cunningham was hit by two rounds in the gut and lay out in the bitter cold—slowly bleeding to death.

When the Ranger rifles were shot up, had malfunctioned, or the men ran out of ammo, the Rangers policed up Al-Qaida weapons and waded into the fanatics, wasting them with their own bullets.

For almost 18 long, blood-soaked hours, it was often hand-to-hand fighting with knives, pistols and rifle butts. That terrible night, the Rangers were supported by USAF C-130 Specter gunships that, according to an Aussie SAS commando on a nearby knob, lit up the hills around them. "It was bloody amazing, the most beautiful—yet fearsome—sight I'd ever seen," he said.

. . . those who were hit never faltered, continuing to put heavy fire on the enemy in the fiercest kind of combat and freezing conditions our forces haven't seen since the Korean War.

Right now you have to develop the will and the resolve to live. Know that if you keep going until medical help arrives, you probably will survive, if you stop your attacker from shooting you again. Understand that with every passing day our evacuation, communication, and medical technology progresses by leaps and bounds. Today, warriors survive horrific gunshot wounds that would have been fatal only 10 years ago. Accept that you might get hit and know that you will survive it.

Being a warrior, living a life of alert readiness and staying in Condition Yellow, means that you notice the good as well as the bad. Consider these anonymously written words found on the wall of a bunker in Saigon:

You've never lived until you've almost died. For those who fight for it, life has a flavor the protected will never know.

At the end of the day when you go home and hug your loved ones and taste that meal prepared with love, it will have a flavor the protected will never know. The sheep spend a lifetime eating grass, but you taste the flavor the protected will never know. That may be the warrior's greatest reward.

Fight for it. Fight for it. Fight for it. Never, never give up. Consider this powerful narrative of survival and determination from a great warrior trainer, Pete Soulis:

As I was in the process of drawing my weapon and ordering the driver to show me his hands, I stepped to the right instead of stepping back and away from his vehicle, thus placing me in what we refer to as a "fatal funnel." I was no more than two feet from his passenger window and looking into the eyes of a smiling cold-blooded killer…that's when he took advantage of my stepping where I had no business being. While seated in his vehicle, the suspect lunged toward the passenger side firing one of two handguns he had concealed…the first round struck me in my vest, causing me to stumble backwards…

Although I knew the suspect was still firing rounds at me, I no longer could hear the shots. Everything was moving in slow motion and my peripheral vision was nonexistent. All I could see at this point was the driver now standing outside his door with a two-handed grip on a black semiautomatic handgun. The slide was recoiling back and forth in slow motion, ejecting spent rounds over his right shoulder. I knew if I were going to survive this attack, I would have to fight through this state of mind and seek cover immediately.

No sooner had that thought entered my mind than I felt a second round impact my left arm just above the wrist, then a third round strike my left forearm causing me to drop my flashlight. Then another round struck my left thigh.

I fell to my knee, now returning fire at the driver who was still smiling at me as if he were enjoying the target practice. Apparently, several rounds I fired hit their mark and caused the driver to seek cover, as he continued to fire.

I sprinted toward the rear of my car, but just as I was reaching it I felt a bullet impact my left shoulder. I saw the material on my shirtsleeve blow open as the bullet passed through my shoulder and exited the left biceps.

The gunfight continued with a volley of rounds exchanged with both of us using our vehicles for cover…The wound I had sustained to my left thigh was now pumping blood onto the trunk of my cruiser. Fearing that a major artery may have been struck, I feared that I was probably going to bleed to death in a short time.

A relative calm came over me. I made the decision to end this deadly confrontation now, regardless if I had to take more rounds to do it. The driver was not leaving this parking lot to hurt anyone else. He had been the predator up to this point and now it was my turn…

I dropped the magazine from my weapon and inserted a fresh one. Apparently, he saw the empty magazine hit the ground and figured I was out of ammunition, or maybe he assumed I had succumbed to my injuries and knelt behind my cruiser to die. Regardless the reason, he left his cover and was coming to finish me off. I was now crouched low behind the left rear bumper of my car. I distinctly remember telling myself to wait; wait until he is closer. I could clearly see the driver's feet as he slowly approached. I waited until he got at least three or four feet from the front of my car before I made my move.

Staying low, I lunged from around my car, firing accurately into the suspect's chest and continuing to fire as I advanced. I remember the smile leaving my assailant's face as he stumbled backward toward his vehicle. He turned, gun in hand, and dove over the rear of the car landing out of my sight. He entered and started his car in an attempt to flee. I stumbled forward, firing through the rear windshield of the suspect's vehicle until it came to a stop, and the suspect sat mortally wounded.

Pete Soulis now trains warriors worldwide, using his experience to teach others.

Survive! Get on with life, and live it to the fullest, savoring every day. That may be a warrior's greatest reward. As David Revore, Second Chance Body Armor Save #777 put it:

That short span of five minutes . . . felt like the longest five minutes in time. Those five minutes have given me the new perspective that Christmas is every day. It has been said that we only get one spin at life, but once in a while we may get another. What we do with it will determine whether or not it is deserved.

Perchance to Dream: The Universal Warrior Nightmare

Like a dog, he hunts in dreams.

—Tennyson
"Locksley Hall"

After you have been in a combat situation it is normal to have nightmares about that experience. Slowly but surely those nightmares should fade away. Years later they might pop up again, sometimes for no obvious reason, and that too appears to be a fairly common part of the healing process. But there is a kind of dream not associated with any real world event. I call it the Universal Warrior Nightmare.

The most common version of the universal nightmare is to dream that you cannot get your gun to fire. The gun jams, the bullets dribble out the end of the barrel, or they bounce impotently off the bad guy's chest. I have interviewed many World War II and Vietnam veterans who had nightmares that their rifles would not work. I asked an audience of SEALs and Green Berets who had just returned from Afghanistan how many had ever had the gun-doesn't-work dream, and nearly all of them raised their hands. When I ask that question of my law enforcement audiences, usually around half of them raise their hands.

The dream can take other variations. People who have spent time training in the martial arts and officers who train extensively in defensive tactics, might consistently dream that their techniques or their blows do not work. People who have been in traffic accidents may dream that their brakes don't work. Usually it is the gun that fails.

This is called a performance anxiety dream. Your handgun, rifle or empty-hand fighting techniques are representative of your ability to deal with danger. You are a warrior and your job is to go into danger. When you truly accept that fact, when there is no denial left in you, it is reasonable to be concerned. And the puppy, your midbrain, your unconscious mind, sends a message into your dreams that says, "Boss, I'm worried. I'm afraid it might not work." Well, who would not be worried?

There is peace in simply understanding that you are not alone, that these kinds of dreams are common among warriors. Many of your brother and sister warriors have such nightmares and there is nothing wrong if you are having them now or you get them in the future. But there is one thing you can do that has helped many warriors to make the dreams go away: train. The puppy is worried, so to calm him you teach him a few new tricks or polish the old ones. Train hard so that he feels confident.

I know an officer who is a member of one of our nation's most elite SWAT teams. He goes into harm's way on a daily basis and is confronted by deadly force encounters on a weekly basis. He tells me that every six weeks, like clockwork, his nightmares return. To make them go away, he goes out to the firing range on a Saturday and fires hundreds of rounds. He particularly likes to shoot at steel targets, the kind that produce an audible clank when struck and then drop down. "My weapon turns into a magic wand. Wherever I point it, things fall down, and my nightmares go away."

For some people, the nightmares pass when they are no longer in danger. Others seem to "learn" how to win in their dreams, to "will" themselves to win, even if it means picking up a big rock and smacking their enemy with it, or defeating an endless stream of attackers until their opponents finally give up. However, if the nature of your work is that every day you face combat or the possibility of combat, one possible solution is to train.

The midbrain or the mammalian brain truly is like having a "puppy" inside. The only way to communicate to your puppy is to train him. I have two dogs, a poodle and a German shepherd: my elite, crack security team. I cannot talk to my dogs, and tell them, "All right, I'm going to be gone for a week, so you guys are in charge. You've got the front door, and you've got the back door." It's not like Scooby Doo where they say, "Rr-all right boss!" and go do it. In the real world the only way you can communicate to your dog is to train him. The same is true with the puppy inside.

The one quality all good police dogs have in common is confidence, verging on cockiness. This is because they have been highly trained and they know that there is nothing the world can throw at them that they cannot handle. Have you ever seen a person that just exudes confidence under stress? You can't fake it, it is a product of training and experience. If you are having performance anxiety dreams, it may mean that the puppy doesn't have that confidence. The only sure way to get it is through training.

The warrior masters his realm. He does not flee from his fear, he conquers it.

chapter **four**

Making the Decision to Kill:

"I Killed Someone. But Someone Lived."

There are two ways to look at it. Some people are so disgusted by the fact that they have killed someone, and further disgusted by the legal system, that they quit. Statistics say that around 50 percent quit. And I can see how that happens. It's a dirty part of the job, and there certainly is no part of me that wants it to happen again. On the other hand, it is a very necessary part of our job, after all, we keep the peace, and sometimes that takes a lot. The other way to look at it is this, "Sure I killed someone. But someone lived. Someone who was not going to live one second longer is instead alive because I did." The woman I killed had two small children who don't have a mother anymore. I'm sorry about that. Regardless of how messed up she was, I'm sure her own children loved her . . . I would have preferred it ended another way, but that wasn't up to me. She made the call. Every single man on my team has kids, too. It was my responsibility to make sure when sugar turns to shit they all went home, and they did. They went home to their families, and no matter what else happens, I can't help but be proud of that fact.

—Russ Clagett
After the Echo

I would argue that we are in the most violent time in peacetime human history. Remember that the murder rate is being held down by medical technology, but the rate at which our citizens are trying to harm and kill each other (the per capita aggravated assault rate) is up five-fold since 1957, and similar increases have occurred in nations around the globe. Meanwhile, we have terrorists racking up the Guinness World Record body count for international terrorist acts (the September 11, 2001, attacks on the World Trade Center), and domestic terrorist activity racking up all-time record domestic mass murder (the Oklahoma City bombing). The result is a "war on crime" and a "war on terrorism," at home and abroad unlike anything seen before.

In these violent times, we must know if we have warriors capable of doing the job. In the area of law enforcement, we need a sure way of screening for shooters so that we know they are going to be able to pull the trigger. Loren Christensen tells of a rookie officer in his agency who was not only incapable of shooting someone, but he would not even wear his sidearm. The officer was hired in the winter and because he wore a long, heavy uniform jacket, his training partner did not know that the rookie was locking his entire web belt and firearm into the car trunk at the beginning of each shift. When the training officer finally caught on—about three weeks later—he immediately drove the rookie back to the precinct. The new man was terminated a few days later, and rightfully so. Now, this man may have been a wonderful husband and father, and an outstanding citizen, but he had no business in police work.

The Skill and the Will to Kill

> Champions aren't made in the gym. Champions are made from something they have deep inside them—a desire, a dream, a vision. They have to have last-minute stamina, they have to be a little faster, they have to have the skill and the will. But the will must be stronger than the skill.
>
> —Muhammed Ali

You need three things to survive in armed combat: the weapon, the skill, and the will to kill.

What if you do not have a weapon? Will that make the people you are sworn to protect safer when someone tries to kill them? No. Even the British police—the famous "Bobbies"—are increasingly armed in order to serve and protect in our modern, ultra-violent world. If there was anything that proves the point of our ever-growning violence around the globe, it is probably the arming of the Bobbies.

What about the skill? Training? Should we take the (all too common) approach that implies that guns are nasty and icky, and not spend any appreciable time training because we do not want "gunfighters"? No, because without training your gun would not do you any good. Indeed, you are likely to be a significant risk to the people you are supposed to protect.

Is it a good thing if you have the weapon and the skill, but not the will to pull the trigger? Of course not, because someone who does have the ability to kill will take that weapon away from you and use it on you or the people you are supposed to protect. If at the moment of truth you cannot pull the trigger, then all your training and all your equipment are wasted, and the lives of those you are sworn to protect will be wasted, and you will be an abject failure.

If you are going to have the weapon, then you must have the will to kill. How is the will developed?

In my co-author's book, *The Mental Edge*, Loren Christensen writes about a champion martial artist who spent decades developing his personal weapons but had doubts as to whether he could use them in the harsh reality of the streets. Christensen writes:

> I know one champion karate fighter who has earned so many trophies that if they were melted down he could build a dozen full-sized cars. He can put his fist or foot wherever he wants and there isn't much his opponent can do about it. In addition to his incredible physical skill, he has a trait rare among champions, especially fighters like him who have graced the covers of martial arts magazines. The trait is honesty. He has told me more than once that he has doubts as to how well he would do in a real fight, a bloodletting, knock down, drag out. "I can play tournament tag," he says. "But if I had to fight for real, I don't know how I would do."
>
> Here is a guy whose techniques are incredibly fast, awesomely powerful, and who can deliver them with the precise timing of a Swiss watch… With the right attitude, my friend could be the terror of the streets… But he doesn't have this attitude because he wasn't born with it, his environment growing up didn't require it, and he has never made an effort to train for it.

Later in *The Mental Edge*, Christensen talks about his own mental preparation to take a life in his job as a police officer. Early in his career, he came to a place in his thinking where he absolutely knew he could shoot and kill with the weapons provided by his police agency. Then the veteran martial artist considered the act of killing with his empty hands in his role as a police officer. He writes:

> It's one thing pulling a trigger when I'm several feet away from a threat, but it is much more personal to beat the life out of someone with my feet and hands. What if a bad guy disarmed me and I had to fight him hand-to-hand? Could I kill him to protect myself? I answered, yes.
>
> I got into a lot of fights as a police officer…While the thought of killing was not a conscious one every time I struggled with a resistor, I was comfortable knowing that if the fight deteriorated and turned into a survival situation, I was mentally prepared to use deadly force with my hands.
>
> Is this thinking sick? No, it is smart. As a police officer, I was paid to protect the community, which meant that in an extreme situation, I might have to use deadly force. That's what I got paid the big bucks for. If I was unable to use that level of force and I was killed, or an innocent person was killed, what good was I as a protector?

How we select police officers is a step in the right direction. Portland, Oregon, had a selection test that is discussed in *Deadly Force Encounters*. Portland does not use it anymore because it has been deemed there as politically incorrect, but it has been picked up by other agencies nationwide. Part of their test involved an interview board that asked how candidates for the position of police officer would handle various situations. One question that really revealed candidates' common sense and their willingness to use deadly force went like this.

> You're a law enforcement officer. You're trained, equipped, and on foot patrol. You come around a corner and find in front of you a chain link fence, topped with barbwire, extending as far as you can see to the left and right. Just on the other side of the chain link fence is a law enforcement officer lying helpless on the ground as someone kicks him repeatedly in the head. What do you do?

The correct answer would be that you would pull your weapon, order him to stop, and if he continued to assault the officer you would shoot him. End of discussion. The candidates, though, were not sure how to answer, so they would hedge their bets. Some would say that they would climb over the fence, and the panel would tell them that the fence was topped with barbwire. "I'm going to go under the fence," a couple of them said, and the panel would say that it was on concrete. "Well, I'll go around the fence." The panel would inform them that the fence goes all the way around the enclosed area. "I'm going to call the helicopter." Sorry, but the helicopter is busy. This would continue as the candidates tried every possible answer to avoid having to use their weapons. In the end, two candidates out of 10 would not tell the panel that they would shoot the assailant, even though there were no other options. Now, these people are probably wonderful human beings and I am proud to be on the same planet with them, but the technical term for their interview is "disqualified."

Lest you think these people answered this way because they were only police applicants, consider a paint bullet scenario that was given to sworn, veteran police officers in Nebraska. In the scenario, they were told that they had received an "officer needs help call," with shots fired. When they got to the scene, they would find the officer down with the suspect pointing a gun at the officer's head. "I'm going to kill him," the suspect says. "I'm going to kill him." The tricky part of this scenario was that the suspect had his back turned to the officer.

When the officers were faced with this situation (one in which they were fully authorized to shoot the man), the majority would not fire, and would do so only after the suspect shot the officer in the head. A significant minority of officers would not even fire then, but would wait until the suspect pointed the weapon toward them. Of course then it would be an action/reaction situation, and the officers would probably lose.

Waiting for the suspect to shoot the officer or point his weapon at you is not an action that saves lives. Warriors need to decide in advance, to the best of their ability, that they can do the right thing when the time comes.

Here is a letter that I received from a SWAT officer:

> I would like to ask you a bit of advice . . . As of late, every SWAT call out, every warrant, and most of the drug buy/busts that I have been involved with, I find myself spending most of my prep time (gearing up, etc.) thinking about how I would handle the aftermath of killing the person we are after. I do not spend any time on the actual event of the shooting/hand-to-hand/knife or act of killing the person, but with thoughts of the aftermath. Is my family going to be all right with what has happened? How is my mother going to handle it? What lawyer should I call, and so on.
>
> I have talked with all of them about killing people before, but until recently I never gave it much thought. I have all the answers and questions pre-answered and they always come out the same. However, I am spending a great deal of mental energy dealing with this. I don't have any regrets or real concerns; however, I get this ever-growing feeling that the actual act is forthcoming.
>
> Is this something that I should worry about? Is this normal or am I going off the deep end? I have been passing it off as just good prep for the possible combat, but then you never know. I may be going loony.

This was my reply:

> I don't think this is loony at all. I think it's part of the growing process that a mature warrior must go through: resolving the issues in your mind, thinking them over, and deciding what you will do ahead of time. Such thinking is the "next step" in officer survival, and I congratulate you on working your way through this level of warriorhood.
>
> I predict in the next couple of months, or even years, that this will resolve itself in your mind and you will come out the other end a superior warrior, functioning at a higher level of preparedness and maturity.

Brigadier General S.L.A. Marshall, in his classic book, *Men Against Fire*, spoke clearly of this resistance to killing in the average, healthy soldier. The army, Marshall says:

. . . must reckon with the fact that he comes from a civilization in which aggression, connected with the taking of life, is prohibited and unacceptable. The teaching and ideals of that civilization are against killing, against taking advantage. The fear of aggression has been expressed to him so strongly and absorbed by him so deeply and pervadingly—practically with his mother's milk—that it is part of the normal man's emotional make up. This is his greatest handicap when he enters combat. It stays his trigger finger even though he is hardly conscious that it is a restraint upon him.

In *Deadly Force Encounters*, Dr. Artwohl and Loren Christensen address this issue head-on:

> An officer who is uncertain whether he can shoot someone, or an officer who for religious or moral reasons knows he will not shoot a human being, should not be in a police car and, for that matter, should not be in police work. Such an officer is a detriment to other officers and to the public he is sworn to protect. They all depend on him to do the right thing when the situation calls for it. If that means taking another person's life, they need to know he will do it, and without hesitation. An unwillingness to shoot is in no way a bad reflection on him as a person, but it does mean he needs to find another line of work.
>
> With the ever increasing dangers on the street, every person considering a career in law enforcement, every rookie just beginning to experience the reality of police work, and every veteran officer who has discovered that his outlook on life and on the job has changed as the years have passed, needs to soul-search to decide whether they can kill another human being. If the applicant answers no, he should not go into a police career. If the rookie discovers this about himself, he needs to talk to the chaplain, a department counselor or a supervisor, someone who can guide him in his next step. If the rookie is unable to change his belief after talking with one or all these people, then he should be fired before more time and money is vested on someone who could get himself or another hurt or killed. The veteran officer, who for whatever reason, realizes he can no longer use deadly force, needs to make this known. He should get counseling and not be allowed to work in a position that will expose him to a deadly force situation.
>
> What is of concern to everyone, however, is when the applicant, rookie and veteran do not express their feelings, or lie about them to get or keep their job. The result can be tragic.

Clint Smith, president and director of a state-of-the-art firearms training facility called Thunder Ranch in Texas said this about the survival instinct:

> Anyone can understand shooting to protect themselves. You give me five minutes and I'll make anyone on this planet mad enough to shoot me. The real question is will they have that much time in a fight? You need to make that decision before you start to fight—your life depends on it.

One officer told me about a young rookie cop in his department who, as a deeply religious man, made it clear to all the other officers that he would never take a human life under any circumstances. Even with all the training he had just undergone and with a total understanding of what might be required of him, he still insisted that he had no intention of ever using deadly force. Yet as a police officer, this is a real possibility. Happily for him and all the other officers, the young man did not last long in that department.

Here is another example, from a letter sent to me, of a warrior who was not prepared to kill:

> I joined the Air National Guard and became a full-time Air Force Security Police officer... One night I was patrolling the tank park and I heard the sound of a tank engine running somewhere in this huge area filled with assorted armored vehicles. I called for the roving MP unit to meet me. "Cowboy," a man with six years of police experience quickly arrived . . . We located an M-113 [armored personnel carrier] with the motor running, one with one of the new, classified weapons system on board. Cowboy and I split up and approached from different sides.
>
> As I got closer, a man suddenly stood up out of a hatch, reached into his overcoat and pulled out a .45 auto, which he began bringing to bear on me. I was only about six feet from him, and Cowboy came running when he saw the man. I had my sidearm out and pointing it at the man, yelling at him to stop and drop his weapon. Cowboy was doing the same.
>
> The man continued turning toward me and I began pulling the trigger on my weapon. It was as if time had slowed down for me; I can still remember vividly watching the cylinder on my revolver rotating as the hammer began to come back. The man froze and I backed off on the trigger. Then he dropped his weapon, and we took him into custody.
>
> At a subsequent hearing, we learned that he was a private in the army and had been ordered there by a lieutenant to guard the tanks, and hadn't informed us. The lieutenant had told him that if anyone came near the tank he didn't recognize, he was to shoot them.

My friend Cowboy was discharged from the army after having a complete psychological breakdown. Even after all his training and experience, he had never pointed a loaded weapon at another human before with the intent to kill. When it hit home just how close he had come to killing, he broke down. All of the training and conditioning had not adequately prepared this young man for the reality of his position.

When the time came, he was unable to perform.

Many warriors have had to work their way through this same process. Vietnam veteran, Tom Hain, talks about his experience:

Sat Cong! [kill Vietcong] I wasn't going to be unsure about killing anymore. I wasn't going to go out of my way to find a target, but I was going to pull the trigger when I got the chance. At least that's what I thought. When the time came, it wasn't that easy. It wasn't a "him or me" choice. I wasn't the target he was firing at, but I was the only one who saw him shoot. When I tried to point him out to the guy next to me, his reply was "shoot da mutha fugga!"

My heart was beating so hard that that's all I could hear. I aimed my M-16 at him and pulled the trigger. No hesitation this time. I fired again, and again, and again. I emptied a magazine on him. When I stopped firing, I started shaking. He was dead and I had done it. "Did everybody see that? I did that." I wanted the guys that he was shooting at to see that I was the one that saved their butts. I didn't want them to see that I was shaking like a scared rabbit. I never saw anyone else shake like that and I was ashamed of myself for being so scared. I wanted to be cool about it, but I couldn't. This wasn't just firing into the bushes like I'd done before. This time someone died. No time for reflections now, back to work!

In my co-author's popular book, *Far Beyond Defensive Tactics,* he writes this about making the decision to kill.

You have to look into yourself to decide what you must do to bring out that politically incorrect term killer instinct. When defending your life, you cannot fight with limitations, you cannot hold back for reasons of etiquette, a sense of humanity, personal religious reasons, fear of Internal Affairs, or of being sued. If you are absolutely convinced that you are fighting for your life, you owe it to yourself, [your partner, the citizens you are sworn to protect] and your family to use whatever personal psychological ploy to help get the job done. If that means you have to view the suspect as a rabid, junkyard dog, so be it.

When the suspect attacks you with viciousness, you must fight back with greater viciousness. Why would you do anything less? For sure, this is not a topic you would discuss at a community meeting, or a woman's canasta club. These people would never understand because it is too far removed from their reality.

It is, however, your reality. As a police officer, you patrol the streets to maintain peace and harmony. But when you or an innocent person in your presence is attacked with viciousness, you must respond with the same, albeit with an objective of getting control. Do not doubt that the killer instinct is there . . . It is a cold entity, but it is also energy producing. It will make you stronger, faster, and resistant to pain.

And it will help you get home at the end of your shift.

Finally, Russ Clagett, in his excellent book, *After the Echo*, put it this way after he had to kill in a life and death situation:

We all know this is part of our job at some point, especially by the time you become a tactical sniper. You should have already answered some basic questions in your own mind and heart. If the time comes, your only consideration is to how best apply deadly force, not whether you can do it. Too much is at stake. You need to be emotionally strong enough to do the hard thing, and if you are, you will do well when your moment comes. On the other hand, if you've already decided just by reading this book that maybe you would rather sell cars, then go sell cars. It's okay.

Response to Killing and the "Joy" of Combat

Combat is of such emotional intensity that strange elations can come from the act of killing. Opponents pit themselves against each other with the certain knowledge that one will be vanquished, one will be victor. The conflict is often at close quarters. You can hear, see, smell, and ultimately touch your antagonist. Sheer terror propels the violence emitting from both sides. All want to live, but one can live only by the death of the other. And when that death does fall to the opponent, there is a great sense of relief.

How curious the fallen look. Instantly their ashen bodies begin to meld with the ground. It is uncanny. As you look, you sense a great deal of pleasure in your being alive. He who was so full of animation a few moments ago now lies eternally inanimate. You are alive; a future is still yours. Countless times the survivor has that sensation until the pleasure of life is confused with the pleasure of killing. The good feeling comes when the enemy is killed, and soon the confusion sets in that the good feeling comes because the enemy is killed, not for the real reason: that you are still alive.

Only by killing is life sustained. This is the way of war. And it is amid this topsy-turvy world of war in which violence provides a chance to live for another day that the combatant must be on guard to preserve his own morality.

—Colonel James R. McDonough, U.S. Army
Quoted in U.S. Marine Corps Leadership MCI-7404

In *On Killing*, I list and discuss a set of response stages to taking the life of another:

-First there is the exhilaration stage in which there might be joy and elation. The common psychological term for this is "survivor euphoria" and combat survivors know that there can be an intense relief and satisfaction that comes from hitting your opponent and knowing that you are alive. This is brilliantly outlined in the preceding quote by Colonel McDonough, author of the superb book, *Platoon Leader*. Here is another example of the exhilaration stage from *Deadly Force Encounters*:

> The suspect gurgled for a few moments, turned gray, and then died . . . I was feeling this tremendous exhilaration. It was a real rush and I'd never felt anything like it. Hey, he tried to kill me, but I killed him first. F— him. Then when the ambulance people started working on him, I remember thinking that I didn't want them to save him.

-Then there is a backlash of remorse and nausea. Many soldiers vomit after their first kill. Sometimes they say, "My God, I just killed a man, and it felt good. What's wrong with me?"

-Finally there is a lifelong process of rationalization and nausea. If this process fails, it can be one of the paths to PTSD.

I spent a great deal of time studying how people respond to what is one of the most significant acts one human being can do to another. The problem is that my data was mostly based on 18- to 20-year-olds who had killed in combat and responded this way.

After *On Killing* was published and had been read by many thousands of warriors, I was informed by some of those who killed that their reactions were somewhat different. They said that they felt the satisfaction, but they did not experience the backlash of remorse and nausea. One veteran police officer who had to shoot and kill a violent criminal said, "All I felt, was the recoil." Some of them were even worried that there might be something wrong with them because they did not feel anything. For example, there was a Green Beret Sergeant Major whose first kill was in Somalia after spending decades of service in the Army; a U.S. Army Master Sergeant with 17 years of experience when he killed his first enemy soldier in Vietnam; a state trooper whose first kill occurred in his ninth year on the job; and a police detective who killed in her 12th year on the job. Each one of them told me that their response to killing had been different.

There were many individuals who were in their 20s, 30s and 40s who did have remorse and nausea after they killed, but there were also many who did not. I believe that the primary reason why their experiences were more positive, if you will, is because they were mature warriors who had done the rationalization and acceptance process ahead of time, before they actually had to drop the hammer on someone. Basically they said to themselves:

> I don't want to have to kill anyone, but if someone gets in front of my weapon and tries to kill me or someone else, I will do what my society employs, equips, empowers, enables and requires me to do.

By having resolved this issue in their minds ahead of time, their responses were healthier and they were able to return to their lives without the residual problems experienced by the young troops I talked about in *On Killing*.

Michael M. Phillips, a reporter for the *Wall Street Journal* covering the 2003 invasion of Iraq, wrote the single most remarkable article I have ever found about the diverse response of men to killing. In this article one young marine responds in the classic manner.

> Corporal Anthony Antista, 29, from Monrovia, California, initially celebrated after he shot dead two Iraqi paramilitary men in a corner of the building site. But the exhilaration instantly gave way to guilt, especially for having felt glad that he had taken lives . . . The life just flowed right out of them, "he said in a pained voice. "They were like Jell-O."

Staff Sergeant Matthew St. Pierre, 28 like the rest of his platoon, had never seen any real combat, but he was a senior NCO, a more mature warrior whose years of training and preparation permitted him to respond slightly differently. He killed one Iraqi, and then he saw a wounded Iraqi reach for his weapon.

> The Staff Sergeant shot him between the shoulder blades. The man again reached for his rifle, this time more slowly. The Staff Sergeant shot him in the back of the head. When the gunfire quieted, the Staff Sergeant "eye-thumped" the Iraqi's body, to make sure he was really dead. The process involved poking the man in the eye with a rifle

muzzle, the theory being that no man alive can avoid scrunching up his face in response to such a provocation.

It was an "eerie feeling," the Staff Sergeant recalled, "like I just did what the Lord in the Bible says not to do." But he added, "we did nothing wrong. They made no attempt to surrender, and we put them down."

Another NCO, Sergeant Timothy Wolkow, 26, had a similar mild reaction when he had to kill the enemy at close range. "For a few seconds there was a kind of eerie feeling," after the first time he shot the man, he said. "It went away, and I shot the guy some more."

Lieutenant Isaac Moore, the unit's platoon leader may have been even better prepared due to the Marine Corps' intensive officer selection and training program and he may have been helped by his experience as a hunter, growing up in Alaska. "He shot his first caribou at the age of seven or eight," he told his platoon during the debriefing.

> It was thrilling to see the animal fall. When he got closer, however, he saw the caribou was still alive, convulsing in pain. The boy was unsure whether he was supposed to feel good or bad. Over years of hunting caribou, bear and other animals, he grew accustomed to eye-thumping and death.

Lieutenant Moore had also worked his way through the rationalization process ahead of time. He told his platoon about an event that had happened earlier in the day:

> A man who had escaped from one of Saddam Hussein's prisons after 13 years walked back to Baghdad to look for his family and somehow got past Marine guards at the Oil Ministry. The Marines found him curled up asleep in a corner. The man, Lieutenant Moore recounted, had acid and electric-shock burns on his legs.
>
> The people who did that to the prisoner, the Lieutenant said, are the sort of people the Marines were killing. "This is not somebody you need to worry about killing," he assured his troops. "When you stand outside the Pearly Gates or whatever you believe in, you're not going to be looked at any differently for what you did here."

Thus, when it came time for him to kill, this mature warrior leader, with a lifetime of hunting experiences, leadership training, and recent rationalization processes firmly established, had the most muted response of all.

When Lieutenant Moore looked down from a staircase in the building in Baghdad and saw three Iraqis below, he didn't hesitate. The men had been wounded by a burst of machine-gun fire, but they were still moving. The lieutenant shot one man point-blank in the head and watched the results; the next man was twitching and got the same treatment.

"It's gross, but here's the thing," the lieutenant told his Marines. "That queasy feeling—I don't get that at all."

There was absolutely nothing wrong with the warriors who responded with guilt and nausea when they killed in combat. There was also nothing wrong with the warriors who were psychologically prepared to kill and did not experience such powerful emotions. But if you had the option, which would you choose?

It is largely a twentieth century affectation, a modern, self-inflicted psychic wound, to believe that you will be mentally destroyed or emotionally harmed by the act of killing during lawful combat. I am convinced, based on interviews with hundreds of men and women who have had to kill, that if you tell yourself that killing will be an earth-shattering, traumatic event, then it probably will be. But if you do the rationalization and acceptance ahead of time, if you prepare yourself and immerse yourself in the lore and spirit of mature warriors past and present, then the lawful, legitimate use of deadly force does not have to be a self-destructive or traumatic event.

The ancient Roman stoic philosopher, Epictetus, stated it well when he wrote, "It is not the thing itself, but the view we take of it which upsets us." Indeed, there is much for modern warriors to learn from Roman stoicism. Thomas Jarrett has led a revolution in the U.S. military, introducing stoicism as both a philosophy and as a powerful form of therapy.

Again, there is nothing wrong with those who are troubled by killing, and such individuals deserve our sympathy and support. But there is absolutely nothing wrong with those who are not troubled or disturbed by it. I believe that not being psychologically injured by socially sanctioned killing has been the norm throughout history, up until the twentieth century.

Combat kills enough; it destroys enough. It is madness to let your combat experiences harm you after the battle, if you could have prevented it through prior preparation. The older you are the easier this rationalization can be. It helps if you have maturity and life experiences under your belt. But most important of all is mental preparation: to have the warrior spirit, the bulletproof mind, in place ahead of time.

When you prepare yourself for killing prior to the event, you are less likely to respond in panic, more likely to deter your opponent, and less likely to take his life inappropriately. You are also better prepared to live with the situation afterward and less likely to take your own after the event.

Once you are forced to kill in your role as a warrior, there is a set of structures in place that society has created to help you live with what you have done. I covered these processes at length in *On Killing*, but I want to give you two of them here. The first structure is that of praise and acceptance from peers and superiors. Warriors do not fight for medals, they do it for their partners, buddies and friends. When Dr. Dave Klinger asked police officers who had shot and killed in combat what was the most important source of support for them afterwards, they said it was their peers and superiors.

Here is an example of what a superior can do for a warrior. Say you are a police officer and you have killed someone in a desperate life and death gunfight. Your gun was the tool, the instrument and the key to your survival. The first thing that will happen at the scene of a police-involved shooting is that an investigator or a superior officer will take away your weapon. Suddenly, you feel naked, vulnerable, exposed, accused, condemned, and no longer having the right to carry your gun.

Fortunately, this procedure is beginning to change. While many law enforcement agencies still relieve an officer of his weapon at the scene, other agencies are now waiting until he has returned to the police station. That helps a little, but there is still another procedure that is occurring more and more around the country that has a positive and powerful impact on officers involved in shootings.

Many police officers have told me that when they had to use deadly force, a sergeant, a captain, or (in one case) even a chief put a hand on their shoulder and asked if they were okay. The conversation would go like this. The superior officer would ask the officer if someone had relieved him of his weapon, and he would say, yes. Then this warrior leader would say, "Here, take mine. I've got a backup."

Metaphorically speaking, you have been standing there buck naked in a howling breeze and a leader has taken off his jacket and wrapped it around your body at a time when you needed it the most. The simple action of your warrior leader removing his weapon from his holster and saying, "Here, take mine," has incredible, affirming power. Many of these hardened warriors choked up a little when they told me about this.

The second structure that helps the warrior is the presence of mature, older comrades who are there for them. Somewhere along your path of warriorhood, you might be forced to take a life. Afterwards, a veteran warrior will be there to help you come to terms with it, so that you grow wiser and stronger. Then someday when another warrior has to kill, it will be your turn to help, and you will say to him, "Welcome to the club," and help him through the process.

When Your Family Is In Harm's Way

Prepare for the unthinkable, as though it was inevitable.

—Tim McClung
Chief of Police, Perkins Township, Ohio

I truly have not done much compared to so many of the warriors I have interviewed, and whose stories I include in this book. But I have done a few interesting, exciting, dangerous and stressful things in my life, and throughout my warrior life, I have worked hard to prepare myself should I have to die. I do not plan on it happening soon, and I am not going down easy. I intend to be very hard to kill. But should it come to that, should I have to die for my country or my family today, I think I am as ready as any man can be. I think I can play the great game with my life as a stake and love every minute of it.

However, what I am not prepared for is some bastard putting my spouse and my kids in danger. I think that I would probably lose my professional objectivity should their lives ever be on the line. That is when it stops being a game . . . and starts becoming deadly serious.

Many warriors have told me that the worse thing that could happen is that they would suddenly be in harm's way while their loved ones were with them. If you agree, if you think that is the worst thing that could happen, then that is the most important thing you should prepare for. Consider this real-life case told to me by one warrior leader and his amazing warrior wife.

An officer got a call on a man rampaging through his house shooting a rifle. The chief of police happened to be nearby with his wife in his personal car, which had a police radio. He heard the officer ask for backup. He told dispatch he would cover the call.

At the house, the officer approached the front door as the chief covered just off to the side. His wife remained in the car, but she could see everything going on. In one explosive instant, the gunman burst from the front door armed with a .30-30 rifle and fired a round into the officer's chest killing him instantly. The chief hurled himself off to the side but a bullet smashed through his shoulder, causing arterial damage and profuse bleeding. He scrambled across the yard as .30-30 rounds kicked up chunks of dirt all around him, and took cover behind a small tree as more rounds ripped away pieces of bark.

Fading fast from blood loss and with his right arm out of commission, he used his left hand to pull his sidearm, braced it on the ground, and emptied his magazine into the wall next to the front door where the man had taken cover. It worked. The bullets penetrated the wall and the suspect collapsed to the floor with a major leg wound, and began bleeding to death. Out in the yard, the chief lay bleeding to death, too.

He was saved, however, by his wife's quick actions. As soon as she saw what was happening, she grabbed the radio microphone and, in a calm and professional voice, provided dispatch and cover cars with all the necessary information. Backup arrived quickly, secured the scene, and took care of the injured parties.

The chief's wife knew what to do because he had prepared her for this very possibility.

Have you prepared your spouse for combat? Your kids? Your parents? Everyone says that the trickiest part of preparing the spouse is when you say, "Do exactly what I tell you." (Just this once!) After that, the priority is:

> Separate yourself from me. I'm going to be drawing and returning fire. If I can, I'll move away, but you must move away from me immediately. Seek cover if you can't get away. Play dead if you can't seek cover.

One law enforcement trainer told me that he has rehearsed two signals with his wife: "Go" and "Stay." "Go" means to get out of there. "Stay" means she must put her hand on the back of his belt and use him for cover. This is one officer's answer, which makes him prepared.

It is vital that you prepare your family members to "Get help." Or, "Call 9-1-1." Or, "Use my radio." Have your loved ones rehearsed dialing 9-1-1? Remember, their fine-motor control will deteriorate, as will their near vision. Your life and their life might depend on their ability to poke 9-1-1 when their world suddenly comes unglued. If you are a police officer and you toss them your hand-held radio, do they know how to use it and know what to say? Do they know how to use your patrol car radio and know what to say? Have you told them how to identify and describe you should something happen when you are off duty? "My husband's a cop. He's got on a white shirt and blue jeans. The guy who is attacking him has on a maroon shirt. Send help for him, please." Have you told your loved ones that if you are down not to go to your body? Tell them you might be playing dead and you do not want them to deliberately enter the kill zone. Preparation, not paranoia.

Preparation. Preparation. Preparation.

Remember that in World War I, World War II and Korea more combatants were disabled by stress than were killed by the enemy. Later we will discuss posttraumatic stress disorder (PTSD) in detail. One of the most important things we will learn is that the *DSM*, the "Bible" of psychiatry and psychology, states that PTSD is caused by "intense fear, helplessness or horror," in a life-and-death situation. By teaching your loved ones what to do at the moment of truth, not only do you save lives physically, but you can also save them from the trauma of fear, helplessness and horror in their moment of truth.

Denial kills you twice: once because you are physically unprepared at the moment of truth and might die in the incident; twice because you are psychologically unprepared and, even if you physically survive, you are likely to be a psychiatric casualty when your "house of cards" collapses. Denial kills you twice, and it can kill your loved ones twice. In the same way, preparation saves you twice, and it may save your loved ones twice.

You also need to prepare your loved ones for the possibility that you may have to kill someone. We would die to protect them from what we have to do, but you also need to prepare them for what may happen, and in so doing you can make them a part of your team.

The head of the SWAT team for a Midwestern city told me how his wife responded to him having to kill someone. The shooting incident happened early in his shift and his wife had not heard about it. Later, he returned home at the usual time. He said,

> I was sitting in my chair after dinner and my wife commented, "You're kind of quiet. What's going on?"
> I said, "I had to kill someone today. I'm not sure how I feel about it."
> "Was it a good shoot? Is everything okay?"
> "Oh yeah. Everything's fine."
> Then she said, "Then what's the problem? That's what you do. I'm proud of you."

There is nothing anyone could have said that would have made it easier for him to live with what he had to do. He told me, "Colonel, my wife could say that because she's listened to the 'Bulletproof Mind' audio tapes and read your books." He had made her part of his team. He had prepared her for the possibility that he would have to kill someone. When it happened, his wife was not stunned or dismayed. She was prepared, and that is the goal.

My dad was a cop, he began his career on a beat and retired as the chief. He and my mother have both passed on and I would give anything to have another 20 minutes with them. My dad bought 20 extra years one day in a supermarket. He carried a gun nearly every day of his life, and he knew that if there was trouble my mom would grab him by his arm. So for a lifetime he always made sure she was on his left side. I almost never saw them together without my dad being on the right and my mom on his left.

One day as they shopped together in a supermarket, a man came around the corner of an aisle, saw my dad and pulled a gun. He was someone who dad had previously put in jail, and he was not a happy customer. As expected, my mom grabbed my dad's arm, his left arm. But his right hand was free and he pulled his gun. Then mom's training kicked in and she cut behind him and dashed off to call for help.

My dad resolved the situation . . . in a satisfactory manner. But I could have lost them both. I got an extra 20 years with them because my dad spent a lifetime preparing for that one day. Their grandbabies would have never known them if their grandpa had not been a warrior who carried a gun and walked the warrior's path for a lifetime in preparation for that one day.

Dr. Piazza says this to all his students:

> If you are feeling that maybe you should forget about carrying a gun or using a gun as a means of self-defense because the responsibility and liability is too great, let me validate your awareness that you do face a great responsibility and huge potential liability. However, let me remind you that there is nothing in this world more valuable than your life and the lives of your loved ones.

Rudyard Kipling put it this way in a poem about the warriors, who he called, "The Sons of Martha":

> They do not teach that their God will rouse them
>   a little before the nuts work loose.
> They do not teach that His Pity allows them
>   to drop their jobs when they dam'-well choose.
> As in the thronged and the lighted ways,
>   so in the dark and desert they stand,
> Wary and watchful all their days that their brethren's day
>   may be long in the land

Can you do that? Can you walk the warrior's path for a lifetime, standing "wary and watchful" all your days to prepare for that one day that will buy your kids and your grandkids 20 extra years with you? You might even buy someone else's grandchildren 20 extra years with them, making your brethren's day "long in the land" because you were there and you were ready.

That is what warriors do.

chapter

five

Modern Paladins Bearing the Shield: *"Go Tell the Spartans . . ."*

> It is in the darkest of times that honor and courage and service shine most brightly. So let us make this our pledge together, you and I . . . that we shall always hold true to our ways, our laws and our traditions. Then centuries yet unborn will look back on us and see, not our darkest times, but our most glorious.
>
> Dave Duncan

I use the terms "warrior" and "warriorhood" throughout this book. When you think of a warrior you might think of a Zulu warrior, an Apache warrior, or some other historic model, and while there are many models for a warrior, I use it to mean those who are willing to sacrifice themselves to defend others, those who move toward the sound of the guns, and those who continue in the face of adversity to do what needs to be done.

The warrior alone advances toward interpersonal human aggression and he is the only sane, rational creature who has any chance of functioning and even thriving in the toxic realm of combat. The degree to which he can understand, master and function in that realm is the degree to which he will survive and accomplish his mission.

There are some people who do not like the term warrior, but if you are in a war are you not a warrior? Do we have a war on crime? Is there a war on drugs? Are we now engaged in a war on terrorism? Are there people who wake up every morning determined to send you home to your family in a box?

If you are in a war then you are a warrior. On a battlefield, there are warriors and there are victims. Decide now which one you are.

Facing the Predator

> When it comes time, sheep bleat, but the knife falls anyway. Do something to survive. Don't let your mind stay with a "this can't be happening to me," attitude.
>
> —Rocky Warren
> Correspondence to Colonel Grossman

There are two types of aggression on the battlefield: defensive and predatory. The zebra is always on the defensive, always living in a constant state of stress. The lion feels no stress. The lion is the stress. Which are you: the zebra or the lion?

The lion's only real enemy is another predator: man. Our worst enemy is also the human predator. Fortunately the true predator, the sociopath who feeds without remorse on his own kind, is rare. Still, you should never assume that he is not out there. Usually, the predator does not give any verbal cues; he stands calmly and then attacks violently, forcing you to react to his action. It is quite possible he will get off the first shot and the odds are that you might get hit. Should that happen, never believe that the fight is over. Your warrior mindset will replace the shock and fear and you will go on; you will continue to fight. When a sheep gets bit they go "Baa," roll over and die. When a sheepdog gets bit, he gets pissed off and bites you back. A warrior meets the predator and survives.

Consider a police-involved shooting that happened in Portland, Oregon, as I was writing this very section. A uniformed officer responded on a radio call to a check-cashing store regarding a 16-year-old male passing a bad check. As the officer was applying the handcuffs, the kid spun around, pulled a pistol from his waistband, and fired into the officer's face. The bullet struck the officer in his left eyebrow, traveled under his skin, and exited behind his left ear. Two subsequent rounds whizzed by his face.

Shots were exchanged in the lobby, and then a running gun battle ensued in which several more rounds were fired. The suspect eventually collapsed in an adjacent driveway with bullets in his pelvis, chest and abdomen. The shot officer kept him covered as he called for backup, and not until other officers arrived on the scene did he collapse.

Later when asked by the press how the officer was doing, the chief said that his head was sore but he was really angry with the kid for shooting at him.

Whether you are a peacekeeper in Bosnia or a police officer on the street, you go where the predator is. When our soldiers go into a cave in Afghanistan, they go into his lair, which means he has the home court advantage. When our police officers go into a predator's house and into his bar, they are going into his lair. In nature the predator in his lair almost never loses because he is going up against predatory and defensive aggression. That is why the lion tamer goes into the cage before the lion. If he did it the other way around, the crowd would be paying to see an entirely different show.

Thus the mission is hard and the deck is stacked against you. But a warrior, with proper training and mindset can and will survive.

Complacency is the Enemy

> Your lifestyle should not be comfortable. It should be comforting.
>
> —Anonymous

You must train to fight with intent and will, not fear and panic, and never with complacency. Consider what happened in a West Coast city to an experienced warrant-delivery team, trained officers who in the past had delivered a hundred no-knock drug warrants a year. In preparation to serve a warrant on one drug dealer, they first met at a local fire station, loaded into the SWAT van, pulled into the suspect's backyard, and streamed up to the backdoor. To their surprise, the door was unlocked, so the officer with the ram just stepped inside, an action that might have confused the rest of the formation. Their regular number two man was in court that morning, which also added to the confusion.

As they shouted, "Police! Search warrant!" the number one man went in to the left, the new number two man, Officer B, went right and the number three man moved in to back up the number one man. The number four man should have been covering Officer B, but he went in the wrong direction. Thus Officer B was moving alone down a hallway when a teenage kid, naked and clutching a high capacity pistol, stepped into the hallway and began firing.

Now, the SWAT team had all been issued Kevlar helmets, but since some of the officers thought they were awkward and bulky they had been made optional. So Officer B, minus his helmet, crouched in the narrow hallway as the naked teenager's bullets punched through the officer's skull, ripping through his forebrain, midbrain, and hindbrain.

Officer B's first shot blew off one of the kid's testicles, and then the officer kept pulling the trigger as he spun down to the floor, putting one bullet into a wall and another into a door. His last, dying shot struck the family television.

When the other team members heard the gunshots, they literally tripped over each other getting out the door. When they realized that Officer B was not with them, they grabbed a shield and streamed back into the house, finding the suspect standing over Officer B's dead body. A spray of bullets dropped the suspect.

The suspect's mother had been in a back bedroom and came out when the shooting ended, screaming, "My son is a cop! What are you doing? My son is a cop. Why is this happening?" Although the suspect's big brother was a law enforcement officer on the same department as the warrant delivery team, the team had a legitimate and lawful reason to go in after the suspect. They got their man, but two law enforcement families were shattered that day. Let's examine what they did wrong.

First, they did not rehearse. U.S. Army evaluation standards require that combat patrols always conduct a rehearsal, no matter how many times similar missions have been conducted. Warriors are required to rehearse two things: actions on the objective and actions on enemy contact. If the team had spent just 30 seconds rehearsing their entry in the fire station prior to going out to the scene, the operation would have gone more smoothly. Yes, 99 times out of 100 the team had performed problem free entries, but this was the one time when things went wrong, a time when there had been no rehearsal.

Nor did they rehearse their actions on enemy contact. So when shots rang out from a back hallway, everyone banged into each other getting out the door, leaving a fellow warrior inside dying on the floor. Always rehearse actions on the objective and always rehearse actions on enemy contact.

Warriors always inspect their equipment prior to a mission. If you are a leader, you check your people to ensure they have all the equipment they need to stay alive, including their helmet. A Kevlar helmet will stop pistol rounds all day long, but only if you are wearing it. If not, it is useless. A warrior will not be caught without his equipment, and a warrior leader makes his people do the right thing.

Warriorhood is infectious—it is communicable. And effective warrior leaders transmit it to their people. When I look back on my years as a military leader, there are a couple of instances that make me shudder. We are all human and complacency tries to seduce us all. Sometimes we fall short of the warrior standard. Fortunately, I had some magnificent warrior leaders who put a boot in my rear whenever I slipped off the warrior path.

Sometimes your warrior peers can transmit a sense of warriorhood. The expectations of your brothers in arms and your responsibility to them can help you do the right thing. Jigoro Kano, the founder of Judo, said that as a warrior, you should, "Train half for yourself and half for your partner." Since warrior comrades and even warrior subordinates hold you to a high standard, you never want to let them down. When you surround yourself with such individuals, they help pull you up the warrior path, and you help each other fight complacency.

Complacency is the enemy, and we must help each other in the battle against this deadly foe. We do our rehearsals. We do our inspections. We are prepared every day. General Peter J. Schoomaker, the U.S. Army Chief of Staff put it this way:

> Real warriors never take their eyes off the horizon. You're like a wild animal in the woods. You pay attention to your instincts. You've always got your rifle within reach.

To be transformed into a warrior, you must study warriors. Now, John Wayne might be an appropriate warrior model, but you must not internalize the Dirty Harry philosophy or any other out-of-control nutcase we see portrayed by Hollywood. These are whackos and avengers. They are great subjects for television and movies, but they make poor warriors. You must dedicate yourself towards doing your job with righteousness and decency.

Dr. Paul Whitesell quotes from a letter by an ancient Greek warrior leader who was writing from the front lines to the city fathers. In it he said this:

> Of every 100 men that they send me, 10 should not be here. Eighty are nothing but targets. Nine are real fighters, they the battle make. Ah, but the one, he is a warrior, and he will bring the others back.

To bring the other 99 back is your job as a warrior. That is what your society calls upon you to do. While every other creature flees from the sound of the guns, you move toward them. Draw from the tradition and the heritage of the past.

On Sheep, Wolves and Sheepdogs

> Honor never grows old, and honor rejoices the heart of age. It does so because honor is, finally, about defending those noble and worthy things that deserve defending, even if it comes at a high cost. In our time, that may mean social disapproval, public scorn, hardship, persecution, or as always, even death itself. The question remains: What is worth defending? What is worth dying for? What is worth living for?
>
> —William J. Bennett
> In a lecture to the United States Naval Academy
> November 24, 1997

One Vietnam veteran, an old retired Colonel, once said this to me: "Most of the people in our society are sheep. They are kind, gentle, productive creatures who can only hurt one another by accident." This is true. Remember, the murder rate is six per 100,000 per year, and the aggravated assault rate is four per 1,000 per year. What this means is that the vast majority of Americans are not inclined to hurt one another.

Some estimates say that two million Americans are victims of violent crimes every year, a tragic, staggering number, perhaps an all-time record rate of violent crime. But there are almost 300 million Americans, which means that the odds of being a victim of violent crime is considerably less than one in a hundred on any given year. Furthermore, since many violent crimes are committed by repeat offenders, the actual number of violent citizens is considerably less than two million.

Thus there is a paradox, and we must grasp both ends of the situation: We may well be in the most violent times in history, but violence is still remarkably rare. This is because most citizens are kind, decent people who are not capable of hurting each other, except by accident or under extreme provocation. They are sheep.

I mean nothing negative by calling them sheep. To me it is like the pretty, blue robin's egg. Inside it is soft and gooey but someday it will grow into something wonderful. But the egg cannot survive without its hard blue shell. Police officers, soldiers and other warriors are like that shell, and someday the civilization they protect will grow into something wonderful. For now, though, they need warriors to protect them from the predators.

"Then there are the wolves," the old war veteran said, "and the wolves feed on the sheep without mercy." Do you believe there are wolves out there who will feed on the flock without mercy? You better believe it. There are evil men in this world and they are capable of evil deeds. The moment you forget that or pretend it is not so, you become a sheep. There is no safety in denial.

"Then there are sheepdogs," he went on, "and I'm a sheepdog. I live to protect the flock and confront the wolf." Or, as a sign in one California law enforcement agency put it, "We intimidate those who intimidate others."

If you have no capacity for violence then you are a healthy productive citizen: a sheep. If you have a capacity for violence and no empathy for your fellow citizens, then you have defined an aggressive sociopath—a wolf. But what if you have a capacity for violence, and a deep love for your fellow citizens? Then you are a sheepdog, a warrior, someone who is walking the hero's path. Someone who can walk into the heart of darkness, into the universal human phobia, and walk out unscathed.

The Gift of Aggression

> What goes on around you . . . compares little with what goes on inside you.
>
> —Ralph Waldo Emerson

Everyone has been given a gift in life. Some people have a gift for science and some have a flair for art. And warriors have been given the gift of aggression. They would no more misuse this gift than a doctor would misuse his healing arts, but they yearn for the opportunity to use their gift to help others. These people, the ones who have been blessed with the gift of aggression and a love for others, are our sheepdogs. These are our warriors.

One career police officer wrote to me about this after attending one of my "Bulletproof Mind" training sessions:

> I want to say thank you for finally shedding some light on why it is that I can do what I do. I always knew why I did it. I love my [citizens], even the bad ones, and had a talent that I could return to my

community. I just couldn't put my finger on why I could wade through the chaos, the gore, the sadness, if given a chance try to make it all better, and walk right out the other side.

Let me expand on this old soldier's excellent model of the sheep, wolves, and sheepdogs. We know that the sheep live in denial; that is what makes them sheep. They do not want to believe that there is evil in the world. They can accept the fact that fires can happen, which is why they want fire extinguishers, fire sprinklers, fire alarms and fire exits throughout their kids' schools. But many of them are outraged at the idea of putting an armed police officer in their kid's school. Our children are dozens of times more likely to be killed, and thousands of times more likely to be seriously injured, by school violence than by school fires, but the sheep's only response to the possibility of violence is denial. The idea of someone coming to kill or harm their children is just too hard, so they choose the path of denial.

The sheep generally do not like the sheepdog. He looks a lot like the wolf. He has fangs and the capacity for violence. The difference, though, is that the sheepdog must not, cannot and will not ever harm the sheep. Any sheepdog who intentionally harms the lowliest little lamb will be punished and removed. The world cannot work any other way, at least not in a representative democracy or a republic such as ours.

Still, the sheepdog disturbs the sheep. He is a constant reminder that there are wolves in the land. They would prefer that he didn't tell them where to go, or give them traffic tickets, or stand at the ready in our airports in camouflage fatigues holding an M-16. The sheep would much rather have the sheepdog cash in his fangs, spray paint himself white, and go, "Baa."

Until the wolf shows up. Then the entire flock tries desperately to hide behind one lonely sheepdog. As Kipling said in his poem about "Tommy" the British soldier:

While it's Tommy this, an' Tommy that, an' "Tommy, fall be' ind,"
But it's "Please to walk in front, sir," when there's trouble in the wind,
There's trouble in the wind, my boys, there's trouble in the wind,
O it's "Please to walk in front, sir," when there's trouble in the wind.

The students, the victims, at Columbine High School were big, tough high school students, and under ordinary circumstances they would not have had the time of day for a police officer. They were not bad kids; they just had nothing to say to a cop. When the school was under attack, however, and SWAT teams were clearing the rooms and hallways, the officers had to physically peel those clinging, sobbing kids off of them. This is how the little lambs feel about their sheepdog when the wolf is at the door. Look at what happened after September 11, 2001, when the wolf pounded hard on the door. Remember how America, more than ever before, felt differently about their law enforcement officers and military personnel? Remember how many times you heard the word *hero*?

And how long did that last? Give credit where it is due: a lot of people stayed alert to the threat and kept their hearts and heads right. But many of them, far too many of them, quickly forgot. They are sheep: they sink back into denial. They are sheep, they have two speeds: "graze" and "stampede."

Understand that there is nothing morally superior about being a sheepdog; it is just what you choose to be. Also understand that a sheepdog is a funny critter: He is always sniffing around out on the perimeter, checking the breeze, barking at things that go bump in the night, and yearning for a righteous battle. That is, the young sheepdogs yearn for a righteous battle. The old sheepdogs are a little older and wiser, but they move to the sound of the guns when needed right along with the young ones.

Here is how the sheep and the sheepdog think differently. The sheep pretend the wolf will never come, but the sheepdog lives for that day. After the attacks on September 11, 2001, most of the sheep, that is, most citizens in America said, "Thank God I wasn't on one of those planes." The sheepdogs, the warriors, said, "Dear God, I wish I could have been on one of those planes. Maybe I could have made a difference." When you are truly transformed into a warrior and have truly invested yourself into warriorhood, you want to be there. You want to be able to make a difference.

While there is nothing morally superior about the sheepdog, the warrior, he does have one real advantage. Only one. He is able to survive and thrive in an environment that destroys 98 percent of the population.

There was research conducted a few years ago with individuals convicted of violent crimes. These cons were in prison for serious, predatory acts of violence: assaults, murders and killing law enforcement officers. The vast majority said that they specifically targeted victims by body language: slumped walk, passive behavior and lack of awareness. They chose their victims like big cats do in Africa, when they select one out of the herd that is least able to protect itself.

However, when there were cues given by potential victims that indicated they would not go easily, the cons said that they would walk away. If the cons sensed that the target was a "counter-predator," that is, a sheepdog, they would leave him alone unless there was no other choice but to engage.

One police officer told me that he rode a commuter train to work each day. One day, as usual, he was standing in the crowded car, dressed in blue jeans, T-shirt and jacket, holding onto a pole and reading a paperback. At one of the stops, two street toughs boarded, shouting and cursing and doing every obnoxious thing possible to intimidate the other riders. The officer continued to read his book, though he kept a watchful eye on the two punks as they strolled along the aisle making comments to female passengers, and banging shoulders with men as they passed.

As they approached the officer, he lowered his novel and made eye contact with them. "You got a problem, man?" one of the IQ-challenged punks asked. "You think you're tough, or somethin'?" the other asked, obviously offended that this one was not shirking away from them.

"As a matter of fact, I am tough," the officer said, calmly and with a steady gaze.

The two looked at him for a long moment, and then without saying a word, turned and moved back down the aisle to continue their taunting of the other passengers, the sheep.

Some people may be destined to be sheep and others might be genetically primed to be wolves or sheepdogs. But I believe that most people can choose which one they want to be, and I'm proud to say that more and more Americans are choosing to become sheepdogs.

Seven months after the attack on September 11, 2001, Todd Beamer was honored in his hometown of Cranbury, New Jersey. Todd, as you recall, was the man on Flight 93 over Pennsylvania who called on his cell phone to alert an operator from United Airlines about the hijacking. When he learned of the other three passenger planes that had been used as weapons, Todd dropped his phone and uttered the words, "Let's roll," which authorities believe was a signal to the other passengers to confront the terrorist hijackers. In one hour, a transformation occurred among the passengers—athletes, business people and parents—from sheep to sheepdogs and together they fought the wolves, ultimately saving an unknown number of lives on the ground.

"Do You Have Any Idea How Hard It Would Be to Live with Yourself After That?"

There is no safety for honest men except by believing all possible evil of evil men.

—Edmund Burke
Reflections on the Revolution in France

Here is the point I like to emphasize, especially to the thousands of police officers and soldiers I speak to each year. In nature the sheep, real sheep, are born as sheep. Sheepdogs are born that way, and so are wolves. They didn't have a choice. But you are not a critter. As a human being, you can be whatever you want to be. It is a conscious, moral decision.

If you want to be a sheep, then you can be a sheep and that is okay, but you must understand the price you pay. When the wolf comes, you and your loved ones are going to die if there is not a sheepdog there to protect you. If you want to be a wolf, you can be one, but the sheepdogs are going to hunt you down and you will never have rest, safety, trust or love. But if you want to be a sheepdog and walk the warrior's path, then you must make a conscious and moral decision every day to dedicate, equip and prepare yourself to thrive in that toxic, corrosive moment when the wolf comes knocking at the door.

For example, many officers carry their weapons in church. They are well concealed in ankle holsters, shoulder holsters or inside-the-belt holsters tucked into the small of their backs. Anytime you go to some form of religious service, there is a very good chance that a police officer in your congregation is carrying. You will never know if there is such an individual in your place of worship, until the wolf appears to slaughter you and your loved ones.

I was training a group of police officers in Texas, and during the break, one officer asked his friend if he carried his weapon in church. The other cop replied, "I will never be caught without my gun in church." I asked why he felt so strongly about this, and he told me about a police officer he knew who was at a church massacre in Ft. Worth, Texas, in 1999. In that incident, a mentally deranged individual came into the church and opened fire, gunning down 14 people. He said that officer believed he could have saved every life that day if he had been carrying his gun. His own son was shot, and all he could do was throw himself on the boy's body and wait for him to die. That cop looked me in the eye and said, "Do you have any idea how hard it would be to live with yourself after that?"

Some individuals would be horrified if they knew this police officer was carrying a weapon in church. They might call him paranoid and would probably scorn him. Yet these same individuals would be enraged and would call for "heads to roll" if they found out that the airbags in their cars were defective, or that the fire extinguisher and fire sprinklers in their kids' school did not work. They can accept the fact that fires and traffic accidents can happen and that there must be safeguards against them. Their only response to the wolf, though, is denial, and all too often their response to the sheepdog is scorn and disdain. But the sheepdog quietly asks himself, "Do you have any idea how hard it would be to live with yourself if your loved ones were attacked and killed, and you had to stand there helplessly because you were unprepared for that day?"

The warrior must cleanse denial from his thinking. Coach Bob Lindsey, a renowned law enforcement trainer, says that warriors must practice "when/then" thinking, not "if/when." Instead of saying, "If it happens then I will take action," the warrior says, "When it happens then I will be ready."

It is denial that turns people into sheep. Sheep are psychologically destroyed by combat because their only defense is denial, which is counterproductive and destructive, resulting in fear, helplessness and horror when the wolf shows up.

Denial kills you twice. It kills you once, at your moment of truth when you are not physically prepared: You didn't bring your gun; you didn't train. Your only defense was wishful thinking. Hope is not a strategy. Denial kills you a second time because even if you do physically survive, you are psychologically shattered by fear, helplessness, horror and shame at your moment of truth.

Chuck Yeager, the famous test pilot and first man to fly faster than the speed of sound, says that he knew he could die. There was no denial for him. He did not allow himself the luxury of denial. This acceptance of reality can cause fear, but it is a healthy, controlled fear that will keep you alive:

> I was always afraid of dying. Always. It was my fear that made me learn everything I could about my airplane and my emergency equipment, and kept me flying respectful of my machine and always alert in the cockpit.
>
> —Brigadier General Chuck Yeager
> *Yeager, An Autobiography*

Gavin de Becker puts it like this in *Fear Less*, his superb post-9/11 book, which should be required reading for anyone trying to come to terms with our current world situation:

> . . . denial can be seductive, but it has an insidious side effect. For all the peace of mind deniers think they get by saying it isn't so, the fall they take when faced with new violence is all the more unsettling. Denial is a save-now-pay-later scheme, a contract written entirely in small print, for in the long run, the denying person knows the truth on some level.

And so the warrior must strive to confront denial in all aspects of his life, and prepare himself for the day when evil comes.

If you are a warrior who is legally authorized to carry a weapon and you step outside without that weapon, then you become a sheep, pretending that the bad man will not come today. No one can be "on" 24/7 for a lifetime. Everyone needs down time. But if you are authorized to carry a weapon, and you walk outside without it, just take a deep breath, and say this to yourself . . . "Baa."

This business of being a sheep or a sheepdog is not a yes-no dichotomy. It is not an all-or-nothing, either-or choice. It is a matter of degrees, a continuum. On one end is an abject, head-in-the-grass sheep and on the other end is the ultimate warrior. Few people exist completely on one end or the other. Most of us live somewhere in between. Since 9-11 almost everyone in America took a step up that continuum, away from denial. The sheep took a few steps toward accepting and appreciating their warriors, and the warriors started taking their job more seriously. The degree to which you move up that continuum, away from sheephood and denial, is the degree to which you and your loved ones will survive, physically and psychologically at your moment of truth.

You're Not a Warrior Until You Taste Them

An SAS Soldier's Prayer

Give me, my God, what You still have;
give me what no one asks for.
I do not ask for wealth, nor for success,
nor even health.
People ask you so often, God, for all that,
that You cannot have any of left.

Give me God, what You still have.
Give me what people refuse to accept from You.
I want insecurity and disquietude;
I want turmoil and brawl.

And if you should give them to me,
my God, once and for all,
let me be sure to have them always,
for I will not always
have the courage to ask for them.

Give me, my God, what You have left over,
Give me what others want nothing to do with.
But give me courage too,
And strength and faith;
For You alone can give
What one cannot demand from oneself.
                    —Prayer found on Lieutenant Andre Zirnheld, SAS
                            Killed in action on July 26, 1941

While the sheep does not always care for the sheepdog, the warrior cares about the sheep. He hurts, suffers and weeps for those he is sworn to protect. Here is a powerful narrative that circulated on several law enforcement forums on the Internet. I have not been able to identify the author, but this anonymous police officer captures the heart and soul of those warriors who lay it on the line for us every day.

The department was all astir. There was a lot of laughing and joking due to all the new officers, myself included, hitting the streets today for the first time. After months of a seemingly endless amount of classes, paperwork, and lectures, we were finally done with the police academy and ready to join the ranks of our department. All you could see were rows of cadets with huge smiles and polished badges.

As we sat in the briefing room, we could barely sit still as we anxiously waited our turn to be introduced and given our beat assignment or, for the layperson, our own portion of the city to "serve and protect."

It was then that he walked in. A statue of a man—6 foot 3 and 230 pounds of solid muscle. He had black hair with highlights of gray and steely eyes that made you feel nervous even when he wasn't looking at you. He had a reputation for being the biggest and the smartest officer to ever work our fair city. He had been in the department for longer than anyone could remember and those years of service had made him into somewhat of a legend.

The new guys, or "rookies" as he called us, both respected and feared him. When he spoke, even the most seasoned officers paid attention. It was almost a privilege when one of the rookies got to be around when he would tell one of his police stories about the old days. But we knew our place and never interrupted for fear of being shooed away. He was respected and revered by all who knew him.

After my first year on the department, I still had never heard or saw him speak to any of the rookies for any length of time. When he did speak to them, all he would say was, "So, you want to be a policeman do you, hero? I'll tell you what, when you can tell me what they taste like, then you can call yourself a real policeman."

This particular phrase I had heard dozens of times. Me and my buddies all had bets about "what they taste like" actually referred to. Some believed it referred to the taste of your own blood after a hard fight. Others thought it referred to the taste of sweat after a long day's work.

Being on the department for a year, I thought I knew just about everyone and everything. So one afternoon, I mustered up the courage and walked up to him. When he looked down at me, I said, "You know, I think I've paid my dues. I've been in plenty of fights, made dozens of arrests, and sweated my butt off just like everyone else. So what does that little saying of yours mean anyway?"

With that, he merely stated, "Well, seeing as how you've said and done it all, you tell me what it means, hero." When I had no answer, he shook his head and snickered, "rookies," and walked away.

The next evening was to be the worst one to date. The night started out slow, but as the evening wore on, the calls became more frequent and dangerous. I made several small arrests and then had a real knock down drag out fight. However, I was able to make the arrest without hurting the suspect or myself. After that, I was looking forward to just letting the shift wind down and getting home to my wife and daughter.

I had just glanced at my watch and it was 11:55, five more minutes and I would be on my way to the house. I don't know if it was fatigue or just my imagination, but as I drove down one of the streets on my beat, I thought I saw my daughter standing on someone else's porch. I looked again. It wasn't her, but it was a child about my daughter's age, six or seven years old and dressed in an oversized shirt that hung to her feet. She was clutching an old rag doll that looked older than me.

I immediately stopped my patrol car to see what she was doing alone outside her house at such an hour. When I approached, there seemed to be a sigh of relief on her face. I had to laugh to myself, thinking she sees the hero policeman come to save the day. I knelt at her side and asked what she was doing outside.

"My mommy and daddy just had a really big fight and now mommy won't wake up," she said.

My mind was reeling. Now what do I do? I instantly called for backup and ran to the nearest window. As I looked inside I saw a man standing over a lady with his hands covered in blood, her blood. I kicked open the door, pushed the man aside and checked for a pulse, but I was unable to find one. I immediately cuffed the man and began doing CPR on the lady. It was then I heard a small voice from behind me.

"Mr. Policeman, please make my mommy wake up."

I continued to perform CPR until my backup and medics arrived. But they said it was too late, she was dead.

I looked at the man, who said, "I don't know what happened. She was yelling at me to stop drinking and to get a job, and I had just had enough. I shoved her so she would leave me alone and she fell and hit her head."

As I walked the man out to the car in handcuffs, I again saw that little girl. In the five minutes that had passed, I had gone from hero to monster. Not only was I unable to wake up her mommy, but now I was taking her daddy away too.

Before I left the scene, I thought I would talk to the little girl. To say what, I don't know. Maybe just to tell her I was sorry about her mommy and daddy. But when I approached, she turned away. I knew it was useless, and that I would probably make it worse.

As I sat in the locker room at the station, I kept replaying the whole thing in my mind. Maybe if I would have been faster or done something different, just maybe that little girl would still have her mother. And even though it may sound selfish, I would still be the hero.

I felt a large hand on my shoulder, and I heard that all too familiar question: "Well, hero, what do they taste like?"

Before I could get mad or shout some sarcastic remark, I realized that all the pent up emotions had flooded to the surface, and there was a steady stream of tears rolling down my face. It was at that moment that I realized the answer to his question: tears.

He started to walk away but then stopped. "You know, there was nothing you could have done differently," he said. "Sometimes you can do everything right and the outcome doesn't change. You may not be the hero you once thought you were, but now you are a police officer."

—Author unknown

The sheepdog is cursed and blessed with the capacity for violence and a profound love for the flock. That is what makes the warrior different from the wolf.

Since all the school shootings, and the terrorist attacks on the World Trade Center and the Pentagon, the sheep have figured out that the wolf is not only at the door, but he is also in the house and in their kids' schools. The wolf is loose and now the sheep—or at least most of them—suddenly like their sheepdog. At least for a while, we are becoming a nation that is appreciating their warriors in a way that has not been seen since the end of World War II. And that is a good thing, as long as they are righteous warriors, noble warriors who love their flock and are truly dedicated to their protection.

Knights and Paladins

Nothing is so strong as gentleness; nothing so gentle as real strength.

—Francis de Sales

The 7-year-old girl clutched a piece of metal wrapped in a handkerchief tightly to her chest as she retold the horrible details of sexual abuse she had suffered four years earlier.

When she glanced at the faces of the jurors or felt the hot stare of the defendant, she squeezed the handkerchief ever more tightly and locked her eyes on the face of Michigan State Police Trooper Jeffrey Miazga.

St. Joseph County Prosecutor Douglas Fisher knew his August 2002 case against the pedophile rested squarely on the testimony of the young girl who had frozen on the stand an hour earlier, unable then to utter anything but her name.

St. Joseph County Circuit Judge James Noecker granted Fisher a recess, but more than an hour of begging, cajoling and reasoning by the victim's adoptive parents and her psychologist were unable to temper her terror and convince her to return to the stand. Fisher watched as his case unraveled, knowing dismissal would free the perpetrator and leave the child's psychological and physical wounds unassailed.

Just as Fisher was preparing to return to the courtroom without his young witness, the man in the blue trooper's uniform pulled his chair close to the girl and acknowledged that he also felt fear at times as a police officer.

"He bent over and spoke to her in a very quiet and private manner," Fisher recalled. "He shared with her his secret that many of the things he had to do as a Michigan State Trooper made him very much afraid."

As the young girl's eyes widened and her tears slowed, Miagza removed the silver shield from his uniform shirt, wrapped it in a handkerchief, and placed it in her hand.

"He told her how his Michigan State Police badge is what protected him and made him safe," Fisher said. " . . . He told her the thought of his badge protecting him gave him the courage to go ahead and do his job. [Trooper Miagza] told her whenever she became afraid, she should squeeze the badge and that would give her the courage to go ahead and testify. She took the badge, held it tightly, and promised him she would try."

Miazga was honored by the St. Joseph County Criminal Justice Council Friday for his empathy and creativity which allowed the young girl to return to the stand in August, delivering testimony which convinced a jury to convict Shaun Roberts of first-degree criminal sexual conduct.

The case, which resulted in a life sentence for Roberts, remains emotional for Fisher who wiped tears from his eyes Friday as Lieutenant Mike Risko, White Pigeon State Police Post commander, read aloud Fisher's commendation letter.

"When he admitted to her his secret fear and the way that he was able to overcome it, he was able to lend her both his badge and his courage."

—"Michigan State Police trooper earns honors"
Kathy Jessup, *Sturgis Journal*, Sturgis, Michigan

The best model for the warrior to internalize is that of the knights of old. The knight donned armor, hung a weapon on his hip and a shield on his left side. On that shield was the authority by which he went forth and did good deeds and administered justice in the land. Eventually, gunpowder defeated armor and the knights went away. Today for the first time in centuries there are warriors (law enforcement officers) who don armor every day, hang a weapon on their hip and a shield on their left side. On that shield is the authority by which they go forth and administer justice and do good deeds. If that is not a knight, a paladin, if that is not a new order of chivalry, then what is?

The ancient knight is part myth, and part truth. Some knights were brutal thugs, but many of them were true paladins, struggling to maintain a standard for nobility and decency that echoes down to this very day. One of those who set a widely accepted standard for knighthood as a protector of the innocent was the Dutch theologian Desiderius Erasmus. He is the author of "Enchiridion Militis Christiani" (which translates roughly to "Guide for the Righteous Protector"), written in 1503. This profoundly influential manual guided the knight (the police officer of the day), by establishing 22 principles for being strong and remaining virtuous in a dangerous world.

In 1514 the artist Albrecht Durer, inspired by Erasmus, carved the image of the "Knight, Death, and the Devil." The subject has been interpreted as the Knight (with his dog) embarking on a righteous mission, invulnerable to the rotting corpse of Death riding beside him (mortality), and the horned Devil behind (temptation). The Knight appears to be riding through the "Valley of the Shadow of Death," yet he fears not. Determined in his righteous mission, the Knight looks ahead, drawing on his faith to give him the moral courage to confront evil.

A full list of Erasmus' 22 principles can be found in the Appendix A at the end of this book. For now, consider these sample guidelines for the behavior of a paladin, written 500 years ago, and see how they still apply to warriors today:

MAKE VIRTUE THE ONLY GOAL OF YOUR LIFE.
Dedicate all your enthusiasm, all your effort, your leisure as well as your business.

TRAIN YOUR MIND TO DISTINGUISH GOOD AND EVIL.
Let your rule of government be determined by the common good.

NEVER LET ANY SETBACK STOP YOU IN YOUR QUEST.
We are not perfect—this only means we should try harder.

ALWAYS BE PREPARED FOR AN ATTACK.
Careful generals set guards even in times of peace.

SPIT, AS IT WERE, IN THE FACE OF DANGER.
Keep a stirring quotation with you for encouragement.

TREAT EACH BATTLE AS THOUGH IT WERE YOUR LAST.
And you will finish, in the end, victorious!

DON'T ASSUME THAT DOING GOOD ALLOWS YOU
TO KEEP A FEW VICES.
The enemy you ignore the most is the one who conquers you.

NEVER ADMIT DEFEAT, EVEN IF YOU HAVE BEEN WOUNDED.
The good soldier's painful wounds spur him to gather his strength.

SPEAK WITH YOURSELF THIS WAY:
If I do what I am considering, would I want my family to know about it?

LIFE CAN BE SAD, DIFFICULT, AND QUICK:
MAKE IT COUNT FOR SOMETHING!
Since we do not know when death will come, act honorably everyday.

Many warrior cultures nurture such values. The Sikhs put it this way:

He is the true hero who fights to protect the helpless.
Great warriors are those whose humility is their breastplate.
Without fear, they advance.
By conquering the vices,
They find that they have also conquered the whole world.

Guarding the Gates and Fighting in the Shade

> Miles to go before we rest. But it is easy for we fight in the shade.
> —Lieutenant Colonel Mark Byington
> Missouri Police Corps

The Spartans are another ancient warrior culture that we can learn from. At Thermoplye, a narrow pass above the crystalline Aegean, in 480 B.C., 300 Spartans volunteered to delay the invading army of Xerxes, King of Persia. For 2,500 years they have been called the "300 Immortals." There was no question the Spartans would perish. The Persians told them, "There are so many of us that when we fire our arrows it darkens the sky."

"Good," replied one old Spartan warrior, "then we will fight in the shade."

The Persians felt great admiration and respect for the Spartan courage and audacity. They told the Spartans that they would be given great wealth and a place of honor in the Persian army if they just laid down their shields and handed over their swords.

"Molon labe," replied the Spartan king: "Come and get them."

So the Persians attacked, and the Spartans fought, buying precious days for the rest of the Greek civilization to prepare. For several days the Spartans held against outrageous odds as wave after wave of fresh Persian troops broke upon the Spartan shield wall. But finally their line collapsed and they died to a man, including their king. The Persians buried them where they fell and moved on. Days later the Greeks defeated the Persian army, and today these words are carved in a plaque mounted to the walls of Thermoplye:

> Go tell the Spartans, stranger passing by,
> that here, obedient to their laws, we lie.

Nearly 2,500 years later, on September 11, 2001, 3,000 of our citizens died in a single day. Among them were more than 300 immortals—firefighters and police officers—who charged up the steps of the World Trade Center, clearing blockage, expediting the flow, saving hundreds perhaps thousands of lives. Peggy Noonan crafted these powerful words to articulate why the actions of these modern day immortals were so remarkable:

> They weren't there, they went there. They didn't run from the fire, they ran into the fire. They didn't run down the staircase, they ran up the staircase. They didn't lose their lives, they gave them.

The first building came down and it darkened the sky. And they fought in the shade. The second building fell, and more than 300 immortals lay buried in the rubble, including their chief.

Go tell the Spartans, stranger passing by, that here, obedient to their laws, we still lie! There are still warriors in the land, who will move to the summons of the trumpet, who will march to the sound of the guns.

"Obedient to their laws . . ." What are the laws to which these warriors remained obedient unto death? Well, the Spartan knights considered their shield to be sacred. It protected not just them, but their brother on their left, their city and their civilization. Steven Pressfield in his superb book, *The Gates of Fire*, translates a Spartan oath about their shield. Read these words, read the "Law of the Shield" and think about those firefighters and police officers bearing the shield as they went up the steps of the World Trade Center.

> This is my shield,
> I bear it before me in battle,
> But it is not mine alone.
> It protects my brother on my left.
> It protects my city.
> I will never let my brother out of its shadow,
> Nor my city out of its shelter.
> I will die
> With my shield before me
> Facing the enemy.

Today, police officers and firefighters are the shield: they bear the shield in defense of their cities and they obey the Law of the Shield. Our military is the sword, rooting the enemy out of their holes in distant lands. They are joined and supported by judges, educators, emergency medical personnel, social workers, and countless other "knights without armor in a savage land." They are all warriors, paladins of all kinds and professions who are willing to risk life and limb for us.

In these new dark ages there is a new warrior who has risen to the occasion. While every other creature flees from the sound of the guns, the warrior goes 100 miles an hour to get to a gunfight, because combat, the universal human phobia, is his realm.

The *Marine Hymn* says that when we get to the gates of heaven we are going to find them guarded by United States Marines. It may be that the highest honor a warrior can aspire to is to guard the Pearly Gates. Here on earth, the highest honor to which a warrior can aspire is to guard the gates of his city and his civilization in this dark hour. To do this formidable task competently, to be successful, the warrior must be the master of his realm—the realm of combat.

On February 15, 2002, about 25 men representing three different Special Forces and three CIA paramilitary units gathered outside of Gardez, Afghanistan, in the East, about 40 miles from the Pakistani border. It was very cold, and they were bundled in camping or outdoor clothing. No one was in uniform. Many had beards. The men stood or kneeled on this desolate site in front of a helicopter. An American flag was standing in the background. There was a pile or rocks arranged as a tombstone over a buried piece of the World Trade Center . . .

One of the men read a prayer. Then he said, "We consecrate this spot as an everlasting memorial to the brave Americans who died on September 11, so that all who would seek to do her harm will know that America will not stand by and watch terror prevail.

"We will export death and violence to the four corners of the earth in defense of this great nation."

—Bob Woodward
Bush at War

six

The Evolution of Combat: *The Physical and Psychological Leverage That Enables Killing in War and Peace*

This is the law: The purpose of fighting is to win. There is no possible victory in defense. The sword is more important than the shield and skill is more important than either. The final weapon is the brain. All else is supplemental.

—John Steinbeck
"The Law"

Humans have proven themselves to be infinitely ingenious at creating and using devices to overcome their limitations. From one perspective, human history can be seen as a series of ever more efficient devices to help us communicate, travel, trade, work, and even to think. Similarly, the history of combat can be seen as the evolution of a series of ever more efficient devices to enable humans to kill and dominate their fellow human beings.

In 1998, I was asked by the editors of the *Academic Press Encyclopedia of Violence, Peace and Conflic*t to write the entry on "The Evolution of Weaponry." This chapter is an expanded and updated version of this encyclopedia entry.

The concept of an "evolution" of combat is appropriate since the battlefield is the ultimate realm of Darwinian natural selection. With few exceptions, any weapon or system that survives for any length of time does so because of its utility, not simply because of superstition. Anything that is effective is copied and perpetuated, and anything ineffective results in death, defeat and extinction. There are fads and remnants (the military equivalent of the appendix) but, over the long run, everything happens for a reason, and that reason is survival and victory in combat.

Ultimately the limitations of our bodies and our minds determines the nature of our weapons. Of these two, the mind is by far the most important, but first, let us examine the nature of man's physical limitations and the evolution of weapons to overcome these limitations.

Weapons as Devices to Overcome Physical Limitations

I've long considered the giving of a weapon to be a solemn obligation and statement. The obligation is from the giver, who has to be sure that he can place his absolute trust in the discretion and judgment of the gifted. The statement is that the giver wishes the gifted warrior to prevail. To preserve themselves and to thrive. A weapon given is a measure of trust from one to another. I give the weapon as protection, as a practical means of survival and as a means to say that the person gifted is important.

Weapons are simple tools. Not engraved. Not pretty. But their importance throughout history is understated. Except in one instance. And that is the rare, right and reasoned use of a weapon by a warrior. Therein ultimately, eventually, and in no other way . . . lies peace.

—Rocky Warren
Police sergeant and law enforcement trainer

The physical limitations of man are a key factor in his search for weapons. The need for force, mobility, distance, and protection has been the key requirements in this realm.

The need for force. Man's physical strength limitations led to a need for greater physical force in order to hit an opponent harder and more effectively, resulting in the development of better methods to transfer kinetic energy to an opponent. This process evolved from hitting someone with a handheld rock (providing the momentum energy of more mass than just a fist); to sharp rocks (focusing the energy in a smaller impact point); to a sharp rock on a stick (providing mechanical leverage combined with a cutting edge); to spears (using the latest material technology—flint, bronze, iron, steel—to focus energy into smaller and smaller penetration points); to swords (which permit the option of using a thrusting, spear-like penetration point, or the mechanical leverage of a hacking, cutting edge); to the long bow (using stored mechanical energy and a refined penetration point); to firearms (transferring chemical energy to a projectile in order to deliver an extremely powerful dose of kinetic energy).

The need for mobility. Limited by the constraints of a bipedal body that could be outrun by a majority of ground-based creatures, man's crosscountry speed created a need for a mobility advantage, resulting in a succession of weapons that provided more efficient means to go around the enemy or to give chase. These weapons evolved from the chariots of the Egyptians, Babylonians, and Persians (which were without horse collars—an invention of the Romans—and were thus quite inefficient since the mounting system choked the horse); to the cavalry of the Greeks and Romans (whose horses lacked stirrups, limiting their ability to strike from horseback); to the cavalry which dominated the battlefield throughout the age of the European knights (since the introduction of stirrups made it possible to deliver a powerful blow from horseback without danger of falling off), and continued to play a key, but ever decreasing, role for over 500 years, up to the beginning of the twentieth century; to modern mechanized infantry, tanks and (the ultimate form of mobility) aircraft. Simultaneously, a similar evolution of evermore effective forms of mobility took place with ships at sea, until the introduction of aircraft originally based on aircraft carriers, to today, with the increasingly, long-range, ground-based aircraft that have come to dominate this realm.

The need for distance. Similarly, man's limited reach created a need for a range advantage in an effort to attack more people than just those in immediate reach (i.e., to increase the zone of influence), and to do so without placing himself in danger. This need resulted in an increasingly more efficient means to kill at a distance, moving from the spear, to the long spear of the Greek phalanx, to the throwing spears of the Roman legionary, to the bow, the crossbow, the English longbow, firearms, artillery, missiles, and aircraft.

The need for protection. Physical vulnerability resulted in a continuous need for armor to help limit an enemy's ability to inflict harm (in the form of kinetic energy). This evolution generally followed the latest development of material technology, to include leather, bronze, iron, and steel. The invention of firearms created a degree of force so great that the human body could not carry sufficient steel to stop a penetration. The only remnant of armor was the helmet, which was designed to stop fragmentation (grenade and artillery) wounds to the vulnerable and crucial brain area. This evolution continues today in tank and ship armor. In recent years, man-made fiber technology (such as Kevlar) has again made body armor practical, so that for the first time in centuries the average combatant, in both law enforcement and military realms, can once again wear a form of body armor.

Weapons as Devices to Overcome Psychological Limitations

Man is the first weapon of battle.

—Ardant du Picq, 1870
Battle Studies

Mobility, distance and protection interact with each other in the evolution of weapons, but man's psychological limitations are even more influential in this process than his physical limitations. Earlier I cited Lord Moran, and it is worth repeating that this great military physician of World War I and World War II, called Napoleon the "greatest psychologist." Napoleon said that, "In war the moral is to the physical as three is to one," meaning that the psychological advantage, or leverage, is three times more important than the physical.

At the heart of the psychological processes on the battlefield is the resistance to killing one's own species, a resistance that exists in most healthy members of most species. This was addressed in far greater detail in *On Killing*, but there is value in a brief recap and update here.

To truly understand the nature of this resistance, we must first recognize that most participants in close combat are literally frightened out of their wits. Once the arrows or bullets start flying, combatants stop thinking with the forebrain (that part of the brain which makes us human) and thought processes localize in the midbrain, or mammalian brain, which is the primitive part of the brain that is generally indistinguishable from that of an animal.

It may be that in conflict situations this primitive, midbrain processing can be observed in a consistent trend toward resisting and avoiding the killing of one's own species. During territorial and mating battles, animals with antlers and horns slam together in a relatively harmless head-to-head fashion, rattlesnakes wrestle each other, and piranha fight their own kind with flicks of their tails, but against any other species these creatures unleash their horns, fangs and teeth without restraint. This is an essential survival mechanism, which prevents a species from destroying itself during territorial and mating rituals.

This resistance can be seen in other places besides mating and territorial battles. Why is it that the biggest kitten in every litter does not smother and kill all the other kittens? Why is it that the biggest puppy does not kill all the other puppies in the litter to enhance its personal survival? Why does the first chick out of the egg not shove the other eggs out of the nest? That chick's personal survival would be greatly enhanced if it did. Now, there is a breed of bird that lays eggs in another bird's nest, and when its eggs hatch it shoves the other bird's eggs out, but those are eggs from a different type of bird. Creatures of the same species never kill their own kind intentionally.

Why is it that you can leave your three-year-old child with your six-month-old infant for a few minutes and the older one does not leap on the little one and smother or somehow kill it? Again, most healthy members of most species appear to have a hardwired resistance against killing their own kind. Any species that did not have this hardwired resistance would cease to exist within a couple of generations. Yes, once every couple of years we may hear of some horrendous incident in which a three- or four-year-old, who has been negatively influenced in some way, murders an infant child, but it is extremely rare. When these incidents occur, it shocks us down to our core because it is a horrible abnormality.

One major, modern revelation in the field of military psychology is the observation that this resistance to killing one's own species is also a key factor in human combat. We have already addressed Brigadier General S.L.A. Marshall's findings in this area in World War II. Based on his innovative technique of post-combat interviews, Marshall concluded in his landmark book, *Men Against Fire*, that only 15 to 20 percent of the individual riflemen in World War II fired their weapons at an exposed enemy soldier.

As I noted earlier, every available, parallel scholarly study of combat firing rates validates Marshall's basic findings. Ardant du Picq's surveys of French officers in the 1860s and his observations on ancient battles; Keegan and Holmes' numerous accounts of ineffectual firing throughout history; Paddy Griffith's data on the extraordinarily low killing rate among Napoleonic and American Civil War regiments; Stouffer's extensive World War II and postwar research; Richard Holmes' assessment of Argentine firing rates in the Falklands War; the British Army's laser reenactments of historical battles; the FBI's studies of non-firing rates among law enforcement officers in the 1950s and 1960s, and countless other individual and anecdotal observations, all confirm Marshall's fundamental conclusion that man is not, by nature, a close-range interpersonal killer.

Somewhere inside our midbrain, at least in the brains of healthy members of our race, we appear to have a powerful resistance to killing our own kind— just like most other species. While this is true, the question begs to be asked: Why then have we been so good at filling up our military cemeteries across the years?

The existence of this resistance can be observed in its marked absence in sociopaths who, by definition, feel no empathy or remorse for their fellow human beings. Pit bulldogs have been selectively bred for sociopathy, that is, bred for the absence of the resistance to killing one's own kind to ensure that they will perform the unnatural act of killing another dog in battle. Breeding to overcome this limitation in humans is impractical, but humans are adept at finding mechanical means to overcome natural limitations. Humans were born without the ability to fly, so we found mechanisms that overcame this limitation and enabled flight. Humans were also born with constraints upon their ability to kill fellow humans, so throughout history we have devoted great effort to finding ways to overcome this resistance. From a combat evolution perspective, the history of warfare can be viewed as a series of successively more effective tactical and mechanical mechanisms to enable or force combatants to overcome their resistance to killing.

Posturing as a Psychological Weapon

> I am sure that not numbers or strength bring victory in war; but whichever army goes into battle stronger in soul, their enemies generally cannot withstand them.
> —Greek General Xenophon, fourth century B.C.
> *Anabasis*

The resistance to killing can be overcome, or at least bypassed, by a variety of techniques. One way is to cause the enemy to flee (often by getting in their flank or rear, which almost always causes a rout), and it is in the subsequent pursuit of a broken or defeated enemy that the vast majority of the killing happens.

It is widely understood that most killing happens after the battle, in the pursuit phase (Clausewitz and Ardant du Picq both commented on this), which is apparently due to two factors. First, the fleeing victim has his back turned. It appears to be much easier to deny his humanity if you can stab or shoot him in the back and not look into his eyes when you kill him. Secondly, in the midbrain of the pursuer, the opponent apparently changes from a fellow male engaged in a primitive, simplistic, ritualistic, head-to-head, territorial or mating battle, to a prey that must to be pursued, pulled down, and killed. Anyone who has ever worked with dogs understands this process. You are generally safe if you face a dog down in a threatening situation. When you have to move, back away from a dog (as with most animals), because if you turn and run, you are in danger of being pursued and viciously attacked. The same is true of soldiers in combat.

The battlefield is truly psychological in nature. In this realm, the individual who puffs himself up the biggest or makes the loudest noise is likely to win. From one perspective, the actual battle is a process of posturing until one side or another turns and runs, and then the real killing begins. Thus, posturing is critical to warfare and the side that does it best will gain a significant advantage on the battlefield.

We have already addressed the Bigger Bang Theory, but it is useful to recap and say that bagpipes, bugles, drums, shiny armor, tall hats, chariots, elephants, and cavalry have all been factors in successful posturing (convincing oneself of one's prowess while daunting ones enemy). But ultimately, gunpowder proved to be the ultimate posturing tool. For example, the longbow and the crossbow were significantly more accurate, with a far greater rate of fire and a much greater accurate range than the muzzleloading muskets used up to the early part of the American Civil War. Furthermore, the longbow did not need the industrial base (iron and gunpowder) required by muskets.

Mechanically speaking, there is no reason why there should not have been regiments armed with longbows and crossbows at Waterloo and Bull Run, cutting vast swathes through the enemy. Similarly, there were highly efficient, air pressure powered weapons available as early as the Napoleonic-era (similar to modern paintball guns) which had a far higher firing rate than the muskets of that era, but they were never used. We must keep in mind Napoleon's maxim that in war the mental factors are three times more important than the mechanical factors. The reality is that if you go *doink, doink,* on the battlefield, and the enemy goes *Bang!, Bang!*, they gain a powerful psychological advantage that ultimately may mean that the "doinkers" lose.

In his book, *War on the Mind*, Peter Watson says that one universal finding of weapons research is that the amount of noise a weapon makes is a key factor in that weapon's effectiveness on the battlefield:

> . . . noise of many kinds, usually incredibly loud, often painfully so— small arms, shells, bombs and aircraft during an attack. This can be prepared for, but the first time in real battle is always different.

This phenomenon helps explain the effectiveness of high-noise producing weapons ranging from Gustavus Adolphus' small, mobile cannons assigned to infantry units, to the U.S. Army's M-60 machine gun in Vietnam, which fired large and very loud, 7.62mm ammunition at a slow rate, vs. the M-16's smaller and comparatively less noisy 5.56mm ammunition firing at a rapid rate of fire. It is important to note that both the machine gun and the cannon are also crew-served weapons, which provides a key factor in killing enabling.

Mobility and Distance as Psychological Weapons

> From a psychologically safe distance, I'm sure I've killed my share of fellow human beings. However, my most traumatic moment was drawing my sidearm on a VC approaching my grounded aircraft... and not being able to pull the trigger.
>
> —Cobra pilot, Vietnam War

Once it is understood that the true destruction and defeat of an enemy happens in the pursuit, then the actual utility of those weapons that provide a mobility advantage becomes clear. First, a mobility advantage often permits a force to get at the enemy's flank or rear. Combatants seem to have an intuitive understanding of their psychological and physical vulnerability when an opponent attacks from their rear, a tactic that almost always results in a mass panic. Secondly, it is during the pursuit that a mobility advantage is needed if a pursuing force is to kill the enemy. An opponent who has cast aside his weapons and armor can generally outrun an armed pursuer, but a man on foot cannot outrun chariots or cavalry. These mobile forces have their greatest utility stabbing and shooting helpless, terrified men in the back.

Another key factor in overcoming the resistance to killing is distance. The utility of weapons that kill from afar cannot be truly understood without understanding the psychological enabling aspect of distance. Simply stated, the farther away you are the easier it is to kill. Thus, dropping bombs from 20,000 feet or firing artillery from two miles away is, psychologically speaking, not at all difficult (and there is no indication of any noncompliance in these situations). But firing a rifle from 20 feet away is quite difficult (with a high incidence of nonfirers) and in hand-to-hand combat there is great psychological resistance to stabbing an opponent.

John Keegan's landmark book, *The Face of Battle* makes a comparative study of Agincourt (1415), Waterloo (1815), and the Somme (1916). In his analysis of these three battles spanning over 500 years, Keegan repeatedly notes the absence of bayonet wounds incurred during the massed bayonet attacks at Waterloo and the Somme. Keegan states that after Waterloo:

> There were numbers of sword and lance wounds to be treated and some bayonet wounds, though these had usually been inflicted after the man had already been disabled, there being no evidence of the armies having crossed bayonets at Waterloo.

By World War I, edged-weapon combat had almost disappeared, and Keegan notes, "Edged-weapon wounds were a fraction of one per cent of all wounds inflicted in the First World War."

Indeed, all evidence indicates that ancient battles were not much more than great shoving matches until one side or the other fled. This can be observed in Alexander the Great who, according to Ardant du Picq's studies of ancient records, lost only 700 men "to the sword" in all his battles put together. This is because Alexander the Great always won, and nearly all the killing happened to the losers, after the battle in the pursuit phase.

The only thing greater than the resistance to killing at close range is the resistance to being killed at close range. Close range interpersonal aggression is, indeed, the Universal Human Phobia, which is why the initiation of midbrain processing is so powerful and intense in these situations. Thus, one drawback to killing at long range is that greater distance has a reduced psychological effect on the enemy. This manifests itself in a constant thwarting of each new generation of air power advocates and other adherents of sterile, long-range, high tech warfare, since it is close-range, interpersonal aggression that truly frightens the enemy and modifies their behavior.

Peter Maass, writing in the *New York Times Magazine,* captured this paradox of the failure of firepower, as it applies to counter terrorism warfare.

> At the outset of the Vietnam War, Colonel John Paul Vann, who would emerge as one of the most thoughtful and ultimately tragic

officers in the war, recognized the paradox and realized his firepower-loving commanders had not. In 1962, he warned David Halberstam, then a young reporter for the *New York Times*, that the wrong strategy had been adopted. "This is a political war, and it calls for the utmost discrimination in killing," he told Halberstam, as recounted in William Prochnau's, *Once Upon a Distant War*. "The best weapon for killing is a knife, but I'm afraid we can't do it that way. The next best is a rifle. The worst is an airplane, and after that the worst is artillery. You have to know who you are killing."

Watson notes in, *War on the Mind* that weapons research has concluded that the weapons that pose a direct threat to the individual are more psychologically effective than "area" weapons. Thus, the sniper is more effective than a hail of machine-gun fire, and the precision-guided bomb is more effective than the artillery barrage. The more accurate the weapon, the greater the fear it inspires. As Watson puts it: "Fear equals accuracy, noise, rapidity of fire—noise being the only truly non-lethal characteristic that is feared."

According to Bob Woodward's book, *Bush at War*, the U.S. armed forces conquered Afghanistan in 2001 with less than 500 Americans on the ground. It should be noted that these 500 Americans were well assisted by elite troops from the British, Australian and New Zealand SAS, and the Canadian JTF 2. The Americans were mostly U.S. Special Forces (Green Berets), and CIA operatives (with the proverbial "suitcase full of money"), who were funding, supplying, guiding and controlling the forces of the Afghani warlords on the ground. Whenever possible, each Green Beret A-Team was supported by a team of U.S. Air Force Combat Controllers (CCTs) who called in the precision airstrikes, which were pivotal to winning that war.

In the Gulf War, just a decade prior, approximately 10 percent of the bombs dropped on the enemy were precision guided. In Afghanistan in 2001 and Iraq in 2003, approximately 70 percent of the bombs were precision-guided munitions that were dropped on the enemy with pinpoint accuracy. In two months, the U.S. led coalition did what the Russians could not do in 10 years. Barely a year later the performance was repeated in Iraq, conquering an entire nation in three weeks. This could not have happened without a vast stockpile of modern, precision guided munitions. But it also would not have been possible without those elite troops on the ground directing and exploiting the air strikes, and working with indigenous forces to provide the Universal Human Phobia, that personal face of death and destruction, which is so effective at modifying human behavior.

Leaders as a Psychological Weapon

> The mass needs, and we give it, leaders who have the firmness and decision of command proceeding from habit and an entire faith in their unquestionable right to command as established by tradition, law and society.
>
> —Ardant du Picq
> *Battle Studies*

We discussed earlier that in World War II only 15 to 20 percent of front-line soldiers would fire. However, almost everyone fired when there was a leader present ordering them to shoot. Lest you think that a leader cannot possibly be that omnipotent, consider the *Milgram Study*. In 1963, Stanley Milgram of Yale University conducted a series of experiments looking at obedience to authority. He instructed his subjects to administer electric shocks to people, who were actually secret confidants of the doctor, whenever they erred on questions given on a test. Milgram found that the subjects followed his orders even when they believed they had actually killed the people they were shocking. Here is how the test was designed.

Two people were chosen for the test, let us call them Lee and John. Lee was in on the experiment, meaning he was the one who supposedly would be shocked. First, John would be shown how painful the electrodes were, and then he would be taken next door where he was shown how to ask Lee questions over a microphone and administer shocks when he received incorrect answers. The test would begin. As the session proceeded, Lee would err on question after question and John would give him, what he believed to be, progressively greater and greater shocks. Lee would scream on each shock and, at one point, he even begged for the pain to stop, claiming he had a heart condition. "Please stop! I can't keep doing this. Let me out. Let me out. Let me out."

Sweating bullets, John would watch the man wearing a lab coat and carrying a clipboard for instructions to stop, but they never came. He would ask permission to stop, but the leader with the clipboard would simply say, "The experiment requires that you continue." Finally, Lee screamed one last time and then there was only silence. Still, the experiment would have to continue because the subject was told that silence was considered a wrong answer. John would zap him again and again with bigger and bigger shots of voltage. There was even a large sign that warned not to go beyond a certain point, but John would continue.

How many people like John do you think were willing to shock a fellow human being to death just because someone with a white lab coat told them to? The shocking answer is that 65 percent were willing! This study has been replicated using only women applying the "electric shocks," it has been duplicated in other cultures and nations, always with a similar, incredibly high percentage of willingness. Now, if a guy with a white lab coat can make 65 percent of all human beings kill another person, as long as they do not have to personally see it happen, what can people with real trappings of authority do? What can a military commander do?

March 16, 1968. The enraged and frustrated troops of Charlie Company, 11th Brigade, America Division, under the command of Lieutenant William Calley, entered the little village of My Lai, Vietnam, nestled in the middle of a densely mined Vietcong entrenchment. Several men in Charlie Company had recently been maimed or killed in the surrounding area, so they were flustered and angry and more than ready for a fight with the Vietcong. They were on a "search and destroy" mission.

Calley ordered his men to enter the village firing, although they had not received information of enemy fire coming from it. As the mission unfolded, it quickly deteriorated into a slaughter of over 300 apparently unarmed civilians, including women, children, and the elderly. Eyewitnesses later said that numerous elderly men were bayonetted, praying women and children were shot in the back of their heads, one girl, possibly more, raped and then killed. Calley, according to reports, ordered a group of villagers into a ditch and then gunned them down with his weapon on full automatic.

Months later, Calley was charged with murder. At the trial, he argued that he was just following orders from his captain to kill everyone in the village.

So a captain can order a lieutenant to kill and the lieutenant can order his troops to kill. And they do it. What power could a satanic coven leader or an urban gang leader exert if they demanded killing behavior? Think about Charles Manson. Think about Jim Jones and the Kool-Aid. Think about the kid in Pearl, Mississippi, who murdered his mother and committed the killings at his school simply because his "coven leader" demanded that he do it.

The modern concept of a combat leader usually envisions a hardened veteran moving behind a battle line of his men, exhorting, encouraging, punishing, rebuking, correcting, and rewarding them. But combat leadership has not always been like this. Armies have always had leaders, but the Romans were the first to take proven warriors and systematically develop them into professional leaders starting at the lowest levels. Prior to this time, leaders were usually expected to get into the battle and lead from the front, but the Romans were one of the first to also place leaders behind their men in an open order of battle.

The influence of this kind of leadership was one of the key factors in the success of the Roman-way of war. The process of having a respected, proven, small unit leader moving behind his men and demanding effective killing activity from them has continued to be a key factor in effective combat in the centuries to follow. (The fact that he does not necessarily have to personally kill the enemy provides a diffusion of responsibility, which also enables the killing.)

This kind of leadership largely disappeared along with the Roman Empire, but it appeared again in the firing lines of English longbowmen, and then it appeared as a systematically applied factor in the firing lines of the successful armies of the gunpowder era, and it continues up to today.

Groups as a Psychological Weapon

We were so close that if one of us was cut, we all bled.

—Anonymous

Groups are another important piece of the equation. Although only 15 to 20 percent of riflemen would fire in World War II, it was learned that when there was a crew-served weapon, that is, a gunner and an assistant gunner, the crew almost always fired. They did so because of mutual support, accountability and diffusion of responsibility. As S.L.A. Marshall put it in his book, *Men Against Fire:*

I hold it to be one of the simplest truths of war that the thing which enables an infantry soldier to keep going with his weapons is the near presence or presumed presence of a comrade.

A soldier can make the decision in his own heart and soul not to pull the trigger, but if he is part of a team, such as a crew-served weapon, he would have to talk to the other soldier about it and they would have to agree not to shoot. That rarely happens.

Think about a drive-by shooting. One gangbanger by himself is an unknown commodity, but two gangbangers leaning out the window become a crew-served weapon. Since they mutually support one another, everyone in the car should be tried for murder. When my co-author worked in the Portland Police Bureau's Gang Enforcement Team, he investigated dozens of assaults perpetrated by skinheads. He said that never once did he investigate a case of one, solo skinhead attacking someone. "These cowardly losers," as Christensen puts it, "always needed the power of the group." In one case, three skins did a shotgun drive-by on a lone black man sitting in the back of a truck. The front passenger fired the weapon, but all three were charged and found guilty. That is the way it should be because they all supported one another.

The two most horrendous school massacres in the U.S. occurred in a Jonesboro, Arkansas, middle school and at Columbine High School in Littleton, Colorado. In both shootings, there were two kids operating side-by-side. If we had taken one kid out of each of those shootings and put him in an alternative school, the remaining kid in each case probably would not have been able to carry out the massacres.

Crew-served weapons have generally been responsible for the majority of the killing throughout the history of warfare, beginning with the earliest crew-served weapon, the chariot. The chariot often employed a driver and a passenger who generally fired a bow (which added the factor of distance in the killing enabling equation), and was most effective in the pursuit when their mobility advantage gave them the ability to shoot large numbers of fleeing enemy in the back. The powerful group dynamics of the chariot (along with its mobility) were to show up again, over two millennia later, in the tanks of the twentieth century.

The Greek phalanx was a mass of spearmen in tight ranks, carrying spears approximately four meters long and protecting themselves with overlapping shields. They were highly trained to move in a formation organized in depth (i.e., moving and fighting "in column," as opposed to "in line") and trained to strike the enemy as a coherent mass. As such, it was a form of crew-served weapon in which newer members were placed in the front, and were thereby under direct observation and accountability by the veteran warriors behind them. The phalanx was of such utility that it has shown up repeatedly throughout history and around the world.

The first systematic military use of gunpowder was in cannons, and these crew-served weapons immediately began to dominate the battlefield. Unlike the early muskets, cannons were effective killers from the beginning. Not only did they provide the best form of posturing (i.e., noisemaking) ever to be seen on the battlefield, they were also a highly effective crew-served weapon, being generally manned by numerous individuals and directly commanded by an officer or a sergeant with sole responsibility for that gun and its crew. Rarely did the crew show any hesitation or mercy in killing the enemy. At close range the cannon fired "grape shot" into tightly packed enemy formations, thus becoming, in effect, a huge shotgun capable of killing hundreds of men with a single shot. Napoleon, that "great psychologist," demonstrated his understanding of the true killing utility of cannon (and the comparative ineffectiveness of infantry) by ensuring that his armies always had a higher percentage of cannon than his enemies, and by massing those cannon at key points in the battle.

In the twentieth century, cannon became an "indirect fire" system (i.e., firing over the heads of friendly combatants from a great distance away), and the machine gun (with its "gunner" and "assistant gunner" or "loader") came to replace the cannon in the crew-served, "direct fire" role on the battlefield. In World War I, the machine gun was called the "distilled essence of the infantry," but it was actually just a continuation of the cannon in its old, crew-served, mass killing role.

The crew-served machine gun is still the key killer on the close-range battlefield, but the evolution of group enabling processes continues in tanks and armored personnel carriers. At sea, the dynamics of the crew-served weapon have been in play since the beginning of the gunpowder era, with crew-served weapons, distance and the influence of leaders.

Conditioning and Stress Inoculation as Psychological Weapons

> It is not the number of soldiers but their will to win which decides battles.
>
> —Lord Moran
> *The Anatomy of Courage*

By 1946, the U.S. Army, full of veteran military leaders fresh from World War II, had completely accepted Marshall's findings of a 15-20 percent firing rate among American riflemen during that war. As a direct result of this, the Human Resources Research Office of the U.S. Army pioneered a revolution in combat training. As we have seen before, this new method of training replaced the old method of firing at bull's-eye targets, with deeply ingrained "conditioning" using realistic, man-shaped pop-up targets that fall when hit. Psychologists know that this kind of powerful "operant conditioning" is the only technique which will reliably influence the primitive, midbrain processing of a frightened human being, just as fire drills condition terrified school children to respond properly during a fire, and repetitious "stimulus-response" conditioning in flight simulators enables frightened pilots to respond reflexively to emergency situations.

Throughout history the ingredients of posturing, mobility, distance, leaders, and groups have been manipulated to enable and force combatants to kill, but the introduction of conditioning in modern training was a true revolution. The application and perfection of these basic conditioning techniques appear to have increased the rate of fire from roughly 15 percent in World War II to approximately 55 percent in Korea and around 95 percent in Vietnam. Similar high rates of fire resulting from modern conditioning techniques can be seen in FBI data on law enforcement firing rates since the nationwide introduction of modern conditioning techniques in the late 1960s.

One of the most dramatic examples of the value and power of this modern, psychological revolution in training can be seen in Richard Holmes' observations of the 1982 Falklands War. I am a graduate of the British Army Staff College in Camberley, where we conducted in-depth studies of the Falklands war. There can be no doubt that the superbly trained (i.e., conditioned) British forces in the Falklands were without air or artillery superiority and were consistently outnumbered three-to-one while attacking the poorly trained but well-equipped and carefully dug-in Argentine defenders. Superior British firing rates (which Richard Holmes estimates to be well over 90 percent), resulting from modern training techniques, has been credited as a key factor in the series of British victories in that brief but bloody war.

I cannot overemphasize the impact of the British Army's success in this instance. Their achievement of repeated, successful attacks against a well-prepared enemy that outnumbered them by a ratio of three-to-one, flies in the face of all military theory. Some would claim that the British success was because the Argentine forces were draftees or conscript troops. But the U.S. Army draftees in Vietnam were trained in the new style, and they had a firing rate of around 95 percent and were generally credited with never losing a major ground engagement in that war. Others point to the M-16 rifle and the close ranges of jungle warfare in Vietnam to explain the high firing rate there; but the Sten, the M-1 carbine and the Thompson submachine gun in jungle warfare in World War II did not have any significant advantage in firing rates as opposed to any other individual weapon. However, key weapons (such as the BAR and flame-thrower) and crew-served weapons (such as machine guns) did have a significant advantage in firing rates in World War II, because of group and leadership influences.

There are still nonfirers. Drew Brown, the *Knight Rider* reporter mentioned earlier who was with 1st Ranger Battalion in the invasion of Panama was one of them.

> I was particularly intrigued when I read how studies show that many soldiers find that they cannot pull the trigger when the moment comes. Despite all of our training, I saw it happen to fellow Rangers in Panama. It happened to me. There were a number of times after our parachute assault on Tocumen Airport when I could have shot what I knew were enemy soldiers. But I just didn't feel the need to. I've rationalized it over the years by telling myself that I was alone and outnumbered at the time, and that since they weren't shooting at me, I wasn't going to shoot at them. Sort of a live and let live attitude. I came across an anecdote a few years ago in Stephen Ambrose's book on D-Day, in which he described how small groups of American and German soldiers knowingly passed within a few feet of each other, yet never fired their weapons. I felt sort of justified then. While I can understand how the average Joe might not pull the trigger, it's always seemed odd to me that the same thing might happen, even in elite, well-trained units. Do you explain it simply by accepting the proposition that most people, even soldiers have a natural aversion to killing?

I responded by telling him that my entire book, *On Killing*, is intended to answer that very question. There are a host of factors, such as groups, leadership, relationship to the target and training, that influence the decision to kill, and almost all of them were working together to reduce the probability that he would fire in this situation. Brown went on to ask,

While out watching an urban warfare exercise a few weeks ago, one of the battalion commanders explained that what they were trying to teach these soldiers was "reflexive shooting." Is the Army's answer to training soldiers how to overcome that aversion?

Of course that is the best answer we have. It seems to work and it appears that this is a revolutionary step forward. I told him that there are still non-shooters (as he is well aware!), but I believe that we have significantly reduced the problem.

We will never achieve perfection on the battlefield, but there can be no doubt that future armies that attempt to go into battle without the kind of psychological preparation provided to the British forces in the Falklands is likely to meet a fate similar to that of the Argentines. The difference between a 15 percent firing rate and a 90 percent firing rate represents a sixfold increase in combat effectiveness, which was repeatedly and consistently sufficient to overcome the Argentine's threefold advantage in raw numbers of troops on the ground.

One additional new development is the use of combat stress inoculation through force-on-force paint bullet training, which has been addressed previously. There is tentative evidence that would lead us to believe that this has reduced the fear-induced spray-and-pray response and increased law enforcement hit rates (as opposed to firing rates) from around 20 percent to approximately 90 percent. This is an additional fourfold increase in combat effectiveness through training, which combines with the sixfold increase in firing rates.

I had the privilege of training numerous combat units associated with the U.S. Army, Navy, and Marines as they prepared for the invasion of Iraq in 2003. All of these troops had incorporated extensively the use of paint bullets in their training to inoculate themselves against combat stress. Additionally, the U.S. armed forces and its allies have integrated state-of-the-art video firearms simulators and laser engagement simulators into unit training.

This systematic integration of simulations technology has made it possible to achieve combat performances such as this:

During the invasion phase of the Iraq War, Captain Zan Hornbuckle, a 29-year-old Army officer from Georgia, found himself and his 80 men surrounded by 300 Iraqi and Syrian fighters. Unable to obtain air or artillery support, Captain Hornbuckle and his unit—*who were never before in combat*—fought for eight hours. When the smoke cleared, 200 of the enemy were dead . . . not a single American was killed. (Emphasis added.)

—Gene Edward Veith
Worldmag.com

This is an achievement that is virtually unprecedented in any previous small unit engagement in recorded history. You simply cannot make a ratio out of 200-to-zero. And there were many similar achievements during the invasion of Afghanistan and Iraq.

Thus modern training has made it hypothetically possible to increase the firing rate of the individual warrior approximately sixfold, and each of these individuals may well be four times more likely to hit their targets. This is a combined effect that represents a potential for a twenty-fourfold increase in the effectiveness of the individual warrior! That hypothetical potential is based on crude estimates, and this full potential may never be completely achieved since a variety of factors will always get in the way. But there can be no doubt that these new forms of training have provided a startling new revolution in combat effectiveness on the modern battlefield.

In the end, it is not about the hardware, it is about the "software." Amateurs talk about hardware (equipment), professionals talk about software (training and mental readiness).

In my science fiction book, *The Two Space War*, I depict warriors 600 years in the future who refer to the period at the end of the twentieth century and the beginning of the twenty-first century as a "Warrior Renaissance." I sincerely believe that future generations will come to think of this period as a renaissance, a period of remarkable progress in which the full potential of the human factor in combat began to be realized. It is entirely possible that elite warriors 100 years from now will be able to selectively control SNS responses, such as auditory exclusion and slow-motion time. If that does happen, they will look back on these years as the era in which we began to discover this untapped human potential.

The final achievement of this renaissance is the nurturing and development of the warrior after combat. The experience of the combat veteran is bought at a great price, and the veteran warrior represents a valuable resource. Conducting critical incident debriefings, training in breathing processes, and training leaders to help warriors through the aftermath of combat are just a few of the mechanisms that have been put in place in recent years. All of this will be addressed in detail in the final section of this book, but for now it is sufficient to say that providing the support structure, the training and the processes that permit the veteran to return to combat represents an important investment in long term human potential for future battlefields, and for the society that must take the returning warrior back into its folds after the smoke clears.

A Brief History of the Evolution of Combat

> O dreadful Forge! . . . more urgent comes our cry . . .
> Brain, sinew, and spirit, before we die,

Beat out the iron, edge it keen,
And shape us to the end we mean!
Burned from the ore's rejected dross,
The iron whitens in the heat.
With plangent strokes of pain and loss
The hammers on the iron beat.

Searched by the fire, through death and dole
We feel the iron in our soul.

—Laurence Binyon
"The Anvil"

Having established an understanding of the physical factors required for effective weapons (force, mobility, distance, and protection), and the psychological enabling factors required to effectively employ these weapons (posturing, mobility, distance, leaders, groups, conditioning, and inoculation), then an overall survey of the "dreadful forge" of combat evolution becomes possible. Although parallel processes have occurred around the world, the evolution of combat is most easily observed in the West. And it is in Western civilization that combat has evolved to a degree of ascendancy that permitted Western domination of the globe, starting as early as the sixteenth century and culminating in total domination in the nineteenth and twentieth centuries.

The Not So Inexplicable Chariot

Arms on armour clashing bray'd
Horrible discord, and the maddening wheels
Of brazen chariots rag'd: dire was the noise
Of conflict.

—John Milton
Paradise Lost

The chariot was introduced to ancient Egypt early in the second millennium B.C. and it was to become the first major, evolutionary weapons innovation. As a system, it was made possible by the domestication of the horse, the invention of the wheel and the invention of the bow and arrow—particularly the recurve bow. The chariot was a two-wheeled platform pulled by horses (usually two) and generally carrying a driver and a passenger. It was of limited value for commerce due to its small cargo capacity, and it was primarily used as an instrument of war. Its mobility gave it a high degree of utility in attacking vulnerable flanks or in the pursuit of a defeated enemy. The passenger was usually an archer who would fire from the platform while on the move, or during brief halts.

For well over a thousand years the chariot was the dominant weapon of warfare. This has been called "inexplicable" by some historians, but an understanding of the chariot's powerful psychological contribution helps to explain its millennium-long ascendancy. The chariot undoubtedly had many limitations: The horses were vulnerable to archers and slingers, and if just one horse was disabled the whole chariot was out of action. The absence of a horse collar meant that the mounting system choked the horse, thus making the chariot's effective range a fraction of that of the cavalry, which would later replace the chariot in its mobility role. Yet, in spite of these limitations, the mobility advantage of the chariot (useful primarily in the pursuit, when most of the killing occurred), combined with some group processes (driver plus archer), and some distance processes (archer firing from a mobile platform), combined to make the chariot the dominant weapon of an era ranging from the Egyptian to the Persian Empires. Ultimately it would be defeated by the phalanx and replaced by cavalry.

The Tried and Trusted Phalanx

Anon they moved
In perfect phalanx

—John Milton
Paradise Lost

One limitation of the chariot (and later of cavalry) was that the horses would consistently refuse to hurl themselves into a hedge of sharp, projecting objects, such as a phalanx, with its deep ranks of tightly packed men carrying four-meter long spears and protecting themselves with overlapping shields. The Greek phalanx required a high degree of training and organization, but starting around the fourth century B.C., the Greeks were able to use it to negate the impact of the chariot in battle. The tightly packed ranks of the phalanx created a group process, which apparently permitted it to act as a vast, crew-served weapon. This factor, along with some distance (through the long spears), and the simplicity and economic viability of the phalanx made it the dominant weapon system of its era. These aspects of the phalanx, combined with the Greeks' subsequent mastery of horseback riding (albeit absent stirrups) enabled them to approach an enemy from its vulnerable flanks and to exploit pursuits, all of which permitted them to conquer a vast portion of the world.

The Greeks were defeated by the Romans, but the inherent simplicity of the phalanx, combined with its psychological fundamentals, were so powerful that after the fall of the Roman Empire the phalanx again became ascendant, with the Swiss achieving the epitome of perfection with it in the Middle Ages and the early Renaissance. The armies of the early gunpowder era continued to use phalanx formations of pikemen combined with formations of primitive, early muskets. The pikemen were replaced with the advent of the bayonet, which made every man a potential pikeman, and a remnant of the psychological dynamics of the phalanx could be seen in the great, column-based bayonet charges of Napoleon's armies.

The Roman System and the Pax Romana

> "The pervasive expansiveness of the Empire which we see today did not come about as a result of some accident nor precipitous good fortune. Legionnaires do not sit around congratulating themselves in the wake of every victory, nor are they idle in peacetime. Rather, they are constantly training and refining their warrior skills, so as to be ready to act at a moment's notice. Indeed, they seem to have been born with weapons in their hands!"
>
> —Josephus Flavius
> circa 90AD

It must be remembered that the Roman Empire lasted for approximately half a millennium (longer if we count the Eastern Roman Empire), and to say "the Romans did this," or "the Romans did that" would generally be inaccurate when referring to a military system that evolved and changed constantly across the centuries. But there were certain aspects that remained constant in the Roman legions, and these factors were key ingredients in the extraordinary military success of the Roman Empire, starting in the second and first centuries B.C., and continuing for another 500 years.

The Greek phalanx required a high degree of training to be effective, but an efficient one could still be produced by a local militia that trained in their free time. The Roman system, however, was a highly complex product that could only be achieved by a professional army that devoted itself full time to the development of its skills and the development of a leadership structure with systematic professional advancement based on merit, taking soldiers from the ranks and placing them in charge of larger and larger groups of men as they demonstrated competence at each level. The Roman open order of battle permitted their small unit leaders to move behind the battle line, holding their men accountable and rewarding skill and valor with advancement and reward.

Most elite modern armies are built around a professional corps of small unit leaders, drawn from the ranks with advancement based on merit, usually operating behind their men during combat to directly influence their actions. While this is the norm for today's successful armies, the Romans were the first to systematically introduce these factors to the battlefield on a large scale over a long period of time.

Another key aspect of the Roman way of war was that each soldier carried a variety of throwing spears (the number and type varied over the years), with which they were highly proficient. An approaching enemy was greeted with volleys of spears, which served to break up their ranks and often stripped them of their shields. These ingeniously designed distance weapons frequently included light javelins, thrown at long range, followed by a standard heavy spear (or pilum), thrown at medium range, and followed lastly by a lead-weighted pilum, which was hurled with enormous force as one final volley before closing with swords.

After shattering an approaching enemy force from a distance with a series of spear volleys, the Romans closed with short swords designed and intended for stabbing. These swords were often qualitatively no different from those of their opponents, but the Romans were systematically trained to use their swords to stab and thrust in a highly effective way that was largely unprecedented prior to this. Like the post-World War II training that would be developed two millennia later to condition men to fire in combat, Roman training used repetition to an extent that could be accurately described as conditioning, to insure that their soldiers would thrust in combat rather than use the more natural hacking and slashing blows. This was a technique that would be used in later centuries to train some elite warriors in fencing and swordsmanship, but never before, nor probably since, has an entire army been trained to this degree of perfection. The small unit leaders walking behind the battle line helped to enforce this. The Roman military chronicler, Procopius, noted that it was necessary for Roman centurions to smack their own troops with the flat of their swords while on the front lines of battle to remind them to thrust instead of slash.

This melding of projectile weapons and intense training, combined with the presence of effective small unit leaders who moved behind their men and demanded effective killing activities, was a devastating combination which (together with the Romans' superior ability to function in rough terrain) smashed or outmaneuvered approaching enemy formations, including the phalanx. The final ingredient in a Roman battlefield victory was the organization of their force into small units with reserves, and dispassionate, highly trained leaders operating behind their men, ready to keep their units in intact formations (even on broken ground, a major advantage over the phalanx) and maneuver their units to exploit any exposed enemy flanks or penetrate deep into the enemy rear. Once the enemy was defeated, the final blow (and most of the killing) was executed by cavalry auxiliaries (still without stirrups and little different from the cavalry of the Greeks) who would pursue and kill a broken, fleeing enemy.

The result of this complex process was the Pax Romana: hundreds of years of relative stability and peace in the Western world. But it was a fragile strength, created through complexity and economic abundance, which was difficult to sustain in the best of times and impossible to replicate (at least in Western Europe) for almost a millennium after the Roman Empire collapsed.

The Introduction of Stirrups and the Mounted Knight

Betwixt the stirrup and the ground,
Mercy I ask'd; mercy I found.

—William Camden
"Remains"

With the fall of Rome, the complex Roman way of war collapsed, to be replaced by older, simpler systems such as the phalanx, and one new system, the mounted knight. The introduction of the stirrup (coming to Europe from China and India around the tenth century, A.D.) made it possible for a man on horseback to strike an opponent with remarkable force without danger of being unseated. Furthermore, careful breeding of horses had developed increasingly larger and more powerful mounts that could carry sufficient armor to make both horse and man virtually invulnerable. A devastating blow could be delivered by a spear or lance, which could be "couched" or semi-attached to the knight. Charging at full gallop, the spear point would strike an opponent with the combined momentum and weight of horse, man and armor. After the initial blow with the lance, the knight could continue to plow into an enemy formation, delivering blows from above with heavy weapons (sword, mace, flail or morning star) assisted by the force of gravity and downward momentum. A formation of such knights, striking together, was extraordinarily frightening and virtually overwhelming, combining high degrees of posturing, force and mobility, which could only be stopped by a hedge of spears and the horse's complete and consistent unwillingness to impale itself.

Thus, the answer to the knight was a phalanx, but the horse's mobility made it possible to maneuver around it, or any enemy formation, in order to attack from a vulnerable direction, and to pursue the enemy after they had been broken. This created the need for spear- or bayonet-equipped ground troops to form a "square" that faced outward in all directions while keeping other units protected inside of it. This was an effective defensive maneuver as long as the infantry kept their nerve (if only a few men broke and ran, the knights could move into that gap and break the entire formation). Until the introduction of the longbow and later gunpowder, the square could be completely neutralized and was often held at bay by a small force of knights.

The longbow, crossbow and gunpowder weapons spelled the doom of the mounted knight and, ultimately, of all individual armor until the twentieth century. Cavalry would continue to exist on the battlefield for centuries, but their economic cost and their increasing vulnerability to small arms fire meant that by the late nineteenth century the utility of cavalry had reverted to that of the Greek and Roman eras. It was useful for reconnaissance, for moving riflemen rapidly to a key location where they would dismount and fight, and for mobility in the pursuit. During the twentieth century, mechanization (trucks, tanks, etc.) would supersede the horse's mobility contribution to the battlefield.

The Age of Gunpowder Weapons

> But I remember, when the fight was done,
> When I was dry with rage and extreme toil,
> Breathless and faint, leaning upon my sword,
> Came there a certain lord, neat and trimly dress'd . . .
> And telling me . . . that it was great pity, so it was,
> This villanous salt-petre should be digg'd
> Out from the bowels of the harmless earth,
> Which many a good tall fellow had destroy'd
> So cowardly; and but for these vile guns,
> He would himself have been a soldier.
>
> —Shakespeare
> *King Henry IV*

Man had always transferred kinetic energy over distances with rocks spears and arrows, but these projectiles could be neutralized by armor. With the advent of the longbow and the crossbow (c. 1400), the average combatant could then single-handedly fire a weapon from a distance, which would penetrate even the best of available, man-portable armor. This was a revolution that introduced a combination of distance and force factors that would continue in its basic format up to the present. The longbow started the process of rendering the knight extinct, but the advent of gunpowder introduced powerful posturing processes into the equation, which quickly (in evolutionary terms) led to the extinction of both the knight and the longbow.

Once individual gunpowder weapons were introduced and widely distributed (c. 1600), the evolution of close-range, interpersonal weaponry subsequently moved along a single, simple path of perfecting this weapon. The early, smoothbore, muzzleloading, gunpowder weapons were pathetically ineffective. They were almost impossible to aim, slow to fire and useless in any kind of damp conditions. Yet their posturing (i.e., their noise), combined with their absolutely overwhelming force (when they could hit something) was so great that they soon came to dominate the battlefield.

Gunpowder was invented in China, but China was under a comparatively centralized government that appears to have seen gunpowder weapons as a threat to the established order, resulting in a conscious decision not to develop them. (Over a millennium later the Japanese would do something similar.) A powerful argument can be made that this single decision in the evolutionary development of weapons resulted in the eventual subjugation of the East and the inevitable domination and colonization of the world by Western Europe.

In Europe, there were constant wars and turmoil, and a complete absence of centralized authority, which created an environment that pursued a continuous development and refinement of gunpowder weapons. This process led to weapons which could be fired in wet weather (percussion caps), fired accurately (rifled barrels), loaded from a prone position (breechloaders), fired repeatedly without loading (repeaters), and fired repeatedly with no other action than pulling the trigger (automatics).

Almost all of the development of gunpowder weapons occurred in the nineteenth century, and by the early twentieth century, the process had reached its culmination. One common myth in this area involves the increasing "deadliness" of modern small arms, which is largely without foundation. For example, the high-velocity, small caliber ammunition used in most assault rifles today, such as the M-16 and M-4 (which fire 5.56mm/.223 caliber bullets) and the AK-74 (which fires a small caliber bullet very similar to the M-16; do not confuse this with the AK-47, which uses the 7.62mm short cartridge) was designed to wound rather than kill. The theory is that wounding an enemy is better than killing him because when one soldier is wounded, it eliminates three people: the wounded man and two others to evacuate him. These weapons do inflict great trauma, but they are illegal for hunting deer in many parts of the United States due to their ineffectiveness at quickly and effectively killing game.

Similarly, after World War I the U.S. military's weapon of choice in pistols was a .45 automatic (approximately 12mm). Most recently the military weapon of choice became the 9mm, which has a smaller, faster round that many experts argue is considerably less effective at killing.

This new, smaller ammunition makes possible greater magazine capacity, which in one way has increased the effectiveness of weapons, while decreasing it in another way.

The Mind is the Final Frontier in Combat Evolution

All things are ready, if our minds be so

—Shakespeare
Henry V

Thus, we can see that there has not been any significant increase in the effectiveness of the basic small arms weapons available today. If we can see the enemy, we can kill them, and we can kill lots of them, very quickly. John Keegan in *The Face of Battle* called this, "An atmosphere of high lethality":

By the beginning of the First World War, soldiers possessed the means to maintain a lethal environment over wide areas for sustained periods . . . where one layer of the air on which they depended for life was charged with lethal metallic particles . . . It was as if the arms-manufacturers had succeeded in introducing a new element into the atmosphere, compounded of fire and steel.

This has been true since World War I, and in the realm of individual, small arms engagements it has not changed significantly since then. The pump-action, 12-gauge shotgun in police cars across America is still the single most effective weapon for inflicting massive trauma at close range and it has been available and basically unchanged for over 120 years. Transportation and long-range killing technology (missiles, aircraft, and armored vehicles) have all evolved at quantum rates, and their availability to the soldier on the ground gives him great power. The ability of one soldier to call in a 500-pound bomb that will land with pinpoint precision makes the individual very deadly, but the weapon he holds in his hand has not really improved by any quantum leap.

It is useful to think of the evolution in combat in the twentieth century as having moved through "solid," "fluid" and "gaseous" phases as the "energy" in the individual "atoms" or "molecules" (i.e., the soldiers) increased.

Solid Phase. The solid phase lasted from the ancient phalanx up to World War I, with compact, crystalline masses of humanity grinding into each other. In the end, whoever had their structure or formation shattered first, lost.

Fluid phase. Late in World War I, in desperation, the Germans introduced fluid warfare with Storm Troopers, or Von Hutier tactics, consisting of small units with heavy firepower and leaders authorized to conduct independent actions. Their objective was to infiltrate high-energy particles through the hard outer shell into soft, vulnerable rear units and key terrain in rear, like water coming through a small gap in a dam, forming what was called an "expanding torrent."

This was refined in World War II into "blitzkrieg" using very high-energy "armor" molecules with closely integrated air and artillery support. Today, this is called "maneuver warfare" (as opposed to attrition warfare), and it is a key doctrinal foundation for U.S. and British tactics.

Gaseous phase. As individual atoms and molecules (soldiers and systems) gain more and more energy (more powerful systems), the result is greater dispersal and a tendency to move upward, into the third dimension. Today, helicopters make whole divisions "air mobile" and "air assault" capable, with transport, attack, recon and command & control from air. Transports, fighters, bombers, and recon aircraft can saturate the upper atmosphere and satellites complete the equation, forming a comprehensive, three-dimensional battlefield, which the U.S. has incorporated as a war fighting doctrine.

The reality of combat is that the enemy gets a vote, too. The enemy also evolves and changes. And the opponents who were quickly defeated in the initial invasion of Iraq and Afghanistan soon converted to the classic "fluid state" of insurgent warfare. The "energy" that insurgent forces can deliver with improvised explosive devices (IEDs) and suicide bombers is nothing new. Previous wars have seen booby traps and kamikaze attacks. But now the "molecules" have increased in both quantity and degree of energy, demonstrating a capacity for sufficient numbers of highly dispersed, high energy "fluid" forces to partially neutralize the advantage of a high-tech gaseous force.

Just as weapons evolution has driven combat from solid to fluid to gaseous states, so too has the increased "energy" of the battlefield increased the area "heated" or affected by combat. The result is an ever expanding battlefield across time and space, progressing from:

-Agincourt in 1415, which was only hours long and covered an area not much deeper than the range of a longbow.

-To Gettysburg in 1863, which lasted three days long (but stopped at night) and covered an area as deep as cannon direct fire (about a mile).

-To World War I (1914-1918), when combat lasted for months on end, day and night and indirect artillery fire extended the depth of the battlefield for many miles.

Today we live in a world in which no place or time is ever truly safe in war. Although the soldier on this modern battlefield is like some ancient demigod calling in thunderbolts from above, the basic technology of the small arms weapons carried by the soldiers, weapons that kill by simply transferring kinetic energy from bullet to body, have reached an evolutionary dead-end in the twentieth and twenty-first centuries.

The basic, close-range killing weapon has not changed fundamentally in nearly a century, but as we have seen in this chapter, there has been a new, evolutionary leap in the conditioning of the mind that uses that weapon to kill at close range. The development of psychological conditioning processes to enable an individual to overcome the average, healthy individual's deep-rooted aversion to close-range killing of one's own species is a true revolution. This is a revolution on the battlefield, and it is a revolution that has also had an unprecedented influence on domestic violent crimes, which will be addressed in the next chapter.

-c.1700BC:	Chariots provide key form of mobility advantage in ancient warfare
-c.400BC:	Greek phalanx
-c.100BC:	Roman system (pilum, swords, training, professional leadership)
-c.900AD:	Mounted knight (stirrup greatly enhances utility of mounted warfare)
-c.1300:	Gunpowder (cannon) in warfare
-c.1300:	Wide scale application of longbow defeats mounted knights
-c.1600:	Gunpowder (small arms) in warfare, defeats all body armor

-c.1800:	Shrapnel (exploding artillery shells), ultimately creates renewed need for helmets, c.1915
-c.1850:	Percussion caps permit all-weather use of small arms
*c.1870:	Breechloading, cartridge firing rifles and pistols
-c.1915:	Machine gun
-c.1915:	Gas warfare
-c.1915:	Tanks
-c.1915:	Aircraft
*c.1915:	Self-loading (automatic) rifles and pistols
-c.1940:	Strategic bombing of population centers
-c.1945:	Nuclear weapons
-c.1960:	Large scale introduction of operant conditioning in training to enable killing in soldiers
*c.1960:	Large scale introduction of media violence begins to enable domestic violent crime
-c.1965:	Large scale introduction of helicopter in battle
-c.1970:	Introduction of precision guided munitions in warfare
-c.1980:	Kevlar body armor provides first individual armor to defeat state-of-the-art small arms in 300+ years
*c.1990:	Large scale introduction of operant conditioning through violent video games begins to enable mass murders in domestic violent crime
-c.1990:	First extensive use of precision guided munitions in warfare (approximately 10% of all bombs dropped), by U.S. forces in the Gulf War
-c.1990:	Large scale use of combat stress inoculation in law enforcement, with the introduction of paint bullet training in U.S. law enforcement training
-c.2000:	Approximately 70% of all bombs used by U.S. forces in conquest of Afghanistan and Iraq are precision guided munitions
-c.2000:	Large scale use of combat stress inoculation in military forces, with the introduction of paint bullet combat simulation training in U.S. Army and U.S.M.C. troops

* Represents developments influencing domestic violent crime.
(Note: Dates generally represent century or decade of first major, large-scale introduction)

Table I: Landmarks in the Evolution of Combat

seven
The Evolution of Combat and Domestic Violent Crime

The evidence is overwhelming. To argue against it is like arguing against gravity.

—American Psychological Association
on the wealth of information linking media violence
and teen violence.
New York Times, May 9, 1999

Through violent programming on television and in movies, and through interactive point-and-shoot video games, modern nations are indiscriminately introducing to their children the same weapons technology that major armies and law enforcement agencies around the world use to "turn off" the midbrain "safety catch" that Brigadier General S.L.A. Marshall discovered in World War II.

In terms of combat evolution, this indiscriminate use of combat conditioning techniques on children is the moral equivalent of giving an assault weapon to every child in every industrialized nation in the world. If, hypothetically, this were done, the vast majority of children would almost certainly not kill anyone with their assault rifles; but if only a tiny percentage did, then the results would be tragic and unacceptable. But it is increasingly clear that this is not a hypothetical situation. Indiscriminate civilian application of combat conditioning techniques as entertainment has increasingly been identified as a key factor in the worldwide, skyrocketing violent crime rates outlined earlier. Thus, the influences of weapons technology can increasingly be observed on the streets of nations around the world.

Weapons Lethality and Murder Rates

God made man, but Mr. Colt made all men equal.

—Anonymous

The resistance to killing addressed in the last chapter also exists in peacetime, and weapons provide psychological and mechanical leverage to enable killing in peace as well as in war. The lethality of weapons, in peace and war, is a contest between a weapon's effectiveness (the state of technology trying to kill you) and medical effectiveness (the state of technology trying to save you). Thus, the difference between murder and aggravated assault (trying to murder someone) is also largely a factor of the effectiveness of available weapons versus the effectiveness of available medical lifesaving technology.

Throughout most of human history, the effectiveness of weapons available for domestic violence did not change significantly. The relative effectiveness of swords, axes, and blunt objects was basically unchanged, and killing (as an act of passion, rather than a premeditated act, such as poisoning or leaving a bomb) was only possible at close-range by stabbing, hacking, and beating. Bows were kept unstrung and, therefore, were not in a state of readiness for an act of passion. It required a premeditated act, plus training, plus physical strength to kill with a bow. Like bows, early muzzle loading gunpowder weapons were generally not kept in a state of readiness because once they were loaded, the humidity in the air could seep into the gunpowder, making the load unreliable. Killing with these weapons generally required time, training and premeditation.

Only in the late nineteenth century, with the widespread introduction of breechloading, brass cartridges, was a true act of passion enabled by state-of-the-art weapons technology. Powerful weapons that could be used with minimal strength and limited training could now be kept loaded. This achievement in weapons effectiveness has been virtually unchanged since the 1860s. The early Colt revolver or a double-barrel shotgun was essentially as effective for close-range killing as any small arms available today.

Thus, the effectiveness of weapons available for domestic violence has remained relatively stable throughout most of human history. It made one, huge, quantum leap in the late nineteenth century, and then has not moved significantly, with the key exception of psychological conditioning methods designed specifically to enable killing.

Advances in Medical Lifesaving Technology

> Without advances in trauma care, there would have been 45,000 to 70,000 homicides nationwide in each of the past five years instead of 15,000 to 20,000.
>
> —"A Hidden Remedy for Murder"
> (reporting new research on the impact
> of medical technology on murder rates)
> By Michael S. Rosenwald, *Boston Globe*, 8/4/2002

Since 1957, the U.S. per capita aggravated assault rate (which is, essentially, the rate of attempted murder) has gone up nearly fivefold, while the per capita murder rate has less than doubled. The reason for this disparity is the vast progress in medical technology since 1957, to include everything from mouth-to-mouth resuscitation, to the national 9-1-1-emergency telephone system, to medical technology advances. Otherwise, murder would be going up at the same rate as attempted murder.

In 2002, Anthony Harris and a team of scholars from the University of Massachusetts and Harvard, published a landmark study in the journal *Homicide Studies* which concluded that medical technology advances since 1970 have prevented approximately three out of four murders. That is, if we had 1970s level medical technology, the murder rate would be three or four times higher than it is today.

Furthermore, it has been noted that a hypothetical wound that nine out of ten times would have killed a soldier in World War II, would have been survived nine out of ten times by U.S. soldiers in Vietnam. This is due to the great leaps in battlefield evacuation and medical care technology between 1940 and 1970—and we have made even greater progress in the years since. Thus, it is probably a conservative statement to say that if today we had 1930's level evacuation notification and medical technology (no automobiles and telephones for most people, and no antibiotics), then we would have ten times the murder rate we currently do. That is, attempts to inflict bodily harm upon one another would result in death ten times more often.

Consider, for instance, some of the quantum leaps in medical technology across the years. Just a century ago, any puncture of the abdomen, skull or lungs created a high probability of death, as did any significant loss of blood (no transfusions) or most large wounds (no antibiotics or antiseptics), or most wounds requiring significant surgery (no anesthetics, resulting in death from surgery shock). Also, consider the increasing impact of police methodology and technology—fingerprints, communications, DNA matching, video surveillance, and others—in apprehending killers, preventing second offenses, and deterring crime.

Each of these technological developments, in their place and time, should have negated the effects of weapons evolution and saved the lives of victims of violence. When assessing violent crime across any length of time, we should ask what proportion of trauma patients survive today, and what proportion of those would have died if they had 1940-level technology (no penicillin), 1930-level technology (no antibiotics), 1870-level technology (no antiseptics), 1840-level technology (no anesthetics), or 1600-level technology (no doctors, no anatomy).

The medical technology continues to move forward, saving ever more lives every year. In an article entitled "New Battlefield Techniques," the *New York Times* reporter Gina Kolata interviewed Dr. Paul K. Carlton Jr., the recently retired surgeon general of the U.S. Air Force. He told of field surgeons who carry everything needed in a backpack, including "sonogram machines the size of cassette recorders, and devices the size of a PDA that can do a complete laboratory analysis on a drop of blood."

Dr. Carlton used the U.S. invasion of Afghanistan as an example of what is now possible.

Of 250 seriously injured patients, only one died. "It was the lowest died-of-wounds rate in the history of war," he said.

One man suffered a catastrophic wound to his rectum, prostate, anus and bladder. The ghastly injury plunged him into shock immediately, but one of the backpack surgical teams got to him right away and did a damage control surgery. Then, he was put on an airplane equipped as a critical care unit and flown a few thousand miles to another hospital for another surgery to stabilize him. Then he was flown to Germany for reconstructive surgery.

"He's home with his family now," Dr. Carlton said. In any other war, he added, "he would have been dead."

A little over a year later, in the invasion of Iraq, new bandages with a powerful clotting agent that can stop arterial bleeding were introduced, providing yet another major leap forward in lifesaving medical technology. That same technology is also holding down the murder rate back home.

-c.1690:	French army institutes first scientific, systematic approach to surgery
-c.1840:	Introduction of anesthesia overcomes surgical shock
-c.1840:	Introduction in Hungary of washing hands and instruments in chlorinated lime solution reduces mortality due to "childbed fever" from 9.9% to .85%
-c.1860:	Introduction by Lister of carbolic acid as germicide reduced mortality rate after major operations from 45% to 15%
-c.1880:	Widespread acceptance and adaptation of germicides
-c.1930:	Sulfa drugs
-c.1940:	Penicillin discovered
-c.1945:	Penicillin in general use, and ever-increasing explosion of antibiotics thereafter
-c.1960:	Penicillin synthesized on a large scale
-c.1970:	CPR introduced on wide scale
-c.1990:	9-1-1 centralized emergency response systems introduced in U.S. on wide scale
-c.2002:	Harris, et al., landmark study by U. Mass and Harvard, published in the journal *Homicide Studies* concludes that medical technician advances since 1970 have prevented approximately three out of four murders

(Note: Dates generally represent century or decade of major, large-scale introduction)

Table II: Landmarks in the Evolution of Medical Lifesaving

Increases in Worldwide Violent Crime

> I think about your work on the effects of violent pop culture when the news tells us of dictators like Saddam and Kim Jong-Il, who are addicted to American "action" movies. One wonders whether the pernicious effects of our "culture of violence" may be extending beyond our borders!
>
> Our toxic products tend to sink to the bottom of humanity, where they will do the worst harm, in our society or elsewhere in the world. The American electronic media has much to answer for.
>
> —Asher Abrams, Gulf War veteran
> Correspondence to Colonel Grossman

Thus, instead of murder, we have to assess attempted murder, aggravated assault or some other consistently defined violent attack as an indicator of violent crime, and by this measure the increase is staggering. The study by Anthony Harris, mentioned above, concluded that in the U.S. the aggravated assault rate reported in the FBI Annual Crime Report is a highly accurate reflection of the problem in the U.S. (This study and many others, however, have concluded that the National Crime Victimization Survey is increasingly inaccurate.)

Consider the following per capita crime rates, as reported by each nation to InterPol. (The U.S. data is from the "FBI Annual Crime Report", and the Canadian data is from their Centre for Justice.)

U.S.	1957-00	5x
Canada	1962-00	4x
Norway/Greece	1977-99	5x
Australia/New Zealand	1977-99	4x
Sweden/Austria/France	1977-99	3x
8 other European nations*	1977-99	2x

(*Belgium, Denmark, England-Wales, Germany, Hungary, Netherlands, Scotland, and Switzerland.)

The increase in violent crime in all these nations occurred during a period when medical and law enforcement technology should have brought murder and crime rates down. Similar increases have been noted in India, Latin America and Japan, and all of these nations have identified media violence as a significant new factor that is contributing to this problem. As we shall see, the same factors that caused a revolution in combat are also causing an explosion of violent crime at home.

Military Conditioning as Entertainment for Children

> What boots it at one gate to make defense,
> And at another to let in the foe?
>
> —Milton
> *Samson Agonistes*

Television, movie and video game violence teaches kids to kill by using the same mechanisms of classical conditioning, operant conditioning and social learning that is employed by modern soldiers, but without the safeguards of discipline and character development. Since this subject has already been addressed extensively in *On Killing* and *Stop Teaching Our Kids to Kill*, and the impact of operant conditioning in violent video games has been updated in this book, I will not address these topics any further here.

One aspect of this problem that should be addressed here is the safety catch used to prevent soldiers from unlawful or unauthorized killing.

I was called as an expert witness and consultant in the case of Timothy McVeigh and the Oklahoma City bombing. The defense contacted me first, explaining that they wanted me to tell the jury how McVeigh's military experience and his Gulf War training had turned him into a killer. I told them that I could not do it. I was still on active duty then, and they argued that the Army could not say, "No." They had a court order signed by the judge in that case, authorizing me $150 an hour to serve as an expert witness. They had the money to pay me, and the authority to make me, but they did not have the facts on their side.

I told them that the reason I could not and would not do it was because they were wrong about how they perceived McVeigh's military experience. The truth was just the opposite, in that the returning veteran is a superior member of society and is less likely to use his skills inappropriately than is a non-veteran of the same age and same sex. Again they said they were willing to pay me $150 an hour, but again I said, "No." Then they told me something that I found to be very interesting. They said, "You don't usually admit this as a defense attorney, but we know that our client is guilty and our primary concern is to prevent the death penalty, and Timothy McVeigh might die if you don't help with his defense." Again I said, "No" . . . with a clear conscience.

Six months later the prosecution got wind of which way the defense was going and quickly secured me as a consultant, on standby as an expert witness, by government order. Which meant they never paid me a nickel. I showed them data from the Bureau of Justice Statistics, which demonstrated that our returning veterans from World War I, World War II, Korea, Vietnam, and the Gulf War were less likely to be incarcerated than non-veterans of the same age and the same sex. While those who learned leadership, logistics and maintenance skills returned home and put their learning to good use in the civilian world, those soldiers who learned only to kill did not.

Now, this does not mean that our veterans do not have problems. The data simply shows that in each of these wars we gave hundreds upon hundreds of thousands of men weeks, months and years of training on how to kill. Then we sent them to distant lands to fight for us, sometimes for years on end, and when they came home they were less likely to use their deadly skill than non-veterans of the same age and the same sex. The finest killers who ever walked the face of this earth were the boys who came home from World War I, World War II, Korea and Vietnam, and yet they were less likely to use those skills than a non-veteran. The reason is clear: Combined with learning to kill, they acquired a steely, warrior discipline—and that is the safeguard.

Across a hundred centuries, the fearsome forge of combat has forced the military to evolve the mechanisms to enable killing. Any nation that does not stay abreast of this dreadful evolution will be defeated and conquered. In that same fearsome forge, with the same tragic consequences of failure, the military has learned how to put safeguards on the returning warrior to insure that he is not a threat to the nation that sent him into battle. Any nation that does not do so, might also face defeat and conquest from its own soldiers.

Discipline is the safeguard in a warrior's life. It is the difference between the sheepdog and the wolf. The military does not dress young troops in uniforms, shave their heads and make them march just for the fun of it. They do these things because if the young warrior cannot submit his will to authority about inconsequential things, such as the way he dresses and how he wears his hair, then he cannot be trusted to submit his will to authority for important things, such as employing deadly force only when a situation calls for it, no matter how bad the provocation. At *least* while the trainee is in the police academy or in military basic training, there is a need for discipline and submission to authority, and that is the safeguard.

Say you are a law enforcement officer or a soldier, and you go to a firing range and shoot at the wrong time or point your weapon in the wrong direction. Or, worse yet, you shoot in the wrong direction. What do you think would happen? A whole world of hurt would come down on your head! The idea of shooting in the wrong direction or at the wrong time is beyond comprehension in the minds of a trained warrior. That is the discipline by which the warrior lives. That is the safeguard.

Media Violence and the "Classroom Avenger" Profile

. . . lieutenant colonel and psychologist, Professor David Grossman, has said that these games teach young people to kill with all the precision of a military training program, but none of the character training that goes

along with it. For children who get the right training at home and who have the ability to distinguish between real and unreal consequences, they're still games. But for children who are especially vulnerable to the lure of violence, they can be far more.
—President William J. Clinton, in his national address in the aftermath of the Columbine school massacre

Psychologist and FBI consultant, Dr. James McGee has conducted the most definitive profile of the school shooters, using extensive data collected from 17 cases. Dr. McGee calls these kids, "Classroom Avengers," and his superb research has been extensively used by local, federal and international law enforcement organizations.

There are many myths about these killers. For example, some individuals claim they were all on Ritalin or Prozac, which is wrong. The truth is that not one of these school shooters was on these drugs when they committed their crimes. One was reported to have been on Zoloft and one had been on Ritalin, but both had been taken off those medications prior to committing their crimes. It may be useful to ask ourselves how many kids (and how many adults) would have committed violent crimes if they were not on powerful, modern antidepressants.

None of the school shooters was on antidepressants, but according to the FBI, all of these Classroom Avengers did have something in common: All of them had refused to participate in any disciplined activity or sport, and all of them were obsessed with media violence.

Consider these facts:

-None of the school shooters was in varsity sports.
-None of them had trained extensively in the strict discipline of a martial art. (One had earned a yellow belt, the lowest rank which took only a few weeks, and after dabbling briefly he dropped out.)
-None of the school killers was in Junior ROTC.
-None of them was a competitive shooter, a very demanding sport with draconian punishments if you fire at the wrong time or in the wrong direction.
-None of the school killers had a hunting license, another activity that requires strict discipline and adherence to the law. (Did you know that if you shoot at a deer from your car, you would lose your car, your gun, your money, and your hunting license? For all you golfers, what would happen if the first time you cheated, they took your clubs and your cart, and banned you from golfing again? There wouldn't be any golfers left! Such draconian discipline and severe punishment is present in hunting because the activity involves deadly weapons, and hunters wouldn't have it any other way.)

-None of them had been avid paintball players, a demanding sport that requires discipline, and one in which the player can get hurt. (You may note that paintball does provide military quality conditioned reflexes and combat inoculation, but no one is attacking this sport, nor should they. The entire medical community—AMA, APA, AAP, and many others—has warned us about the health impact of violent video games, but not one scholarly study has indicated that paintball is harmful for kids. Again, discipline seems to be the safeguard.)

The video game industry is particularly incensed by this school shooter profile, and have gone to extreme levels to provide some exceptions. For example, they claim that the Columbine killers were reported to have gone bowling. Which is a pretty pathetic example, and I believe it simply proves the point if this is the best they can come up with. The primary point to remember is that it is not me saying this about these killers—it is the FBI.

It should be mentioned that there was one disciplined activity in which several of the school shooters did participate (although several of them later dropped out), and that was band. But no one is sure what to make of that. I am not taking a cheap shot at band, an excellent activity in which all three of my sons participated. This is a puzzle that many good people have examined with sincere concern, developing theories involving such factors as the absence of discipline in some band programs, possible bullying in the band environment, and the non-athletic nature of this activity.

With a few minor exceptions, none of the school shooters were willing to participate in disciplined, structured activities, but all of them were infatuated with media violence. In the end, the profile of the school killer is that of a sad, pathetic little kid who is obsessed with violent movies, TV, and/or video games, but who will not participate in an activity in which he might be hurt or have to submit to discipline.

I am not necessarily recommending any of these activities for children, nor am I condemning them. But I am joining our medical community in stating that, from the perspective of my area of expertise in enabling killing in combat, the impact of violent TV, movies, and (most especially) video games on kids should be condemned. Like the Al-Qaida terrorist, or the kamikaze pilot, or the Nazi SS, these kids have immersed themselves in a sick culture, and they have convinced themselves that what they are doing is good, appropriate and necessary. The school shooters are all products of our sick culture, and those who immerse themselves in the sickest part of our sick culture have potential to be very sick indeed.

Warrior Training: Violence Can be Good and It Can Be Needed

> To be prepared for war is one of the most effectual means of preserving peace.
>
> —George Washington
> First annual address to Congress, 1790

While discipline is the safeguard in a warrior's life, the other half of the equation is violence. When Private Grossman stepped off the bus in Ft. Ord, California, in 1974, a man named Drill Sergeant Garito was there waiting for me. I still have nightmares about that man upon occasion. The Stockholm Syndrome set in, I identified with my captor, and he convinced me, beyond a shadow of a doubt, that violence can be good.

In the law enforcement and military environment, can violence be a good thing? Yes, because it is often the only thing that will save your life. When done right, it is honored above all else. In the military, every barracks, range, street, weapon system, and ship is named after military heroes who killed lots of people, and young soldiers know that if they perform the same, they too will be famous.

My co-author tells about a man who took a woman hostage in her mobile home. At one point he inserted the barrel of a shotgun into her vagina and duct taped it into place. When negotiations failed and the man's agitated threats to kill the woman reached a peak, a police sharpshooter fired through the window, disintegrating the man's head. Was violence the solution in this situation? Was violence a good thing? Yes, because today an innocent victim is alive as a result of that action.

Drill Sergeant Garito convinced Private Grossman that violence was good and that violence was needed because there were people out there who would hurt me—and he was at the top of the list. When a soldier or police officer is convinced that violence is good and needed, when he is convinced deep in his gut that violence is valued and that there are people who need it used on them, then the foundation is established for that person to be a killer. When we add the ingredient of discipline with the capability of violence, we create a warrior.

The Media's Influence: Violent Kids Without Discipline

> Thou hast most traitorously corrupted the youth of the realm.
>
> —Shakespeare
> *King Henry VI*

What if we convinced our children when they were two, three or four years old that violence was good and needed, but we did not teach them discipline?

Then we would have created killers, little homegrown sociopaths, as in Moses Lake, Bethel, Pearl, Paducah, Jonesboro, Springfield, Littleton, Taber (Canada), Edinborough, Conyers, Ft. Gibson, Santee, San Diego, and Erfurt (Germany).

We have had a fivefold increase in per capita violent crime in America, Norway and Greece; and a fourfold increase in Canada, Australia and New Zealand. Violent crime has tripled in Sweden, Austria and France, and doubled in eight other European nations. Although there are many factors influencing this, let's examine one new ingredient in the equation: the media.

Until children are six or seven years old, they have great difficulty differentiating between fantasy and reality. That is why we do not use them as witnesses in court. We do not send people to prison on the word of a five-year-old, since kids at that age are so malleable and suggestible. When children between two and six years of age see someone on television getting shot, stabbed, brutalized, degraded, and murdered, those images are real to them, as real as anything in their young lives.

Wise men understood this over 2,000 years ago. Socrates wrote, in *The Republic*:

> What is this education to be, then? Perhaps we shall hardly invent a system better than the one which long experience has worked out, with its two branches for the cultivation of the mind and the body. And I suppose we shall begin with the mind, before we start physical training.

> And the beginning, as you know, is always the most important part, especially in dealing with anything young and tender. That is the time when the character is being molded and easily takes any impression one may wish to stamp on it.

> Then shall we simply allow our children to listen to any stories that anyone happens to make up, and so receive into their minds ideas often the very opposite of those we shall think they ought to have when they are grown up?

> No, certainly not.

> It seems, then, our first business will be to supervise the making of fables and legends, rejecting all which are unsatisfactory; and we shall induce nurses and mothers to tell their children only those which we have approved, and to think more of molding their souls with these stories . . . Most of the stories now in use must be discarded.

> The worst of all faults, especially if the story is ugly and immoral as well as false—misrepresenting the nature of gods and heroes.

> A child cannot distinguish the allegorical sense from the literal, and the ideas he takes in at that age are likely to become indelibly fixed; hence the great importance of seeing that the first stories he hears shall be designed to produce the best possible effect on his character.

Think of the impact of violent media as a boot camp for kids, their own little basic training. As they sit before the tube, hour after hour, they learn that violence is good and violence is needed. They see it, experience it—and they believe it. They are inundated with the violence factor, but they never get the discipline. Now, if it troubles you that our young soldiers have to go through a process of traumatization and brutalization, you should be infinitely more troubled that we are doing the same thing indiscriminately to our children without the safeguard of discipline.

Police officers see horrible things every day: car accidents, gunshot victims, suicide victims, fights, violent death, and suffering. Soldiers in combat see unconscionable acts of man's inhumanity to man. Would you want your child to see these things? No. Then why would you let them see it on television? Understand that what they see is real to them, and by watching all the blood, gore and revenge, they learn that that is the way the world works.

I was once on a national radio talk show discussing the effects of violent media on kids. A man called in to say that he agreed that it is a violent world and that he wanted his son to be able to function in such a world. To "help" his boy do so, he would take him to see violent movies every chance he got. In fact, the man had just taken him to see "Saving Private Ryan," a movie that is probably the most realistic depiction of the horror of combat that has ever been put on film. I asked the age of his son. "Six," the man said.

Six! Maybe a mature teenager seeing that extraordinarily violent movie with his father would be appropriate, but a six-year-old? Never. I said, "Brother, do you understand that for a six-year-old that movie was real? Do you understand that the real soldiers depicted in that movie traveled to a distant land and laid their lives down in the sand by the thousands to prevent the horrors of war from coming to American children? If those young warriors who died on that beach could see you intentionally inflicting the horror of that beach upon your six-year-old son, they would roll over in their graves."

Our job is to protect our children, not rape their innocence when they are six. We can no more share our favorite violent movie (or TV show or video game) with our kids than we can share sex with them.

The Effects of Violent Media on Children: Fear, Bullying and Murder

The oldest sins the newest kind of ways.

—Shakespeare
King Henry IV

Most children who are traumatized and brutalized through their exposure to violent media do not become violent, but they do become depressed and fearful. If you were in the service or are in law enforcement, you no doubt remember people who were washed out of basic training or the academy. These people wanted to be there, but the rigid discipline and the intense violence was just too much for them, and they became depressed and dropped out. Likewise, when two-, three-, four- and five-year-old children are exposed to this environment via media's realistic depictions of death and mayhem, it becomes too much for them and most of them just become depressed and fearful. They "drop out" of this "boot camp" violentization process, but they are forever scarred by their experience.

Most of those who do become violent will not become criminals, they will become bullies. Bullying is the law of the jungle. The alpha male in every tribe, in every herd and in every flock is a bully, which means he gets whatever he wants. In every environment on earth, being a bully is a perfectly adaptive, appropriate and desirable behavior—except in a civilization. In a civilization we must punish and prevent bullying.

Through their early exposure to bloody violence, we convince our youngest children that it is a dark, hard, brutal and desperate jungle out there and, as a result, most of them become victims and others become bullies. Have we got a problem with bullying in our schools? Yes, numerous studies demonstrate this fact, and it is a situation that is getting worse.

It is not just one big kid hassling one little kid, now it is gangs of bullies pecking away at one poor little kid. If you have been around chickens, you know there is always one chicken being pecked by the others, sometimes pecked to death. If you pull the victim chicken out and eat it for dinner (not much of a save from the chicken's standpoint), the remaining chickens will simply choose another to fill that one's place. The same thing is happening in our schools.

Not every child is being bullied. Some children are blessed with wonderful teachers who make school a positive environment that they look forward to. And others have such a toxic environment at home that school is an escape. For many kids, however, school has become a corrosive, toxic, fearful environment.

The Secret Service says that in 1998 we had 35 murders in American schools, but that is just the tip of the iceberg. Remember, medical technology is saving more and more lives every year. Besides the 35 deaths, there were around 257,000 serious injuries caused by violence in our schools that year. How many kids have been killed or seriously injured by school fires in the last 10 years? None. But a quarter of a million were seriously injured by school violence in 1998 alone.

Then there were nearly one million thefts and larcenies in those same months. Many of the kids who lost their bikes, skateboards, lunch money, and backpacks were victims of bullies, alpha males who committed criminal acts, using intimidation and physical force to take what they want. There were 1,500,000 reports of fighting. If you have not been a kid for a while, you should know that fighting is far different today than it has ever been. It is far more brutal and more likely to involve weapons.

My co-author investigated a case where a Vietnamese gang member was angered because another kid "looked at him hard" (meaning the kid glared) as they passed each other in the hall. The gang member skipped his next class and went to a nearby Vietnamese grocery where he bought a meat cleaver. He returned to the school, found the kid who had glared at him, and hacked a large wedge out of the boy's shoulder. As the other kids screamed and panicked, the gang member walked calmly back to store, cleaning the blood and bone chips from the blade on the way, and got a refund, telling the clerk he decided he did not need the cleaver anymore.

In the "good ol' days," it was always boys fighting boys, but about 20 years ago it began to change, with girls fighting girls and, in the last 10 years, girls fighting boys. To the boys' chagrin, the girls are winning. This is because the average girl can kick a boy's tail in junior high, since boys and girls develop at different rates. When they get into high school, though, and the boys have had a developmental spurt, they are fighting the girls and administering a degree of violence and brutality upon them like nothing we have seen before.

There is also a different nature to the ritualistic fight-after-school. Today, it is epidemic and extraordinarily violent. Statistics show 18 million incidents of bullying. Do we have a moral obligation to prevent this? Of course! Just as firefighters have an obligation to prevent fires, law enforcement has an obligation to prevent bullying and violence in the schools.

While there have always been bullies and bullying, there is something new going on, something fueling the fire. The AAP says that violence is a learned skill, and it is learned most pervasively through violence in the family and through—what is the new and toxic addition—violence in the media. The result: bullying and cruelty. What are television programs, violent video games and movies teaching kids about how to respond when being bullied? Payback. It is no longer just fighting back, now it is payback in the extreme. Remember the old television programs and old movies where the sheriff faced down the lynch mob? He would tell them that there is going to be justice in the town, and then he sent them home in shame. Sadly, those old themes are gone.

Hollywood voluntarily submitted to a written code, beginning in 1930 and continuing through 1968 when the Motion Picture Association of America (MPAA) rating system was set up. This "Hays Code" said that:

> . . . the MORAL IMPORTANCE of entertainment is something which has been universally recognized. It enters intimately into the lives of men and women who affects them closely; it occupies their minds and affections during leisure hours; and ultimately touches the whole of their lives. A man may be judged by his standard of entertainment as easily as by the standard of his work.

Movies like *Casablanca* and *Gone With The Wind* were made under a code that a criminal was not rewarded, violent behavior and lawlessness was always punished, and the criminal was never the hero. Well, that code went away in the late 1960s and then we got *Dirty Harry*, Charles Bronson in the *Death Wish* series, and Richard Roundtree in *Shaft*.

Today, there is a new type of hero in action, adventure and horror movies, in plots that almost always play out the same way. They begin with horrific death and destruction so vivid, so in-your-face that audiences, kids included, are virtual witnesses to bloody celluloid realism. Then the audience sits through the rest of the movie as the hero desperately seeks vengeance. Toward the end, it is often the bad guys who are shown playing by the rules, as the hero turns into an avenger, violating codes of ethics and breaking laws along the way. Anthropologists and sociologists say there is great power in the stories we tell ourselves, so when we tell tales of vengeance, we are going to reap avengers.

Say we have a kid being bullied. He feels helpless and powerless to fight back. He is not into sports, martial arts or any activity other than playing video games. He associates only with friends who feel the same way he does. He is, in fact, exactly like all the school killers who shared one common trait: an obsession with media violence. Like all the others, this kid becomes convinced that the right response is anger followed by revenge. What began as an outrageous act of bullying, soon begets an even more outrageous act of revenge. It is an all too common vicious cycle that is happening inside our kids' schools right now.

The 15-year Phenomena: A Generation Later, You Pay the Price

A boy's will is the wind's will,
And the thoughts of youth are long, long thoughts.

—Longfellow
"My Lost Youth"

Most kids inflicted with media violence do not become killers, they just become depressed and fearful. Those who do become violent turn into bullies. Still, enough kids do become killers that we now have this alarming statistic: Anywhere in North America where television has appeared, the murder rate doubles 15 years later. This has happened in South Africa, Brazil, Mexico, and Japan, but it has been best measured in North America. Television appeared first on the East Coast and then on the West Coast. It appeared first in the cities, then later in the countryside. It appeared first in the white community and then later in the African-American community. We got it first in America, and then later in Canada. No matter where it appeared, 15 years later the murder rate at least doubled. Why 15? That is how long it takes kids to grow up. We exposed them to violent media between the ages of two and six, which convinced them that the world is a dark and violent place, and then 15 years later, when they are teenagers or in their early 20s, we reap what we sowed.

The murder rate in America today is six per 100,000 per year. If six more out of 100,000 people were convinced to kill, the murder rate would double. Remember, murder is just the tip of the iceberg because for every homicide there are tens of thousands of injurious assaults, hundreds of thousands of thefts, millions of acts of bullying, and untold millions who live their life in fear.

The June 10, 1992, issue of *The Journal of the American Medical Association (JAMA)*, the world's most prestigious medical journal, reported that violence depicted on television "caused" (caused is a powerful scientific word) a subsequent doubling of the homicide rate in the United States 15 years later. The AMA is so convinced of the impact of violent media, that they said if television technology had never been developed in the United States (or if we had kept our kids away from it) there would today be 10,000 fewer homicides each year, 70,000 fewer rapes and 700,000 fewer injurious assaults.

I was on *Meet the Press* with Surgeon General David Satcher two weeks after the Columbine High School shooting in Littleton, Colorado. The moderator, Tim Russert, held up our book, *Stop Teaching Our Kids to Kill* and asked the Surgeon General who could possibly deny, in light of what happened at Columbine, that we are indeed teaching our kids to kill. During the panel discussion, the Surgeon General was asked if he could do a report on the link between media violence and violence in our society, and give us a warning just as his office did about tobacco. He said that he could do "another report," but first we should read the "1972 Surgeon General's Report", which had already established the link. He said we could also read the report by former Surgeon General C. Everett Koop that shows a link between media violence and violence in our society. "We don't need more research," he said. "We need action."

The Media Cover-up: Censoring News That Will Make Them Lose Money

> When organizations representing all of America's doctors, all her psychiatrists, and millions of parents, call upon an industry to change (i.e., reduce violence on the public airwaves), and then that industry does exactly the opposite (i.e., increases the violence), this can be viewed as nothing short of complete and total contempt for the people of the United States.
>
> —Dave Grossman & Gloria DeGaetano
> *Stop Teaching Our Kids to Kill*

No doubt you know that the surgeon general says that tobacco can cause cancer. Most people, though, are unaware that he has also said that media violence can cause real violence in our society. It is not surprising why so few people have heard of this when you consider that we count on the media for our information. If you were to ask the tobacco industry about the link between tobacco and cancer, they would most likely lie. Some might even believe their lies, but that does not change the fact that what they tell us is untrue. In the recent past, the tobacco industry has presented a stooge researcher and a tamed scientist on a leash to say that tobacco does not cause cancer, and that the AMA and the Surgeon General do not know what they are talking about. What was the one way you could tell when the tobacco industry was lying? Their lips were moving.

So, if you ask the television industry about the health impact of their product, what do you think they would do? They would move their lips. They would bring out their stooge researcher and their tame scientist on a leash, all to say that there is no link between violent media and violence in America. The AMA, APA, the surgeon general, and the AAP all cry from the mountain about the grave harm being done, but the media systematically censors their cries. The reason is clear: They are just another industry, like the tobacco industry that refuses to give out information that will cut its own throat.

The American Family Association (AFA) has done good work organizing people to boycott various elements of the media. They publish a monthly bulletin in which they outline what they consider to be the worst television programs, along with addresses and phone numbers of the sponsors. Not surprisingly, the media censors the information about these boycotts. Here is an example.

In early 2000, the Southern Baptist Church, which is the largest protestant denomination in the United States, representing millions of people, along with several other denominations, joined together to boycott Disney, primarily because of the violent, sexually explicit movies that they produce under another name. For several years Disney took quite a beating and their family movies consistently flopped, so the boycott was somewhat effective. But after the initial media report on the boycott there was never a follow-up story. There were plenty of other news and business articles about Disney's problems, but not one mentioned that there was an effective, ongoing boycott of Walt Disney by the nation's largest protestant denomination. Such boycotts are effective, but they are tough to get off the ground because the media refuses to give them coverage.

Here is another example of this censorship (can it really be called anything but that?). In July of 2000, there was a bipartisan, bicameral congressional conference at which the AMA, the APA, the AAP, and the AACAP—those are all of our doctors, pediatricians, psychologists, and child psychiatrists—made a joint statement to congress. They reported that the media is a causal factor of violence in our society, and violent video games are particularly dangerous. If you are like most people, you did not hear about that, though you probably did hear about the deadly problems with Firestone tires.

It is clear what is going on. On one hand everyone has heard and read that Firestone tires may have been a causal factor in approximately 250 deaths across several years (it has not been proven as of this writing). On the other hand, the *JAMA* says that the product presented by the media is a key, causal factor in 10,000 murders a year, yet no one hears a word about that. The reason is clear: We do not have a free press. When it comes to the media's liability, negligence and culpability, the information is systematically censored.

I was on the now defunct television program *Politically Incorrect*, sharing the stage with three Hollywood media types. Their big argument was this: "Well, people buy it, so we sell it." They admitted that it might hurt people, but their only defense was to blame the buyer. I told them that was "drug dealer logic," except that most drug dealers do not sell their product to little children.

The media also argues that it is the parent's job to control what kids watch. Do not regulate our product, they say, because it is the parent's job to monitor their children. Well, what if the pornography industry tried that? We know that the First Amendment protects adults to view porn, but what if a six-year-old child walked into a porn shop with a $10 bill, and the proprietor shrugged and rented him a video, arguing that it is the parent's job to monitor want he watches? What if the gun industry tried this? They could argue, "We're protected by the Second Amendment. Don't you dare regulate children's access to guns; that is the parent's job." What if the automobile industry used this argument, or the alcohol, or tobacco industries tried it? What if the child abuser tried that line? "I know that little girl was only eight, it's the parent's job to keep her away from me."

It is indeed the parent's job to protect their kids from guns, alcohol, tobacco, pornography, sex, drugs, and cars, and we have laws that help them do that. So why are parents being left to their own devices when it comes to violent media? The information exists about its toxicity, but the media uses their control over the public airwaves to censor it. Sadly, this censorship is impacting us at the cost of 10,000 murders a year.

The AAP says that of all the causes of violent crime in American, media violence is "the single most remediable factor." Just as there are many causal factors to, say, heart disease, there are also many causal factors to violent crime in our country. However, out of all the factors that influence it, media violence is the single most remediable.

In that joint statement made to the U.S. Congress by the AMA, the APA, the AAP, and the AACAP, they said: "Well over 1,000 studies point overwhelmingly to a causal connection between media violence and aggressive behavior in some children."

Until 2001, no one had demonstrated that when media violence is removed from the lives of children that their violent behavior goes down. That is, until the "Stanford study."

The Stanford Study: The Light at the End of the Tunnel

Long is the way
And hard, that out of hell leads up to light.

—Milton
Paradise Lost

In the spring of 2001, Stanford University released a landmark study that showed less television equals less violence. The study found a 50 percent decrease in verbal aggression and a 40 percent decrease in physical aggression, just by encouraging kids to turn off their televisions and video games. Thomas N. Robinson, an assistant professor of medicine at Stanford and the study's lead author, said, "What this says is there is something you can do in a practical way, in a real-world setting, and see the effects."

The Stanford data was gathered at two similar San Jose elementary schools. Researchers first carefully assessed the baseline level of aggressive behavior in 192 third- and fourth-graders through playground observations and interviews. They then introduced a curriculum at one school meant to encourage children to cut back on video games and watch less television. Two-thirds of the pupils agreed to participate in an initial, 10-day effort to turn off their televisions, which was monitored by slips signed by parents. Over half of them limited their television watching to less than seven hours per week during the next 20 weeks.

After 20 weeks, the researchers found a 40 percent reduction in physical aggression, and a 50 percent reduction in the level of verbal aggression in the overall population at the experimental school, compared with the other that did not follow the curriculum. The children who were the most aggressive at the outset of the study had the most to gain, and did in fact show the greatest benefit. The researchers also noted a significant reduction in obesity and overeating problems in the school where the curriculum was introduced.

Remember, according to the U.S. Secret Service, in 1998 alone there were 35 kids murdered in acts of school violence and a quarter of a million "seriously injured." However, it has been many years since a single child has been killed or seriously injured by school fire. This means that the likelihood of your child being killed or injured by school violence is thousands of times greater than the probability of them being killed or injured in a school fire. Thus, we have the moral obligation to spend at least as much time and energy on school violence as we do on school fires. Every school has sprinklers, alarms, drills, and extinguishers in preparation for fires, so why don't we prepare for what is killing our kids?

If we had a quarter of a million kids seriously injured by school fire every year, and we knew that fire drills would reduce that by 40 percent, would we have a moral obligation to conduct fire drills? You bet. So, if we have a quarter of a million kids a year seriously injured by school violence, and we knew that educating them about the health impact of media violence would reduce that by 40 percent, would we have a moral obligation to conduct media violence education? You better believe it.

When I was in first grade and the teacher told us that cigarettes could kill people, I thought immediately of my dad who smoked. I loved my dad and did not want him to die, so I hid his cigarettes (he convinced me that that was not a good idea). The generation in elementary school that was first taught about the health risks of tobacco is the same one that grew up and played pin-the-tail-on-the-donkey with the tobacco industry.

Today we are on the threshold of a generation that is being informed of the health impact of media violence, the result of which, if corrective measures are implemented, will be a major victory for America's children and for the American people. We have never had anything that demonstrated a fraction of the result of the Stanford study. We have wonderful programs in place, such as aggression replacement, peer mediation, Drug Abuse Resistance Education (DARE) and Gang Resistance Education and Training (GREAT), all outstanding efforts, but not one has demonstrated a fraction of the impact of simply teaching kids to just turn off the television. Turn off the toxic culture.

Here is what I call my "milk and cookies equation." Say there is a kid hooked on some kind of an addictive drug. We could give him all the milk and cookies in the world but he would still do everything he could to get his fix. If the drug were suddenly yanked out of his life, he would suffer and struggle through the withdrawal process until he returned to normal. It is only then, when he is no longer hungry for his fix, that he would be ready to accept the food. The Stanford study made it clear the positive impact that happens when we take the addictive drug of violent media out of children's lives.

I had the opportunity to work with a wonderful lady who runs a state sponsored school in Canada for violent Native American boys from the backwoods country. The kids in this Canadian school were placed there because they are prone to violence, so much so that the Mounties had to be called almost daily. The program was designed so that kids would attend the school for a short while and then get cycled out at the end of the semester.

With one group of boys, the principal removed television and all violent video games from their lives. Remember that the Stanford study found that the most violent kids were impacted the greatest when television was taken out of their lives. At the Canadian school, there was a 90 percent reduction in violence among the boys who had television and video games removed, compared to any previous group of boys who had been through that school.

Today this curriculum is essentially free, thousands and the Delta-Schoolcraft school district in Escanaba, Michigan, is now the national distributor for the Stanford "SMART" Curriculum. Twice a year they hold training conferences to distribute and familiarize educators with the curriculum. You can get information about the next conference at www.warriorscience.com.

Hollywood vs. America: "Anyone Who Thinks the Media Has Nothing to Do With It Is An Idiot."

The dream factory has become the poison factory.

—Michael Medved
Hollywood vs. America

Has there always been violence? Will there always be violence? Of course, but we know now that when the ingredient of media violence is added to everything else, violence skyrockets. After the slaughter at Columbine High School, the president of CBS television made a slip. When asked if he thought the media had anything to do with the Columbine shootings, he answered, "Anyone who thinks the media has nothing to do with it is an idiot." How much clearer can it get?

Shortly after the Littleton killings, the California Senate unanimously approved a resolution on media violence. By chance did you read or hear anything about this unanimously approved senate resolution? Probably not, because it was censored. Here is what Ted Turner said: "Television violence is the single most significant factor contributing to violence in America." He didn't say it is the only factor; he said it is the most significant one. Now, if Ted Turner knows that but he keeps selling it to kids, what does that make him? A hypocrite? A child abuser? An accessory to murder?

So why does he keep doing it? Money. It makes him rich. Rich like a drug dealer. Does a drug dealer know he is hurting people? Of course. Does he care? Not one bit. Do the media people know that they are hurting people? Of course. They even admit it. Do they care? Apparently not.

We are dealing with an industry functioning at the moral level of drug dealers; in fact, one of their objectives is to convince us to legalize drugs. Once they sell out to drug dealer logic, then the next natural step is to legalize drugs and identify with the dealers and other criminals. How low can they go? There is a wonderful, insightful book by Michael Medved called, *Hollywood vs. America,* and I encourage you to read it. I have been on Michael's national radio show several times. He is a brilliant man who writes a weekly column for *USA Today* and is one of our nation's most respected commentators on the media. *Hollywood vs. America*. That really says it all.

On one occasion, I was on CNN's *Larry King Show* and then later served as a member of a panel at a national conference chaired by King. He is a great man and his program is not hurting anyone—except maybe the occasional crooked politician. Still, he is part of the media industry, so his first response to its culpability was denial.

At one point in the program, King said, "Colonel, there's violence in the *Bible*. Why don't we take the *Bible* away from kids, too?"

"The difference," I told him, "is that the American Medical Association has not identified the *Bible* as a key causal factor in half of all the murderers in America. No one should be talking about very young children and the written word because they cannot process it until they are around eight years old. What they see goes into their eyes, it is decoded in their logic center, and it trickles and filters into their emotional center." I went on to explain oral communication. "No one should be talking about the spoken word, as it cannot be processed until around age four. Spoken language goes into the kids' ears, where it is decoded in the logic center, and then trickles and filters into the emotional center." Then I explained the dramatic difference with what the child sees. "Violent visual imagery can be fully processed as young as 14 months. The images seen by an infant go straight into the eyes, and then into the emotional center where they have an immediate impact on how that baby views the world."

Now, one or two violent shows will not immediately transform a young mind, but the average child in America spends more time in front of the tube than he does in school. In school, he learns reading, writing, arithmetic, and every other academic subject, but it is from television that he learns about death, horror and destruction.

Violent imagery can have a profound and tragic impact on a child. Comparing it to *Grimm's Fairy Tales* or comparing it to the *Bible* is like comparing cigarettes and chocolate.

Loren Christensen knows a young couple whose daughter was 17 months old on September 11, 2001. Like most people in America, the couple sat transfixed by the horrific images on their television: planes flying into the sides of the Twin Towers, smoke, screams, panic, the collapse of buildings, more screams, sirens, more panic, the urgency in the reporters' voices, and bellowing black smoke and lapping flames shooting from the Pentagon. Their 17-month-old daughter watched, too, sitting amongst her toys on the floor, her large innocent eyes glued to the violent images. Within an hour, she began to whine and wanted to be held, and by mid-afternoon the little girl was clearly anxious and clingy, her eyes large with fear. It finally dawned on her mother that her daughter had been watching the television screen, too. After that, the parents no longer watched the news when she could see it.

Here is another look at how kids process information at different ages:

-Your eight year-old is away at camp. He gets a letter from home that informs him that the dog was hit by a car and died.

-Your four-year-old child comes home from daycare and you sit him down and tell him that the dog was hit by a car and died.

-Your two-year-old child is standing out in the front yard and witnesses a car run over the family dog. The dog whines, cries and dies as it messes itself and bleeds a big bloody spot in the middle of the road, all the while the child watches with wide eyes.

Which do you think is going to have the most profound impact on the child? Obviously, the violent visual imagery is much more harmful to the child, because of the age at which each child processes the information and because of the visual nature of the information .

Learning Violence: We Are Biologically Primed to Seek Survival Data

Base is the slave that pays.

—Shakespeare
King Henry IV

The International Committee of the Red Cross (ICRC) invited me to join a handful of experts in Geneva, Switzerland, for a conference on the impact of media violence on atrocities worldwide. One of the attendees was a British biologist who discussed how living creatures are biologically primed to learn certain things at specific ages. For example, if a little bird does not hear its species' song in the first year of its life, it will never sing it later. This is because the bird is primed to learn only one song, and if he fails to learn it when it is supposed to, it never will.

Human beings have a capacity to learn violence the same way. We do not need violence any more than we need crack, nicotine or alcohol, but if we are exposed to it at a young age we become hooked. Humans are biologically primed to seek survival data, and violence is the ultimate survival data. What is the one event on the playground guaranteed to draw every child like a magnet? A fight. Children fight to see a fight, because if there is violence in their environment, they must witness it so they can adapt to it as quickly as possible.

Your brain, a self-programming computer that fills the space between your ears, is designed to help you survive. You do not have strong limbs, deadly fangs or sharp claws, but you do have a brain, and your survival depends on it adapting quickly to changes in your environment. If violence occurs in your presence, you have to learn to run or use violence in self-defense. Most kids run, or they become fearful and depressed. A few, however, learn to adapt to violence, and to use it.

When a boy between the ages of two and five years of age watches his father beat his mother every night, he probably learns to hate that behavior and to hate his father. Fifteen years later, when he is grown and has a wife and kids, it is probable that under stress he will beat his wife, too.

We know that not every kid who watches his father beat his mother will grow up to be a spousal abuser, but that kid is more likely to repeat the behavior than one whose father did not abuse his mother. This is because any behavior observed in the first six or seven years of a kid's life is hard to unlearn. As the child's brain develops, Mother Nature is a harsh gardener, pruning the unused, fertilizing the useful. That seven-year-old does not hide his eyes as his father strikes his mother, but he huddles in the corner, watching and learning. His biological drive for survival and to adapt to his environment demands that he watch and learn.

Once puberty begins, a second biological drive kicks in, one that is immensely attractive: sex. Procreation. Say you show a porn movie to a three-year-old; don't do it, it's not good for him, but the truth is that the kid could care less. He would just flip to another channel since the images wouldn't mean anything to him. Show porn to a 12-year-old, however, and he is riveted. His heartbeat goes up, his respiration goes up, and other things go up. He has an immediate and profound biological response to the pornographic images. Violent visual imagery is to a two-year-old as pornography is to a 12-year-old. The two-year-old boy's heartbeat goes up, his respiration goes up, and he is riveted. It is what he is biologically primed to seek.

I had an opportunity to talk with one of the vice presidents at Random House, the publisher of *Stop Teaching Our Kids to Kill*. He told me that he believes that television is the single greatest threat to the book industry today. When television viewing goes up, reading goes down. When the number of television channels goes up, the number of newspapers goes down. We spent 5,000 years struggling to become a literate society and now, for the first time in history, we are stepping backwards.

I had the occasion to be interviewed by Katie Couric on NBC's, *The Today Show*. She looked at me with those big eyes (which were kind of . . . distracting) and asked, "Colonel, I watched all that stuff when I was a kid and I'm not a killer. Why should I worry about my kids?"

I said, "Katie, when I was a kid I never buckled my seatbelt and I'm just fine. So why should I buckle up my kids?"

"Oh," she said.

Although she was playing the devil's advocate, there are many parents who live by that logic. Imagine some bubba from my home state of Arkansas driving through your state with his kids in the backseat, unbuckled and bouncing around like high-speed molecules. A police officer pulls him over, and says, "Sorry, but I'm going to have to give you a ticket because your kids are not buckled in. It's the law." Not surprisingly, my homeboy is going to try to get out of that ticket with a little Arkansas logic. "Well, officer," he'll say, "When I was a kid I never buckled my seatbelt and look at me. I'm just fine. In fact, everybody I know never buckled their seatbelts. And I bet you never buckled your seatbelt, and look at you. You're just fine, too." Do you think that logic will get him out of a seatbelt ticket? I don't think so either. In fact, ol' Bubba should get two tickets: one for not buckling his kids in and the other for, being "felony dumb," as we call it in Arkansas.

I have to admit that at one time I was felony dumb. I heard about the issue of media violence years ago, but I just ignored it. I thought that since it had not hurt me why should I worry about it hurting my kids. Today, I look back and I am ashamed of what I let my kids watch. By the grace of God they turned out all right. Most kids do, in spite of us. But what a stupid risk!

It is important that we learn from our mistakes. My mom did. She never buckled us kids into our seatbelts and we turned out okay. But when my mom had grandbabies, she "got religion." One time when my kids were little she came to visit me. I was a tough paratrooper then, a sergeant, a man of the world. I went to the airport to pick up my mama, as my two little boys bounced around in the backseat. The first thing she did after she got in the car was to try to take charge. She turned to me, and said, "Dave, buckle those babies up." Well, I figured I didn't have to take that anymore, so I said, "But ma, you never buckled us up when we were kids and —" Bam! She smacked me right up side of the head. End of discussion!

That is the kind of grandparent I am going to be. No, I am not going to thump them, but I will bribe them. My wife and I have cut a deal with our kids and they fully agree. We are going to pay them $1,000 a year towards the grandbabies' college funds for every year they promise to keep them television-free for the first six or seven years of their lives. I admit this might be over-the-top, but if they can keep those kids violence free, we will have done wonders for them during these most impressionable years.

When the military wants to put together an effective psychological operations message, they often go to those who make commercials, the people on Madison Avenue. In the field of behavioral sciences, more money has been invested in designing commercials than in any other. It is not a perfect science. If it were, we would all be eating "Big Macs" three times a day, but it is not for a lack of trying. Madison Avenue has spent billions of dollars to determine the right color and shape of a product, the most effective number of times to show the commercials, and the right flicker rate to ensure that your child walks away from the television screen with two things in his mind: a desire to overeat and dissatisfaction with his possessions.

Besides a pronounced reduction in violence, the Stanford study showed two other interesting side effects when television viewing was eliminated for a semester: A significant decrease in obesity and a decrease in nagging parents for toys. There is a national problem of obesity among our kids, not only because they sit on their chubby tails for long periods doing nothing but watching television, but also because they are victims of junk food commercials. While there are numerous studies that link television viewing with obesity, there is no study that shows a link between obesity and playing video games. The key factor in the equation is that they sit and watch television commercials that advertise tantalizing burgers, shakes, sugarcoated cereals, fat-laden chips, and sugar-saturated sodas.

Television gives our kids massive amounts of toxic and addictive violence and tweaks their minds with sophisticated psychology to make them overeat and feel a sense of dissatisfaction with their possessions. It is imperative that we protect them during the first six or seven years of their lives.

Violent Female Role Models and an Explosion of Violent Girls

Oh woman, woman! when to ill thy mind
Is bent, all hell contains no fouler fiend.

—Homer
The Odyssey (Pope transl.)

Why do you think males are the biggest perpetrators of violent behavior? Testosterone poisoning? That might very well be part of the reason, but arguably a more significant factor comes from the impact of role models. At about the age of two, a little boy and a little girl look at their naked selves in a mirror and discover their specific sexes (wow, look at that!). Shortly after this discovery, they start seeking same-sex role models, and they usually find it in the media. The little boy turns on the television and he sees male behavior manifested in violence. When he sees this depicted repeatedly on the tube, he begins to think that that is what the male species is all about.

Females are most often depicted in the media as passive and helpless victims. When a little girl sees that over and over, that behavior becomes a role model to her. The *Teenage Mutant Ninja Turtles* movies, last produced in the 1990s, were the last generation of all-male preschool violent role models. They were replaced with the Power Rangers, half of which were females. Let's call it gender equity in preschool violent role models. That generation grew up with the Power Rangers, which cocked and primed them for Xena the Warrior Princess and Buffy the Vampire Slayer, and many others.

It was even predicted a few years ago that there would be an increase in violent behavior by young females from their exposure to the bombardment of violent, female role models in the media. Well, the best measure of a scientific theory is its power to predict. In just 10 years, from 1990 to 1999, the aggravated assault rate for juvenile males went down five percent, while the juvenile female aggravated assault rate took a 57 percent hike. Juvenile weapons violations for males went down seven percent, but for females it went up 44 percent. Why are these numbers so dramatic?

To answer that, consider what the tobacco industry did. For years, they primarily marketed tobacco to males but then one day the ad men said, "Wait a minute. Half the population out there isn't smoking as much as they should. We need to hit them, too." So, they started marketing to females and, a few years later, there was a resultant explosion of cancer among women. It was even predicted that if there were an increase in smoking among females that their cancer rates would soar. A few years later, it was predicted that if there were an increase in violent female role models in the media, violent female behavior would soar—and it did.

The Future: Kids, the Internet and Bombs

> The childhood shows the man,
> As morning shows the day.
>
> —Milton
> *Paradise Lost*

Today, we are seeing a dramatic increase in incidents of planted explosives and suicide/homicide bombers causing massive death and destruction in war torn countries. Is it likely that international terrorists will do the same thing in the United States? I am afraid so, and I am afraid that we are going to see it perpetrated by homegrown terrorists, too.

With all the aforementioned violence enablers in place for our kids, we are going to see bloodletting manifest itself in new ways. The future is bombs, and the kids are going to get the information to make them from the Internet. Once an angry, sick kid downloads the simplistic instructions, he will go to Radio Shack to buy the electronic means, and to another store to buy a propane tank and a candle. That is all he needs to blow up his ex-girlfriend's house, or "pay back" the kids who bullied him at school and anyone else who happens to be in the vicinity.

While it may be impossible to keep the information and tools out of kids' hands, we must make every effort to understand what is in their heads and hearts. We know that the goal of every terrorist is media coverage, and to get it they need a body count. With that in mind, consider that video games are won by accumulating points. At the start of most games the player is armed with a knife or pistol, and if the player kills enough people, the kid is rewarded with bigger weapons. When he advances to the upper levels of the game, he is given the ultimate in weaponry: bombs, rocket launchers, grenades and grenade launchers, sticks of dynamite, barrels of gunpowder, and pipe bombs, instruments to kill large quantities of people all at one time. Once they have worked up to a place where they have killed in mass, the game is still not over. Now they use their arsenal of guns to kill whoever is left standing.

The old model terrorist, such as the IRA, planted bombs and then quickly departed the area. In Oklahoma City, Timothy McVeigh left a bomb at the Federal Building and then walked away. Today, there is a new generation of killers who are inspired by video games, and they too will plant bombs, but then they probably will not just walk away. Case in point: If it were not for one flaw in their bombs, the Columbine High School shooters would have caused death and destruction of unthinkable proportions. Their plan was to detonate large propane tank bombs in the cafeteria to kill a mass of kids, and then use guns and secondary bombs to kill the survivors when they fled out the exits. Their goal was to kill everyone in the school. One subtle flaw in their bomb making techniques prevented this video game-scripted model from making that tragedy many times worse than it was.

While we should feel relief that they failed to get the huge body count that they desired, we cannot sit back and get too comfortable, because the mistakes made at Columbine have been analyzed and corrected. The investigating fire chief at Columbine told me that within a week of the shooting there were Web sites around the world identifying errors the Columbine killers made in building their bombs—and correcting them.

Our Violent Future: Respond with Caution

> We will not anticipate the past; so mind, young people,—our retrospection will all be to the future.
>
> —Richard Brinsley Sheridan
> *The Rivals*

Since Columbine, there have been several cases of kids with bombs and guns caught by the police before they could inflict massive death in their schools. There will be more attempts, and some will succeed. Police, teachers and emergency crews need to be courageous and rescue the wounded, but they need to do so with great caution and with security in place. They need to be alert for a gunman in the middle of the kill zone with a shotgun, or an entrenched sniper gunning down survivors.

There are two lessons regarding bombs that we all need to learn and apply. First, whether the scene is a workplace or a school, never evacuate into a parking lot. Car bombs are the most simplistic type of explosive. While a killer might be able to sneak a 20-pound bomb into a school in a backpack, a car parked next to the building can hold and hide hundreds of pounds of explosives. Do you remember the car bomb at the Sari nightclub in Bali that killed nearly 200 people in October of 2002? This is why people need to be cautious about evacuating a school every time it receives a bomb scare. There will be lives lost should a bomb explode inside a school, but if everyone then rushes out into a parking lot, a well-placed car bomb could kill vast numbers of people, with a sniper picking off any remaining survivors. If students must be evacuated into a parking lot, make it the faculty lot. The second lesson is to stay away from any vehicle, box, bag, pipe, or freshly upturned dirt, objects and locations where secondary explosives might have been planted to continue the carnage.

Paranoia? Over the top? Not at all. These two lessons were learned at the price of blood and lives in nations such as Israel, England, Ireland, Spain, France and Russia. The most significant terrorist act in human history—September 11, 2001—happened to us, on our watch, in our lives. We must be ever vigilant to more possibilities. School violence could be worse than it already is, but now kids, teachers, administrators, parents and police officers are all working together to do the right thing. Concerned people are hurling themselves on this grenade and trying desperately to contain it.

The majority of kids in our schools are good, but the kids who are bad are the worst we have ever seen. We did it to them; we allowed it to happen, but it is not too late. Education is the most important solution strategy, and if we teach kids about the unhealthy impact of violent media and encourage them to turn it off, it will have an enormous impact. We know this from the results of the Stanford study and others.

Many of our so-called problem kids do not live with their parents but are in the custody of juvenile parole and probation services or a foster parent by court order. On my Web site, www.warriorscience.com, there is a link to a model juvenile parole and probation order written by a judge. When the judge writes such an order, he not only has the authority to mandate appropriate media viewing for the kid, he has the responsibility to do so. Remember, the Stanford study and others done in Canada revealed that the more violent the kid, the greater were the results when the viewing of violent movies, television and video games was eliminated.

Making the Media Link: Ask What They Watch

> Find out the cause of this effect,
> Or rather say, the cause of this defect.
>
> —Shakespeare
> *Hamlet*

Police officers investigating crimes committed by kids or even by mentally disturbed adults who have committed, say, massive workplace shootings, should ask the perpetrators if their crime reminded them of a specific video game, television program or movie. They should not be asked if they were inspired by a movie or a video game, as that often makes them angry. Many of them have great pride in what they have done and they do not want to give credit elsewhere. For example, when the detective in the Paducah, Kentucky, school shooting case asked the young shooter if he was inspired by the movie *Basketball Diaries*, the kid became enraged. Later, he told his psychologist, "This is the only real adventure I've ever had and now they are trying to accuse me of being a copycat." The two Columbine High School killers even said in their videotape that no one should think they were copycats. "Those other kids were the copycats," they said, "We had this idea first."

These killers denied they were copycats because deep inside they knew they were. The detective in Paducah backed off and then came back with a softer and slightly different approach. "What movie was it like?" he asked, and just like that the kid connected the dots. That is the key question officers should ask: What video game or what movie was it like?

Brain Scan Research: The Final Nail in Hollywood's Coffin

> Next time you find your child playing a violent video game or watching an action movie, think. Because you want them to be able to do so.
>
> —Center for Successful Parenting
> Brochure on Indiana University Brain Scan Study

The final nail in Hollywood's coffin will be the brain scan studies that are now coming out around the world.

Once upon a time I could show you two X-rays: one of a smoker's lung, and one of a healthy lung. End of discussion.

Now I can show you two brains scans: one of a healthy child, and one of a child "whacked out" from media violence. End of discussion.

This research has been replicated in Texas and Japan, and as time goes by we will see more and more of it, but the true pioneer in this field was the Center for Successful Parenting, which funded the brain scan research conducted by the Indiana University Medical Department. Not that this is medical research. I cannot over emphasize how important it is that we listen to the AMA and not Hollywood or the video game industry. When it comes to our children's health we must listen to the medical professors, not the journalism professors.

I'd like to tell a little story to demonstrate how foolish I think it is to give any credibility to the industry that sells this stuff, or to the journalist or the sociology professor, instead of listening to the medical profession.

A police officer told me about two felons fleeing in a car. When the police finally got the car stopped there were cops in front of the suspects' car, so if it pulled forward it would be a clear deadly force threat. The officer said that he went up to the driver's side window with his gun drawn. It was a hot day and the windows were open, so he commanded to the driver, "Stop the car or I will shoot."

He said,

> I distinctly heard the guy in the passenger seat say, "Go ahead, man. He won't shoot." So the car started to pull forward and "Blam! Blam!" I put two holes in the driver. Then I distinctly heard 'Einstein' in the passenger seat say, "Whoa! Sorry man."

The moral of the story is this: Be very careful who you get your advice from. If you are getting advice about the health effects of screen violence from Hollywood, the TV industry, the video game industry, the journalism professor, or the sociology professor, then you are about as "swift" as the driver in that car.

So listen to what the Indiana University Medical Department's brain scan research has to tell us. The following is an extract from the Center for Successful Parenting brochure designed to inform the public about this important research.

PARENTAL WARNING
VIOLENT MEDIA EXPOSURE HAS A NEGATIVE
EFFECT ON YOUR CHILD'S BRAIN

You probably think that the video game your child is playing every afternoon isn't affecting their behavior. Think again. Researchers at the Indiana University School of Medicine recently conducted a study that demonstrated otherwise.

The Study

Over a two-year period, researchers at Indiana University School of Medicine studied two groups of adolescents between the ages of 13 and 17.

The first group was made up of normal teenagers. The second group consisted of teenagers who had been diagnosed with disruptive brain disorder or DBD. A DBD diagnosis is given to children who have shown significant aggressive behavior and resistance to authority. Subjects from the two groups were paired according to age, gender and IQ.

Step One

In step one of the study, the teenagers and their parents were surveyed about the teenagers exposure to violence in video games, movies and television.

Some of the teenagers had viewed a lot of media violence throughout their lives and some had viewed very little.

Step Two

In step two, the teens were tested in a very sophisticated MRI, called fMRI. The fMRI produces pictures of the activity in the logical part of the brain, the pre-frontal cortex. This part of the brain produces what we think of as adult behavior.

The pre-frontal cortex is responsible for controlling behavior, moderating impulsive urges, thinking about future consequences and decision-making. If children do not fully develop their pre-frontal cortex, they can become problem adults.

The Brain Scans

The following two sets of the fMRI pictures or brain scans show the differences in brain activity between teenagers who had been exposed to a lot of media violence and those who had been exposed to very little.

To understand the pictures, you need to know that the scans on the left are teens with low exposure to media violence and the scans on the right are teens with high exposure. The larger the black area, the more brain activity is occurring in the logical, adult part of the brain.

This is the area that parents want to develop in their children. Conversely, the smaller the black area, the less brain activity is taking place.

The Video Game

This set of scans shows brain activity when the teenagers were viewing a video game inside the fMRI. The low media exposure teens are using more of the logical part of their brains than the high exposure teens.

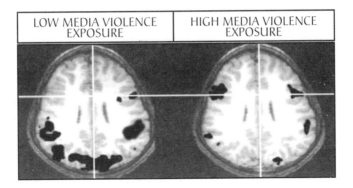

| LOW MEDIA VIOLENCE EXPOSURE | HIGH MEDIA VIOLENCE EXPOSURE |

Decision Making

This set of scans shows brain activity during a decision making exercise, called Go-No-Go. When it comes to looking into the future, weighing consequences and making decisions, the low media violence exposure group is using a lot of the logical part of their brain; the high media violence exposure group is using very little.

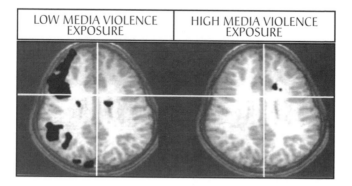

The Conclusion

After studying and comparing all of the brain scans of all the teenagers, what did the researchers conclude?

The most surprising result was that normal teenagers with a high amount of exposure to media violence had reduced activity in the logical part of the brain similar to those of teens with disruptive behavior disorder.

All of the teens with DBD—disruptive behavior disorder—had less activity in the logical part of their brains than normal teens. The more violence they had seen, the more pronounced the deficit.

The normal teens that had seen very little media violence had the most activity in the logical part of the brain—the part that parents want to develop in their children.

All of these results indicate that there is a correlation between the amount of media violence children see and their ability to think logically.

Next time you find your child playing a violent video game or watching an action movie, think. Because you want them to be able to do so.

What YOU Can Do As A Parent

-Provide a media-free zone in your child's bedroom—no TV, video games, computer, VCR or DVD players.

-Reduce the exposure children have to violent content in movies, TV and video games.

-Refuse to expose children under the age of 7 to ANY violent content in entertainment.

-Make TV viewing a family activity and have the TV in a common area.

-Turn off the television before school.

-Don't let your children play violent video games. Check www.moviereports.org for reviews of video games.

-Know the content of movies before your child goes to the theater. Check www.moviereports.org for information on violence, sexual content and language in movies.

-Don't let a child under the age of 17 go to an "R" rated movie.

-Monitor your child's use of the Internet. Don't let your child have unlimited access to the Internet.

-Get involved in the Parents Awareness Campaign. All 70 million families in America must become aware of this national health hazard—your child is not really safe until they and their friends are media violence free.

This was just the conclusion based on "Phase One" of a major, three phased research project. More information will be available on the Center for Successful Parenting (CSP) Web site, www.sosparents.org, in the years to come. For now it is sufficient to know that the CSP has concluded that:

-Media violence stunts, or "retards," kids' brain development: Kids with violent TV, movie, and video game exposure had reduced cognitive brain function.

and

-Media violence makes violent brains: Violent TV, movies, and video game exposure had an effect on normal kids that made their brain scans the same as kids with documented, diagnosed Disruptive Behavior Disorder.

The Future: Peace Warriors and a Reckoning for the Media

> Yet sometimes glimpses on my sight,
> Through present wrong the eternal right;
> And, step by step, since time began,
> I see the steady gain of man
>
> —John Greenleaf Whittier
> *The Chapel of the Hermit*

Kids' access to violent media is not the only factor attributing to raging, escalating violence. There is also child abuse, poverty, gangs, drugs, breakdown of moral structure, lack of moral training, easy access to weapons, and mental illness. These are all factors, too. Keep in mind, though, what Ted Turner and the AAP say is the most "remediable," the most "significant" factor: media violence. Yes, you can just turn media violence off in your house, but there will be millions of other households where kids are watching it because their parents allow them to. They are watching it because it is available to them.

The good news is that we have a joint, moral responsibility to fix this wrong and we are working hard to get more and more people to join the fight with us. One hundred years ago it was legal to sell alcohol to a nine-year-old and the alcohol industry did exactly that, and they even murdered people in their battle to keep doing it. Fifty years ago it was legal to sell tobacco to a six-year-old and the tobacco industry did, and they had an army of people battling any law that would keep tobacco out of the hands of kids. Why was the tobacco and alcohol industry working so hard to keep selling their product to underage customers? Money. The younger the consumers are when exposed to the toxic and addictive substances, the more likely they are to have an addictive response for a lifetime.

Today, television, movie and video game industries are doing the same thing as they sell their toxic and addictive substance to kids. Just as tobacco manifested in an explosion of cancer and heart disease, media violence has manifested itself into the most violent times in peacetime history. Even if we could stop all the media violence today, it would take at least 15 years to see long-term, positive results, though we would experience an immediate impact, just as was found in the Stanford study when television viewing was curtailed for one semester.

I truly believe we are on the threshold of positive change, but it is going to take time. The brain scan research findings are coming out and schools across America are embracing the Stanford study and investing themselves in it. Their curriculum has been released nationwide and is available to anyone in any school through The Center for Successful Parenting (www.SOSparents.org).

To win this battle we need peace warriors. We have peace officers in America and we have peacekeepers in distant lands. We have activists, educators, students and parents, all working together for peace. You have a choice between the culture of death, or the side of the peace warriors. Chose your side.

The peace warriors will succeed, and for those who sold death and destruction to our children there will be a reckoning. But first there will be many violent years in front of us, years that will make what we have experienced thus far pale in comparison. We can survive those years, but to do so we need educated, informed warriors. Warriors who remember the dead children they have held in their arms and who understand the causes of violence in our society.

> For they are the sparrows around God's door,
> He will lift them up in His own great banner.
> But the folks who made them suffer so sore,
> He will deal with them in a different manner.
> —Stephen Vincent Benet

Section Four

The Price of Combat:
After the Smoke Clears

To Live As A Warrior

So live your life that the fear of death
can never enter your heart.

Trouble no one about their religion;
respect others in their view,
and demand that they respect yours.

Love your life, perfect your life,
beautify all things in your life.

Seek to make your life long
and its purpose in the service of your people.

Prepare a noble death song for the day
when you go over the great divide.

Always give a word or a sign of salute when
meeting or passing a friend, even a stranger,
when in a lonely place.

Show respect to all people and grovel to none.

When you arise in the morning give thanks
for the food and for the joy of living.
If you see no reason for giving thanks,
the fault lies only in yourself.

Abuse no one and nothing, for abuse turns
the wise ones to fools and robs the spirit of its vision.

Live right so when it comes your time to die,
you will not be like those whose hearts are filled with
the fear of death, who weep and pray for a little more
time to live their lives over again in a different way.

Sing your death song and die like a hero going home.

—Tecumseh

The Great Shawnee Warrior and Statesman

(Courtesy of The United Tribe of Shawnee Indians)

one

Relief, Self-blame and Other Emotions:
"My World Was Turned Inside Out"

The mind is its own place, and in itself
Can make heaven of hell, a hell of heaven.

—Milton
Paradise Lost

"Thank God It Wasn't Me"

Then my world was turned inside out. One of the guys that I had come to know and respect, and I called a friend, was killed. He died in front of me and I couldn't do anything about it. All of the ways I'd dealt with death up to that time were of no use to me now. I felt guilty that I couldn't do anything to prevent it. I felt "better him than me," and then I felt guilty about feeling that. I felt alone. I felt the loss of a friend. I felt that if it happened to him, it could happen to me. I was sickened by the way he died. I was pissed that the enemy could do this to my friend. But we were in the middle of a firefight. I didn't have time to dwell on it so I had to put off feeling anything until later. At his memorial service I cried.

—Tom Hain, Vietnam veteran

The first response of most people upon seeing sudden, violent death is relief; they are relieved that it did not happen to them. Say your partner or buddy is killed and your first thought is, "Thank God it wasn't me." Later, when you reflect on your first response, how do you think that will make you feel? Guilty. You are consumed with guilt because no one ever told you that the normal response of most people upon seeing sudden violent death is to focus on themselves, and to feel relief. The puppy is in charge (your midbrain, that part concerned about your survival), and it sends out a message, "Hey, that could have been me."

The day after a major school shooting, I was in the school explaining the debriefing process to the teachers who had just survived that horrific event. I explained that they should not feel guilty about any initial concern they had for themselves during the tragedy, because such an emotion was a perfectly normal response to such extraordinary violence. I told them that it is similar to when the stewardess on an airliner tells them that if there is a loss of cabin pressure, oxygen masks will drop down, and they should put on theirs before they help small children. The first response of the organism is to take care of itself first, and that is okay, because that is simply the law of nature. After I explained this to those teachers, several of them laid their heads down on a table and began to sob with relief. They were relieved and comforted to learn that what they had experienced was normal.

If you know in advance that it is normal upon seeing trauma and death, to think, "Thank God it wasn't me," then that thought will not have the power to hurt you later. That is the first debriefing principle: "You are only as sick as your secrets." Just like when you know ahead of time that a loss of bowel and bladder control is normal, then that too no longer has the power to hurt you.

The Catholic Church has understood this for over a thousand years. They call it, "confession." They know that when you confess your secrets and lay them on the table, so to speak, you come to terms with them so that they have far less power over you.

"It's All My Fault" and the Power of Debriefing

With *Plato's Republic* and the *Bible*, *Oresteia* (a trilogy of 3 plays about the hero cycle of Orestes) is one of the three most important works of Western literature. Orestes must avenge the murder of his father by killing his father's murderer: his mother. It drives him to psychosis.

The conflict of the *Oresteia* is between the ancient tribal code of vengeance and the new law of forgiveness. The ancient tribal gods of blood-guilt are the furies, who drive Orestes to mental illness through the violence he must do to fulfill their law of revenge. The new law is given by Athena, patron of the young democracy of Athens. She casts the deciding vote in the Athenian assembly to acquit Orestes of his guilt after a long and passionate discussion and trial, which frees him from his debilitating "PTSD." The work ends with a hymn of praise to holy Peithous.

Peithous, not pathos. No, it's not divine Mercy, not Faith, not even Justice. Peithous simply means . . . dialogue! It is the power of telling our stories honestly in a trusted circle of compatriots. What a remarkably unmiraculous salvation, yet profound as Grace: men can be healed through telling their stories in community! Your book can be that community, "no judgment, no condemnation, just the remarkable power of understanding."

—Alfred LaMotte
Chaplain, Charles Wright Academy
Correspondence to Colonel Grossman

In the stress of a violent situation, the tendency to accept responsibility for what happened can be a powerful one. The midbrain can hit you with an it's-all-my-fault response. For example, kids of recently divorced parents are often convinced at some gut level that the demise of the marriage is because of them. They think that if they had just been better kids the divorce would not have happened.

After one horrendous massacre at a middle school, many of the 11-, 12- and 13-year-old children said in their debriefings that they believed that what had happened was all their fault. "If I had just been nicer to him on the bus on Friday maybe he wouldn't have been mad at us." "If I had just said something to him in the hallway on Monday, maybe he wouldn't have done this." "If I had not let the fire door shut behind us . . . ." "If I had only pulled her down to the ground when I went down." On and on it went. If the kids were thinking this way, finding some convoluted probability path by which they could have prevented some aspect of what had happened, what do you suppose the teachers were thinking? They were eating themselves alive. This brings us to the second debriefing principle: pain shared is pain divided.

Say we are going to debrief the individuals involved in a police shooting. All the participants are present—including the dispatcher, who should always be included, since she could be living in hell and very much in need of "filling in the gaps" through the debriefing process. Many of the participants walk into the debriefing with the weight of the world on their shoulders, thinking, "It's all my fault." One might even say it out loud. "Man, I think this was all my fault." Another says, "No, I think it might be my fault." Still another says, " No, I blew it, because I should have done it differently." As the debriefing unfolds, each member figures out that it cannot be everyone's fault and by the time it ends, each person walks out with his fair share of the blame. They came in with the weight of the world on their shoulders, and they walk out with their fair share. Pain shared is pain divided.

Much more will be said about critical incident debriefings in later chapters, but for now it is important to point out that the authority, ability and responsibility to divide the pain falls on the shoulders of the people who shared the event. They are the ones who can sift through what happened and help each person understand the totality of the event. They must be there for each other to "divide the pain." By the way, the rest of the equation is "joy shared is joy multiplied." First the pain is divided and then the joy is multiplied.

Sometimes just being educated about the it's-all-my-fault response can help put things in perspective and send someone down the path of healing. Here is an example of a warrior who accepted responsibility for a death that was not his fault, and found healing afterward by being trained and informed about this common response:

In 1992 I was a young correctional officer at the county jail. In the MAX unit was an inmate named . . . Green. He was a sex offender and was in jail for a parole violation and was going to be sent back to prison in a few days.

Green was a model inmate, never caused any problems and did what he was asked to do. One day . . . he asked how my day was and when I thought I would be back into the block. I told him that . . . I would be back soon and asked if he needed something. Green stated that he was writing a letter and that he would give it to me to mail later.

I walked into the MAX cell block where Green was housed just as another officer went into Green's cell to get him for commissary. I heard the officer yell and I ran to the cell. I observed Green with a sheet around his neck hanging. His face was purple, his eyes red and bulging and his tongue was sticking out of the corner of his mouth.

Me and the other officer got Green down and laid him on the cell floor. I started to do CPR on Green and was soon joined by another officer. Medical arrived and Green was transported to the hospital where he was pronounced dead.

I did not want to admit to my fellow officers that this incident had shook me up. I also felt responsible for not having found Green sooner, for not being able to save him or knowing that he intended to harm himself. He was one of the inmates in my block.

Although Green had never threatened or showed any signs that he was planning to kill himself, I felt that it was my fault that he had done so. For months after the incident, Mr. Green would come to me in my dreams. He would be wearing a jail uniform and looked just as he did the day we found him hanging. In my dreams his face was purple and his eyes were red and bulging out of his head. He would try to speak to me but could not because of his tongue hanging out of the corner of his mouth.

I never told anyone before about this not even my wife. I felt as a law enforcement officer such things should not bother me and was ashamed that it did.

I have been transferred out of the jail and into patrol for some time now. Since then I have seen many dead and dying people and none affected me the way Mr. Green did. The difference, I believe now, is because Mr. Green was an inmate who was in a cell block where it was my job to make sure things were okay and to protect the inmates .

As the years went on the dreams came less and less. Now I only dream about Mr. Green about 2 or 3 times a year.

Sitting in your training the other day, it all came pouring back to me and now I understand why I felt the way I did.

I understand now that Mr. Green's death was not my fault and that he chose his own fate. I believe Green asked what I had going on that day to find out the best time to hang himself and prevent me from interrupting him.

I feel that I have come to accept this memory and I don't think I will have any more visits from Mr. Green.

Thank you ever so much for helping me put this incident to rest.

—Correspondence to Colonel Grossman

"Thank God It Wasn't You"

> To each his suff'rings; all are men,
> Condemn'd alike to groan,—
> The tender for another's pain,
> Th' unfeeling for his own.
>
> —Thomas Gray
> "On a Distant Prospect"

Although I live in Jonesboro, Arkansas, my wife and I heard about the school shooting that happened there from my aunt who called us from Florida. When she told me that she had just heard on CNN that there had been a mass murder in a middle school in Jonesboro, my first thought was of my son who was attending middle school there. I turned on CNN and there it was. My God! A mass murder in the middle school in our town. I was paralyzed; I didn't know what to do.

My wife told me that I needed to go there. "But what could I do?" I asked. She told me I could help and gave me a nudge out the door. I rushed to my son's school, only to discover that the shooting had not happened there, but rather at another middle school. I sped over to that one, and spent the entire day and evening working with a group of magnificent people and helping to train and prepare mental health professionals. In my own hometown I was applying the lessons of mass critical incident debriefings learned from the battlefield.

When I got home about one o'clock in the morning, I headed straight to my boy's bedroom. He was a tall, gangly kid then, but I rolled him out of his bunk and hugged him as hard as I could, saying to myself, "Thank God it wasn't you." There were probably few parents in Jonesboro who did not do the same thing that night.

My co-author said that he did it often as a police officer. On one occasion, for example, he found a dead, one-month old baby in a chest of drawers in a rundown apartment. Christensen's son was just a year old at the time, and that boy got a big hug from his dad that night, and a whispered, "Thank God it wasn't you." If you have not said it, can you understand how someone would? It is important to understand that you could utter those words and that it is okay if you do. And if it is okay for you to say it to them, then it is okay for them to say it to you.

After a horrific experience, such as the loss of a partner or buddy, it can be a powerful shock to hear yourself think, "Thank God it wasn't me." Then the shock changes to shame, which makes you think, "I wish it was me. I want it to be me. I wish I were dead." In addition to this, you might very well be convinced that "it's all my fault" and you have not had the debriefing that will help you fill in the gaps and divide your pain. You are at one of the lowest points in your life.

Something horrible has happened in your life, but for your family something wonderful has happened: You walked in the door. What words might they say to you? "Thank God it wasn't you." Though they say this with heart felt love, you might find it hard to accept, especially in light of your confused thoughts. Many returning veterans of combat also deal with similar survivor guilt. When they hear these words from their families it can cause them to distance themselves from their loved ones at a time when they need them the most.

Right now, while you are calm and rational, you need to understand and accept the fact that your loved ones might say this. As always, prior preparation is the key. Should it happen to you, you will recognize it and say, "Grossman warned me that this might happen. It's okay. I can say it to them, and they can say it to me." It is important that you mentally prepare for it because their words and their love can be hard to accept when you do not like yourself at that moment. It is important to understand that in your world, something horrible happened, but in theirs something wonderful happened: You walked in the door.

There is one other response you might get from your loved ones: anger.

Dr. Elisabeth Kubler-Ross, author of nine books dealing with the natural phenomenon of dying, says there is a set of response stages to death: denial, anger, bargaining, and acceptance. You might walk in the door after your horrible day and run smack into an angry spouse! Someone tried to kill their loved one and they feel helpless and frustrated that there is nothing they can do. At first they denied what happened but then they feel anger. It is important, therefore, that right now, while you are calm and rational, you ask yourself: "Who are they really angry at?" Are they angry at you? No. They are angry at the world that tried to harm their loved one, and in their confusion they might displace that anger onto you. Once again, can you see how this might distance you from your loved ones when you need them the most?

You are a warrior. We talked before about surviving gunshot wounds. If you can take a bullet and drive on, you can certainly take a little displaced anger and drive on. Do not let your loved one's confusion and misplaced anger distance you from them at a time when you need them most. Hug them, hold them and cherish them. Wait for their emotions to pass, and know that they will still be there when you need them. And you will be there for them in the years to come, because your warrior spirit prepared you to survive this challenge.

Always hug and kiss your loved ones goodbye

Every day when you leave your loved ones to go to work, or when you go on a trip (whether to a combat zone or on business), never forget to kiss that special person in your life, and say, "I love you," even if you have been fighting. As a warrior, you know that every day is a gift. If you should fall today, you do not want to leave your loved ones with guilt or anger, feeling: He didn't even kiss me goodbye or tell me he loved me.

Upon reading the first edition of On Combat, a police officer sent me his thoughts on this important subject.

I would like to add a suggestion to warriors who walk the razor's edge every day. Before a warrior leaves on a mission – whether it's an eight-hour shift as a police officer or a year-long deployment in the military - he or she should go to their family and give them a heartfelt hug coupled with the words, "I love you."

My wife and I are both police officers. She understands that even when we are arguing and one of us is leaving for work, we follow this ritual. It strengthens us and lets us know that when we are out there, we have something to come home to. And when the warrior comes home, he should kiss his significant other again, and tell them that he is glad to see them.

In his book, Anatomy of a Riot, my coauthor Loren Christensen writes this about a Southern Ohio Corrections officer.

On, April 11, Easter Sunday of 1993, Peggy Vallandingham kissed her husband Robert goodbye in the kitchen as he left for work at the Southern Ohio Correction Facility where for the past two years he worked as a correction's officer. Robert walked out into the garage, then paused. He turned, ran back inside his house to do something he had never done before: he kissed his wife goodbye a second time.

She would never see him alive again.

Within hours, he became a hostage under the control of rioting inmates. Four days later, they would strangle him to death and drop his body out of a window into the prison yard.

Make it a habit. It is one of the best things you can do for your family and it is a powerful gesture for yourself. And never doubt that a warrior has strength enough to love, and courage enough to show it.

chapter **two**

Stress, Uncertainty, and the "Four Fs":
Forewarned is Forearmed

I've been in four shootings and while they all have left lasting memories, I often think about another incident in which I did not shoot. My partner and I got a call about a man running through the halls of one of our nicer hotels holding a revolver. The caller said he "seemed mentally out of it."

There was a torrential downpour as we pulled into the hotel parking lot, so it took us a moment to grasp that the blurred, distorted image we saw through the windshield was the suspect, shirtless and barefoot, standing out in the downpour, his arms down at his sides, his head angled upward. His hands were empty. We scrambled from the car and took cover behind our doors. I shouted for him to put his hands behind his head, but he just lowered his head slowly and laughed at us.

Then the scene took on a surrealistic look as he moved his feet together and stretched his arms out to his sides in sort of a crucifix pose. "I got a gun in my pocket," he yelled over the rain. "I'm going for it. You'll have to shoot me."

It was then that I knew that I would have to kill him when he reached for the weapon. I had pointed my revolver at a lot of people at that point in my career and I'd shot at one, but this time I just knew in my mind and soul that I was going to kill this guy.

"Here I go," the guy yelled, reaching downward toward his pocket. I squeezed the trigger on my revolver at least half way back. The guy laughed and raised his hand back out to his side. Then he yelled the threat again and began lowering his hand. I decided I'd wait until I saw his hand come out with the weapon before I fired. I was so very ready.

He plunged his hand into his pocket, laughing loudly, insanely. When he jerked it out I could see the gun, and I began to complete the squeeze on my trigger, when my partner shouted, "It's not a gun. It looks like…a bunch of match books."

The rest of the day I felt horrible: anxious, shaky, as if I needed to run really hard or punch something. I was just so extraordinarily wired. My psychology 101 take on it is that I didn't get a release. I was absolutely ready, mentally, spiritually and physically to kill him. But then it didn't happen. I thank God I didn't have to do it, but not getting the release after being so ready, so full of fight, felt awful.

—A police officer

The Fog of Uncertainty

> For if the trumpet give an uncertain sound, who shall prepare
> himself to the battle?
>
> —I Corinthians 14:8
> *The Bible*

There are many burdens that weigh upon the warrior, and one of the greatest is uncertainty. Remember that the Universal Phobia is interpersonal aggression, and for a warrior in combat, this toxic event can happen at any time. This can seem like an insane roller coaster: riding up to the brink of death and destruction, and then back, up and back, over and over, knowing with absolute certainty that at any time you can go over the edge to personal death and destruction.

The constant anticipation of being attacked can have a profoundly toxic effect, especially when this stress continues over months and years. For the police officer or soldier, there is the constant possibility that just around the next corner there might appear an individual who will dedicate all the noxious cunning and destructive venom of the most deadly opponent on the face of the earth toward snuffing your life out and sending you home to your family in a box.

Consider this experiment that one of my old psychology professors told me about, conducted on three groups of rats.

-For seven straight days, the first group got random shocks via electrodes tied to their tails. They would just be standing around doing whatever rats do, licking their little rat parts, and *Bam!* they would get zapped.

-The second group of rats got a warning first. As they went about doing rat things, a bell rang and 10 seconds later they would get zapped. Later on, the bell rang again and the rats would think "Uh-oh" and they got zapped. The third time the bell rang, the rats chorused "Oh, no!" and again they got zapped. For an entire week at random intervals: bell-shock, bell-shock.

-The third batch of rats was the control group. They got the bell, but were never zapped.

At the end of the week, just as the rats were giddy with excitement that their lousy duty was over, the scientists killed them and dissected their bodies to see if they had ulcers, a good indication of stress.

The control group that received only the bell tone showed the least indication of stress, while the majority of rats in the group that received random zaps showed ulcers. The group that received the warning bell first had just a few more ulcers than the group that was not shocked at all, thus demonstrating that what caused the ulcers was not the shock, but rather the absence of a warning of an impending shock.

When you are warned that something might happen, you can more easily control the amount of stress you receive. However, if you spend your life in denial and then something happens, it hurts you, and hurts you seriously. That is why the sheep are destroyed by combat. The sheepdog, who expects the wolf and is prepared for it, thrives in the combat environment. The fog of uncertainty will dissipate when you are mentally prepared, and accept the fact that on any given day there are bad people in the world who are able and willing to hurt you.

This does not mean that the sheepdog's job is easy. It simply means that he can exist in a realm that destroys the sheep. Even the sheepdog must learn to live with and manage stress.

The Bathtub Model of Stress

> Stress applied to the individual is not necessarily harmful. It is only when the stress is prolonged or overwhelming and the individual is not able to cope with it that it becomes harmful physically and/or psychologically.
>
> —Davis & Friedman
> "The Emotional Aftermath of Crime and Violence"

The "bathtub model of stress" is a useful tool for understanding the long-term effects of stress. We use this to help West Point freshman, the plebes, deal with the stress of their new environment, and believe me they definitely need it.

Think of your body as a bathtub and stress is the water that pours in. Now, the drain can only release so much, so if water comes in so fast that the drain cannot handle it, the water begins to rise. If it rises too high, it overflows and damages the floor. If five gallons are suddenly added to the tub, you have got to get out from under the faucet for a couple of days to let the water—the stress—subside.

You have to be able to control your stress throughout your entire life. Life is a paced marathon, not a sprint; think of it as a four-quarter game. If you are in good physical shape, your tub is a little larger and you can handle a little more water before you overflow. The best way to make your drain bigger, so that you process stress out faster, is to engage in appropriate management dynamics, specifically, daily vigorous physical exercise.

The stress hormones flooding through your body are made for fight or flight, and cannot be ignored. They need to be used, and hard exercise is the best way to do it. When you get busy, however, it is often your workout program that is the first thing to go. Do not let this happen to you, because exercise is the very thing you need. A daily run, 45 minutes pumping weights or a basketball game are the kind of things that can help burn off the stress hormones flooding through your body. Be sure to work out with positive, quality people who can help you blow off steam. You do not get anything from your workout when you exercise with bitter, trash-talking or quick-tempered people. Such individuals only add to your stress.

The Four Fs

> The natural man has only two primal passions, to get and to beget.
> —Sir William Osler
> *Science and Immortality*

Several of my professors have told me about one 1950s psycho-physiology text book that has a dry joke imbedded in it. It says that the function of the midbrain can be thought of as the "four f's: fight, flight, feeding, and . . . mating." There is value in understanding that this is, indeed, what the midbrain—the puppy—does.

I have already talked about fight or flight. You know that if you are under stress there is a distinct possibility that you might respond with inappropriate levels of aggression, which is something you must guard against. You also know that one of the healthiest ways to deal with stress is to get out from under it. Now let us look at the remaining two realms of the midbrain, feeding and . . . mating, functions that generally manifest themselves after combat.

Some people lose their desire for food when overly stressed, but the more common response is to develop an enhanced appetite. The midbrain is a simple organism, and it can only do one thing at a time. When anxiety eats away at you, the puppy pokes his nose through the screen door, whining and whimpering. So you eat a big piece of chocolate cake, which is the same as giving him a bone to gnaw on for a while. While you overeat, the puppy stays busy and you get a break from your anxiety. When you stop, however, he is back at the screen door whining and whimpering, as once again your anxiety gnaws away at you. It is a vicious cycle because not only are you not dealing with the cause of your stress, your attempt to placate it with food leads to obesity and the many health problems associated with it.

This is why daily vigorous exercise is so vital. Pumping iron, running, and basketball burns off the stress hormones that motivate you to eat. It also burns off a few calories, which makes the body healthier (or the "tub" a little larger) so that you can more easily handle the incoming stress. The better shape you are in, the more motivated you are to continue to burn off stress hormones in a healthy way, rather than trying to appease it with comfort food.

Food has a powerful calming effect. I think that it may be virtually impossible to be in Condition Red and eat at the same time. When I train at national hostage negotiators conferences, I encourage them to use food as a calming tool with hostage takers. While a person is eating he is usually in Condition White or Yellow, which can be one of the best times to make rational arguments. This can also be one of the best times for the SWAT team to roll that flashbang grenade in the door. When the suspect is in Condition Red, his auditory exclusion, and other stress responses we have discussed, greatly limit the sensory overload caused by this device. Pick your time well, such as when he is eating, and there is a better chance that flashbang will stun the suspect and no one will have to die that day.

The Fourth F: Sex

The sex is ever to a soldier kind.
                              —The Odyssey *(Alexander Pope transl)*

Some people lose their appetite for food in response to stress, but many have an enhanced craving to eat. In the same way, some individuals can lose their sex drive in response to great stress, but other people experience a tremendous sex drive, especially after a combat situation in which they were triumphant. Faced with death, destruction and horror all around, there can be a powerful life affirming drive toward sexuality. Frank Herbert, in his book, *Dune*, referred to this as: "The fertility drive of the species . . . that profound drive shared by all creatures who are faced with death—the drive to seek immortality through progeny." Others believe that it may just be the drive of a male, having defeated another male in a "mating" battle, to claim his "prize."

Understand that if this should happen to you, it is perfectly normal. There is nothing wrong with you if it doesn't happen, and there is absolutely nothing wrong with you if it does. Once I had the pleasure of training a large group of FBI agents and their spouses at a conference in Reno. I told them about this common response and that it was perfectly normal, and there was a sudden roar as many of them turned to their spouses and said, "See. I'm okay. It's all right."

That great pioneer in the field of warrior science, Bruce Siddle, tells about a state trooper that he had trained who was forced to kill someone in the line of duty. Bruce called him the next day to see how he was doing. Bruce says, "I heard about the shooting and I wanted to be sure you're okay." The trooper said, that he was doing fine. "As a matter of fact," he said, "I'm a little worried how fine I am, because last night my wife and I had the best sex we've had in months."

I tell the law enforcement officers I train that there are not many perks that come with the job. So if you find one, relax and enjoy it.

On the other hand, when I work with school resource officers I have to give them a little warning. After a traumatic incident on or near the campus, there might be a tendency for the female to be drawn to an alpha male who can protect her, and there might be a tendency for the male to spread the genes around in the face of anxiety and sudden death. I tell the officers that "forewarned is forearmed," and "biology is not destiny." If we know that these things might happen then we can avoid being blindsided by them.

Physiological Stress Responses in Females

It is all right for a woman to be, above all, human.

—Anais Nin
Diary of Anais Nin

Before we leave the issue of sexuality in combat, let's look briefly at one other aspect. We know that it is common for junior high or high school female athletes to stress their bodies in training to the extent that they stop having their monthly periods. It is logical, therefore, that junior high or high school girls, who witness the horror of their friends being gunned down, may also experience a cessation of their periods. It is a normal response.

Now, we know there is an ongoing level of sexual activity among high school and middle school students, and after a horrific incident, such as a Columbine or a Jonesboro, there is going to be an even greater level of sexual activity. How do you think the girls are going to react when they fail to have their periods? Stressed? Do you think it might stress those boys out, too? We think some of the extreme stress response, and perhaps even some of the suicides that occur in the first two months after these horrendous events, might be linked to this phenomenon. These young girls' lives are already stressful (i.e., their tubs are already full) just dealing with all that goes into being a teenager, so when they experience a traumatic event, and a few weeks later think they are pregnant, it can be just too much for some of them.

This is a relatively easy problem to deal with. When we were working in the school after the Jonesboro massacre, I was first made aware of this possibility by my old battalion sergeant major, Jeff Shearman. He knew about it from his time as a drill sergeant in charge of a platoon of female recruits. After the shootings, we advised the girls' physical education teachers to tell their girls' PE class that their periods might stop in response to what they had experienced. The girls should know that if it happens, it does not necessarily mean they are pregnant.

That is all it took to shortstop the problem. (Incidentally, our adult female warriors need to know that the same thing could happen to them as a result of a deadly force incident.)

As warriors, if we did not know this could happen, there would be no way for us to protect these little lambs from the aftershock stressors that can occur. A firefighter knows all about the many stages of fire, including the cleanup and toxic effects afterward. Likewise, it is important that warriors know all about interpersonal human aggression, because, sadly, it is many times more likely to kill or injure our children than fire. That is our job and we must be masters of the realm.

chapter

three

PTSD: *Re-experiencing the Event,*
and Fleeing from the Puppy

Thaine High of Oceanside can't stand the smell of meat on a barbecue. High was a graves registration officer in Europe [in World War II]. He and his eight-man squad picked up more than 1,700 corpses from the front lines in France, Belgium, Germany and Czechoslovakia. "The worst thing were the tank battles," he explains. "If a tank was hit and burned, you had to wait until the tank cooled down, sometimes two or three days. We'd get the five names of the men who were in it from the tank commander. After the tank cooled down, we'd go in and open the hatches and try to get some kind of remains from the bodies. If we were lucky, we'd find an arm, a leg, or a foot, sometimes a skull." His voice quivers. "To this day I can hardly stand to have a barbeque because it reminds me of burnt flesh."

—David Weddle
"Secrets at the Bottom of the Drawer"

To begin our examination of Posttraumatic Stress Disorder, PTSD, let us draw straight from the *DSM-IV*. This is truly the "Bible" of psychiatry and psychology, or the "Big Book of Crazy," as one of my psychology professors used to put it.

If you look at the extract from the *DSM*, it looks a little complex at first, but it is really straight forward and simple. To have PTSD you must have two from column A, one from column B, three from column C, and two from column D. Kind of like a Chinese menu.

First, look at paragraph A. To be at risk for PTSD, you must be exposed to a traumatic incident in which two things occur. First, the incident must be a life and death event that involves actual or threatened death or serious injury to you or to others. As a warrior, exposure to such events is not preventable. Your job is to move to the sound of the guns, to deliberately go into the realm of violence, death and destruction.

The second element that must occur is for you to respond to the exposure with intense fear, helplessness or horror. When I am training police officers they usually have copies of my handouts, and I always tell them to underline those

Diagnostic Criteria for Posttraumatic Stress Disorder
(Extracted from the Diagnostic and Statistical Manual (DSM-IV)
of the American Psychiatric Assn.)

A. Exposure to a traumatic event in which <u>both</u> of the following were present:
1. Experienced, witnessed, or was confronted by event(s) involving actual or threatened death or serious injury . . . of self or others
2. Response involved intense fear, helplessness, or horror
   The disorder may be especially severe or longer lasting when the stressor is of human design (e.g. torture, rape). (DSM-III-R notes that: some stressors frequently cause the disorder (e.g. natural disasters or car accidents).
B. Traumatic event is persistently reexperienced in <u>one or more</u> of the following ways.
1. Recurrent, intrusive, distressing recollections of the event . . .
2. Acting or feeling as if the event were recurring including: "sense of reliving" the experience, illusions, hallucinations and flashbacks— including while awakening or intoxicated
3. Intense psychological distress at exposure to internal or external cues that symbolize or resemble an aspect of the traumatic event
4. Psychological reactivity on exposure to internal or external cues that symbolize or resemble an aspect of the traumatic event
C. Persistent avoidance of stimuli associated with the trauma, or numbing of general responsiveness, as indicated by <u>at least 3</u> of the following:
1. Efforts to avoid thoughts, feelings or conversations associated with the trauma
2. Efforst to avoid activities, places, or people that arouse recollections of the trauma
3. Inability to recall an important aspect of the trauma
4. Markedly diminished interest or participation insignificant activities
5. Feelings of detachment or estrangement from others
6. Restricted range of affect (e.g. unable to have loving feelings)
D. Persistent symptoms of increased arousal (not present before the trauma), as indicated from <u>2 or more</u> of the following:
1. Difficulty falling or staying asleep
2. Irritability or outbursts of anger
3. Difficulty concentrating
4. Hypervigilance
5. Exaggerated startle response
   [Self medication]
E. Duration of the disturbance (symptoms in B, C, and D) of at least one month
F. The disturbance causes clinically significant distress or impairment in social, occupational, or other important areas of functioning

<u>Acute:</u> if duration of symptoms is less than 3 months
<u>Chronic:</u> if duration of symptoms is 3 months or more
<u>With Delayed onset:</u> if symptoms were at least 6 months after the trauma.

four words. A little bit of fear can manifest itself as Condition Red, and this can be a useful response, but intense fear, helplessness and horror is what we have defined as Condition Black, and we know that this is not a desirable thing. As S. L. A. Marshall noted, fear in combat is ever present, "but it is uncontrolled fear that is the enemy."

Now, you cannot do anything about the exposure to a life threatening situation, as a warrior, it is your job to go into danger, but you can do something about how you respond to it. This is critical because if you do not feel a sense of intense fear, helplessness or horror, there is no PTSD.

You create fear, helplessness and horror by being a sheep. You prevent it by being a sheepdog, a warrior. If there is no sense of helplessness because your training has taught you what to do, there is no PTSD. If there is no horror because you have been inoculated against seeing blood, guts and brains, there is no PTSD. If there is no intense fear, meaning that your heart rate does not shoot up to 175 bpm because you use tactical breathing, there is no PTSD.

Reexperiencing the Event: The Puppy Comes for a Visit

> . . . we must admit that what is closest to us is the very thing we know least about, although it seems to be what we know best of all . . . it is just because the psyche is so close to us that psychology has been discovered so late.
>
> —C.G. Jung
> *Modern Man in Search of a Soul*

Next, look at paragraph B, re-experiencing the event. Think of it as when the puppy comes for a visit. Anyone can re-experience the event after a traumatic episode. Many police officers and soldiers, warriors who purposely go into the toxic realm of violence, have experienced this. It is important to emphasize here that just having the puppy come for a visit (re-experiencing the event) is not, by itself, PTSD.

My co-writer, Loren Christensen served as a military policeman in Saigon, Vietnam, in 1969 and 1970, perhaps the most dangerous city in the world at that time. He had to contend with rocket attacks, snipers, terrorist bombings, anti-American riots, bar fights, racial violence, and a host of other deadly stressors. He said that after he returned home and bought a house in a quiet neighborhood, a large community of Vietnamese sprang up about a mile from where he lived. He never thought much of it. He drove by the housing projects every morning on his way to the police precinct.

One morning, almost 10 years to the day after he had returned from the war, he drove by the projects on his way to the firing range where he worked as an instructor. As he waited at a stoplight, he said a dozen Vietnamese children crossed the street in front of him. "Panic hit me like an overwhelming wave," he said. "I looked at those kids, especially the girls who were wearing ao dai, the traditional white tunic over black pants, a sight I saw every day in Vietnam, and my first thought was, 'I have to get more guns.'" Sweating profusely and breathing as if he had just run a mile, he turned his truck around and returned home to get two more firearms. He had the presence of mind to take a different route to the firing range, and eventually his heart rate, trembling hands and profuse sweating went away.

About two weeks later, he had a similar experience while shopping in a military surplus store for backpacking gear. When he bent over a large bin to rummage through a pile of used fatigue pants, he smelled the familiar odor of the material, and he again began to sweat heavily, breathe raggedly and became nearly overpowered with a sense of unexplained panic. As before, it took Christensen several minutes to return to normal. He says it was not until he had two more episodes in the following weeks that he began to research the symptoms of PTSD. With a new understanding of what was happening to him, he was able to "make peace with the memory" and has never had such intense episodes since.

Christensen was like every returning soldier from Vietnam in that he was not debriefed. One day he was in a war torn environment and the next day he was stepping off an airplane in Oakland, California. He got a steak dinner, a fresh uniform, and a discharge. Four hours later he was sitting in his parent's living room.

Reexperiencing the event can be caused by extended periods of danger and stress, as happened with Christensen after his tour of duty in Vietnam. Or, the puppy might come for a visit after a single, significant, traumatic event. Robert Speer, an Arkansas State Trooper who is now in command of their state SWAT team, tells about when he had to kill a gunman in a desperate and explosive gunfight at point-blank range. He had difficulty sleeping for a few nights, but otherwise he was fine; at least he thought so until one evening a week later when he and his wife were watching his daughter at a swimming competition. "Maybe it was one of the starter's guns that set me off," he said. "All of a sudden out of the blue my heart started pounding, I began hyperventilating and I was drenched with sweat." His reaction was so powerful that his wife thought he was having a heart attack.

This was a classic example of a powerful, postcombat response, commonly called a panic attack. Sometimes it is referred to as an anxiety attack, but that term is not appropriate. He was not feeling a little anxiety; the puppy inside his head was panicking!

During his gunfight, his heart rate skyrocketed and a neural network was established when the puppy "blew a hole through the screen door." That neural network was still in place when a week later the unexpected sound of the starter's pistol at a swim meet caused the trooper's puppy to burst through that hole in the screen door, jump into his lap, pee, gnaw at his throat, and cry out, "Gunfight! Gunfight! Where's the gunfight? Where? Where? Where?"

Robert is fine today, a true warrior leader with a lifetime of successful combat experiences behind him. But at that time he had two things working against him: First, no one warned him that he might have such a reaction. Second, no one taught him what to do should it happen. Untold hundreds of thousands of other people over the millennia have been through traumatic events and have later relived their experiences. They too had two things working against them: No one warned them that they might re-experience the event, and no one taught them what to do should it happened. So, I'm warning you now that it might happen, and here is what you should do if it does happen.

Again, do not think that everyone who gets in a deadly force encounter will get a "visit" from the puppy. In Dr. Dave Klinger's research of 113 SWAT team members who had shot and hit an adversary in real combat, approximately 40 percent of them re-experienced the event. If you are stress inoculated, know how to use our breathing techniques and are properly trained in survival tactics, then you can reduce the possibility that it might happen. Still, even mature, world-class warrior leaders with a lifetime of experience under their belts (like Robert Speer in this case, and Randy Watt who we will meet later in this chapter) can re-experience their traumatic event and have the puppy come for a visit.

It is important that you understand that a visit from the puppy does not necessarily mean you have PTSD. Reexperiencing the event can be a normal reaction to an abnormal event. You need to make peace with the memory and get on with your life. PTSD, as you will see later, occurs when you try to flee from the memory.

The Grassy Meadow and the Widow of 50 Years

Memory, the warder of the brain.

—Shakespeare
Macbeth

Your brain has billions of neurons, like spaghetti noodles in a bowl. Everywhere the "noodles" touch there is a neural connection, forming a vast, three-dimensional neural network.

For our purposes, let us create a two-dimensional model of your brain. Think of your mind as a vast meadow filled with waist-high grass. Each time you walk on it, you leave a path behind you. That path is your memory. If you walk up and down that path several times, you begin to beat a trail. That is learning and training. Thus, we can think of your brain as a vast meadow that is filled with trillions of paths and trails, some shallow, and some deep.

Now imagine a lady who has been married to someone for 50 years. Every day of her married life, she got up with her husband, and every night she went to bed with him. He is not just a path or a trail in her meadow, he is a valley that has been carved deeply across the decades. He is the dominant terrain feature in her meadow.

Then one day he dies.

It can take our widow of 50 years a long time to "rewire" her brain around this new reality. Although she will mourn her husband at the funeral, the grieving process will take far longer than just the funeral. For the first few days she might begin to set a place for her husband at the table and then realize that he will not be coming to dinner, which devastates her all over again. For months after she might see motion out of the corner of her eye, turn expecting to see him, and then remember that he will not be there.

Slowly but surely she will rewire her brain around the fact that her companion and lover of 50 years is gone. In general, the grieving process will probably take less time for other members of the family, because their paths are not as deep. There will always be an ache and a hollow spot in their hearts, but the actual neuronal adjustment to the new reality will be over in a comparatively shorter period. But our widow of 50 years needs more time.

There are two rules by which she has to operate during this process, rules that we all intuitively understand. First, she must come to terms with the reality of his death. She cannot pretend he never lived. She cannot pretend he is not dead. She cannot refuse to ever talk about him again. She cannot refuse to let anyone mention him. She must accept the reality of what has happened. To think any other way would be pathological.

Second, our widow of 50 years must separate the memory from the emotions. If she is still sobbing hysterically a year later every time someone mentions her husband, something is clearly wrong. It is normal and healthy for her to weep at first, but a year or two later, she will hopefully be able to bounce her grandchild on her knee and tell him a story about his grandpa without losing control. A tear might leak from her eye, but she will not lose control of her breathing and her speech. This is the end state of healthy grieving: to fully come to terms with the reality of what has happened and to separate the painful emotions from the memory.

Now, imagine a disruptive force underneath your meadow, an earthquake that suddenly rips open a canyon that is as deep as the one formed by our widow's memory during her 50 years of marriage. This is what can happen when fear, helplessness and horror are experienced during a life-and-death situation. I have likened this to a puppy ripping a hole through a screen door, but in extreme cases it can be much more than that.

When a canyon has been ripped into your meadow, you must operate by the same two rules as our widow. First, you cannot pretend that the incident did not happen. You cannot refuse to let anyone talk about it and you cannot refuse to ever talk about it. That would be profoundly unhealthy. Second, after a year has passed you should not still be weepy, angry or emotional every time you are reminded of the event. Do not fool yourself into believing that it is okay to get angry because that is the same as getting weepy. Both are uncontrolled manifestations of the puppy, or the sympathetic nervous system. Likewise, fleeing from the memory is unhealthy, as it will only drive you down the path of PTSD. Your healthy, long-term survival requires that you do the same as our widow, and make peace with the memory.

Making Peace with the Memory

Macbeth:
> Canst thou not minister to a mind diseas'd,
> Pluck from the memory a rooted sorrow,
> Raze out the written troubles of the brain,
> and with some sweet oblivious antidote
> Cleanse the stuff'd bosom of that perilous stuff
> Which weighs upon the heart?

Doctor:
> Therein the patient
> Must minister to himself.

—Shakespeare
Macbeth

Here is an example sent to me in an e-mail from Randy Watt, Assistant Chief of Police for the Ogden, Utah, Police Department. For years he was the commander of their SWAT team, and he had many deadly force encounters during his decades of experience in law enforcement. He is also a Green Beret in the U.S. Army Reserves, with an unprecedented amount of time on an A-Team as a sergeant and officer. In 2002, this seasoned, veteran warrior was sent to Afghanistan, where he saw considerable action and was subsequently nominated by U.S. Army Delta Force operators for a Silver Star for gallantry in combat. He explained in his e-mail what happened to him when he got home and the puppy came for a visit.

> Thought I'd share an interesting experience with you . . . Yesterday was our semiannual FATS [Fire Arms Training Simulator] shoot [a realistic video game-type training device that uses a large movie screen and high-quality sound]. I went out to the simulator and they had laid out six scenarios of varying degrees. You know the drill. The first three were standard L.E. stuff, like buy/bust, bar fight, etc. No problems. The fourth one was an ambush on the police officer (me). The setting was a

suspicious Jeep parked in a rural area with large rock piles and small trees surrounding the area. I immediately was struck by the thought that this location looked familiar. [i.e., it reminded him of Afghanistan.]

During the check of the vehicle, four suspects come up from behind the rock piles, two with long guns and two with pistols, and open fire. I reacted properly and engaged, moved to cover, etc., however, the physiological response was something I had never experienced before. My palms were instantly sweaty, my chest was constricted, my breathing was ragged and my pulse was racing. I was breathing rapidly and shallowly. The trainer/evaluators didn't notice anything but I sure did. I completed the next two, again standard L.E. scenarios, and then asked to do the ambush one again. I wanted to see if I could desensitize my response to it. After all, it's not real, it's just a video. I couldn't desensitize, it evoked the very same physiological response, which had not dissipated in anyway. I finished up and left, but it took two to three hours for the physical effects to subside. [Adrenaline dump not burned off.] Then, last night, I had a very restless night. I had weird dreams, all about combat situations but with unrealistic and disconnected responses.

I am one of those guys you talk about in terms of being macho. When I came home, I told everyone I was fine and that the war had no effect on me. I've been back about three-and-a-half months now and I'm beginning to see that I've been lying to everyone, especially myself. Two weeks after I came back to the PD [police department], one of my friends came to me quietly and asked if I was all right. He said that he and some of my friends were worried about me, that I wasn't the same guy as before I had gone over. He said that I was quieter, less aggressive in nature and not at all outspoken. Having been a serious extrovert all my life, I wasn't sure what he meant so I asked my wife about it. She said they were right. Anyway, I told him that I was fine, just that I was readjusting to the change in environment.

It appears to me, now, that the war and the activities we were involved in over there had more effect than I want to admit. I'm fine, I'm not crazy or anything, I'm just now realizing that time is going to be my best friend.

This was my response:

My brother, this is a classic example of a kind of "sensitivity" that is very common after an intense combat experience. We saw lots of examples after World War II, Korea, and Vietnam. Most commonly, we heard stories of GIs who "hit the deck" reflexively when they heard an unexpected, loud noise, like a car suddenly backfiring.

What happened with these GIs, and with you, is that the midbrain, or the unconscious mind (or the "puppy inside" as I put it) has learned to bypass logical thought processes and established conditioned reflexes, or sympathetic nervous system (SNS) responses, instantly, without having to be told to do it. This can be a powerful survival mechanism in combat. For example, your unconscious mind hears the incoming artillery and you hit the ground without having to spend time thinking about it, saving vital milliseconds in the process.

It just takes time for this kind of conditioned "reflex" to "decay." Using your breathing exercises and gaining conscious control over these SNS responses is like putting a "leash" on the puppy. But remember, to the puppy (and we really do have a puppy inside) that gunfight in that FATS simulator was real! We have hit the level where our simulations can be real enough to fool the puppy (the unconscious mind) and that is pretty damned real!

You can think of it as being like a kid who touches a hot stove. After being burned just one time by that stove he will stay far away from it in the future, because the kid's "puppy inside" will immediately come on alert whenever he comes close to it. The way to deal with this is to spend a lot of time around the "stove" and learn how to remain calm in spite of the potential danger, which is exactly what most of us do. Sure the stove can burn you, but it also can provide good food. In the same way the warrior can say, "Sure combat can hurt you, but it can be the means by which I save lives and help to preserve my civilization, and that can be very rewarding."

Here is another example that a lot of guys can understand. On a football team, a defensive lineman can come to associate the rising inflection of the opposing quarterback's voice with getting hit by 300 pounds of offensive lineman. After a while, he can get pulled "offsides" by a tricky quarterback who goes, "Hut, hut, hut HUT!" but does not snap the ball. His "puppy" has been tricked!

Trying to Not Think About It

> To think that I am not going
> To think of you anymore
> Is still thinking of you
> Let me then try not to think
> That I am not going to think of you
>
> —Takuan
> Seventeenth century Japanese Zen Buddhist monk, writer and poet

Take a look at paragraph C from our *DSM* extract. The puppy is coming for a visit and since it scares the hell out of you, you try to not think about it. You might try to avoid all stimuli associated with the traumatic event as well as any thoughts, feelings, or conversations associated with the trauma. Is this even possible? Can you really avoid a thought? Choose a topic and try not to think of it again for the rest of your life. It is impossible.

This is what I wrote next in my answer to Randy Watt:

How would a good coach deal with this problem of a lineman being pulled offsides by his past associations and that tricky quarterback? Well, in practice, he would probably put the defensive line through lots of plays, and in many plays he would have the offensive quarterback try to pull the defensive line offsides. If a player had a particular problem, the coach might even put him through hours of drills designed to teach him to react to the snap of the ball, and not to the quarterback's voice.

In the same way, you need to go through that FATS scenario (and other scenarios), as many times as you need to until you can remain calm. Then try it with paint bullet scenarios.

The response that you have told me about is very common in law enforcement officers who have been in deadly force encounters. Many law enforcement trainers have told me about officers who were in gunfights, and then later, when they were in FATS or paint bullet training scenarios, they had powerful SNS responses. Some of them went into Condition Red too soon, like you did. Others went right into Condition Black in their first training simulation after combat, and could not perform properly. These trainers have learned that they must "ease" these combat veterans back into the business, sometimes running the scenarios repeatedly until they feel calm and collected while shooting in a combat simulation.

You boys out in Utah understand this, it's called "Gittin' back on the horse." You instinctively knew to do this the first time, when you went back through the scenario again. Now keep on doing it.

A seasoned veteran is a very valuable commodity, to say the least! But that "seasoning" was expensive. Lives may have been lost in combat to buy that seasoning. We don't want those lost lives to have been in vain! We need that veteran warrior in coming battles. So it is a small expense to be sure that they have been properly eased back into combat. We'll put them back on the horse, but it will be a horse we know they can master, not one that will just buck them off again and reinforce the negative associations.

For World War II vets who jumped when the car exhaust went off, it just took time for the reflex to decay. Most of them laughed it off, and got on with life. Some of them, unfortunately, did not understand what was happening and they were deeply concerned about it. They thought they were losing their mind (and nothing scares us more than that!) so they tried all kinds of things to prevent the response from happening. Like avoiding situations with loud noises or trying not to think about or talk about their combat experiences. When what they really needed to do was to spend so much time around the stimulus (the noise) without the bad stuff (death and injury) that it no longer excited the "puppy." Remember, just having the puppy come for a visit is NOT PTSD. According to the *DSM*, the "Bible" of psychology and psychiatry, PTSD happens when:

1) You feel "fear, helplessness or horror" (i.e., have a powerful SNS response) in a life and death situation, AND

2) You "persistently re-experience" the event (i.e., the "puppy" keeps coming for a visit in flashbacks, dreams and/or SNS arousal in response to events or "cues that symbolize or resemble an aspect of the traumatic event"), AND

3) You persistently avoid "stimuli associated with the trauma" including, "Efforts to avoid thoughts, feelings, or conversations associated with the trauma," and/or "Efforts to avoid activities, places, or people that arouse recollections of the trauma," AND

4) The disturbance lasts for "at least one month," and it "causes clinically significant distress or impairment in social, occupational, or other important areas of functioning."

Number 3 is the important part. We can't avoid going in harm's way, and there is always a chance that we will get highly excited when people are fighting and dying (this may be especially true when you are wounded), which may cause the puppy to come for a visit. But we can prevent the "persistent avoidance" of things that bring the puppy for a visit! And that means plenty of range time, FATS time, and paint bullet force-on-force scenarios, every chance you get, combined with breathing (the "leash") until the puppy gets under control.

Preventing "fear, helplessness and horror" through previous training is step one in preventing the potential for a PTSD response. In your case, you have done that about as well as any human being could do! But still there is a leftover, "mental residue" of combat that can bring the puppy for a visit (i.e., unwanted SNS responses) in even the most well prepared warrior. It is worth repeating: when that happens, the key is to focus on preventing Number 3. Spending a lifetime trying to "avoid" stimuli—thoughts, feelings, conversations, activities, people or places—that make the puppy come for a visit can literally make you crazy!

The World War II vets did not have force-on-force paint bullets scenarios and FATS simulators to go back to. So, for some, their combat responses slowly decayed. Others never made "friends" with the memory/puppy, and they lived in fear of their responses for a lifetime. But you do have that opportunity to engage in realistic training, and you should.

As to becoming more introverted, and other personality changes, note Number 4 above. You do not have a full blown case of PTSD unless it lasts for at least a month, and you have significant impairment in some important part of your life.

In your case, it may be that some of the personality changes will go away with time. However, it is normal and healthy for an extroverted person to grow more introverted as they get older (we get more comfortable with ourselves) or for an introverted person to get more extroverted (we get more comfortable with others). If you are troubled by what is happening, and are not satisfied with your progress, there is absolutely no shame in going to a licensed counselor who specializes in this area, and talking it over with him. There are other tools which can help. For example, a lot of combat vets (in law enforcement and military) have been helped by EMDR [which I will discuss later in this chapter]. For now, you have hit it right on the head: Time is your best friend.

Randy understood all of this, and this was his wise response:

> As a result of what happened last week, I've also begun a personal "therapy" program. I'm starting to train my SWAT guys again, including SIMS [Simunition brand paint bullets] and FATS, to talk about my experiences (that seems to really help), and I'm spending a couple of days per week on the range, going through the mechanics of shooting but now I'm going to add some visualization aspects . . . I'll keep you apprised of how things are going. I'm not worried or concerned about what's happening to me, your lectures from the past prepared me well. I just thought you might enjoy seeing your doctrine validated.

Later in the book we will talk more about how you can delink the memory from the emotions and make peace with the memory, which are positive and

healthy responses to the re-experiencing phenomena. For now I want to hold up
Randy Watt as a model for others.

First, he educated and trained himself ahead of time so that he had a good
idea of what was happening to him. He is a true warrior of the highest caliber,
and he has nothing to prove to anyone in the law enforcement or military worlds.
But even with all his experience and credentials, he was still affected by his
combat experiences. Warrior that he is, when he saw what was happening to him,
he took immediate corrective action. No denial, no shame, just action.

Second, by sharing this experience with others, he was able to help with his
own healing while also using his experience to guide others down the warrior
path. Again, no guilt trip, no denial, no pity party, just decisive action to help
himself and others.

Rejecting the Gift That Keeps on Giving

> But after the fires and the wrath,
> But after searching and pain,
> His Mercy opens us a path
> To live with ourselves again.
>
> —Rudyard Kipling
> "The Choice"

Now look at items 4, 5, and 6 under paragraph C in our PTSD extract from
the *DSM*. Not only are you impacted by posttraumatic stress disorder, but your
spouse and kids are also affected as you begin to lose interest in the things you
used to enjoy. In an effort to control your bubbling and boiling emotions, you
shut them off, or at least you think you do. The reality is that you build a wall
around them. Your fear and anxiety still bubbles and boils, but now they are
walled in. You cannot shut down just the bad emotions, so you try to shut them
all down. That means you no longer experience joy or happiness because you
have become Mr. Control Freak when it comes to your feelings. Maybe the only
way you can have a good time is when you are drunk. If that is the case, you have
a serious problem.

With your emotions walled in, you feel detached and even estranged from
others. Although you have loving feelings for your family and close friends, you
cannot communicate them. You are unable to say the "L" word because it cannot
climb over that high wall. Consider this case study:

> Early in the morning, two other officers and I were talking in a
> parking lot when one of the officers, Howard, said he was going to
> check a car on a nearby street. He was a veteran officer of 13 years who

had just transferred from narcotics to patrol. I didn't think much of him going to check a car, assuming it was unoccupied, so I didn't go with him.

About 10 minutes later, I received a call of gunshots in an area about a mile from my location. At first I didn't think anything of it since those calls come in all the time, often only backfires. Howard was dispatched as my follow unit, but he didn't answer the call. Seconds later, I was told by dispatch that a citizen was calling and saying that he heard gunshots in front of his home and there was a police unit out front with its overhead lights on.

As I tore away from the parking lot and was rolling Code 3 to get there, one of the most chilling things I've ever heard came over the radio: A citizen's voice telling us that an officer had been shot and was down in the street.

As I turned onto the street, I saw Howard on the ground in front of his unit with a small crowd of citizens nearby. I tried to comfort him, but I was unsure what to do for him. He had wounds to his face and below his vest in back. He gave me a description of the shooter as the paramedics arrived.

I helped load him into the ambulance, rode with him to the hospital and was with him in the operating room. When they wheeled him out, I thought he was going to be okay, but when I went into the recovery room, I was told he was dead.

I broke down and cried as I stood there in operating scrubs. Detectives ushered me out before they brought in his wife. I was driven back to the police department still wearing the scrubs, which I objected to. I wanted to walk in the same way I walked out: as a police officer in uniform not a crying lump in scrubs with all my peers looking.

They called in our department psychologist, who I had not seen since he made the decision whether I was to be hired as a police officer. In my mind, I thought if I showed weakness they would fire me, so I said I was okay, and essentially refused to talk to him.

Over the next few months I changed drastically. My work performance came almost to a halt as I spent most of my time drinking coffee and bullshitting. I was short tempered and moody and I began to slowly withdraw from my wife. Then I decided I didn't love her anymore and wanted a divorce.

I drank heavily and experienced flashbacks to the night of the shooting. Once, I drove by the scene of Howard's shooting and I saw a police unit with its lights on in the same position as Howard's had been. But when I turned down the street, it was dark and empty. Several times I saw Howard sitting in the briefing room and I also passed him driving another police car.

I went to see the psychiatrist again and he did help me a little, though I wasn't completely up front with him. A while later, I moved out from my wife and in with a single officer. I drank and chased women and drove myself in debt. Several times, as I sat alone in my room, I put my gun barrel against my head. I'm still amazed I didn't pull the trigger. After a few months of this, I realized I was killing myself. My wife, wonderful woman that she is, held on through all of this and kept in touch through mutual friends, since I rarely returned her calls. I called her one day and told her I would go to marriage counseling with her; we eventually got back together.

Today, I take my job much less seriously. I still do it to the best of my ability, and take survival seriously, but the job no longer consumes my life. My wife and I have a 10-month-old son now who I love. It scares me to think how close I came to losing my wife and never knowing my son.

—Officer Jim Holder
Correspondence to Colonel Grossman

Persistent Symptoms of Arousal

Heat not a furnace for your foe so hot
That it do singe yourself.

—Shakespeare
King Henry VIII

Now look at paragraph D in our *DSM* extract. You might begin to have persistent symptoms of increased arousal and difficulty falling or staying asleep. Since your wall prevents you from dealing with the memory of the event during the day, it haunts you in your dreams. Of course, it is normal to have nightmares about the event, but in time they should go away. However, if you do not make peace with the memory during the day, they will come back in your dreams and those horrific images will disrupt your sleep for months, even years after.

You might become increasingly irritable and have outbursts of anger. Now, a normal, healthy person deals with his anger every day: Hey that bothered me. Please don't do that again. Expressing your feelings about something is a healthy response but your emotions are walled in, so you cannot express them. Each day you get a little angrier until you explode in an outburst of rage, and everyone wonders where it came from. The outburst might even surprise you, too, since you thought you no longer had emotions. Well, they were there all along; you were just deceiving yourself by holding them in.

My co-author tells of a fellow officer who was forced to kill two people in two separate incidents. In the last one, he shot and killed a teenager in a lawful self-defense situation or, in police vernacular, a righteous shoot. Two years later when Christensen asked if he could interview him for his book, *Deadly Force Encounters*, the officer refused, saying that he was still having trouble coming to terms with his last shooting.

Other than that statement, there were no other outward indications that he was having problems. Until a few months later. As was his usual, the officer walked into the precinct and then into the locker room. Then, seemingly from out of nowhere, he exploded into a tremendous rage, screaming, punching lockers, and throwing benches about. When a sergeant approached him, the officer threatened him with deadly force. The man was quickly relieved of duty and subsequently placed on disability.

You might also have difficulty concentrating because your mind is so busy trying to not think about this painful memory. This might cause a state of constant hyper-vigilance and an exaggerated startle response. Yes, a warrior should be vigilant and alert and he should be the one who sits with his back to the wall, but this extreme vigilance and exaggerated startle response are aspects that did not exist before the traumatic event.

This unabated tension, which begins as a psychological issue, can cause long-term physical health problems as your endocrine system pours out a steady stream of hormones and other chemicals, attacking the body over a period of years. To combat this over arousal, you might self-medicate with alcohol, cannabis or tranquilizers. That, of course, is not the solution and will only lead to new problems.

It is quite normal to experience some of these symptoms after a traumatic incident. Consider it a normal reaction to an abnormal event in your life. Should one or more of these last only a few days it is not PTSD. But when they last longer than a month and cause clinically significant distress or impairment in your life, you just might have posttraumatic stress disorder.

Our Fathers' Pain

> When I got home from the war and someone would ask if I had killed anyone, I asked them why they wanted to know. Did it make me more macho, or scary, or loathsome? Did you want all the details? Or did you just want to see me shake like a leaf? Tell me what's in your head and I'll tell you what's in mine. If it's just morbid curiosity, go away! I don't need this and you don't either! I'm not ashamed of what I did in Vietnam but I don't need to brag about it.
>
> —Tom Hain, Vietnam veteran

Many of us have fathers who are veterans of World War II, Korea or Vietnam. When these warriors came home and experienced many of the manifestations discussed here, most of them did not have PTSD. They were able to live fully functional lives with their social and occupational areas under control. Still, their problems did have a restricted range of effect, since they held much inside. Michael Pritchard, an ex-cop, a great professional speaker and comedian, says this about these men: "You want to see a World War II vet let it all hang out? Here it is." (Nothing happens) "You want to see it again?" His point is that these vets never let it all hang out; instead they hold it all in. That is not necessarily healthy, but it is not necessarily PTSD. It is just how they manifested their experience in the war.

While some people do suffer from full-blown PTSD, most cases are mild. What often occurs is that a doctor tells a patient that his symptoms look like PTSD, and that diagnosis impacts that person right between the eyes as if he were told he had cancer. Well, it is not like cancer; it is more like being overweight. If you weigh 30 pounds more than you should, those extra pounds, while tiring to lug around, are probably not life threatening. To get rid of the poundage, you just do a little dieting and you are fine. On the other hand, should you be 400 pounds overweight, your life is greatly impacted. In fact, it just might kill you tomorrow.

Most cases of PTSD are like carrying 30 pounds of extra weight around: It is extra work, but you can live with it, and if you make the effort to rid yourself of the PTSD, you are going to be fine. To reiterate, some people do suffer from full-blown PTSD, but it is comparatively rare. There are also other people who have all of the manifestations, but they are mild. It is important that you bring the issue into perspective and think of it more along the lines of being overweight than being stricken with cancer and all that that means. Put it in perspective and make peace with the memory.

No Macho Men and No Pity Parties

> In this author's work with many combat and postdeployment veterans, in order for a person to feel normal while still suffering the sequels of trauma, s/he must be able to view the symptoms as a normal reaction to an external threat, rather than an illness . . .
> —Dr. Jacques J. Gouws
> "Combat Stress Inoculation, PTSD Recognition,
> and Early Intervention"

One danger in studying PTSD is that we might be tempted to identify all the ways that things did not go perfectly, and then use that as an excuse to have a sulking, pity party. However bad it was for us in combat, we must understand that our reactions are normal.

Try to keep your combat experiences in perspective. If you feel like you received no support from your community or your chain of command, then consider the plight of the Vietnam veterans. Though they were spit on and condemned upon their return from a year of combat, most of them dealt with it and have gone on to make great contributions to our nation. How America abused and mistreated our Vietnam veterans is covered in much greater detail in *On Killing.* Many Vietnam veterans were truly harmed by this process, but this needs to be put into perspective. B. G. Burkett's book, *Stolen Valor,* is an extremely valuable resource to help us understand that, in spite of what we did to them, the Vietnam veterans have done very well. The stereotype of the emotionally marred, psychologically destroyed Vietnam vet is, in most cases, a myth.

This is not to belittle anyone's experiences or to say that your pain is not as bad as someone else's. The goal here is to recognize that the warriors of these past great battles did not have critical incident debriefings and all the other progressive techniques we have now, and most of them were just fine. Likewise, most of today's warriors will be fine. We just need to be sure that our study of psychiatric illness in combat does not turn us into psychological hypochondriacs, or "psychochondriacs."

Although most veterans of World War I and World War II were okay, our goal today is to do things better. For example, they did not have antibiotics in World War I and most of them were okay in spite of that. But that doesn't mean that we want to go into combat without antibiotics available to our doctors. Each passing year and each generation, step by step, we learn to do a better job.

Across the years there has developed an appropriate warrior ethic of not complaining. Our forefathers who fought in two World Wars, Korea and Vietnam returned with a group ethic of close-mouthed pride. The son of one veteran put it this way:

> My father survived the Bataan death march, escaped to Kabanatuan, was recaptured and spent three and a half years as a Japanese POW. He never spoke of the war that made a sad man of him. The very pride that helped him survive also made him unable to seek help. He died many years later from damage done by bayonet wounds and beatings he endured. Some have said he never really came back from the war.

A "suck it up and drive on" ethos has great survival value in the heat of battle, but it has also kept us from seeking helpful treatment after the battle. One veteran police officer who survived a shooting experience told me, "Colonel, you tell all these young guys, 'Don't try to be a macho man.' Tell 'em to get help if they need it. I tried to macho it out after my shooting and didn't get help when I needed it, and it damned near killed me."

No sane person would turn down antibiotics if the doctor prescribed them, and no reasonable warrior should turn away from psychological help if it is available and needed. Totti Karpela, the head instructor of the Helsinki, Finland, Police Department says it well: "It's a sign of strength to admit that you're not always strong enough."

The presence of new tactics and new medicines saves lives in modern combat, but lives are still lost. Doing a better job in the area of psychological debriefings and bulletproofing the mind will reduce psychiatric casualties, but it is no guarantee.

Do you see how we can walk that middle road between the mindless macho man on one side, and the pity party on the other? The bulletproof vest does not stop everything; it is not a guarantee. Likewise, the bulletproof mind is not fail-safe, but we are far better off with it than without it. As Dr. Jonathan Shay, author of the superb book, *Achilles in Vietnam*, says:

> In my own preaching on prevention of psychological and moral injury, I emphasize that we are talking about flak jackets, helmets, and well-made and well-sited fighting positions—not godlike invulnerability.

No macho men, and no pity parties. As long as we walk that middle road, applying the best tools we can, while not permitting ourselves to sink into self-pity when things are not perfect.

But in this age of sensational tabloid journalism, the media can encourage our returning warriors to wallow in the pity party by presenting endless reports and exaggerated "news" pieces implying that virtually every veteran of the war in the Middle East is suffering from full-blown PTSD. This can create dire consequences, as we shall see in a moment.

Here is a letter that I often send the press in response to their queries about the military and PTSD. It's taken in part from an article of mine that appeared in Greater Good magazine:

> Today I am on the road almost 300 days a year speaking to police agencies and numerous military organizations deploying and returning from combat. I teach them that there are two dangers they must guard against. One is that of the "Macho man" mentality that can cause a soldier to refuse to accept vital mental health services. The other danger is what I call the "Pity party."
>
> Interestingly, the very awareness of the possibility of PTSD can increase the probability that it will occur. There is a tendency for human beings to respond to stress in the way that they think they should. When soldiers, their spouses, parents and others are convinced that the

returning veteran will suffer from PTSD, it can create a powerful self-fulfilling prophecy.

I decline most requests for media interviews because of my time-intensive traveling and teaching schedule. I also decline them because I refuse to be part of that "drumbeat of voices" that tells veterans that they are doomed to a lifetime of psychological trauma. I tell the media the truth but then they edit out anything that does not support their belief that "the war will destroy all the soldiers and we'll pay a price for generations to come." This sensationalist "if-it-bleeds-it-leads" journalism is irresponsible because it can cause more harm to our warriors.

Sadly, it is not difficult to find people in the mental health community to support the thesis that anyone who kills, experiences combat, or witnesses violence (or any other fill-in-the-blank 'victim du jour') is doomed to lifelong PTSD and, consequently, needs lifelong mental health care. Too few mental health professionals communicate to their patients that 1) they can recover quickly from PTSD and that 2) they will become stronger from the experience. Yet that expectation must be there if there is to be hope of anything other than a lifetime of expensive counseling.

Here is what I tell all my military and law enforcement audiences:

PTSD is not like pregnancy. You cannot be "a little bit pregnant;" either you are, or you are not. PTSD is not like that.

PTSD is like being overweight. Many people carry around 10, 20, or 30 pounds of excess weight. Although it influences the individual every minute of every day, it might not be a big deal health wise. But for those people who are 500 pounds overweight, it will likely kill them any day now. There was a time when we could only identify people who had "500 pounds" of PTSD. Today we are better at spotting folks who carry lesser loads, 30, 40 or 50 pounds of PTSD.

I have read statistics that say 15 percent of our military is coming home with "some manifestation of psychological problems." Others claim it is 20 percent and still others report 30 percent. Well, depending on how you want to measure it, 30 percent of all college freshmen have some manifestation of psychological problems. Mostly what is being reported on today are people with low levels of PTSD (30, 40 or 50 pounds of PTSD) who in previous wars would not have been detected. We are getting damned good at identifying and treating PTSD and, when the treatment is done, most people are better for the experience.

PTSD is not like frostbite. Frostbite causes permanent damage to your body. If you get frostbite, for the rest of your life you will be more vulnerable to it. PTSD is not like that.

PTSD can be more like the flu. The flu can seriously kick your tail for a while. But once you shake it off, you probably are not going to get it again for the rest of the year. You have been inoculated. PTSD can kick your tail for a while (months and even years). But once you have dealt with it, next time it will take a lot more to knock you off your feet because you have been stress inoculated.

When I was a kid, World War II veterans were everywhere. They were our police sergeants, captains and chiefs. They were our battalion commanders and our senior NCOs. They were our business leaders and our political leaders. The idea that a World War II veteran was a shallow, fragile creature who would break under pressure was ridiculous. (There were some people like that; everyone knew of a few, but they were rare.)

Nietzsche said, "That which does not kill me makes me stronger." The Bible says something similar many times. For example, Romans, chapter five says: " . . . we glory in tribulations . . . knowing that tribulation worketh patience; And patience, experience; and experience, hope: And hope maketh not ashamed." Throughout history, we have understood that bad things can make us stronger.

The World War II generation was the "Greatest Generation" and today a new Greatest Generation is coming home. That is, if we do not screw them all up by telling them (and their families, their neighbors and their employers) that they are ticking-time-bombs doomed to a lifetime of mental illness.

Here is what I believe is the heart of the matter. To harm and destroy people you have to lie:

Lie Number 1: Ignore the vast majority who are just fine and report only on the minority with problems.

Lie Number 2: Fail to report that most PTSD cases are people with only 30, 40, or 50 pounds of PTSD, people who in previous wars would have gone undetected.

Lie Number 3: Fail to report that we are damned good at treating PTSD and that we are getting better at it every day.

Lie Number 4: Fail to report that PTSD can be a step on the path to stress inoculation and that one can be stronger when they come out the other end.

Lie four times over. Lie the worst kind of lie: the lie of omission that gives only the distilled essence of the bad news. Create an expectation in veterans (and their families, employers and neighbors) that they are all fragile creatures who could snap at any time and are doomed to a life of suffering. Get veterans invested in their grievance and in their role as victim. Get them to draw disability from PTSD and convince them that they will never recover.

I want the media to care, but I am convinced that most of them are part of a mob-mentality, a pile-on, if-it-bleeds-it-leads profession that does not care about the harm they do. Remember, this is the same profession that put the Columbine killers on the cover of Time magazine twice – yes, twice – thus giving those brutal mass-murderers the very fame and immortality they wanted. This in turn inspired the Virginia Tech killer who also appeared on every news show and on the front pager of every newspaper in the nation. Sadly, this too inspires countless others as the media continues to be their happy co-conspirators in a murder-for-fame-and-immortality contract.

Please forgive me if I have been harsh but the situation calls for us to be passionate. Yes, some of our veterans will suffer from PTSD and we have an obligation to give them the best possible support. But we also need a balanced, tough love, that creates an expectation that they will get over it, get on with it, and be better for the experience. That they will be the new Greatest Generation

I prefer to emphasize the positive expectations. Positive self-fulfilling prophecies. Now there is a nice concept. But will we ever see it in the news?

EMDR: When You Cannot Make Peace With the Memory

Days of darkness still come o'er me,
Sorrow's path I often tread

—Francis Rowley
"I Will Sing the Wondrous Story"

There is a tool being used now that appears to have proven itself to be helpful in many cases of PTSD. I will just mention the treatment briefly here and suggest that you research it further if you are interested. Although Eye Movement Desensitization and Reprocessing (EMDR) treatment sounds mystical, there are studies that show an 85- to 90-percent success rate with it. Let me say first that it has been my experience talking with thousands upon thousands of police officers and soldiers that these warriors have the most finely tuned BS meters (nonsense gauges) in the world. If something works for this cynical, conservative, hard-nosed bunch – then it works. Period. Well, it is still controversial, and there is still much to be learned, but the reports from the trenches are that EMDR works.

EMDR is an innovative therapeutic treatment introduced by Dr. Francine Shapiro in 1989. Police psychologist Dr. Alexis Artwohl (co-author of *Deadly Force Encounters*) is one of the early psychologists to use EMDR in the

Northwest. She says that many others are now on board with this "strange, but very effective tool." In fact, there are over 50,000 practitioners worldwide using it today.

It is not clear how EMDR works because neuroscience researchers are still exploring how the brain works. Research suggests that when a person is extremely upset, the brain cannot process information as it does normally. A traumatic event that sparks intense emotion becomes "frozen in time" in the information processing system. Then as the person goes about his normal day he runs into external reminders of the experience that triggers a re-experiencing of the sights, sounds, smells, thoughts, body sensations or emotions of that event that often feel as intense as they did at the time it really happened.

The EMDR trained mental health professional follows a procedure based on the specifics of each person. First the clinician helps the client identify an image that represents the target situation, say a shooting, and the emotions and body sensations associated with the memory. The client then works through these memories while he watches the clinician's moving hand, or a moving set of lights, which causes voluntary eye movements. In some cases, auditory tones or hand taps are used instead. After each set of eye movements, tones, or taps, the client is asked to briefly comment on what he felt. While the results of the EMDR session are different for every person, most find that they get a reduction in the negative feelings they had been experiencing.

Here is what we think is happening with EMDR and your personal puppy. The midbrain is a simple mechanism. It can only do one thing at a time. Now the puppy is out in the yard and is so busy watching the clinician's visual stimulus that he does not charge through the whole in the screen and pee in your lap. For the first time since the traumatic event, you are able to work your way through the memory without interference from the puppy. The result is that you begin to patch that hole in the screen door.

The clinician is highly supportive during the processing of upsetting memories, emotions and so on. Should difficulties arise, he makes clinical decisions about needed interventions to achieve the most positive outcome possible during the session. A specific traumatic memory or disturbing situation may resolve in as few as one to three sessions. It is a powerful tool and works incredibly fast. If you are having trouble with persistent re-experiencing of a traumatic event (i.e., the puppy keeps coming for a visit), I encourage you to look into it.

The Next Frontier

The last and hardest conquest of the mind.

—Alexander Pope
The Odyssey of Homer

Unresolved trauma predisposes you to combat stress and PTSD. As Gavin de Becker puts it, "Your past is buried, but for some people it is buried alive." When you are faced with a traumatic, frightening incident, you might revert to whatever level of unresolved residual fear you have from past experiences. In that case, de Becker says, "It will be at least as bad," as the worst thing you experienced before. Which can be pretty bad!

Techniques such as EMDR, used ahead of time, to confront and defuse your ghosts, might be a tool that can negate or preempt this possibility. After we have mastered stress inoculation, incorporated the breathing exercise, understood and applied the prevention of PTSD by delinking the memory from the emotions, the next step in developing warriors and healthy human beings may be this systematic preemption of trauma before combat.

I first met Dr. Per Hamid Ghatan, a brilliant M.D. and Ph.D. specializing in cognitive neurophysiology, when I was presenting at a conference in Stockholm, Sweden. Large numbers of Gulf War veterans came home in the early 1990s and began having serious problems, commonly known as Gulf War Syndrome. Dr. Ghatan believes that the exposure of young children to profoundly frightening movies at an early age might have interacted with a host of other stressors and toxins to predispose these Gulf veterans to become stress casualties.

As discussed earlier, we are truly abusing children by exposing them to images of horrific, brutal murders on television, movies and video games, during an age when they cannot tell the difference between fantasy and reality. Link that with de Becker's theory that your traumatic experience will be "at least as bad" as your worst unresolved residual fear, and we can begin to understand that Dr. Ghatan may very well be right.

In the Gulf War, Afghanistan and Iraq our warriors performed superbly, but could it be that many of them were predisposed to stress casualties due to the toxic nature of our modern culture? Perhaps. This is only a theory and must be viewed with extreme caution, but it is one more reason why we must study this realm. More than ever before, we must make sure that all the variables we can control have been manipulated so that the degree of stress and trauma our warriors encounter before, during and after combat have been reduced as much as possible.

Concern for man himself and his fate must form the chief interest for all technical endeavors. Never forget this in the midst of your diagrams and equations.

—Albert Einstein

chapter

four

A Time to Heal: *The Role of Critical Incident Debriefings in Preventing PTSD*

> To everything there is a season,
> And a time for every purpose under the heaven.
> There is a time to be born and a time to die.
> A time to plant and a time to reap.
> A time to kill and a time to heal.
>
> —Ecclesiastes Chapter 3
> *The Bible*

Pain Shared = Pain Divided, Joy Shared = Joy Multiplied

Well, it has happened here in the city of Elgin. A man, thrown out of a bar for harassing women and arguing with employees over his bar tab, went home, shaved his head, put on camo fatigues, gathered up two shotguns, two handguns, and 220 rounds of ammo and went back to the bar.

First, he shot into a car in the parking lot, injuring two women, and then he walked into the bar and shot a male patron, who died. He then began screaming lines from *Natural Born Killers* and shot an additional 20 people, including the bartender, who died. The offender was apparently first targeting people wearing purple shirts, which the employees wore, and then he began shooting randomly.

The body count: 23 injured, 18 of those shot, two dead. One woman will lose the use of the lower portion of her arm; she took a contact hit from a shotgun when she raised her arm to defend herself. Her limb was just hanging by a shred of flesh.

I was called in for a critical incident debriefing that night before the officers were released to go home. I have never seen more officers shaken up after an event that did not include an officer-involved shooting, especially the young officer first on the scene who could hear shots still being fired inside when he arrived.

—Correspondence to Colonel Grossman
From Commander Dave Barrows

What is this "critical incident debriefing" that Dave Barrows conducted after this horrific incident? This is still a new, developing, evolving field, and there is much to learn. In some areas it is still considered controversial, but it is really quite simple, and in the military and law enforcement fields where lives are on the line and lessons have been learned the hard way, this concept has been embraced and widely accepted.

In *Deadly Force Encounters*, Artwohl and Christensen tell us that:

> A debriefing is any discussion after an event that helps the participants come to terms with it, and learn from it. Hopefully, it helps to gain closure so that event will not continue to cause emotional distress. An informal debriefing can simply be a discussion that arises spontaneously after an event, while a formal debriefing takes the discussion one step further because it's organized and facilitated to ensure it helps everyone.

Dr. Greg Belenky is a U.S. Army Colonel and psychiatrist working at the Walter Reed Army Institute of Research. He is also one of the Army's leading experts and a true pioneer in PTSD treatment and critical incident debriefings. I have had the honor of being a co-presenter with Dr. Belenky at several conferences. He teaches that there are two primary functions of a critical incident debriefing.

First, it is needed to reconstruct the event from the beginning to the end, to learn what was done wrong, what was done right, and to help develop operational lessons. The Army believes that the majority of the learning on a tactical exercise comes afterwards in what is called an "after action review," where all the participants talk about what took place. This phase is so important that to not do it is to have essentially wasted the exercise. If this is true of a training event, how much more important is it to learn from what happened when blood was shed and lives were lost?

Second, the debriefing is a time to put everyone back together. Remember there might be memory loss, memory distortion, irrational guilt, and a host of other factors clouding the ability of the combatants to deal with everything that happened to them. The debriefing is a tool to sort out these matters, and to restore morale and unit integrity. It can make lives healthier and sometimes it even saves them.

Another way to look at the objective of the debriefing can be found in an old expression by E.E. "Doc" Smith, a Ph.D., and famous science fiction author in the 1930s. Smith presented this as an equation:

$$\text{Pain Shared} = \text{Pain} \div$$
$$\text{Joy Shared} = \text{Joy X}$$

Pain shared is pain divided, and joy shared is joy multiplied; that is the essence of the human condition. Historically, we have always gathered together after a traumatic event to divide each other's pain, and to multiply our joy. We do this in wakes and in funerals, and we have always done it after battles to lift up, multiply and amplify the valor, the sacrifice and the professionalism of the living and the dead.

There has always been time for a remembrance, a time to touch on that which was good and fine about a fallen comrade. Across the centuries, in funerals, wakes and around the campfire, warriors would tell of their fallen comrade: the noble deeds that they had personally witnessed, the lessons in life that had been taught, and how their lives had been shaped by the life which was now departed.

They also found humor in what happened: a strange, twisted, dark humor at times; simple and childlike at other times; but always they found the peace and healing of humor in what they did, and this was an important part of multiplying the joy. At the same time they also shared and divided the suffering, the grief and the pain, breaking it into manageable chunks, grieving intensely and briefly so that they could bear it and get on with life.

We conducted these debriefings every night around the campfire, throughout history. You see, up until the twentieth century, warriors almost always took the nights off. After Agincourt, Waterloo, Picket's Charge, Bunker Hill and San Juan Hill, the winners and the losers sat around their separate campfires that night and debriefed. After ten thousand battles across thousands of years, warriors have always gathered to put together the pieces and figure out what happened.

Combat is a corrosive, toxic environment, but someone has to do it. Just as surely as someone has to go into blazing buildings, toxic waste sites and hospitals full of infectious diseases, so too does someone have to go into combat to confront those who would do us harm. George Orwell said, "We sleep safely in our beds this night, because rough men stand ready in the night to visit violence on those who would do us harm." Someone has to do it. So, across the centuries, over thousands of years, slowly, painfully, we found a way to be able to live with ourselves after combat and then go back into the heart of darkness again, and again.

In my fiction book, *The Two-Space War,* there is a young private who has had all the bad experiences of most green recruits in combat. At the end of the book, he tells his captain, "The part that bothers me is the lies. It's all a lie. The poetry and the glory and the honor, it's a lie. I've seen war, and it's not like that."

The captain replies,

No, my friend, it's not a lie. It's men making the best of a dirty, nasty job that has to be done. There are times when evil comes, when darkness falls, and good men must fight. Then we make a virtue of necessity. Pain shared is pain divided. Joy shared is joy multiplied. Every night around the campfire, or with our mess mates over dinner, we talk about the battle. Each time we divide our pain and we multiply our joy. Until in the end we've turned combat into something we can live with, something we can keep on doing. It would be a lie if we completely forgot the pain, the suffering and the loss. But it's not a lie to recognize that there is good to be found in battle. And it's not a lie to focus on the good parts, to magnify the joy and divide the pain so that we can live with it. There is glory, if we give it to them. There is honor, if we honor those who do it. Sometimes wars have to be fought. It destroys enough, it harms enough during the war. It is foolishness, it is madness to let it destroy us after the war. So we turn it into something we can live with. And we turn ourselves into creatures who can do this dirty, desperate job, do it well, and live with it afterward.

In *Henry V*, Shakespeare wrote, "There is some soul of goodness in things evil," and men would "observingly distil it out." War is a great evil, but upon occasion it may be a necessary evil. Perhaps we should not judge those who must partake of that evil and attempt to distill some goodness out of it.

Warriors Weep at Funerals . . .

. . . According to reports, in one 10-minute period on Omaha Beach, a single rifle company of 205 men lost 197, including every officer and sergeant. These were not pointless or avoidable deaths. The price was very high – but for that which they died was sacred. We remember. Their comrades in arms remember. And those who could, came back.

—William J. Bennett
From a lecture to the United States Naval Academy

Across countless thousands of years, men have developed two rules of behavior after combat. These rules are not mindless, macho nonsense, they are valuable tools that have evolved at great cost.

The first rule is that it is okay to weep at the funeral of a beloved comrade or family member. We mourn briefly, intensely and unashamedly, and then we get on with life. Lord Wavell, the supreme commander of the British forces in World war II wrote in his book, *Other Men's Flowers*, that "Heavy mourning, deep black edges, long widowhood, unrestrained grief are out of fashion, as they must be to a generation which has indulged in . . . war."

Sir Henry Taylor said it this way:

He that lacks time to mourn, lacks time to mend.
Eternity mourns that. 'Tis an ill cure
For life's worst ills, to have no time to feel them.

After the battle we must find "time to mourn." There is no shame in it; we need it. Our long-term survival demands it, and the dead have earned our tears.

You have the right to mourn any way you choose. Strength and even denial are forms of mourning, but you should know that most warrior societies, across the ages, have found it appropriate and healthy to shed tears for their fallen comrades. Whatever you do, don't blot them out. Don't leave them behind. I think you will agree that they deserve to be mourned.

> If you are able, save for them a place inside of you, and save one backward glance when you are leaving for the places they can no longer go.
>
> Be not ashamed to say you loved them, though you may or may not have always. Take what they have taught you with their dying and keep it with your own.
>
> And in that time when men decide and feel safe to call the war insane, take one moment to embrace those gentle heroes you left behind.
>
> —Major Michael O'Donnell
> KIA March 24, 1970, Dak To, Vietnam

. . . But Not at the Memory of Battle

There has something gone wrong
    My brave boy, it appears,
For I see your proud struggle
    To keep back the tears.
That is right. When you cannot
    Give trouble the slip,
Then bear it, still keeping
    "A stiff upper lip!"

Though you cannot escape
    Disappointment and care,
The next best thing to do
    Is to learn how to bear.
If when for life's prizes
    You're running, you trip,
Get up, start again —
    "Keep a stiff upper lip!"

> Through childhood, through manhood,
>   Through life to the end,
> Struggle bravely and stand
>   By your colors, my friend.
> Only yield when you must;
>   Never "give up the ship,"
> But fight on to the last
>   "With a stiff upper lip!"
>
>   —"Keep A Stiff Upper Lip!"
>   Phoebe Cary, 1824-1871

The second rule is that it is not okay to weep at the memory of battle. A warrior who does is like a firefighter who weeps at the memory of fire or a pilot who weeps at the memory of flight. The firefighter and the pilot can mourn comrades killed in fires and crashes but still find satisfaction in what they do. Combat is what warriors do, and if the memory of battle is unbearably painful to them, then they will have great difficulty doing it again. Like the widow of 50 years mentioned earlier, the veteran must come to terms with what has happened, and he must delink the memory from the emotions.

We have always conducted critical incident debriefings. We did them every night around the campfire, and the "Old Sarge" always led them. There was always an old sarge, an old captain, or an old chief who was the survivor of past battles. We knew that if we were going to be survivors, if we were going to be there for our village or our nation in the years to come, then we had to be like him. Old Sarge modeled survivor behavior, and Old Sarge was calm.

Across untold thousands of years, we learned that the man who became weepy or angry when he talked about his combat experience would not be there for his village next year. Unless he was able to get his emotions under control. Other than in funerals, warriors have always been embarrassed to weep in front of their brothers, and they were embarrassed to see a brother weep because it showed a character flaw, a true weakness which meant that he might fail his comrades in the future. If he was not able to get his emotions under control.

The laconic Spartans modeled this behavior. The inscrutable samurai epitomized this code. The quiet plainsman, woodsman and cowboy who were products of the American Civil War, the Indian wars and the harsh frontier, symbolized this ethic. And the sang-froid that marked the height of the French Empire; or the ethic of British imperturbability, the "stiff upper lip" that sustained the British Empire; was more than just an affectation: it was a vital survival skill.

The stoic Romans exemplified this ethos, but today, almost 2,000 years later, they have evolved into the wonderful, colorful, flamboyant, emotional and militarily incompetent Italians. Homer talked of this falling off of martial skills, this military fall from grace, over 2,500 years ago in *The Iliad*:

Chiefs who no more in bloody fights engage,
But wise through time, and narrative with age,
In summer-days like grasshoppers rejoice,—
A bloodless race, that send a feeble voice. . .
Like leaves on trees the race of man is found,—
Now green in youth, now withering on the ground;
Another race the following spring supplies:
They fall successive and successive rise.

—(Alexander Pope transl.)

Perhaps the secret to long-term survival as a civilization is to develop and nurture a group of stoic, laconic, stiff-upper-lipped warriors. Always the standard has been there for us, set by the Old Sarge, because only someone like him would survive across the years. Perhaps now we can understand when we observe such behavior that it is not some mindless macho affectation but a vital warrior survival skill.

One classic example can be seen in the real-life character of Sergeant Major Plumley in the movie, "We Were Soldiers." That movie was drawn from the book, *We Were Soldiers Once and Young*, written by the battalion commander and the journalist who were there in America's first major battle in Vietnam. The movie is about the experiences of the real warriors who fought in that battle, and it is one of the most accurate depictions of the behavior of men in combat that you will ever see. Sergeant Major Plumley (played by Sam Elliot in the movie) was a veteran of combat in World War II and Korea, so when it came time for him to engage in combat in Vietnam, how did he behave? He was calm. The definition of courage is "grace under pressure." We have always honored the ability of a warrior to control his emotions and demonstrate grace under pressure.

Do you think Private Plumley was like that in his first battle? No. It took many battles and years of combat experience for him to grow into that warrior. And there can be no doubt that there was an "Old Sarge" who modeled that behavior and taught him to remain calm in the heat of battle.

Neitze said, "What does not kill me only makes me stronger." But this concept was communicated long before Neitze, almost 2000 years before, when it was written:

. . . we glory in tribulations . . . knowing that tribulation worketh patience; And patience, experience; and experience, hope; And hope maketh not ashamed.

—Romans 5:3-5
The Bible

The young warrior fails, and picks himself up, dusts himself off and drives on, year after year, to become the veteran that others can depend upon in their hour of need. And always the lesson he learns is to remain calm, to have grace under pressure.

So you see, the debriefing is not some "Kumbayah sobfest." We can weep at funerals, but we strive not to weep at the memory of battle. The tool that we use to control our emotions, to keep the puppy from coming through the screen door, is the tactical breathing exercise, which will be covered in the next chapter. For now, understand that the goal is to maintain control of your emotions and remain calm, before, during and after combat.

This does not mean that the warrior knows no joy. The process of multiplying the joy includes finding humor and laughter in your memories. Often with an earthy, even bawdy humor.

Controlling your emotions does not mean you have no emotions. There can be a deep and abiding joy in the warrior's life, as long as he keeps the puppy under control. As Shakespeare wrote:

> Give me that man
> That is not passion's slave, and I will wear him
> In my heart's core, ay, in my heart of heart . . .
>
> *—Hamlet*

For centuries we divided the pain and multiplied the joy, striving *not* to be "passion's slave" and learning, always learning from the Old Sarge, how to survive in this toxic realm of combat.

The Twentieth Century: "Farewell to Tranquil Mind!"

> Farewell the tranquil mind! farewell content!
> Farewell the plumed troop and the big wars
> That make ambition virtue! O, farewell!
> Farewell the neighing steed and the shrill trump,
> The spirit stirring drum, the ear piercing fife,
> The royal banner, and all quality,
> Pride, pomp, and circumstance of glorious war!
>
> —Shakespeare
> *Othello*

The twentieth century has seen a "farewell to tranquil mind," for the warrior. Not only have there been horrendous, brutal wars unlike anything before in history, but the combatant has also been increasingly denied whatever small solace there was to be found in the sad, wretched duty that his nation sent him to perform. As Winston Churchill said, "War which was cruel and glorious has become cruel and sordid."

The era of debriefing around a nighttime campfire ended with the beginning of World War I. The profoundly different nature of combat in World War I is superbly captured in John Keegan's classic book, *The Face of Battle*, which I highly recommend as a primer for understanding this dramatic change. Suddenly warriors could no longer take the nights off, because combat was now taking place day-and-night for months on end. There was no escape from the danger, so the warriors did not get a chance to make peace with the memory every night.

In his book, A *History of Warfare*, John Keegan notes how this debriefing process changed during the twentieth century:

> There was debriefing, of a sort, after the battle, in World War I, World War II, Korea, and Vietnam, but it was often after weeks and months of continuous combat, rather than on a daily basis. There was also a form of debriefing when the troops sailed home, which had great value, but this did not occur in Vietnam when the soldiers flew home as individuals after their tour of duty was finished.

Throughout history the veteran has learned to make peace with his memory, often they even made friends with their memory. Steven Pressfield speaks of this in his book, *The Gates of Fire.*

> I have heard it said that for the lover the seasons are marked in memory by those mistresses whose beauty has enflamed his heart. He recalls this year as the one when, moonstruck, he pursued a certain beloved about the city, and that year, when another favorite yielded at last to his charms.
>
> For the mother and father, on the other hand, the seasons are numbered by the births of their children—this one's first step, that one's initial word. By these homely ticks is the calendar of the loving parent's life demarcated and set within the book of remembrance.
>
> But for the warrior, the seasons are marked not by these sweet measures nor by the calendared years themselves, but by battles. Campaigns fought and comrades lost; trials of death survived. Clashes and conflicts from which time effaces all superficial recall, leaving only the fields themselves and their names, which achieve in the warrior's memory a stature ennobled beyond all other modes of commemoration, purchased with the holy coin of blood and paid for with the lives of beloved brothers-in-arms. As the priest with his graphis and tablet of wax, the infantryman, too, has his scription. His history is carved upon his person with the stylus of steel, his alphabet engraved with spear and sword indelibly upon the flesh.

The American Civil War veterans were no different than all those who had gone before. They too had "ennobled" the memory of their battles. They came home and told war stories. They bounced their grandbabies on their knees and proudly told of shooting Johnny Reb or killing the damned Yankees. They wrote their memoirs by the thousands, in intimate detail.

The returning World War I veteran was different. The returning veterans of this war did not talk about his experiences. He didn't make peace with his memories immediately after the battle. Later they were too painful to touch, so he tried to not think about them. He tried to bury his memories, but sometimes they were buried alive. Many veterans of World War II, Korea and Vietnam did the same thing.

Throughout the 20th century the old rule of "warriors don't cry" was still in place, personified by John Wayne and Clint Eastwood and a host of other laconic, stoic models. But this new generation of warriors did not always understand that it was okay to weep at funerals, and they tried to live by the don't-cry rule without making peace with the memory. Sometimes it worked, but sometimes it festered, swelled and ate away at them.

> Before and after the war he was a farmer, never married, never discussed the Army, yet wore the issue khaki while riding the tractor, kept his bedroom as Spartan as a barracks, ate only vegetables and drank well water. The day before he died at eighty-three of the old man's friend, pneumonia, his mind flashed back to the Philippines. He shouted out "Get down! Get down!" and flung his shit-stained boxers against the threatening enemy wall, thrashed and clawed and yelled and spat so much the nurses had to strap his hands, sedate him.
>
> Two months before he died he told a story, only war story that he ever mentioned: he and a Jap, not twenty yards apart, faced each other with weapons aimed, not fired. Nip Arisaka, his M-1 Garand.
>
> They stood that way for nearly thirty minutes, then parted, like lovers for the first time.
>
> —Collie H. Owens
> "Uncle Joe"

Fighter Pilots as a Model

> Fierce fiery warriors fought upon the clouds,
> In ranks and squadrons and right form of war.
>
> —Shakespeare
> *Julius Caesar*

During the twentieth century, only the fighter pilots got the chance to do it right. In the horrific, violent wars of that century, the ground troops often found themselves in day-and-night combat operations, unable to debrief every night. But the fighter pilots did debrief after every battle. In both formal and informal debriefings, they multiplied the joy and divided the pain, and their attitude toward killing in combat was much healthier.

When a fighter pilot got a kill, his buddies toasted him and his crew chief proudly painted a small enemy flag on his aircraft. When he killed five of the enemy, he was called an "ace" and was honored and respected. When he killed an all-time record number of the enemy, he was given the highest honor and lifted up as an example for all.

This idolizing and adoration of the fighter pilot has held true throughout the twentieth century, but for the poor infantryman who kills an enemy soldier, the situation has become quite different. Very successful snipers or soldiers who receive major awards for valor sometimes have the number of enemy killed carefully set forth in their award citations, but the individual rifleman who kills "only" a few enemy soldiers is often ashamed to tell how many kills he has made.

Why should there be such a remarkable difference between the way a fighter pilot and an infantryman feel about their kills? Perhaps it is because sometimes the enemy pilot is able to bail out so that the fighter pilot can occasionally defeat his opponent without having to actually kill him. But the rifleman also wounds or captures many enemy soldiers, defeating them without having to kill them. Perhaps this difference exists because the pilot kills at a distance and is only shooting at a machine, which allows him to partially deny the reality of his killing. (I address the difference created by distance in detail in *On Killing* and will not go into the subject in detail here, other than to say that although this is an important factor, I do not believe it is the major one in this case.)

I think the major difference between the fighter pilot and the "poor bloody infantryman" is how he feels about what he has done. The fighter pilot has always formally processed what he did with approving, supportive leaders after every day's work, and then that night he did it again over a beer with complimentary friends. Usually the infantryman did not get the chance to do any of this, and he never made peace with the memory. Unless he was a Medal of Honor recipient, who was lauded and lionized, he never got a chance to multiply the joy, and all too often he never divided the pain. Instead he multiplied the pain and divided the joy.

Instead of a magnificent tiger striding proudly in with his prey in his mouth, many infantrymen and police officers have been turned into cowed, shamefaced dogs who slink in and lick their wounds. They are often ashamed of what they did, and all too often our society acts like we are ashamed of them. The fighter pilot who paints 21 enemy flags on his aircraft is a proud hero, but the infantryman who puts 21 notches in his rifle is considered to be deviant and deranged. Why? Because the fighter pilot and his comrades are proud of his heroic action. They tell the world of what he did and all his friends affirm to one-and-all that there was honor and glory in his deeds. Their leaders mirror and magnify these attitudes, and (perhaps most importantly) they will vigorously, righteously and happily channel their warrior spirit into a swift punch in the nose for anyone who is foolish enough to claim otherwise. It should be dangerous to attack a warrior, but when we turn our protectors into cowed puppies, they sometimes do not even have the spirit to defend themselves from the kicks of an ungrateful public. And in the end, they may not be able to protect us and our loved ones at the moment of truth.

It may trouble us to think that we should congratulate, praise and reward a man who kills someone in honorable combat, but the alternative is to have disposable soldiers and one-shot, throwaway police officers. The alternative to honoring them is to destroy them for doing exactly what we told them to do. We employ them, equip them, enable them, and empower them to kill, and then when they do, we act ashamed of them. This is a shameful and inexcusable thing to do and the first step in correcting this is for the warrior and his comrades, like the fighter pilots, to honor themselves.

I had the privilege of witnessing a powerful affirmation and honoring of a young warrior one day when I was training at a state SWAT conference. The head of the state police SWAT team, an old sergeant with many gun battles under his belt, introduced a young officer from a rural police department, and told how he who had recently been shot in the face and was still recovering from his wounds. He told how the young officer had been shot and survived. "Best of all," the Old Sarge said, "he got back up and killed the bastard who shot him." There was a growling roar of affirmation from the crowd upon hearing these words, and I could see the young warrior hold his head high with shining eyes.

There is honor, if we honor them. There is glory if we give it to them, and the process starts within the warrior community, and then it works outward.

Two Case Studies: "How Not to Leave Our Mentally Wounded Behind"

I just wanted to thank you again for leading the way and teaching us how not to leave our mentally wounded behind. It was an honor to finally meet you and to tell you thanks for being a major part of my recovery and helping to save my career, marriage and life (not in that order).

—Correspondence to Colonel Grossman

The first case study is a tragic tale in which the warrior failed to debrief, and the other is a life-affirming story in which a warrior did get a chance to tell his tale among his comrades. The first is about a Vietnam veteran named Tim.

In the spring of 1991, a group of West Point psychology students spent their summer conducting interviews for me at the Boston V.A. Medical center. I used the data that they collected in *On Killing*. Tim and another Vietnam veteran had come to the U.S. Military Academy at West Point for me to interview them in front of my cadets so that I could model the process that I wanted them to use in their interviews. We sat in my living room with Tim, his wife, my wife, a dozen West Point cadets, and me, as Tim told his story.

Tim said he had never told anyone this story. This is a statement that should always set off alarm bells, since it usually means that the person has not made peace with the memory and the experience has been eating away at him for many years. Tim was in an infantry unit in Vietnam. On one occasion they had been out "rocking and rolling" all day, and then that night he was assigned extra duty, which kept him from sleeping. The next day he was out doing the same as the day before, and then that night the company went into a defensive position on a hilltop.

There were two covered and concealed avenues of approach, two wooded draws that came close to the top of the hill. Although he was exhausted, Tim was ordered to go out with three other troops at dusk to establish an observation post (O.P.) as part of the security plan. They were ordered to establish their O.P. in one of these draws, and another group of four soldiers would set up an O.P. in the wooded draw on the other side of the hill. So at the last flickering of twilight they slipped out to their position, scratched out shallow foxholes, and hunkered down.

Tim said he was so tired that he turned to one of the other individuals in his position and said, "I had duty last night and I didn't get any sleep." He slipped off his watch, which had a luminous dial, and handed it to him. "Just give me 30 minutes and then wake me up and I'll give you a break." The soldier agreed, and Tim went to sleep.

Tim says that he had no idea how long he had been asleep before he felt a hand cover his mouth and someone shaking his shoulder. "I woke up," he said.

> I groped for my weapon, and by the moonlight trickling through the forest canopy, I can see this guy pointing down the hill. When I look, I see North Vietnamese soldiers, lots of them, crawling past us and moving toward the perimeter. I pulled him over to me, and whispered in his ear, "Fire their asses up and run."

The soldier obediently popped up and emptied a magazine of ammunition from his M-16 on full automatic at point-blank range, and then all hell broke loose. It was a major regimental attack coming at them from multiple directions.

Tim and one other man went running into the perimeter shouting, "It's the O.P. It's the O.P. We're coming in. Don't shoot."

As soon as they got in, a corporal grabbed Tim and asked where was the rest of his O.P. Tim realized that just he and one other individual had made it in. Again the corporal asked him where the other men were. Then, "You left them out there," the corporal screamed. "You left them."

For the rest of the night the battle raged with artillery and air strikes all around the perimeter. Tim says he spent the entire night behind an M-60 machine gun, firing all around the area of the O.P. to keep the enemy at bay. At dawn, the North Vietnamese finally pulled out.

At first light Tim went with a patrol to check the O.P.s. The men assigned to the O.P. on the other side of the hill all had their throats cut. They had fallen asleep on guard and had paid the price.

Then they went to Tim's O.P. and found the two remaining members of his team. One was dead and the other was badly wounded. "I jumped into the hole," Tim said,

> . . . and I saw that the wounded one was the guy I had given my watch to. He tried to give it back to me, but I said, "No buddy, you keep it. You keep it." To this very day, I can't wear a watch.

Tim's wife had been sitting beside him as he told his story and when he finished, she said, "It's been almost 20 years and I never knew this. I never understood why you wouldn't wear a watch."

Tim looked at me with pain in his eyes and tears running down his cheeks, and said, "Do you understand? I abandoned those men. I left them."

I shook my head and said,

> Tim, listen to me. I'm an airborne ranger. I'm an infantry officer. I teach tactics at West Point. Believe me when I tell you that an O.P. is a sacrificial lamb staked out to bleat once as the tiger comes through. Your only job was to warn everybody else in the company. You went out there and you set up a sleep plan, and then when you saw the enemy at point-blank range, you gave the order to open fire. Do you know how easy it would have been to hunker down and wet your pants and do nothing? You saved the lives of every man in that company that day and you got 50 percent of your people out of there. You provided cover fire all night long and you came back and got another 25 percent of your people out of there. You should have gotten a medal for what you did that night.

He looked at me for a long moment and then said, "I never looked at it that way."

For over 20 years, this had been a cyst in Tim's brain, a cyst filled with guilt and self-loathing, and it had swollen and festered across the years. He had never had the chance to lay it out and examine what exactly had happened that horrific night. He had never debriefed; he had never even talked about it before. It was an event that impacted the mind of a terrified, sleep deprived 19-year-old kid and had eaten him alive, year after year.

Tim was truly a victim of, as Thomas Hardy put it,

Aggressive fancy working spells
Upon a mind o'erwrought.

The Dynasts

We will come back to Tim, but let us move ahead to the first Gulf War in 1990. This was two decades after Vietnam, and the U.S. military had begun to understand that there was a moral, medical and legal obligation to conduct these debriefings. The Army had combat stress teams assigned at the brigade level, and these individuals were true pioneers in conducting critical incident debriefings.

Dr. Greg Belenky, the psychiatrist and U.S. Army expert on PTSD mentioned earlier, was in command of a combat stress team during the Gulf War. During one conference that I attended with Colonel Belenky, he told the story of what happened after a soldier was killed.

This soldier had stepped on an unexploded bomblet (which had become essentially a landmine) in one of the little outlying camps. Colonel Belenky grabbed a helicopter and flew out to the site, where he learned that the medic, who had treated the fatally injured man, was still in deep shock 24 hours later. When the helicopter had evacuated the body, the medic had just sat there, muttering how the man's death was his fault. He said it so often and so intensely that everyone else accepted it as the truth.

Then Dr. Belenky gathered all the participants for a debriefing. Once they began talking, it turned out the platoon sergeant and platoon leader felt guilt over errors they had made calling in the medivac helicopter. The group learned that the kid who died had been carrying an M-203 grenade on his chest, ammunition he was supposed to have turned in but the squad leader and team leader had let him keep it. When he stepped on the ICM bomblet, it exploded and set off the grenade on his chest. This was a source of guilt for the team leader and squad leader, since they had failed to follow procedure. Then the medic told his story.

He had raced across what could have been a minefield, dropped down beside the victim and began CPR, though there was no heartbeat or respiration. Bloody air gurgled out the man's cheek, so the medic slapped his hand over the wound and continued to apply mouth to mouth. Bloody air gurgled out the guy's chest, so the medic ripped open his shirt and tried to cover the gaping wound with his arm while continuing with CPR. Then bloody air gurgled out of the guy's eye sockets. For over 20 minutes, the medic applied CPR to a bloody corpse, his own body becoming drenched in the man's blood. Finally, the medivac bird came, the man was placed into a body bag, and the helicopter whisked him away into the sky. On the ground, the medic cried, "It's my fault. It's all my fault. I should have done more."

His friends sat stunned with tears in their eyes. They hugged him and said, "We never understood what had happened. We never understood. It's not your fault. You did all you could do." His peers were the only ones who could convince him that it was not his fault. Dr. Belenky said that when the others said those words and embraced him that the medic blossomed like a rose. They gave him his life back. The doctor did a follow-up on him later and he was just fine.

It was too late, though, for Tim my Vietnam veteran friend. Although he did get a chance to talk with me and debrief about what had happened, the memory had festered and eaten away at him for too many years. About two years later I got a call on the 5th of July from another Vietnam veteran. He said that I needed to call Tim's family. I had a sickening feeling why, but still I asked. "Yesterday, on the 4th of July," the man said, "Tim put his gun in his mouth and blew his brains out."

Tim was a great American, a good father and a noble man who answered his nation's call. He was my friend. He killed the enemy and saved the lives of many Americans, but then his society told him to be ashamed of what he did. He was not alone. For years after, the citizens of his nation attacked and condemned the returning Vietnam veteran, pouring salt on his festering PTSD. (The shameful degradation and condemnation of the Vietnam veteran by the American public is addressed in detail in *On Killing*.)

All warriors are responsible for their own actions; you cannot lead a warrior life any other way. But from one perspective, Tim's chain of command, his buddies, and his fellow citizens killed him that night just as surely as he killed himself, though it was done largely out of ignorance. Today, we know that debriefings are critical. In these violent times, we hold each other's lives in our hands, and we are morally obligated to be there for each other. Pain shared is pain divided, but Tim never got a chance to share that pain. We know that you are only as sick as your secrets, but Tim never got a chance to share his secrets. So they ate him alive. It does not have to be this way. We have a moral, medical and legal obligation to be there for each other after the fact.

Getting It Right Again: ". . . and the Deep Roots Are Not Touched by the Frost."

> Let us sing the old songs,
> When all the new songs have been sung.
>
> —Finnish Proverb

Throughout the twentieth century we did it wrong. When the nature of combat changed and we could no longer conduct nighttime debriefings, no longer multiply the joy and divide the pain after the day's battle so we could live with ourselves after, we inadvertently multiplied the pain and divided the joy.

Now let us reach back into our past with wisdom and understanding to find the warrior heritage, the deep roots that sustained our forefathers across the centuries. J.R.R. Tolkein, writing in *The Lord of the Rings*, wrote powerfully and eloquently about the need to tap into the deep roots of our heritage after the long, bitter years of hard frost:

> Not all that is gold doth glitter,
> Not all those who wander are lost.
> The old that is strong does not wither,
> and the deep roots are not touched by the frost.

So now as we enter into the twenty-first century we are finally getting it right again. The two case studies we just examined are more than just two warriors, one destroyed by combat and one who lived. These are two models, two paths. One leads to death and destruction, the other to healing and redemption.

In his book, *A War of Nerves: Soldiers and Psychiatrists in the Twentieth Century*, Ben Shephard emphasizes the importance of social and cultural responses to combat stress. In particular, he emphasizes immediate, local help given by those who understand concepts of military group bonding, underpinned by supportive leaders and affirming comrades. He also points out the importance and value of sex, memories of sex, singing, and humor. Far from being placebos, these are actually powerful survival mechanisms that have been developed across the millennia to help defuse traumatic situations by reasserting normality into our lives.

Critical incident debriefings have come under academic scrutiny, and even a degree of attack and condemnation by some psychologists and psychiatrists. Those who have been in a stressful incident can find value in coming together as a group, sorting out the memory distortions, filling the memory gaps, confronting the irrational guilt, recognizing the achievements, learning the lessons, multiplying the joy and dividing the pain of the traumatic event.

Warriors have done this throughout history. This is very similar to what happens in funerals and wakes. To say that a debriefing is harmful is like saying that funerals and wakes are harmful.

Those who are members of the critical incident stress management (CISM) community sometimes feel that these attacks are really a "turf battle" motivated by therapists and counselors who believe that their source of income and prestige is being threatened. There can be no doubt that the empowerment of individuals and groups to conduct debriefings has intruded on some of the turf that was once solely owned by the psychiatrist and psychologist, and some may be threatened or offended by this. However, it is quite appropriate to constantly examine the process being used, to ensure that we do the best job possible.

If we are going to do these debriefings and provide this cultural, social support (and we must), then we are obligated to do it right. This means that we need to constantly research and study to develop the best methodology. Recent research on the effectiveness of critical incident debriefings in military units returning from peacekeeping missions found that the debriefing can potentially do harm, just as any medical procedure can if it is done incorrectly. Research (and common sense) indicates that there are several things that we must consider:

-We must not force individuals to participate. Experience has shown that they will participate voluntarily if we explain why this is important. There are two key pieces of information that need to be communicated: (1) Stress is a key disabler and destroyer of warriors and, (2) although some may not need the debriefing, it is a tool that can help them save their buddies' lives in the years to come.

-It is important that soldiers are not required to conduct their debriefings after returning home. The soldier's departure from the war zone can be delayed (there are always legitimate reasons for transportation delays), so that the debriefing can be conducted in-country, as soon after the battle as possible. It is extremely demoralizing for a soldier to be forced to stop and debrief when his wife and children are waiting for him right outside the gate.

-If at all possible, outsiders should not conduct the debriefing. Someone they know, trust and respect, someone with the same background and the same warrior ethos, and someone who has been with them in the past should do it.

-The debriefing should not stand alone. It should be part of a continuum of psychological support, which includes referrals for counseling, education, and follow up for those who need it. Remember, no "macho men." A warrior makes use of all available resources to win the battle, and it just makes sense to use state of the art, medical and psychiatric assistance if you think you might need it.

-Try to avoid having a "sob fest." We understand if our brothers and sisters weep, but the participants should go into the debriefing knowing that one key objective is to delink the memory from the physiological arousal. The breathing exercise should be used to help accomplish this.

Today, the military has standardized critical incident debriefings in the form of comprehensive after-action reviews (AARs), which are conducted by unit leaders in-country. The law enforcement community has also learned to follow these rules by conducting their group debriefings as soon as possible during duty hours, and by using respected and trained superiors and critical incident stress management (CISM) teams from within the department. In both the military and the law enforcement community, it is understood that these debriefings are vital to develop valuable operational lessons. I am happy to report that today's warriors are becoming increasingly aware that there is a moral obligation to participate since the debriefing is also a tool that can help save their comrades lives in the years to come.

Remember Dr. Dave Klinger's interviews with over 100 SWAT team members who shot and hit a suspect in a gunfight? The police officers in his research said that it was their friends and superiors who helped them the most. This is what the debriefing can provide for police officers, soldiers and other warriors in dangerous and stressful professions: an opportunity to put the pieces together, figure out exactly what happened, make peace with the memory, and provide a structured environment to provide support from superiors and peers, when it is most needed.

A Time to Heal

> The universe is change; our life is what our thoughts make it.
> —Marcus Aurelius
> *Meditations*

The *Bible* tells us that, "There is a time to kill, and a time to heal." Let there be a time to heal. Let us actively seek and choose the path of healing from this point on. Whether we approve of the combat or not, no reasonable observer could wish more pain and suffering upon those warriors who answered their nations call as peace officers in our streets and soldiers in distant lands.

> We have come over a way
> that with tears has been watered,
> We have come treading our path
> thru' the blood of the slaughtered,
> Out from the gloomy past,
> till now we stand at last . . .
> —James Weldon Johnson
> "Lift Every Voice and Sing"

Throughout the twentieth century the price has been horrific. We sent young men forth and they waded through rivers of tears and blood, only to be destroyed long after the battle was over. If there must be war, if there must be "rough men to stand watch in the night," let us do it in such a manner that we do not destroy the individuals who we have trained, equipped, enabled and empowered to kill. Now let us come out from the gloomy past to stand at last in a time to heal.

five

Tactical Breathing and the Mechanics of the Debriefing: *Separating the Memory from the Emotions*

On April 28, 2001, at 2038 hours, I was involved in my sixth officer-involved shooting with a man intent on killing his wife, daughter, and four-year old granddaughter. His plan was to shoot them, and he had armed himself with a .357 mag., 9mm, and a 12-gauge pump shotgun.

When I arrived, the suspect immediately began firing at me with the handguns while I evacuated the daughter and granddaughter. While attempting to evacuate the wife, the suspect aimed the shotgun at us. I pushed the lady on the ground and covered her with my body. The suspect fired and four pellets struck me in the head, two entered my brain.

The blast of the shotgun flipped me over, and I got up off the ground and pulled the lady behind cover. I engaged the suspect in a running gun battle wounding him seven times (five fatal wounds), but he would not go down. As with most head wounds, I was bleeding profusely and felt as though I would soon lose consciousness, when I saw the suspect coming towards the lady and me. I had fired 39 of the 40 rounds that I carry. So, using the breathing technique that you teach, and that I learned in the U.S. Army Infantry [marksmanship training] 15 years ago, I slowed myself down, got a good sight picture, and fired the fatal headshot.

The bullet struck him in the left eye, my exact point of aim, and ended the threat. I was wounded, bleeding profusely, and firing with only one hand, as I had to hold the lady down behind cover.

This was my sixth officer-involved shooting, all have been fatal for the bad guys. I have been shot in three of those six shootings, and my body has seven bullet holes in it. I have been stabbed once and have lost a partner in the line of duty—but we must fight the good fight.

—Correspondence to Colonel Dave Grossman
From Officer Keith Nelson Borders

Now let us examine the application of the breathing exercise to control the puppy and rein in the sympathetic nervous system. In order to do this, let us first establish a foundation of understanding the body's physiological response after the smoke clears and then see how the critical incident debriefing and breathing exercise can fit in.

In their book, *Deadly Force Encounters* Dr. Alexis Artwohl and Loren Christensen have done a great job discussing post-combat responses. These are typical reactions that many survivors of a traumatic event experience in the minutes, hours, and days after.

Immediately afterwards, you might experience trembling, sweating, chills, nausea, hyperventilation, dizziness, thirstiness, an urge to urinate, diarrhea, upset stomach, and jumpiness. Later that night, you might experience sleep disturbance and nightmares. Some people do not suffer from any of these symptoms, some experience several of them, while others experience all of them. No matter how you react, it is important to understand that your reactions are normal.

In the days following the event, you might be preoccupied with what happened as you relive it over and over in your mind, second guessing yourself, and thinking you did something wrong, even when you did everything right. If you are a police officer, you might doubt your ability to function on the job, and you might be unwilling to continue in your career. You might be angry, sad, irritable, hypersensitive, vulnerable, anxious, scared, self-conscious, paranoid, and afraid of being judged by others. You might feel elated that you survived, but guilty because others did not. You might feel numb, robot-like, unnaturally calm, and alienated from those who "haven't been there." Your thinking might be confused, you might experience difficulty concentrating, and you might have an impaired memory.

Overall, I think we can agree that it is not necessarily a pleasant time, and the individual who is experiencing this needs our help.

Memory Retention and "Critical Incident Amnesia"

All things are taken from us, and become
Portions and parcels of the dreadful Past.

—Alfred, Lord Tennyson
"The Lotos-Eaters"

In the military community, it is often said that the first victim of combat is truth. Another truism is that the first report from the battlefield is always wrong. Let's say that you have the task of getting information from those involved in a deadly encounter. Your first objective is to capture and preserve the event in the minds of the participants, so you can dissect the information and learn what happened. The first step in maximizing memory retention is to have everyone involved make a report immediately after the occurrence.

To get detailed information, you have to do all you can to keep the participants calm and collected. Remember, from the very beginning the goal is to delink the memory from the emotions. Initially, you want to remove them from where the stressful event took place, as there are many associations there that can act as powerful stressors. Do not offer them coffee or other caffeinated beverages, as the stimulant might hype them even more. Even after taking these precautionary measures, many of them might be so shaky that they have difficulty writing. In those cases, consider having them tape-record their initial reports.

Sometimes, for legal purposes, investigators are concerned about "contaminating" the memory process. In those situations you should encourage everyone involved not to go out drinking and rehashing the event with their buddies, but rather go home and get a good night's sleep to help recover additional memory. Sleep helps them achieve a calmer mental state, which in turn helps them consolidate information into their long-term memories. For those who are single and have no one to go home to, it may be helpful to spend the night with a friend. The next day you can conduct a second interview, and then they can conduct their own informal debriefings with each other. To prevent their memories from being contaminated, instruct the participants not to read the paper or watch the news.

After the first night's sleep, you can conduct an interview at the location, but you need to be ready to help the participants separate their emotions from their memories. Anticipate that you might have to stop to help an especially emotional person through the tactical breathing process, because by returning to the scene, the participants are exposed to memory cues that facilitate their recall of how the event unfolded. For example, they might see a mailbox at the scene, or some other object that played a critical role that they had forgotten was there. Objects that seem to be inconsequential to people who were not involved just might provide the missing link that brings all the information together.

The day after the incident, law enforcement agencies should conduct a group "critical incident debriefing" and the military should conduct the "after action review." Everyone directly involved in the incident and even those on the periphery should attend. If it is a police incident, include the police dispatcher and the call taker. If it is a military incident, you should consider including those soldiers who were nearby, though not directly involved, and include those at the command post, such as radio operators. The idea of a group critical incident debriefing is to "get back on the train" and derive specific memory cues from each other. You will likely hear participants say such things as, "So that's what you did?" "Oh, I forgot about that." "So, when you did that, that's when I did this. Now it makes sense." Like a jigsaw puzzle that had been scattered with pieces missing, it all begins to come together as everyone adds their one or two pieces.

All this is not without its flaws. A process called "memory reconstruction" is unavoidable in a group debriefing. What happens is that some participants reconstruct, or fill in their missing pieces of memory with information learned from other participants. The mind hates a vacuum, so they might fill in the gaps and "remember" it as if it had actually happened to them. Some degree of memory reconstruction is inevitable, but the group debriefing is still the best possible tool for giving participants accurate information to help them remember, for helping them learn from mistakes, and for helping them on the path to returning to normal after a horrific incident.

Consider conducting a second debriefing 24 to 48 hours later. This allows participants to get another night or two of sleep, which often provides for further memory consolidation. The second debriefing can also be done on location. (Bruce Siddle and I co-authored an article on this topic, entitled "Critical Incident Amnesia." It was published in the *Journal of the International Association of Law Enforcement Firearms Instructors (IALEFI)* and is posted (complete with footnotes and scholarly references) on my Web site, www.warriorscience.com.

Consider these steps a valuable, scientific method to collect information and to help the participants prevent or overcome trauma from a stressful event. Now let us continue to examine the mechanics of the debriefing and how this tool can be used to help the warrior avoid the debilitating effects of PTSD.

The Moral Obligation to Participate in a Debriefing

Beat-up warriors return safely,
Marry and have children, and make a new life,
But pass their suffering to those they love—
Families, children and wife.

Wives and children should be chosen –
Nominated for purple hearts,
Wounded by war they've never seen,
Disadvantaged from the start.

Another daddy just started his 40th job,
He can't get close – and he can't get free,
What ghostly memory holds him?
Society pays for war, and so does he.

—Fred Grossman
"A Purple Heart For You"

The first thing all warriors must understand is their moral obligation to participate in a critical incident debriefing. We know that unmanaged stress is a major factor that can destroy our warriors and devastate their families. It has been mentioned before that PTSD is "the gift that keeps on giving." When you are impacted by stress symptoms, your spouse and your kids are also impacted and if it is left unchecked, all of you will continue to be affected in the years to come. One key tool to prevent PTSD is the critical incident debriefing.

There are always those people who say something like: "Debriefing? I don't need no stinking debriefing!" and we believe them. But the debriefing is not necessarily for them; it is for their buddy, partner, spouse and their children. What would they not do to save a buddy's life? A partner's? Or the lives of their spouses and kids? Remember, the probability of loss of life after the event can be far greater than the loss of life during the event. Think of a debriefing this way: It is a mechanism that makes it possible to save lives.

Remember: Pain shared is pain divided, and you are only as sick as your secrets. In a debriefing, you have the opportunity to share those secrets and to share your pain as you come together to help each other through a traumatic event. Those who say that they do not need to participate need to ask themselves if they would withhold their fire in the middle of a life and death gunfight just because they were not in danger. Would they withhold medical support for someone gushing blood just because they were not hurt? Of course not. Nor should they withhold their support of others in a critical incident debriefing just because they do not think they need a debriefing.

After one of the major school shootings, I taught first responders about the importance of participating in a debriefing for their friends. There was a fire chief there who, after hearing my explanation, became angry with the people who had debriefed him and his crew. "Why didn't they tell us that?" he said. "A lot of our guys [thought they] didn't need a debriefing so they came in with an attitude. If they had told us that we were there for our friends, they would have had a completely different attitude. We would have done anything for our friends. But they treated us like children. They packed us all in and they debriefed us, without explaining what we were going to be doing and that we were doing it for our friends."

Objective of a Debriefing: Delinking the Memory from the Emotions

Give sorrow words: the grief that does not speak
Whispers the o'er-frought heart and bids it break.

—Shakespeare
Macbeth

It is important to let participants know that any thoughts or reactions they experienced during a critical incident debriefing are okay. For example, they need to know from the outset that if they lost their bowel and bladder control during their incident that this is a normal response shared by many others who have gone through the same experience. You can spend a lifetime debriefing people and few if any will admit that they soiled their pants. If they learn up front, though, that it is normal and okay, it is amazing how many people will reveal that it happened.

The same is true for those who experienced the "Thank God it wasn't me" response. Having this thought race through your mind upon seeing violent death is arguably one of the deepest, darkest, most shameful of all human responses. However, when you tell people that it is a normal thought, it is as if a huge weight has been lifted, and their sense of shame no longer has power to hurt them.

But the most important objective of a debriefing is to sever, separate and pull apart the memory from the emotions, delinking the memory of the event from the sympathetic nervous system arousal. You want to make peace with that memory, so every time the puppy tries to blow through that screen door, and barks, "Gunfight? Gunfight? Where? Where? Where?" you stop and use the tactical breathing method that will be outlined in this chapter. The idea is to patch that hole in the screen door, because if you do not, every time the puppy blows through, he makes it bigger, more ragged, and harder to patch.

As the debriefing unfolds and you work your way through the memory of the event, know that anything and everything is permitted. The only thing not permitted is anxiety. If you begin to perspire, your voice begins to quiver, your eyes begin to well up with tears, your face becomes white and blotchy, and your hands begin to shake, you need to stop and do tactical breathing. After just a few cycles of this incredible technique, you experience a wave of calm and relaxation that begins to help you delink the physiological arousal from the memory of the event. In short, you begin to make peace with the memory.

Let's look at this powerful and versatile tool that helps you before, during and after a critical incident.

Tactical Breathing: A Leash on the Puppy

On September 6, 2001, while working on a Robbery Task Force, I used [tactical breathing] seconds prior to shooting and killing a masked armed robber in a grocery store. The detectives had received information that this guy was going to rob a grocery store in town, so my partner and I were assigned to be in the store as the take down team. He was going to use the M-26 Taser [stun gun] to subdue the subject. In the previous six robberies, the suspect had been armed with a revolver, a semi-auto handgun, and a sawed-off shotgun. My job was to cover my partner.

Detectives saw the suspects leave in a vehicle and they began a moving surveillance on them. We could hear what was going on over the police radio. The suspects drove by the store several times and stopped a couple of times to see if anyone was following them. Eventually, one of them was dropped off nearby.

We had surveillance set up in the parking lot and he could see the suspect at the end of the building. Surveillance was giving us play-by-play of what the suspect was doing: He would crouch down behind a dumpster to conceal himself when cars drove by the store. We had plenty of time to think about what was going to happen.

I realized my heart rate was elevating. You know when you smash your finger with the hammer or slam your finger in the car door, and the finger starts throbbing? That's how my heart felt. I told myself that it was time to start breathing. I kept breathing the way you instructed until I felt my heart stop pounding. I'm not sure how long it took, but I knew when I was ready. So I thought. It took half a second to fire seven rounds from the MP5 [submachine gun] on full auto. Six rounds struck the moving target. The next thing I remember was standing over the suspect thinking, 'BRING IT ON!' and 'HOLY SHIT!' at the same time.

—Correspondence to Colonel Dave Grossman
From Officer Rick Lanoue

Tactical breathing is an easy-to-do technique that can be used in a stressful situation to slow your thumping heart beat, reduce the tremble in your hands, deepen your voice so you do not sound like Mickey Mouse, and to bathe yourself with a powerful sense of calm and control. In other words, it is a tool to control the sympathetic nervous system. One police officer who used tactical breathing in a confrontation with an armed robber, summed it up with these succinct and powerful words: "Using the breathing technique…I slowed myself down, got a good sight picture, and fired the fatal head shot." After a critical incident, tactical breathing is a highly effective tool to help you delink your physiological arousal from your memory of the event.

Here is what is happening inside your mind and body and why this simple breathing method quickly restores your calm and control. For our purposes, let us divide your body into two parts: the somatic nervous system and the autonomic nervous system. The somatic nervous system is involved in those actions you have under conscious control, such as moving your arms and kicking a stone out of your path. The autonomic nervous system is involved with those things that you do not have under conscious control, such as your heartbeat and perspiration. Indulge me for a moment and try a little physical demonstration that will help you completely grasp the differences in these two nervous systems.

First, let's test your somatic nervous system. Raise your right arm. Excellent. You have demonstrated your mastery of the somatic nervous system. Okay, you can lower it now. Stay with me, it will get harder.

Now, let us test your autonomic nervous system. When I say, "go," I want you to raise your heart rate to 200 bpm, start perspiring, and see if you can manifest a little stress diarrhea. Ready. Go! What happened? You failed because you cannot consciously control your heart rate, make yourself perspire or have stress diarrhea, even if you wanted to. It is called the autonomic nervous system because these actions are automatic; they are not under conscious control.

As you read the last two sentences, your inhalation and exhalation were also autonomic actions. If you had to consciously control your breathing, you would die when you fell asleep. That said, please take a deep breath and then let it out. With that conscious action, you just pulled your breathing from autonomic to somatic control. Breathing and blinking are the only two actions of your autonomic nervous systems that you can bring under conscious control anytime you choose. As such, your breathing is the bridge between your somatic and autonomic nervous system.

Think of your autonomic nervous system as a big, shuddering, shaking machine that has only one control lever sticking out from its side. Your breathing is that control lever, the one thing you can reach out and grab. When you control your breathing you control the whole autonomic nervous system. As discussed earlier, the autonomic nervous system has two branches: the sympathetic nervous system and the parasympathetic nervous system. Through proper breathing, you can control your sympathetic nervous system response, the fancy term for fear and anger. As mentioned earlier, uncontrollable fear and anger are the same thing, they are just two different manifestations of the puppy getting out of control. Tactical breathing is a leash on the puppy. The more you practice the breathing technique, the quicker the effects kick in, as a result of powerful classical and operant conditioning mechanisms.

Although we continuously find new uses for the power of tactical breathing, it is really nothing new. The yoga, Zen and martial arts community have used breath control for centuries. The rifle marksmanship community has used it for over 100 years, and the Lamaze community has used it for the last several decades. (I tell my warrior audiences to think of tactical breathing as "combat Lamaze.") Yoga, Zen, and the martial arts may have some mystical connotations, but when you strip away the mysticism, all that is left is a simple process that allows you to gain conscious control over your unconscious nervous system, and then puts it to work for you.

It is really just common sense. Have you heard of these expressions? "I was scared out of my wits," "I was so scared that I couldn't see straight," or "I got the crap scared out of me." These are all common expressions to communicate some of the things we have been talking about in this book. In the same way, when we were children and overly excited about something, many of us were told by our mother, "Just take a deep breath." Well, mama knew what she was talking about, except for us it will be three, deep belly breaths.

The technical term for the procedure is autogenic breathing, but in the warrior community it is typically called tactical breathing or combat breathing. Though it is derived from many places, Calibre Press and Gary Klugiewicz should be credited for pioneering it and spreading it throughout the warrior community.

Due to poor planning on my part, I once found myself in front of an abortion clinic where a hundred sign-waving protesters wanted a piece of me. Half were pro-choice and half were pro-life; more were arriving every minute. There was shouting and pushing and when a couple of big guys tried to push me aside, I pushed back, inadvertently knocking one man, a national leader, down a set of steps. That ignited his people and they began screaming hysterically, some threatening to get me.

My eyes were watering profusely, I was trembling, and my chest was heaving as if I had run a mile.

I held my position and, imperceptible to the crowd, I drew a long, deep quiet breath, held it for a fourcount moment, and then slowly and quietly released it for a four count. I paused empty for a four-count and then repeated the procedure. After the third cycle, my trembling had stopped, my breathing had quieted, and my eyes cleared.

I remained calm until my backup arrived.

– A police officer

I teach tactical breathing to Green Berets, federal agents and even surgeons in hospitals so they do not lose their fine-motor control in the middle of an operation. (My definition of a bad day is when my surgeon begins to lose his fine-motor control.) I also teach it to basketball players to improve their free-throw rate and to college kids suffering from test anxiety. I know of one martial arts instructor and two police officers who used it in the middle of their heart attacks. Four deep belly breaths and they were able to pull their heart rate down.

Many police officers have contacted me over the years to relate how they have used tactical breathing to make desperate life and death shots, or how they have taught it to their kids to use when they get hurt, but my favorite story comes from one of my college students. I taught this young man the breathing exercise when he was in my intro-psychology course; in fact, I taught it to all of my students in order to help them with test anxiety.

A couple of years later, this student came up to me in a supermarket in Jonesboro, Arkansas, and said, "Hey, Colonel Grossman, you remember that breathing exercise you taught us? That stuff really works." I asked him what happened. "I got into a traffic accident," he said, "and my car flipped over and I was trapped with a broken leg. I began to panic and then out of the blue I remembered what you taught us."

The mind is like that: What you need will be there for you, and sometimes it seems to come out of the blue.

"I began to panic," the young man said, "and then it was just like you were there in class making me do it during a test. I began breathing in through my nose, holding it as you had taught, exhaling and then holding empty. You know what? That worked, it calmed me down."

I asked the young man what happened next.

"What could I do? I'm trapped in my car! I reached over, turned the radio on my favorite station and waited for somebody to come get me. They eventually got there with the Jaws of Life, pried the car apart, and pulled me out. They told me that if I had panicked I would have probably killed myself."

If he had panicked, he would have killed himself. What did Yoda teach us about fear? "Fear leads to the dark side . . . Fear leads to anger, anger leads to hate and hate leads to much suffering." The degree to which you control your fear and anger is the degree to which you control your hate and suffering. Your goal is to prevent fear, prevent anger, prevent hate, and prevent suffering. The degree to which you control your fear is the degree to which you have mastered yourself as a warrior.

The Mechanics of Tactical Breathing

The devil is in the details.

—Old German military maxim

There is still a need for extensive research to see how long each phase should be held, but for many years now the four-count method has worked wonders for warriors around the globe. Once you start using it, you can tailor it to your body's needs. For example, you might find that you need to hold each count for five seconds and that you need five cycles of the procedure to achieve the desired effect. This is fine. It is like adjusting a tuning knob: Grab hold of the knob and keep tuning it until you get "dialed in" to the level that works for you. For now, let us use the four-count method. Begin by breathing in through your nose to a slow count of four, which expands your belly like a balloon. Hold for a count of four, and then slowly exhale through your lips for a count of four, as your belly collapses like a balloon with its air released. Hold empty for a count of four and then repeat the process. That is it. Short, but effective. Now, follow along as I guide you through the procedure.

In through the nose two, three, four. Hold two, three, four. Out through the lips two, three, four. Hold two, three, four.

In through the nose deep, deep, deep. Hold two, three, four. Out through the lips deep, deep, deep. Hold two, three, four.

In through the nose two, three, four. Hold two, three, four. Out through the lips two, three, four. Hold two, three, four.

Maybe you are feeling a little mellow now or maybe you didn't notice a difference since you were already relaxed. But in a life and death situation, we know this simple exercise can be a true revolution in human development. For the first time in human history we are teaching large portions of our population to consciously control the unconscious part of their body.

Tactical Breathing in Warrior Operations

Our tactical unit was involved in the fatal shooting of a suspect recently during a protracted barricade situation. The suspect was a former prison gang member, wanted for homicide, and had become trapped during a home invasion while fleeing the police. One of our shooters [after the incident] made some comments that I thought you might find interesting.

[The officer] was in a position approximately 40 feet from the suspect when he ultimately fired and struck the suspect with his M4 [carbine]. The area was dark and the officer was wearing a protective mask because of chemical agents [tear gas] previously fired into the structure.

Over time, the suspect made numerous statements to negotiators that he was going to "come out shooting" and that the officers had "better get ready because I'm going to blow away the first ones I see."

The officer who ultimately shot the suspect spoke afterwards of the "up and down" mental preparation he went through prior to the suspect's eventual exit at a full sprint. He said that during the time leading up to the shooting, all he could think of was "the things Colonel Grossman told us about visualizing a deadly confrontation," and how he did "those breathing exercises that he discussed and demonstrated." The officer is adamant that your lecture and book *On Killing* helped him prepare for the critical incident that he knew was about to unfold in front of him.

Thank you for your significant contributions in the preparations of my officers to do what was right, just, and necessary and for their mental/emotional well being afterwards.

—Correspondence to Colonel Grossman
From a SWAT lieutenant

Tactical breathing can be used before, during and after a combat situation. When used before, it quickly calms and prepares you to function at your best in a hostile environment. Say you are a member of a tactical team and your heartbeat is racing in high Condition Red as you prepare to crash through a door. With a heart rate at such a high level, the slightest stimulus is going to put you over the top and possibly cause you to overreact. While you wait in those minutes or even seconds for the "doorman" to smash the entry point, use the four-count breathing technique to get your heart rate down to the target range in low Condition Red or high Condition Yellow.

Many police officers have told me that they have done really stupid things in high-speed chases, and every week we hear of another jurisdiction somewhere in the country no longer allowing their officers to engage in pursuits. Officers drive fast to hot calls all the time, so why do they get tunnel vision and stop thinking when driving in a high-speed pursuit? If you said it is the puppy's fault, you are correct. When the driver's heart rate gets too high, tunnel vision sets in, depth perception goes out, fine and complex motor control shuts down, the forebrain shuts down, the midbrain takes over, and the puppy is driving the car! An excited little dog is now careening that car through the streets, making all kinds of bad decisions and scattering terrified citizens.

Trainers of emergency vehicle operation courses who have introduced tactical breathing into their curriculum, report that the quality of performance among their trainees have broken all previous records. Charles E. Humes has pioneered a powerful and effective training process in which police officers are taught to breathe automatically, as a conditioned reflex, in response to the sound of their siren.

When an officer is calm, you can hear it in his voice on the police radio, even while driving 80 mph in pursuit of armed felons. He sounds like that famous transmission from Apollo 13: "Houston, we have a problem." The crew was in outer space—outer space!—and when they saw a warning light flash suddenly, followed by a loud bang, Jack Swigert announced calmly over the radio, "Houston, we have a problem here." The astronauts remained calm because most of them were drawn from fighter pilots and test pilots, and the only way they had stayed alive across the years was to function with steely calm in the face of great danger. If a test pilot blows his cool, he dies. When a police officer or any warrior blows his cool in a life and death event, he too might die.

If you are in an administrative supervisory position, and you are listening to a high-speed chase on the police radio, pay close attention to the officer calling the pursuit. If the officer is losing fine-motor control in his voice, then he is probably also losing fine-motor control in his hands. If his voice sounds like Barney Fife or a 12-year-old girl—high-pitched and over-the-top excited—pull that officer off the chase. If you hear the calm and in-control voice of an astronaut, a fighter pilot, on the radio, let him proceed.

Tactical Breathing in Court

The first thing we do, let's kill all the lawyers.

—Shakespeare
Henry VI

You can and must use this breathing technique after the event, especially during the critical incident debriefing discussed earlier, to delink the memory from the physiological arousal. The worst response you can have to a traumatic event is to have fear of its memory. The example of the Arkansas State Trooper who had a powerful SNS response upon hearing a starter pistol is typical of hundreds of untold thousands of other people who have lived through a terrifying experience. The first time that memory comes rushing back it can scare the daylights out of you because no one warned you that it might happen. You expect to be scared in combat, but you do not expect to be scared later, for what seems like no good reason.

After it scares you the first time, you live in fear of it happening again. The next time it is going to be even worse, because when the puppy comes through the screen door, you are going to run from it and he is going to chase you. If you continue to allow this to happen, you create a vicious cycle that will spin you downhill. Instead, use tactical breathing to control the puppy by putting a leash around his neck and staking him out in the front yard so he cannot come through that door again.

Take a deep breath. Do it right now, as you read this. There, see? You have the power to do this any time you want. If you let anger or fear control you, it is because you have made a conscious choice to not use the breathing technique. You have a leash around your puppy's neck and you have chosen not to use it. If uncontrollable anger or uncontrollable tears start to happen, remember that they are not really uncontrollable, because if you control your breathing, then you can control the emotions.

Some people would say that PTSD is a self-inflicted malady. To a certain degree, from one perspective, there can be some truth to this. We must never "blame the victim," but some aspects can result from ignorance, and now you are no longer ignorant.

If you have not made peace with the memories, if you have not done a group critical incident debriefing and worked your way through that memory and made peace with it, there is a good possibility it will come back to bite you when you testify in court. You have been fleeing from the memories, refusing to come to terms with them, but in court you cannot avoid them, and the result can be very traumatic.

A slick lawyer in a thousand-dollar suit will stand in front of you and conduct a cross-examination. But he does not want you to testify, he wants the puppy on the stand. He wants that neural network to activate so that you hyperventilate, your heart pounds, your brow perspires, your voice quivers, and your face turns white and blotchy. Keep in mind that the lawyer has been trained to play head games with you, and he is paid big bucks because he is very good at what he does. He wants to create stress and trauma in your life, and he does it by whistling for the puppy. If he is successful the jury will think you are a liar or, at the least, unreliable.

As a warrior you have three goals in life that you strive to accomplish. First and foremost, protect the innocent; second, convict the guilty; and third, draw your retirement. These are three honorable objectives, but now you are confronting a slick lawyer in a shiny suit wanting to prevent you from doing all three by trying his best to spin you down the path of PTSD.

The best advice I was ever given for testifying in court was simply to "Take . . . your . . . time." You have all the time in the world, so use it. I relate it to my competitive pistol shooting, when I have lots of time to make a shot. I take a nice deep breath, let it out, and caress the trigger. When you are on the stand and that lawyer asks the first question and your heart pounds in your chest, just take . . . your . . . time. Think of it as going into battle. Take a deep breath, hold it, let it out, and then slowly, calmly, professionally, put the answer right between the lawyer's beady little eyes.

You control your body; your body does not control you. And the lawyer? He is not even in the equation.

Other Useful Times to Breathe

"I have not yet begun to fight!"
"Now would be a good time to start!"

—Terry Pratchett

There are many good times to breathe. Sometimes tactical breathing works to bring relief from health problems. Co-author Loren Christensen knows a woman who suffers from migraine headaches, an affliction she did not have prior to her tour in the Gulf War. When she feels a migraine coming on, she immediately begins the four-count breathing process and, if caught in time, she wards it off.

This is not a panacea. Breathing will not solve all of life's ills, but it can help in many cases. Consider this example.

> I know that this may sound strange, but have you had anyone tell you that the combat breathing technique you teach may help with physical ailments such as heart burn? In the past I used to be devastated by an intolerable amount of pain from heart burn, no matter what I did (a bottle [literally] of Pepto, Tums, or any other antacid would not help at all) I was about resigned to the fact that I would have to go to the doctors office for a prescription. One day in the middle of such an attack I used the technique to take my mind off of the pain, and almost immediately it was gone. Since then, when I feel an attack coming on, I use the technique and I avoid an attack all together.
>
> —Correspondence to Colonel Grossman
> From Ron C. Danielowski

One of the most important things we can do is to use the breathing exercise to help others in their time of need. I was first introduced to it as Lamaze which my wife used in childbirth, and I was so impressed with the combination of visual concentration, relaxation, coaching, and breathing, that I have continued to use it for a lifetime.

On one occasion, one of my young soldiers was in a motorcycle accident and I went to the hospital to check on him immediately after the accident. He was strapped to a hard wooden backboard, in great pain as he waited to be X-rayed. It was a good feeling to have a tool to give him to help in his moment of need, and I coached him through the full Lamaze process with great success.

On another occasion I used the breathing, tied in with the other Lamaze techniques, with my son when he split his eye open and needed stitches. The doctor at the emergency room was amazed at his calmness as the numbing shots and stitches were applied. Many individuals have been able to use this tool to help their children when they were injured. One law enforcement officer wrote to me and gave a classic example.

> A few weeks ago, my nine-year-old daughter fell from our swing. She let out a bloodcurdling scream that brought my wife and I to investigate. She was lying on her back, screaming and holding her right arm. One look told me that it had been broken in at least two places.
>
> I remembered what you had taught on breathing and immediately started her on "Combat Breathing." She immediately calmed down . . . I drove her to the hospital and made her continue to breathe in a proper military manner . . . After being treated and her arm being put into a

cast for three broken bones, the staff told me that they had never had such a calm child in their hospital with such a severe break."

—Correspondence to Colonel Grossman

As a warrior, your concern is always to help others, and to do that you must be the rock of calm. When the whole world is coming unglued and all about you are losing their heads and blaming it on you, your job is to be that rock that others can anchor themselves to, and tactical breathing is one powerful tool that helps make this possible.

We know that attitude can be contagious. Panic can be contagious, and so is calm. As a warrior, you must be an example of calm and, in that capacity, you can and must pass on the calming benefits of this exercise to others.

Soldiers, police officers and educators are often the first to debrief a person after a traumatic event. Say you are a police officer and you arrive at the scene of an armed robbery where the Seven-Eleven clerk has been beaten; or you are an Army officer getting a combat report from one of your units; or you are an educator and a kid has just been in a fight. In each of these cases you are going to ask what happened, and you have both a professional and a moral obligation to insure that the individual reporting to you remains calm.

An agitated and anxious person has trouble recalling facts and might even lose pertinent pieces of information. You do not want to interview the puppy, because once it has taken over, your efforts can be in vain. When you are in the business of gathering information, you need to first get the subject calm so you can conduct the most productive interview possible. Not only will you get better information, you will have made a giant step in helping that person avoid lasting psychological trauma and from spinning down the path of PTSD. Remember this: the probability of loss of life after a traumatic event can be greater than loss of life during the event. Here is what you can do to help prevent that.

You want to calm the victim as you begin to get information or as you just reach out to offer a helping hand. Place a comforting hand on his shoulder, speak calmly and quietly, and ask him to take in a deep breath to your count of four and then hold it in while you again count to four. Tell him to let it out to your count and hold again to your count. When done correctly, this interview can be an initial debriefing that will begin the process of patching the hole in the person's screen door and helping him down the path of healing. If not done correctly, say you too become excited and agitated, you just might allow the victim's puppy to make the hole in the screen door even larger. Your actions need to be calm, helpful and in control to help close down the neural network linking the memory of the event with the emotions, so that he can begin the process of healing.

Gary Klugiewicz is a law enforcement trainer who does a lot of work in corrections, especially cell entries, where two or more corrections officers charge into a cell to take a violent or threatening prisoner down onto the floor.

Gary says that many prisoners, having nothing better to do, initiate lawsuits at the drop of a hat, most often when force has been used against them. To try to prevent this, he now includes tactical breathing techniques whenever he has to use physical force. He charges into the cell, takes the con down, sits on his back, and says, "Listen, I want you to breathe. I'm not going to get up until you breathe. Breathe in, two, three, four. Hold it, two, three four. Let it out, two, three, four. Hold it, two, three, four. I'm not getting up until you do this." The prisoner obeys (since he has no choice), and within seconds the effect from the breathing procedure kicks in and mellows him. "You know," Gary says, "these guys sue for anything, but I've never had anybody sue me for making them breathe."

On March 24, 1998, I walked in the door of Westside Middle School in Jonesboro, Arkansas, after an 11 and 13 year-old boy had gunned down 15 people. I offered my services to Jack Bowers and Linda Graham, the two crisis counselors who had been put in charge. Jack and Linda were two of the most remarkable, competent and compassionate people I have ever met. They immediately accepted my offer, and it was one of the highest honors of my life to be able to work under their supervision, along with the other magnificent members of the crisis team during that crisis.

I taught tactical breathing to mental health professionals and clergy the night of the shootings. The next morning, I conducted the initial briefing for all of the teachers and established a cognitive foundation for their debriefings, which included training and rehearsing the tactical breathing procedure. Later, the survivors were broken into small groups and began to work their way through their experiences. During this debriefing, only anxiety was forbidden. As soon as anyone began to show anxiety, as soon as the puppy began to come through the screen door, the person was made to stop and do tactical breathing. This process allowed the survivors of this deadly event to confront their memories and emotions, and begin to delink them from their physiological responses.

The next day, the mental health professionals, clergy, and teachers conducted debriefings with children using the same rules and techniques. The results were excellent. Of course, we cannot measure success in such circumstances, but there were immediate and observable positive responses from counselors and subjects, and a host of anecdotal support later to show the effectiveness of the breathing technique. In one case, a mother complained to a counselor that she was so anxious that she had been unable to sleep. The counselor said that he had her do just one cycle of tactical breathing and, to the woman's amazement, she yawned.

I am happy to report that, to the best of my knowledge, there have been no suicides associated with the Jonesboro shootings, although there have been some resulting from the Littleton, Colorado, school shootings, and the Oklahoma City bombing. The national team of experts who arrived 36 hours after the shootings, under the very competent supervision of Dr. Scott Poland, stated that the procedures we had set in place had established a "national standard" for posttrauma responses.

Using this breathing technique to help calm people is a simple, compassionate and decent thing to do, just like our mama did for us when she told us to calm down and take a deep breath. It makes people feel better in just a matter of moments, and it helps them to regain control so that you, as an interviewer, can interact with the adult upstairs, not the puppy out in the front yard.

six

What to Say to a Returning Veteran, and What to Say to a Survivor

He who did well in war just, earns the right
To begin doing well in peace.

—Robert Browning
Luria

As a writer, sometimes you are lucky enough to find something that perfectly and powerfully communicates what needs to be said on a vital topic. When it comes to the question of "What to say to a returning veteran?" Colonel Timothy C. "BT" Hanifen, USMC, wrote that "perfect" piece upon returning from Iraq in 2003. With his kind permission, Colonel Hanifen's vital, wise and timeless words are included here.

Three Gifts You Can Give Returning Veterans: That Will Last Them a Lifetime . . .

The combat phase of the campaign in Iraq is winding down and now the hardest job of all begins—winning the peace. Soon many of our fellow citizen-Soldiers, Airmen, Sailors, Marines and Coast Guardsman, both active and reserve, will return home with their units or as individuals. All have served and participated in an extraordinary campaign of liberation, fought in a manner that reflected not only the determination of the American people to do what was necessary, but also reflective of our value to spare life whenever and wherever possible.

As these veterans begin returning home, people are asking themselves what they can do to celebrate their return, honor their service, and remember those who have fallen in the performance of their duty. After every war or major conflict, there are always concerns about the emotional state of returning veterans, their ability to readjust to peaceful pursuits and their reintegration into American society. People naturally ask themselves, "What can we do or what should we do?" The purpose of this message is to offer that there are three very important gifts that we personally, and collectively as a society, can give to these returning veterans. They are "understanding, affirmation and support."

With "understanding," I am not speaking of sympathy, empathy, consoling or emotional analysis. Rather, I offer that we, to the best of our ability, need to comprehend some of the combat truths learned and experienced by these returning servicemen and women. Their perspectives and their personal experiences will shape each of them and our society in large and small ways for years to come. Though we were not there, our comprehension and respect for their "truisms" will be part of the gift that will truly last them and us for a lifetime.

The truth every combat veteran knows, regardless of conflict, is that war is about combat, combat is about fighting, fighting is about killing and killing is a traumatic personal experience for those who fight. Killing another person, even in combat, is difficult as it is fundamentally against our nature and the innate guiding moral compass within most human beings. The frequency of direct combat and the relative distance between combatants is also directly proportional to the level of combat stress experienced by the surviving veteran. Whether the serviceman or woman actually pulled the trigger, dropped a bomb or simply supported those who have, I've yet to meet any veteran who has fought and found their contribution to or the personal act of killing another human being particularly glorious. Necessary—Yes. Glorious or pleasurable—No.

In combat, warriors must psychologically distance themselves from the humanity of their opponent during the fight. The adversary becomes a target or an objective or any number of derogatory epithets that separates "them from us." Combat becomes merely business—a job that has to be done, part of your duty and killing—a necessary result. It's a team job that needs to be done quickly, efficiently, unemotionally and at the least cost in lives to your unit, to innocents and with the most damage inflicted in the least time to your adversaries. Then you and the team move forward again to the next danger area and fight. The only sure way home is by fighting through your opponents as quickly and efficiently as possible. Along the way you quietly hope or pray that your actions will: be successful; not cause the loss of a comrade; not cause the death of an innocent; and that you won't become one of the unlucky casualties yourself. You stay despite your fears because the team, your new family of brothers or sisters, truly needs you and you'd rather die than let them down. You live in the moment, slowly realize your own mortality and also your steadily rising desire to cling to and fight hard for every second of it. You keep your focus, your "game face" on, and you don't allow yourself the luxury of "too much reflection" or a moment's "day dreaming" about home, loved ones, the future or your return. You privately fear that such a moment of inattention may be your last, or worse, because of you, a comrade's last.

So if I may caution, please don't walk up to a combat veteran and ask him or her if they "killed" anyone or attempt well meaning "pop" psychoanalysis. These often-made communication attempts are awkward and show a lack of understanding and comprehension of the veteran. They also reveal much about the person who attempts either one. Instead, please accept there is a deep contextual gap between you both because you were not there. This chasm is very difficult to bridge when veterans attempt to relate their personal war experiences. Actual combat veterans are the one's least likely to answer the question or discuss the details of their experiences with relative strangers. Most likely they will ignore you and feel as though they were truly "pilgrims" in a strange land instead of honored and appreciated members of our Republic. So accept and don't press . . .

Don't ignore them or the subject. Please feel free to express your "gladness at their safe return" and ask them "how it went or what was it like?" These questions are open-ended and show both your interest and concern. They also allow the veteran to share what they can or want. In most cases, the open door will enable them to share stories of close friends, teammates or some humorous moments of which they recall. Again, just ask, accept—but don't dig or press.

The second gift is "affirmation." Whether you were personally in favor of the war or against it no longer matters at this point. As a Republic and a people we debated, we decided and then we mustered the political and societal willpower to send these brave young men and women into combat in hopes of eventually creating a better peace for ourselves, for the Iraqi people and for an entire region of the world. More than anything else, the greatest gift you can personally give a returning veteran is a sincere handshake and words from you that "they did the right thing, they did what we asked them to do and that you are proud of them." We need to say these words often and the returning combat veteran truly needs these reassurances. Also please fly your flag and consider attending one or more public events with your families as a visible sign of your support and thanks. Nothing speaks louder to a returning veteran than the physical presence of entire families. Those Americans attending these events give one of their most precious gifts—their personal time. Numbers matter. Personal and family presence silently speaks volumes of affirmation to those you wish to honor.

The third gift is "support." Immediately upon return there will be weeks of ceremonies and public praise applauding the achievements of the returning units and their veterans. But the pace of life in America is fast and it will necessarily move rapidly onward towards the next event. Here is where your support is most needed to sustain the returning veteran and you can make the most difference in their lives for years to come. Continue to fly your flag. If you are an employer, then simply do your best to hire a veteran who is leaving service or if he or she was a Guardsman or Reservist, welcome them back to a new job within the company. All reserve personnel know that the economic life of the company has continued in their absence. It has to do so in order for the company to survive and prosper. They also know it is likely their jobs have since been filled. Returning veterans are always unsure whether or not they will find or have employment upon return. As an employer, if you can't give them an equivalent job because of downsizing, then extend them with your company for three to four months so they can properly job hunt. Please take a personal interest in them and their families and use your extensive list of personal and professional contacts to help them land a better job—even if it is with one of your competitors. The gratitude they will feel for you, your personal actions and your company is beyond words.

For everyone else, the greatest gift you can give to continue support will take 10 seconds of your time. In the years to come, if ever your paths cross with one of the hundreds of thousands of veterans of this or any other conflict, then simply shake their hand and tell them "thanks" and that "they did a great job!" Your words show you understand, you affirm their service and you continue to support them. Teach your children to do the same by your strong example. Though veterans may not express it, every one of them will be grateful. If this message rings true with you, then let us each give these returning veterans these three gifts that will truly last them a lifetime.

—"Home of the Free, Because of the Brave!"
Colonel Timothy C. "B.T." Hanifen, USMC

Who is a Veteran, Who is a Survivor and What is a Trauma?

What is food to one man may be fierce poison to others.
—Lucretius (first century B.C.)
De Rerum Natura

Many people are not sure how to relate to a fellow human being who has experienced a traumatic incident. One major purpose of this book and books such as *On Killing*, *The Gift of Fear*, and *Deadly Force Encounters*, is to teach you how not be a victim after a traumatic incident, and how to help others in their hour of need.

Traumatic incidents are not limited to those where you have been shot or shot at. Consider the following events that are just some examples of incidents that are so far out of the norm of our daily experiences that exposure to them could be toxic under some conditions.

-You witness another person shooting someone
-You witness someone getting hurt or killed
-You witness a horrific traffic accident
-You find a dead child
-You are unable to rescue someone from a fire or from drowning
-You receive a debilitating or life threatening injury

Here are a few other influences that can affect how a critical incident impacts a warrior. Let us use a police officer as an example, one who has gotten into a shooting on a day when—

-he is having problems in his personal life
-he was chewed out an hour earlier by his sergeant
-he is coming down with a cold
-it is a slow media day and the press attacks him
-headquarters decides they need to make an example of someone
-he is severely sleep deprived
-he has not recovered from the impact of his last critical incident

Any one of these, or any combination of them, might be the impetus that causes the officer to be psychologically impacted by the event. If the shooting had occurred the week before, when the influence was not present, is it possible the officer would have gone through the experience without a problem? Maybe, maybe not. It is hard to say because there are other, deep-rooted, personal issues that exist in every person. We do know, however, as has been discussed throughout this book, that prior mental and physical preparation can dramatically decrease the emotional impact of a critical incident.

Always keep in mind that we are all different. Do not decide which incident should or should not be traumatic and who should or should not be traumatized. Do not think that every person is going to have problems after an incident, and do not conclude that a person should not have a problem because the incident is not one that you consider traumatic. Always remember that what might seem to you to be a "no big deal," just might be an event that has a powerful, psychological impact on another, and one that seems to be a big deal to you, might not be to someone else.

What to Say to a Survivor: "I'm Glad You're Okay," and "The Worst is Over."

> The military gives human beings opportunities to be at their amazing bests while doing terribly hard stuff. Personnel get permission to be unabashed, demonstrative friends and helpers to one another. They have to be. They get to be.
>
> —Jane Toleno
> Correspondence to Colonel Grossman

Chris Pollack is a law enforcement officer and writer who has written on this very issue. He has "been there" and he has talked to others who have been there. He says that the right response to a survivor is to say simply, "I am so glad you're okay." That the person survived the ordeal and he is okay is all that matters.

I had the honor of training every sheriff in one major state. A few weeks later, one of the attendees contacted me, and said,

> Nobody in our department has ever had to use deadly force and then the week after you trained us, one of my deputies had to kill someone. It was just like you said, social paralysis. I didn't know what to say. I didn't know yet if it was a righteous shoot. I couldn't commit myself, so I didn't say anything to him. Then, I remember what you'd taught us. I walked up to my deputy, put a hand on his shoulder and said, "Hey man, right now I just want you to know what's important to me is that you're okay."

That was all that officer needed to hear. Not, "Good shooting." Not, "The bastard had it coming." And not, "We'll get you a good lawyer." But, "I give a damn about you, and I'm glad you're okay."

I call this the "ready round." It is the round in the chamber ready to go when you do not know what else to say or do. You simply let the person know that you care about him and are glad he is okay.

A friend of my co-author's called Christensen one evening, and it was apparent in his voice that he was shaken and distraught. An hour earlier, a car full of thugs had, for some unknown reason, pulled up next to him and yelled threats out their windows. Frightened, Christensen's friend drove off, but the car followed close behind, and continued to follow his every evasive move as he drove down side streets, alleys, and across parking lots. At one point when he got jammed in traffic, the thugs scrambled from their car and charged toward him. A sudden break in the line of cars allowed Christensen's friend to change lanes and speed off, successfully losing them.

It was clear to Christensen that his friend had made several mistakes in his flight to safety, but that was not the right moment to point out his errors. Instead, Christensen said, "Hey, I'm just glad you're okay," and just like that, the simple comment calmed his friend.

What if they are not okay? We used to teach people to provide "psychological first aid," usually coaching them to say something like, "Hey, man you're going to be okay." But we don't teach that any more, because all too often people are not okay. My brother was a paramedic who had some serious PTSD problems resulting from his job. One time he told me, "Dave, I cannot tell you how many people have died, and the last thing they ever heard was a lie coming out of my lips." This is a terrible burden to put on our first responders. Authors Judith Acosta and Judith Simon Prager have lead the way to a different response with their book, *The Worst is Over: What to Say When Every Moment Counts*. Although there is much of value in the book, for our purposes here, the title pretty much says it all. In their book Acosta and Prager tell us that:

> An altered state is like fertile soil. We can either plant healthy seeds that grow into fruit-producing plants, we can let the weeds overrun it, or we can let erosion wash it away in the storm. We can either say and do nothing, use our words and our presence to heal, or use our words to harm.

These contributions by Chris Pollock, and by Acosta and Prager, help us to determine, ahead of time, what to say at the critical moment in order to, "use our words and our presence to heal." These are not trite or hollow phrases because they come from the heart. Since we truly do care about our friends, it is absolutely sincere to tell them, after they have had a brush with danger, that we care and are glad they are okay. And there really is value in reminding someone that the worst is over, because it is the truth and that has power.

Thus we have two ready rounds worked out and prepared ahead of time. If the victim is okay, we rejoice with him in that fact. If he is not okay, we help to put the situation in perspective so they can look to a better future. It is all about working things out in advance.

Assume Nothing . . . and Treat Everyone With Respect and Compassion

> Knowledge is proud that he has learn'd so much;
> Wisdom is humble that he knows no more.
>
> —William Cowper
> *The Task*

You cannot go wrong if you assume nothing and treat everyone with respect and compassion. Here are some tips on how to approach someone who has been involved in a traumatic incident, which has been adapted from the recommendations written by Dr. Alexis Artwohl on how cops can best support their fellow officers after a critical incident.

Initiate contact in the form of a phone call or a note to let the person know you are concerned and available for support or help. Say, "Hey, I'm just glad you are okay . . . " If the spouse answers the telephone, respect that person's decision whether to let the traumatized person talk to you.

If the person lives alone, offer to stay with him the first few days after the traumatic event. If you cannot stay, help find another friend who can.

Let the person decide how much contact he wants to have with you. He may be overwhelmed with phone calls and it could take a while for him to return your call. Understand that he may want some "down time" with minimal interruptions.

Do not ask for an account of the incident, but let him know you are willing to listen to whatever he wants to talk about. People often get tired of repeating the story and they find curiosity seekers distasteful.

Ask questions that show support and acceptance, such as "How are you doing?" and "Is there anything I can do to help you or your family?"

Accept the person's reaction to his event as normal for him and avoid suggesting how he should be feeling. Remember that people have a wide range of reactions to different traumatic incidents.

Apply nonjudgmental listening. Monitor your facial expressions and simply nod your head at whatever he tells you.

Do feel free to offer a brief sharing of a similar experience you had to help him feel like he is not alone and that you understand what he has been through. This is not the time, however, to work on your own trauma issues. If your friend's event triggers emotions in you, find someone else to talk to who can offer you support.

Do not encourage the use of alcohol. If you go out, drink decaffeinated beverages, not coffee and not alcohol. In the aftermath of trauma, it is best for people to avoid all use of alcohol for a few weeks so they can process what has happened to them with a clear head and with true feelings. For some, drinking coffee immediately after the incident may not be a good idea because it stimulates an already stimulated system.

Do not call him "killer" or "terminator" (even as a joke) or make lighthearted comments about his actions. Even your best buddy, who you often banter with and tease, may find such comments offensive.

Although you are likely to find yourself second-guessing your friend's actions, keep your comments to yourself. Your words have a way of getting back to him and might do additional harm as he struggles to recover. Besides, your second-guesses are usually wrong anyway.

Do encourage him to take care of himself. Be supportive of his need to take time off work and encourage him to participate in debriefing procedures and professional counseling. Support him by going to the right people to talk with them about what your friend is experiencing.

Do confront him gently with his negative behavioral or emotional changes, especially if they persist longer than one month. Encourage him to seek professional help.

Do not refer to a person having psychological problems as "a mental" or other derogatory terms. Stigmatizing someone might encourage him to deny his psychological injury and not get the help he needs.

Do educate yourself about trauma reactions by reading written material or consulting with someone who knows the topic. Get the traumatized person to read this book, as well as *Deadly Force Encounters*. *On Killing* has also proven itself to be of value, having been used by many mental health professionals, and by the United States Department of Veterans' Affairs counselors to educate themselves and their veterans in this critical area.

The person wants to return to normal as soon as possible. Do not pretend like the event did not happen, avoid him, treat him as fragile, or otherwise drastically change your behavior. Simply continue to treat him as you always have.

It is worth repeating: When in doubt as to what to do or say, simply say, "I'm just glad you are okay.

When you care about someone, let him know it; that is the first round in the chamber, ready to go. For example, when my son was in his final year of high school and on spring break, he drove with some friends to Texas. Later in the week I got a collect phone call from him (never a good sign). The first words out of his lips were, "Dad, the car is totaled but everyone is okay."

Well, as a parent there were a lot of things I could have said at that moment, but for once I was able to practice what I preach. I said, "Buddy, I love you dearly, and I'm so glad you're okay." Later on we did discuss the other things, but it was important at that moment that the first words that came out of my lips was that I cared.

When my son came home from Iraq in 2003, I hugged him and told him I was proud of him, and then proceeded to follow Colonel Hanifen's advice on "What to say to a veteran," which was fresh in my mind.

Sometimes, having the right words to say can be the most important thing of all.

Thou Shalt Not Kill?

The Judeo/Christian View of Killing

chapter seven

"Courage is really fear that's said its prayers," says Father Vincent J. Inghilterra, a top Army Colonel and Catholic priest who has been a military chaplain for 34 years . . . Talking to these [chaplains], one is struck by their moral realism, and how starkly it contrasts with the effete sentimentality you find among so many clergymen today. Theirs is a sterner faith, a more manlier piety than mainstream America is accustomed to . . .

Clerical pacifism leaves many soldiers angry, confused, betrayed, and even spiteful toward faith. "These pronouncements tend to reinforce the notion that religion is for wimps, for prissy-pants, for frilly-suited morons— and those are among the more gentle statements I hear," says Chaplain [Eric] Verhulst. "It frustrates me, because I know that notion is false, but all I can do is provide a counter-example."

—Rod Dreher
"Ministers of War"

My dad died in 1999. He was born on Easter Sunday and he was buried on Easter Sunday, 63 years later. He had been an MP in the Army, served in the CIA, and as a career law enforcement officer he started on the beat and retired as a chief. He was holding a beer in his hand when he died and he never spilled a drop. I think that is how he would have wanted to go.

My mom died a year before that in the middle of the night wrapped in dad's arms; she never woke up. I think that is how she would have wanted to go.

I believe that most families, when burying their parents, want a minister, priest, chaplain or rabbi to help them deal with eternal factors. Even a family that has not darkened the door of a place of worship for many years will turn to the clergy at this time of need. That is just the way we are wired. We cannot help but feel that there is still a piece of our parents out there keeping an eye on us, and we want to come to terms with that.

In the same way, when you have killed another human being, when you have watched the mystery of life and death flicker in front of your eyes, and a living, breathing person has become a piece of meat, and you are the one that caused that, you cannot help but think, "I'm going to have to answer to my maker for what I did."

Early in World War I, young Alvin York, an Army recruit, went up his chain of command during his basic training to explain to his leaders that he was a Quaker. He told them that because he had always been taught, "Thou shalt not kill," he did not think he could do what they were asking of him. So one of his officers took him aside and explained the other side of the story so the recruit could make his own decision. Well, York went on to receive the Medal of Honor by acting with great valor and killing many enemy soldiers. At a critical, crucial moment in our nation's history, when he was needed, Alvin York was on the battlefield, with his heart and mind prepared for combat. So, let me tell you what that young leader said to York to change his thinking and help him make such an incredible contribution to his country and his fellow soldiers.

"Thou Shalt Not Kill" or "Thou Shalt Do No Murder"

> Are you ready to kill another human being? If you have not made spiritual peace—in advance—with your moral decision to take another life to save your own life or those around you, then you may . . . find it difficult to make the decision when time is of the essence.
>
> —Dr. Ignatius Piazza
> Founder of Front Sight Firearms Training Institute

I have been a keynote speaker at the annual convention of Vietnam Veterans of America, I was a co-speaker with General William Westmoreland at an international conference of Vietnam Veterans and I have trained the Veterans Administration rehab counselors at the regional and national level. Whenever I speak to veterans, they tell me that what I am about to tell you is the most useful, powerful and healing information I have to teach them. Do the veterans of our wars have anything to teach us about living with killing? I think they do. So, if this information is so vital to them, perhaps it can be of value to you. Even if you do not need it, maybe you can use it to help some future Alvin York in his moment of truth.

You have heard the commandment, "Thou shall not kill." With few exceptions, however, most major modern translations, and all Jewish translations of the original Hebrew, interprets the commandment as, "You shall not murder" (Exodus 20:13). Have the rabbis, ministers and priests of the Judeo-Christian ethos been hypocrites for the past 5,000 years when they sent men off to war? Did they say, "Thou shall not kill" one day and then send them off to battle the next? Now, the Seven Day Adventists, Mennonites, Shakers, and Quakers believe in the strict, literal interpretation of this translation of the Sixth Commandment, and in the end they may be right. The vast majority of the Judeo-

Christian ethos, however, understand it to mean, "Thou shall not murder."

While we are here on earth, we all place our "bets" in the great "spiritual lottery" of the afterlife. After we die, everyone from the atheist to the most devout believer will know if their bets have paid off. For the sake of argument, let us assume that there is a God and He is the God of the Judeo-Christian heritage. If God is powerful enough to have His will manifested on earth by the majority of his believers, then maybe the "truth" should be found in the overwhelming majority of believers who went to war against Hitler, or who bless the police officers who guard them with deadly force every night. And that great majority of believers have felt that God's commandment is "Thou shalt not murder."

Do you know the difference between murder and killing? If you do, maybe God does too.

The King James Version (KJV) of the *Bible*, published in 1611, translates the Sixth Commandment from the original Hebrew in the Old Testament, as "Thou shalt not kill." But in Matthew 19:18 (in the New Testament, translated from Greek) Jesus cites the Commandments from the KJV, as "Thou shall do no murder."

If you have to kill in the lawful act of your duty, in defense of yourself or another, is that murder? No. The *Bible* says that King David was a man after God's own heart (Acts, 13:22). It says, "Saul hath slain his thousands, and David his ten thousands" (I Samuel, 18:7). David killed tens of thousands of men in combat and was honored for it. It was not until he murdered Uriah to get at Bethsheba that he got himself into trouble (II Samuel Chapter 11).

Can you tell the difference in killing 10,000 men in lawful combat and murdering one man to get at his wife? If you can, maybe God can too.

In Proverbs 6:17 it says, "These six things doth the Lord hate, yea seven are an abomination." If you have even a remote sense that there is a God and that he is the God of the *Bible*, you might want to know what he hates. Near the top of God's list are "shedders of innocent blood," and we know that those who have fought to preserve innocent lives have received the highest honor during 5,000 years of Judeo-Christian ethos.

On Warriorhood: "The Lawful Bearer of Arms"

The bounds of civilised warfare are defined by two antithetical human types, the pacifist and the 'lawful bearer of arms'. . . . Their mutuality is caught in the dialog between the founder of Christianity and the professional Roman soldier who had asked for his healing word to cure a servant. 'I also am a man set under authority,' the centurion explained. Christ exclaimed at the centurion's belief in the power of virtue, which the soldier saw as the complement to the force of law which he personified . . . Western culture would, indeed, not be what it is unless it could respect both the lawful bearer of arms and the person who holds the bearing of arms intrinsically unlawful.

—Sir John Keegan
A History of Warfare

Jesus told the rich young man to sell everything he had because his wealth was coming between him and God (Matthew 19:21). Now, you can make a good argument from the *Bible* against being rich, but you cannot make much of an argument against being a warrior. When the centurion came up to Jesus, Jesus said to him, "No greater faith have I found." Not only did he not tell the centurion to lay down the sword (as he told the rich young man to give up his possessions), he said to his disciples just before he was arrested and executed, "He that hath no sword, let him sell his garment, and buy one" (Luke, 22:36).

We know that Peter had a sword, because when the authorities came to arrest Jesus, Peter drew it, which prompted Jesus to tell him that they were a lawful authority. Jesus said that if you "live by the sword," if you raise your sword against them, then "you shall die by the sword," rightfully administered by the lawful authority (Matthew 26:52). That is reinforced in Romans 13:4—probably the single most important chapter and the single most important verse for a warrior. It says: "For he is the minister of God to thee for good. But if thou do that which is evil, be afraid; for he beareth not the sword in vain: for he is the minister of God, a revenger to execute wrath upon him that doeth evil." Whether the sword bearer is a peacekeeper in a distant land under international authority, or a law enforcement officer at home, he is under the authority of law and "he beareth not the sword in vain."

I am privileged to do a lot of work with the peace community. My book, *On Killing*, is required reading in many "peace study" courses in Mennonite and Quaker colleges. These are magnificent people who are sincerely struggling and striving to find a path to peace. They are much like the law enforcement officers and soldiers I train, only they have chosen a different path. On one occasion, I was in a Mennonite college talking to a group of professors, and I asked if they were serious about being pacifists. When they said that they were, I pointed out that there was an armed guard out front defending their campus, and I asked how they could justify having him there. They told me that there had been much debate about it, with many people arguing that there was a different standard for a peace officer in Romans 13. Some Mennonites felt that they could not support soldiers, but they had to support peace officers. They know that; do you?

The first non-Jew we know of who became a Christian is Cornelius in Acts 10. He was a Roman centurion, a soldier, a police officer of the Roman Empire. Never once is it implied that it was inappropriate for him to be a warrior and still be at peace with God.

Finally, Jesus said these powerful words that apply to all professional warriors who put their lives on the line every day: "Greater love hath no man [or woman] than this, that a man lay down his life for his friends" (John 15:13). Clearly, the men and women who walk out their doors into the mean streets of this country and go to dangerous lands abroad to lay down their lives for people they have not even met are deserving of the highest honor from 5,000 years of the Judeo-Christian ethos.

Whether we want it or not, most of us are influenced by Judeo-Christian ethos. Should you have to lawfully kill in self-defense or in defense of another, and all you know of the Judeo-Christian ethos is an image of someone waving a book and shouting "Thou shalt not kill," your lawful act might cause you great mental and spiritual harm. Hopefully, there is healing and understanding in the verses outlined in the preceding paragraphs.

> And when our time has run out,
> And we're facing our own end,
> We will walk a beat in Heaven,
> With our loved ones and our friends.
>
> —Joseph "Lil Joe" Ferrera
> "The Thin Blue Line"

eight

chapter

Survivor Guilt: *Life Not Death and Justice Not Vengeance*

The Germans were retreating, and there was this raised railroad track. They were going over this track, and the one guy, I hit one guy and – what bothered me – he never, he tried to get up and I took him out again and I – you know, that, that's nasty. I kept thinking, "Don't stand up, please don't stand up." I felt anger that the guy didn't have sense enough to stay down – that's about all that I can – I don't really – you're trained, you're trained for. You knew, I mean, the one thing that an infantryman knows and is drilled into him is that if somebody points a gun at you, kill him first before he kills you . . .

I wonder if he had a family, if he had a girlfriend. I had a girlfriend before I went overseas and I married her – we've been married for 50 some years. You not only wonder about that one person that I killed, but all the young men on both sides that lost so much of the future.

—David Weddle
"Secrets at the Bottom of the Drawer"

Much has been written about survivor guilt among Holocaust survivors, war veterans, police officers, and even relatives spared from an illness that has struck down other family members. It is not unusual for the survivor to think that he was spared at the expense of another and feel a heavy sense of debt to the one who is gone. Some survivors make every effort to stay in the shadows to avoid drawing attention to the fact that they survived. Some may feel some distorted sense of not being worthy, and that their daily concerns are of little matter; they may even feel guilty for having needs at all. Survivor guilt can be extraordinarily toxic.

There is a bond of love among the men and women who put their lives on the line that the average person cannot comprehend. Shakespeare wrote about this when he said,

> We few, we happy few, we band of brothers;
> For he to-day that sheds his blood with me
> Shall be my brother; be he ne'er so vile,

This day shall gentle his condition:
And gentlemen in England now a-bed
Shall think themselves accursed they were not here,
And hold their manhoods cheap whiles any speaks
That fought with us upon Saint Crispin's day.

—King Henry V

That is the bond of the men and women who put their lives on the line every day. Lose one and it is the same as losing a spouse or a brother, and when it is a human who causes the loss of a fellow warrior's life, it becomes personal. If you let survivor guilt destroy you, then you have given the enemy one more life, one more victory. And we will not give them that life!

If you are a survivor and you do not proceed carefully, there are two ways you can spin out of control: through inappropriate aggression towards others and inappropriate aggression towards yourself. Warriors must guard against both. Let us now put two last pieces of the bulletproof mind into place. The first piece is the concept of "justice not vengeance." The other is "life not death."

Justice, Not Vengeance

Don't dehumanize those who disagree with us, or even hate us. Filling ourselves with hate is neither necessary to combat those who hate us, nor is it productive. The professional soldier is one who is cold, dispassionate and regretful in his duty when forced to kill.

Those Operators, they didn't hate the Somalis anymore than they loved them. They were there to do a job that they didn't question, not because they're mindless cogs, but because soldiers do what they're told to. They were surgically dispassionate in how they executed that job. That is what makes somebody truly dangerous to an enemy, not a berserker rage fueled by hatred for what they did to 19 Americans. The steady trigger finger kills a lot more enemy than the one that trembles with hatred. Take pride in the fact that we live in a country where we should treat Americans from all clans as Americans first and foremost; don't stoop to the level of hating those that hate us. Just keep giving us ammo and we'll take care of them, coldly, dispassionately and without malice.

We don't execute murderers out of a need for vengeance; we do it out of a need to protect others from them. Same reason we put down rabid dogs. The hate mongers of the world should be treated the same way. And we shouldn't become rabid dogs in the process.

Respectfully, Souleman

—From a "Black Hawk Down" online discussion group

For our purposes, "justice not vengeance" simply means that the soldier and police officer swear a solemn oath to justice. Should they violate that oath and seek vengeance, it will destroy them. The surest way to a dose of posttraumatic stress disorder is to commit an atrocity or a criminal act that violates your code of ethics.

Now, as we come to the end of the book, let us "review the bidding" and look at the factors that can contribute to stress disorders so that we can place the impact of atrocities into the equation.

-First, remember that unmanaged stress is a major destroyer and disabler of warriors.

-Ahead of time, the way to be psychologically predisposed to become a stress casualty is to be a sheep: live in denial, fail to stay on the warrior's path, avoid training, don't prepare and don't equip yourself for that moment when the wolf comes.

-Physically, the way to predispose yourself to be a stress casualty is to have your body already stressed when the traumatic moment arrives. This includes malnutrition, dehydration and, most importantly, sleep deprivation.

-At the moment of truth, the key to avoiding stress casualties is to avoid Condition Black. This is done ahead of time by developing stress inoculation in training, learning to apply tactical breathing, and through training that develops an autopilot response to insure that even under high stress you will do the right thing.

-Ahead of time, the warrior must confront that dirty four-letter word "kill" and the responsibility to use deadly force when the situation requires it. This insures that at the moment of truth you will not panic, you will be more likely to deter your opponent, and you will be better able to live with your actions afterwards.

-Thus the warrior's mind and body must be ready, but there is one other component we have covered: the spirit. Your mind, body and spirit must be prepared before combat, and thus we have addressed the spiritual or religious aspects of killing.

-Afterward, the key to preventing a stress disorder is to conduct the debriefings, delinking the memories from the emotions, multiplying the joy and dividing the pain.

There is one last ingredient in the equation, and that is to understand that of all the actions you could take in combat, the one most likely to destroy you is to commit an atrocity or a criminal act. Your unconscious mind, your "puppy" knows that you are not at peace with the "pack" and that can eat you alive. This concept was communicated most eloquently, by a warrior leader on the eve of invading Iraq in 2003:

It is a big step to take another human life. It is not to be done lightly. I know of men who have taken life needlessly in other conflicts. I can assure you they live with the mark of Cain upon them. If someone surrenders to you then remember they have that right in international law and ensure that one day they go home to their family.

The ones who wish to fight, well, we aim to please . . .

If you harm the regiment or its history by over-enthusiasm in killing or in cowardice, know it is your family who will suffer. You will be shunned unless your conduct is of the highest, for your deeds will follow you down through history. We will bring shame on neither our uniform or our nation.

—Lieutenant Colonel Tim Collins
1st Battalion of the Royal Irish Regiment
22 March 2003

Two centuries earlier Longfellow said:

Every guilty deed
Holds in itself the seed
Of retribution and undying pain.

—"The Masque of Pandora"

You can almost think of "justice not vengeance" as what the *Bible* calls the "Breastplate of Righteousness." As long as you are doing the right thing, as long as you are following the rules and doing what your duty calls you to do, then there is true legal and mental protection in that. Again Shakespeare said it best, calling this "A peace above all earthly dignities, a still and quiet conscience." For those seeking more information on this topic I strongly recommend Jonathan Shay's excellent book, *Achilles in Vietnam*, which is a superb analysis of the tragic price that warriors pay for committing atrocities, engaging in berserk behavior, and violating the ancient code of the honorable warrior

Earlier, I talked about how pain shared is pain divided. This is a powerful tool, but when a warrior commits a criminal act, he cannot share that pain. I also talked about how you are only as sick as your secrets. If as a warrior you commit a crime or an act of vengeance, you cannot share that secret with anyone, and it will only eat away at you.

When we are young and hard, we think we can get away with anything. A World War II veteran once sat across from me, wracked with sobs. He was, to my mind, a magnificent noble American, but he had made one tragic, horrific mistake in his life and it was eating him alive. He looked at me, tears streaming down his cheeks, and said, "Colonel, I'm an old man now, and I'm going to have to answer to my maker soon. I'm going to have to answer for that day it was inconvenient to take those German soldiers back. The day we shot them while they were quote, 'trying to escape.' I murdered those men that day; we murdered them. We didn't have to kill them. We murdered them, and soon I will have to answer to my maker for what I did."

What do you tell a man like that? No one is beyond redemption, but I know what that old soldier would advise us: "Don't do it."

Now, many will say, "Colonel you're crazy. I'm not going to commit some criminal act." Good, but the reality is you do not know what you are going to do when your world comes unglued unless you prepare your mind, soul and spirit ahead of time. You do not know for sure that you can dial 9-1-1 when your world is coming unglued, and you do not know for sure you can make a magazine change in your weapon unless you have rehearsed it ahead of time. Likewise, when you have rehearsed and prepared to always do the right thing at the moment of truth, you are more apt to deal appropriately with whatever comes your way.

The key is to work this matter out ahead of time, because at the moment of truth making the right decision might be difficult.

> I had to figure out, am I a cop right now or am I somebody that's mad because someone did something to my family. You don't know if you want to go for vengeance or for justice. When it happens to someone you work with, it makes a different impact.
> —A police officer's comment
> after his partner was shot in an ambush

Justice not vengeance. You have sworn a solemn oath to justice. Some of you swore it as a peace officer, but all Americans swore it from their youngest days. It went like this: "I pledge allegiance to the flag of the United States of America, and to the republic for which it stands, one nation under God, indivisible with liberty and justice for all."

Vengeance will destroy you. Remember, PTSD is the gift that keeps on giving. It impacts not only you in the years to come but also your spouse and your kids. So now, ahead of time, while you are calm and rational, think it through: whoever you think you are avenging would not want you to pay the price of your life and your loved ones' lives in the years to come.

Consider this incident that happened to a young Marine captain in Beirut in the spring of 1982. The Israeli Army was advancing, into Lebanon, with tanks in the lead, when word came down to a small band of Marines to stop the Israelis. An entire army, one of the most competent in the world, was rumbling up the road with tanks in the lead, and the American Marines were waiting for them, armed with nothing bigger than M-16 rifles. But orders are orders, and Marines are Marines, so a young captain, holding an M1911, .45 automatic pistol in his hand, walked out into the middle of the road before the advancing army. He stopped the lead Israeli tank, turned it around and sent them all back.

Did that pistol in his hand deter and frighten the entire Israeli army? No. But that pistol represented the might, the majesty and the authority of the United States of America in the hands of a very brave man who was doing what his nation wanted him to do. Those Israelis knew that if they continued forward, they would have to kill that young marine, and along with him came all his friends, a whole nation of friends bringing a whole world of hurt, and the price was too high for the Israelis to pay.

As a warrior, understand that when you awaken every morning, strap on your weapon, and take it into combat, it represents the might, the majesty and the authority of your city, your county, your state, and your nation, but only as long as you do what your nation wants you to do. Step out from under the umbrella of your authority and you become just another criminal. As Shakespeare wrote:

> What stronger breastplate than a heart untainted!
> Thrice is he armed that hath his quarrel just,
> And he but naked, though locked up in steel,
> Whose conscience with injustice is corrupted.
> —*King Henry VI*

Not too many years ago a police officer used to be given a lot of leeway. Perhaps there was a day when, if a man was asking for an ass-whooping, it was a cop's job to give it to him. Well, that day is gone. If it ever existed, it is gone today.

The Nazis and the Imperial Japanese in World War II committed many, horrendous, brutal and large scale atrocities. Unfortunately, the allied side also committed some. Many prisoners were "shot, trying to escape" when it was inconvenient to take them back, and that was often winked at. That day, too, is gone. Like the police officer, the modern soldier is likely to have his every act videotaped and reported on national TV, and there is no tolerance for any deviation from the rules of war. Today our soldiers are held to the highest standards, and that is a good thing.

It's as if we had been playing football but now it is basketball season, and some fool is out there trying to tackle people on the basketball court. He is tackling people on the basketball court! What's going to happen? He's going to foul himself out of this game. And if he's not careful, he's going to lose this game.

Whether you are a soldier or marine in close combat, a peacekeeper in a distant land, or a police officer working in the mean streets of America, you are held to a far higher standard than that of the average person. As such, you must dedicate yourself now, ahead of time, to the concept of justice, not vengeance. As individuals and as a society, we must walk the path of justice, not vengeance, lest we wake one day and find ourselves, as Edward Young put it 300 years ago, with:

Souls made of fire, and children of the sun,
With whom revenge is virtue.

—"The Revenge"

Life Not Death: "Earn It."

We cannot fill his shoes, nor replace him, but we can do the things that he did. We can remember and honor him by being good officers, good husbands and fathers, and good friends. We can take seriously our life's work and be faithful servants.

—Officer Greg Pashley
"Huffy: Cop, friend and hero"

When someone gives his life to save your life, you must not waste it. Let me repeat that: If someone buys your life at the price of his life, you do not dare waste it. Your moral, sacred responsibility is to lead the fullest, richest, best life you can.

Think about this, right now, ahead of time, while you are calm and rational. If you were the one to die and your partner lived, you would want him to have the best life possible. You died to give him that.

Now, should your partner or your buddy die in combat, leaving you to drive on, what would he want for you? The same thing. He would want the fullest, richest life you can have. That is what he died to give you, and that is your moral, sacred responsibility. Your mission.

That means that right now you need to make a conscious effort to set aside all self-destructive thoughts and dedicate yourself to leading that full life. Now, you might say, "Colonel, you're crazy, I'm never going to eat my gun." Good. But according to the National Police Suicide Foundation, the number of suicides among police officers is two to three times greater than line of duty deaths. And many other warriors in their hour of despair have done the wrong thing, seeking a permanent solution to a temporary problem. They too would have sworn that they would never consider suicide. At the moment of truth, however, they did the wrong thing because they had not, with all their heart and soul, worked through it ahead of time.

So tell yourself this: "Nobody takes my life without one hell of a fight ... including me!" Say it to yourself, right now. "I will fight for my life. I will seek counseling. I will get medication. I will leave no rock unturned. I will fight for my life like I would fight for my child's life! Because I'm a warrior! And nobody takes my life without one hell of a fight. Including me." If you pound it into your soul now, then at the moment of truth you will do the right thing.

Steven Spielberg's motion picture *Saving Private Ryan* gives us an incredibly realistic depiction of the violence and horror of combat. This movie is something which, like sex, can be child abuse if inflicted upon children, but for adults it can provide us with a wonderful model for behavior when we talk about choosing life not death. Let me tell you what *Saving Private Ryan* means to me.

A band of U.S. Army Rangers go behind enemy lines, where each man, one by one, dies to save one young paratrooper: Private Ryan. To me that band of Rangers represents every American warrior who ever willingly gave his life to give us the freedom, the lives and the liberty that we have today. Those Rangers are the boys who fell at Lexington and Concord, and they are bloody windrows of bodies at Shilo and Gettysburg. They are trenches full of blood in the Ardennes Forest, and they are a bloody tide of bodies at Normandy Beach and Iwo Jima. They are more than 300 police officers and firefighters rushing up the steps of the World Trade Center, and they represent the cop who died yesterday, alone and afraid on a dirty street, somewhere in America. That band of Rangers is every warrior who ever died to give us what we have today.

Private Ryan is us. He is every citizen who is alive and free today because two centuries of warriors have gone before us and purchased at the ultimate price what we have today.

Do you remember the end of the movie, when the last ranger, Captain Miller, lay dying on the bridge? He looks up at Ryan, he looks up at us, and what are his dying words? "Earn this. Earn it."

Earn it. Be worthy. Don't waste it. Two centuries of warriors look up from their graves in this dark hour, they look up from the rubble of the World Trade Center, and their message is, "Earn it." We can never truly earn what has been purchased at the ultimate price, but we can do our best. Our model is Private Ryan.

Do you remember the old man at the very end of the movie standing over the grave of his comrades with his grandbabies and his great-grandbabies bouncing all around him? He looks over at his wife, and says, "Tell me I've led a good life. Tell me I've been a good man."

As a warrior, your mission is to man the ramparts of our civilization honorably and well in this dark hour; to retire honorably and well; to raise your grandbabies and your great-grandbabies straight, tall and true; to raise the next generation, straight and tall and true; to crack the bones and suck the marrow from every single day that you have been blessed with; and at the end of your days, to look into the eyes of your loved ones and say, "Tell me I've led a good life. Tell me I've been a good person."

As warriors, we dedicate ourselves toward a lifetime of service to our civilization. We make the choice, the conscious decision to take the path of justice not vengeance, and life not death. Almost 2,500 years ago, the Greek poet and philosopher, Heraclitus, talked about making this choice.

> The soul is dyed the color of its thoughts . . . The content of your character is your choice. Day by day, what you choose, what you think, and what you do is who you become. Your integrity is your destiny . . . it is the light that guides your way.

In my presentations I show a photograph of a young firefighter wearing his heavy protective equipment and helmet. You can see vasoconstriction causing white areas around his eyes, nose and mouth, clearly the face of a frightened young man. The photo also shows several other people in the background, their backs to the camera as they scramble down a stairwell. What makes this firefighter—this young warrior—different from everyone else in the photograph is that he is going up the stairs. The photo was taken in a stairwell in one of the Twin Towers on September 11, 2001, where in one horrific morning 3,000 of our citizens died. Most of them did not have a choice that day, but there was a group of warriors—police officers and firefighters—who did. They were willing to go up the stairs, because that was their job, because that was what they were trained to do, but most of all they went up those stairs because they held the lives of any citizen in that building to be more precious than their own. "Greater love hath no man than this . . . " They went up, but most of them did not come back down. Many lives were taken on that tragic morning, but some were freely given.

How can we equip ourselves, train ourselves, and prepare ourselves so that we will not be found wanting at our moment of truth? How can we "earn" this? As warriors, we can learn, strive and prepare ourselves but in the end we can never truly earn it. None of us can ever be worthy of what two centuries of men like the frightened, courageous young firefighter in that photo have done for us. We can, however, strive to do our best, like Private Ryan, and dedicate ourselves, ahead of time to master survivor guilt and lead the full, rich and productive life that has been purchased for us at such a dear cost.

Conclusion

Are warriors leaders? I think so. I think they pretty much have to be. Unfortunately, rank and leadership do not automatically go hand-in-hand. Rank also does not automatically make one a warrior. Here is an example.

Five years ago I was selected to test for a sergeant position with my police department. Part of that process was a long oral board interview with upper-level police supervisors from outside agencies in the area. One of the first things they asked me was this: What is your supervisory philosophy?

I responded that I didn't see this as a supervisory position, which seemed to confuse them slightly. So they asked me what did I see it as. I told them that I saw it as a leadership position. They chuckled politely and asked me what my leadership philosophy was. This is how I responded.

This is leadership responsibility. You have to lead from the front. You cannot stand in the back and yell, "Follow me!" You have to stand tall and set an example. You have to take care of your troops and never ask them to do anything you are not willing to do. If you cannot do the job then you must find someone who can and give that person the opportunity to do it. You take responsibility for the actions of your men and you accept responsibility for your own actions. You never ever point a finger at your men for your own shortcomings and you make damn sure they know it when they do something good. If you do these things, your men will follow you anywhere you want to go.

This was met with a stunned silence. I was subsequently unanimously recommended for promotion and I have tried my very best to live the words I spoke.

It's up to people like you and I to seek out those young men and women and to teach them, lead them, and to provide them with everything they need to become our future warriors and leaders. These people truly are our future. I realize that I haven't got the education and the experience guys like you have, but I have some pretty good ideas that I've learned from guys like you.

I try to pass those things on every day to those young men and women I have taken under my wing.

—Dave Bergquist
Correspondence to Lieutenant Colonel Dave Grossman

It may well be that we are at a turning point in history, a new era, a time for warriors. In this dark hour, our mission is to rise up and nurture the next generation of warriors. And, as Sergeant Chris Pascoe shows us, there is reason to believe that a generation of mighty warriors is rising to the challenge.

Sergeant Pascoe, a remarkable warrior-scholar working for the Michigan State Police, e-mailed me concerning a book called, *The Fourth Turning: An American Prophecy* by William Strauss and Neil Howe. Chris was rightfully excited about the book, saying that it is an analysis of cycles in human development that have repeated themselves throughout history. I agree with Chris that this book has powerful considerations for today's warrior and for the next generation of warriors. Here is his explanation of the four turning points.

The First Turning is a high new civic order, an upbeat era of strengthening institutions and weakening individualism (i.e., Truman, Eisenhower, and the Kennedy era). The Second Turning is an awakening and passionate era of spiritual upheaval where the civic order comes under attack (i.e., the turbulent 1960s). The Third Turning—is an unraveling or culture war, a downcast era of strengthening individualism and weakening institutions, when the old civic order decays and new values are planted (i.e., Reagan, Bush, and Clinton era). The Fourth Turning—is a crisis or upheaval that propels a new civic order, eventually leading to another First Turning.

At the time the book was written in 1997, the authors predicted a possible Fourth Turning in the year 2005, initiated by a "fiscal crisis, global terrorism, and growing anarchy."

The result, according to the authors: "Armed confrontation usually occurs around the climax of crisis. At home and abroad, these events will reflect the tearing of the civic fabric at points of extreme vulnerability; problem areas where, during the unraveling, America will have neglected, denied, or delayed needed action. Many Americans won't know where their savings are, who their employer is, what their pension is, or how the government works. Anger at mistakes we made will translate into calls for action.

"From this trough, and from these dangers, the making of a new social contract and new civic order will arise. National issues will break clear of the Unraveling-era circus, Republicans, Democrats, or perhaps a new party will decisively win the long partisan tug-of-war, ending the era of split government. Trust will be reborn. American society will be transformed. The emergent society will be something better, a nation that sustains its Framers' visions with a robust new pride. Or it may be something worse. The Fourth Turning is a time of glory or ruin."

Then Chris asks: "Are we in the Fourth Turning now?" Could the attacks of September 11, 2001, the invasions of Afghanistan and Iraq and the ongoing war on terrorism, combined with all-time record violent crime rates at home and around the world be the crisis period of the Fourth Turning that will open the door for a new period of revival, regeneration and renewal in our society?

If so, then warriors may well be the "midwife" of this crisis phase, giving birth to a new era of stability and civic order. If that is our challenge, then now, more than ever, we must become masters of our realm, embracing the warrior concepts of life not death, and justice not vengeance.

In recent years, there has been a segment of our society that does not like using the term warrior. For them the noble heritage of the knight paladin is not what they think of when they hear the word. They are not bad people, but they do not understand.

So let us all work together to help them see that in a republic or a representative democracy such as ours, the role of the warrior is not to kill; it is to protect, preserve, and defend. Yes, upon occasion, peace warriors may be called upon to take human life, but that is never their goal. The goal of the "moral warrior" can best be summed up in one last model for action, one final true story.

This is not a story about killing. Killing is what we do if we must, and if we must, we do it well. Nor is this a story about dying. Dying is what we do if we must, and if we must, we do it well. It is just a simple story about a young warrior standing in the snow.

During the Battle of the Bulge, the Nazi SS spearhead units had broken through American lines in the Ardennes Forest in December of 1944, and the demoralized American units were fleeing in terror down the little roads coming out of the Ardennes Forest with the Nazis on their heels. My old unit, the 82nd Airborne Division, was brought out of reserve to help stop the enemy advance. The paratroopers of the 82nd marched day and night to establish blocking positions on the roads leading through the Ardennes Forest, and they had the mission, the authority and the responsibility to rally together the fleeing Americans and stop the Nazi advance. And that is exactly what they did.

There was an American tank, 30 tons of death, fleeing down one of the little roads leading through the forest. One lonely paratrooper stood beside the road. A photographer captured the image of this young man with hollow sunken eyes, a three-day growth of beard, an M-1 Garand in one hand, and a bazooka slung over his back. He raised his hand to stop the fleeing tank. After it had ground to a halt, the weary paratrooper looked up at the tank commander, and asked, "Buddy, are you looking for a safe place?"

"Yeah," the tank commander replied.

"Then park your tank behind me, because I'm the 82nd Airborne, and this is as far as the bastards are going."

Do you understand how this story applies to you, my fellow warriors?

For the rest of your lives you are going to be faced with people who are fleeing. They will be fleeing drugs, crime, poverty, violence, terrorism, and the fear that lurks in the hearts of every man and woman. And you have the mission, the authority and the responsibility to stand up and say, "Friend, neighbor, brother, sister, buddy . . . are you looking for a safe place?"

And they will say, "Yeah."

So you tell them, "Then get behind me, because I'm a cop—because I'm a soldier—because I'm a warrior—and this is as far as the bastards are going!"

You see, it is not about killing, and it is not about dying. We are not all called to kill, and we are not all called to die, but we are all called to serve our civilization in this dark hour. It's about preserving and protecting. It is about serving and sacrificing. It is about doing a dirty, desperate, thankless job, every day of your life, to the utmost of your ability, because you know that if no one did that job our civilization would be doomed.

So now as you do that, for the rest of your lives, may God bless you, your families and your every endeavor. Amen.

The Final Inspection

The warrior stood and faced God,
    Which will always come to pass,
He hoped his shoes were shining,
    Just as brightly as his brass.

"Step forward now, old warrior,
    How shall I deal with you?
Have you always turned the other cheek?
    To My Church have you been true?"

The warrior squared his shoulders and
    said, "No, Lord, I guess I ain't,
'Cause those of us who carry guns
    Can't always be a saint.

"I've had to work most Sundays,
    And at times my talk was tough,
And sometimes I've been violent,
    'Cause the world is awfully rough.

"But, I never took a penny
    That wasn't mine to keep.
Though I worked a lot of overtime
    When the bills got just too steep,

"And I never passed a cry for help,
    Though at times I shook with fear,
And sometimes, God forgive me,
    I've wept unmanly tears.

"I know I don't deserve a place
    Among the people here,
They never wanted me around
    Except to calm their fears.

"If you've a place for me here, Lord,
    It needn't be so grand. In life
I didn't expect nor need too much,
    So if you don't, I'll understand."

There was a silence all around the throne,
    Where the saints had often trod,
As the warrior stood quietly.
    For the judgment of his God.

"Step forward now, my warrior,
    You've born your burdens well,
Walk peacefully on Heaven's streets,
    You've done your time in Hell."

—Author Unknown

Appendix A

Erasmus' Twenty-two Principles on How to Be Strong While Remaining Virtuous in a Dangerous World

From the *Enchridion Militis Christiani: A Guide for the Righteous Protector,* by Erasmus, 1503, extracted by Sergeant Chris Pascoe, Michigan State Police.

First Rule
INCREASE YOUR FAITH.
Even if the entire world appears mad.

Second Rule
ACT UPON YOUR FAITH.
Even if you must undergo the loss of everything.

Third Rule
ANALYZE YOUR FEARS.
You will find that things are not as bad as they appear.

Fourth Rule
MAKE VIRTUE THE ONLY GOAL OF YOUR LIFE.
Dedicate all your enthusiasm, all your effort, your leisure as well as your business.

Fifth Rule
TURN AWAY FROM MATERIAL THINGS.
If you are greatly concerned with money you will be weak of spirit.

Sixth Rule
TRAIN YOUR MIND TO DISTINGUISH GOOD AND EVIL.
Let your rule of government be determined by the common good.

Seventh Rule
NEVER LET ANY SETBACK STOP YOU IN YOUR QUEST.
We are not perfect—this only means we should try harder.

Eighth Rule
IF YOU HAVE FREQUENT TEMPTATIONS, DO NOT WORRY.
Begin to worry when you do not have temptation, because that is a sure
sign that you cannot distinguish good from evil.

Ninth Rule
ALWAYS BE PREPARED FOR AN ATTACK.
Careful generals set guards even in times of peace.

Tenth Rule
SPIT, AS IT WERE, IN THE FACE OF DANGER.
Keep a stirring quotation with you for encouragement.

Eleventh Rule
THERE ARE TWO DANGERS:
ONE IS GIVING UP, THE OTHER IS PRIDE.
After you have performed some worthy task, give all the credit to someone else.

Twelfth Rule
TURN YOUR WEAKNESS INTO VIRTUE.
If you are inclined to be selfish, make a deliberate effort to be giving.

Thirteenth Rule
TREAT EACH BATTLE AS THOUGH IT WERE YOUR LAST.
And you will finish, in the end, victorious!

Fourteenth Rule
DON'T ASSUME THAT DOING GOOD ALLOWS YOU TO
KEEP A FEW VICES.
The enemy you ignore the most is the one who conquers you.

Fifteenth Rule
WEIGH YOUR ALTERNATIVES CAREFULLY.
The wrong way will often seem easier than the right way.

Sixteenth Rule
NEVER ADMIT DEFEAT EVEN IF YOU HAVE BEEN WOUNDED.
The good soldier's painful wounds spur him to gather his strength.

Seventeenth Rule
ALWAYS HAVE A PLAN OF ACTION.
So when the time comes for battle, you will know what to do.

Eighteenth Rule
CALM YOUR PASSIONS BY SEEING HOW LITTLE THERE IS TO GAIN.
We often worry and scheme about trifling matters of no real importance.

Nineteenth Rule
SPEAK WITH YOURSELF THIS WAY:
If I do what I am considering, would I want my family to know about it?

Twentieth Rule
VIRTUE HAS ITS OWN REWARD.
Once a person has it, they would not exchange it for anything.

Twenty-first Rule
LIFE CAN BE SAD, DIFFICULT, AND QUICK:
MAKE IT COUNT FOR SOMETHING!
Since we do not know when death will come, act honorably everyday.

Twenty-second Rule
REPENT YOUR WRONGS.
Those who do not admit their faults have the most to fear.

Appendix B
Board of Advisors for On Combat

Many people have had a hand in this book, and many others would have been happy to help if I had asked them. Space does not allow me to mention everyone, and our publishing schedule did not permit me to touch base with all these dear friends and comrades who would have happily assisted. But one particular group of individuals did go the extra mile, on a very tight schedule, reading the manuscript and providing detailed feedback and assistance. They are listed below. If there is anything wrong in this book, I accept full responsibility, but if there is anything right, the credit goes to them and all the others who have shared and assisted across the years.

Loren W. Christensen
Loren's bio is included elsewhere, but I want to take this opportunity to recognize an awesome friend, partner, warrior, scholar, and wordsmith. We began with the transcript of a two-day class that I conducted, and a stack of hundreds of pages of notes, all of which were dumped in Loren's lap. He worked long and hard to turn this mass of information into something readable, and he deserves much credit. Again, if anything is wrong, it is my fault, but if it is right and readable then Loren is first and foremost among those who deserve the credit.

Alexis Artwohl
Alexis Artwohl, Ph.D., is a public safety trainer and consultant who provides training and consultation across the U.S. and Canada. Her areas of training include: achieving peak performance in high stress situations, preparing to survive deadly force encounters, investigating officer-involved shootings, and managing the psychological damage caused by trauma and organizational stress. Dr. Artwohl is co-author of the book *Deadly Force Encounters: What Cops Need to Know to Mentally Prepare for and Survive a Gunfight,* written with retired police officer Loren W. Christensen. During her 16 years as a private practice clinical and police psychologist, she provided traumatic incident debriefings and psychotherapy to numerous public safety personnel and their family members. She was an independent provider of psychological services to public safety agencies throughout the Pacific Northwest. In January 1999, she closed her clinical practice office and joined her husband, Assistant Chief Dave Butzer of

the Portland Police Bureau, in his retirement. They are continuing to pursue careers as public safety trainers and consultants. www.alexisartwohl.com.

Ron Avery

Ron Avery is president and director of training at the Practical Shooting Academy, Inc., and a full-time professional firearms/defensive tactics trainer and consultant. He has over 20 years' experience in law enforcement in both an active and reserve capacity. During his years of law enforcement, Mr. Avery was trained in special weapons and tactics (SWAT) and has worked as head firearms instructor/program director, defensive tactics trainer, field training officer, and countersniper. The practice of martial arts has been a part of Mr. Avery's life since the age of 16 and he incorporates martial arts' concepts and principles into his firearms programs.

Ron is a world-class professional shooter and has won numerous matches and awards over the past 20 years. Ranked among the best shooters in the world in international practical shooting competition, he represented the United States as part of the USPSA Gold Team in Standard Division at the 2002 World IPSC Championships in Pietersberg, South Africa, placing third individually and helping to secure the first place team trophy.

Mr. Avery is nationally and internationally recognized as a top level firearms trainer and researcher. He has developed training programs and models that represent some of the most sophisticated work ever done in the firearms training field. He has worked as a consultant and trainer for top level federal agencies as well as law enforcement agencies across the U.S. www.practicalshootingacad.com.

Massad Ayoob

Massad Ayoob has been a sworn law enforcement officer for 30 years, and since the American Society of Law Enforcement Trainers (ASLET) was founded in 1987 has been chair of ASLET's firearms committee. An expert witness for the defense in numerous homicide cases, he was certified as a police prosecutor in 1988 and served two terms as co-vice-chair of the forensic evidence committee of the National Association of Criminal Defense Lawyers. Ayoob founded the Lethal Force Institute in 1981 and still serves as its director at this writing. The author of numerous books on defensive use of force and thousands of articles, he is presently handgun editor of *Guns* magazine, law enforcement editor of *American Handgunner* magazine, and associate editor of *Combat Handguns* magazine.

Jack Beach

Colonel Johnston "Jack" Beach, U.S. Army (ret.), is currently a leadership development consultant for IBM. As such, he works with that corporation's senior executives to further develop individual leadership capacities, more effective organizational climates, and grow a culture of leadership throughout IBM. Colonel Beach is also the CEO of his own consulting group, The Leadership Difference. Prior to retirement from the military, Colonel Beach lead an illustrious career. Starting as a combat medic in 1969, he rose from private to colonel. In 1981, he joined the faculty in the Department of Behavioral Sciences and Leadership at the United States Military Academy where he remained until his retirement in 1999. He received numerous awards and decorations for service to his country.

Gavin de Becker

Gavin's bio has been placed with his foreword to this book, but he has also been a key contributor to this book, from the very beginning, and I want to take this opportunity to recognize and thank him.

Tony Blauer

Tony Blauer is founder and CEO of Blauer Tactical Confrontation Management Systems (BTCMS) a consulting firm specializing in research and development for combative training for the military and law enforcement communities. Mr. Blauer has over 20 years' of teaching experience and is an internationally sought-after instructor. His expertise, to only name a few, has been sought by the U.S. Navy SEALs, U.S. Army Special Forces, U.S. Air Marshals, numerous state tactical police associations, United Nations Security Services, and various organizations in Venezuela, Australia, the United Kingdom and Germany. Mr. Blauer is a member of the American Society of Law Enforcement Trainers (ASLET) and the International Association of Law Enforcement Firearms Instructors (IALEFI). www.tonyblauer.com.

Jim Bray

Mr. Bray is a writer and pragmatic peace activist. He assisted in writing the National Green Party defense platform.

Steven C. Bronson

Steve Bronson is a retired U.S. Navy Chief, a decorated combat veteran, a Naval Special Warfare (NSW) instructor and a combat craft patrol officer. He is the director and founder of Tactical Watreborne Operations (T.W.O). Chief Bronson has been asked to sit on several regional and state tactical response advisory boards as they relate to the emerging possibility of terrorist threats against maritime targets. Chief Bronson was one of the former program managers for the NSW's Special Warfare Craft (SWCC) school and continues to work closely with NSW and Special Forces personnel through training and development of special equipment for

Special Operations. Chief Bronson's latest equipment development project has resulted in the CBR-pack requested by the Navy's Office of Disaster Preparedness. Chief Bronson has contributed numerous articles on water operations to magazines such as *Police, Law and Order, Tactical Response,* and *The Tactical Edge.* He is the official maritime operations and counterterrorism adviser to *Police* magazine and serves on the board of directors for the southeastern SWAT conference. www.twoboatguy.com.

John D. Byrnes

John Byrnes, D. Hum., founded The Center for Aggression Management, a division of Aon Corporation's Crisis Management Practice, in 1993. Dr. Byrnes' provides comprehensive training to assist organizations in the management of aggressive behavior in the workplace. He is a successful businessman, lecturer, and author sought after, to name only a few, by such national organizations as the U.S. Postal Service, NASA, American Society of Law Enforcement Trainers (ASLET), National Association of School Boards (NASB) and many state government organizations. Dr. Byrnes has been interviewed by or has been published in the *Wall Street Journal, Risk Management* magazine, *Denver Post,* and the *Wall Street Journal Radio Network: Work & Family,* to name only a few. Dr. Byrnes is the author of *Before Conflict: Preventing Aggressive Behavior.* He was selected by the U.S. Department of Labor to represent the United States at the Violence as a Workplace Risk conference being held in Montreal, Canada. www.AggressionManagement.com.

Andy Casavant

Andy Casavant is the Associate Director of the University of Illinois Police Training Institute and the President of the Midwest Tactical Training Institute. Andy is a Lieutenant Colonel in the U.S. Army Reserves Military Police and is nationally recognized as an innovative SWAT trainer and speaker on tactical and training subjects. He is currently Chairman of the Board of Directors for the American Society for Law Enforcement Training (ASLET) and is on the Board of Directors for the International Association of Law Enforcement Firearms Instructors (IALEFI). Andy has won numerous awards including the Silver Star for Bravery from the Police Hall of Fame as well as several TOP COP awards from the U.S. Army. Andy has a master's degree in technology in training and development as well as in work performance improvement from Eastern Illinois University.

Jeff Chudwin

Jeff Chudwin is Chief of Police for the Village of Olympia Fields, Illinois. He is a founding member and current president of the Illinois Tactical Officers' Association (ITOA), which is comprised of over 1,700 emergency response officers throughout the State of Illinois. He serves as a regional co-chairman of the Illinois Law Enforcement Alarm System, the ad hoc terrorism committee of the South Suburban and Will County Chiefs' of Police Association, and is a member of the Illinois Chiefs' of Police Association Terrorism Committee. Since 1978, Chief Chudwin has trained officers on issues of police use of force, firearms skills, and has been a presenter on officer survival issues at conferences throughout the country. He speaks on issues of personal safety, school violence, and counterterrorism to both law enforcement and civic groups.

Kevin Dillon

Lieutenant Kevin Dillon is a 23-year law enforcement veteran having served in various capacities. He is presently the Detective Bureau Commander at the Police Department of Hartford County, Connecticut. Lieutenant Dillon is often called upon by internal affairs and civil courts as an expert in the use of force. He has developed an intensive nine-day Arrest and Control Instructor's course for the Connecticut Police Officers' Standards and Training Academy. For the past 27 years, Lieutenant Dillon has studied numerous martial art systems. He has appeared in the *Encyclopedia of Self-Defense* video/DVD produced by Turtlepress and has recently released another series entitled *Police Combat Tactics*.

Ron Donvito

Ron Donvito is a 20-year veteran of the U.S. Marine Corps. During his distinguished career, Mr. Donvito was the SME for the Marine Corps from 1989-1998, as well as the advisor to the Armed Forces Medical Examiner on all close combat related homicides. Mr. Donvito has earned Black Belts in 9 styles of martial arts including a 10th degree Black Belt in his own style of Kobushi Sessen-Jutsu. Mr. Donvito is the founder of the LINE system of close combat training and has been responsible for the training of over 475,000 military personnel in the last 15 years. Currently Ron Donvito is the owner and chief instructor of the Close Combat Institute in Fayetteville, North Carolina, where he is responsible for all entry level close combat training for the U.S. Army Special Forces. www.ccimartialartsacademy.com or www.linecombatives.com.

Mark Dunston

Mark Dunston is a consultant and trainer specializing in research, development and delivery of specialized training, policy and liability reduction needs for law enforcement, military, international and corporate communities. Mr. Dunston is a former chief of police and has been active in the law enforcement and security professions since 1981 serving in various capacities. He has appeared on the Law Enforcement Television Network (LETN), ABC, CBS, and FOX as a content expert on training, management and issues on use of force by police. His is an internationally sought-after expert who has written two books and numerous articles. He has served as a lead instructor for the Calibre Press Street Survival Seminar and is a member and past board member of the American Society for Law Enforcement Training (ASLET).

Kevin Ellis

Kevin Ellis is a police officer currently working within the Firearms Department of the Thames Valley Police in the United Kingdom. He has been involved in all aspects of use of force and control, from conflict resolution to police use of firearms—including public order/riot control. Kevin is an international instructor in PR24, defensive tactics, straight baton/CASCO and Quickuff. He is a master instructor in M26 TASER, and PAVA/OC/CS. He has been intensely involved in research, development and preparation of policy for various elements relating to use of force. Kevin is an independent member of the Expert Witness Institute.

John S. Farnam

John Farnam is one of the top defensive firearms instructors in the nation. He has personally trained thousands of federal, state and local law enforcement agency personnel, many private security agencies, foreign governments, and hundreds of civilians in safe gun handling and the tactical use of the defensive firearms. Mr. Farnam is the author of numerous magazine articles, three books, and several handgun manuals. He has produced numerous training videos and has written a model "Use of Force Policy."

His books, The Farnam Method of Defensive Handgunning and The Farnam Method of Defensive Rifle and Shotgun Shooting are standard texts on the subjects.

After graduating from Cornell College with a B.A. in biology, Mr. Farnam entered the U.S. Marine Corps Officer Candidate Program. After being commissioned a Second Lieutenant, he was sent to Vietnam as an infantry platoon leader. For 51 days he was involved in heavy fighting and was awarded three Purple Hearts. He served the remainder of active duty time in the United States training Marines. During his three years' of active duty he lived in Virginia, California, and Illinois. He now resides in Ft Collins, Colorado. Until his retirement in 1987 as a major, Mr. Farnam remained in the Reserves. His branch was infantry.

John has been a policeman since 1971, when he joined the City of Elroy Police Department as a patrolman. He is presently a fully commissioned deputy sheriff (training officer) for the sheriff's office of Park County, Colorado.

William Gambino

Will Gambino is a long-time martial artist and graduate of numerous military and civilian firearms courses with expertise in scenario-based training combining combat marksmanship and combative skills.

Jacques Gouws

Dr. Jacques Gouws is a clinical psychologist who relocated to Ontario, Canada, from South Africa in 1995. He has two clinics, one in Cambridge and one in Hamilton, Ontario, where psychologists and other mental health professionals provide assessment/treatment of motor vehicle accident and work accident victims, as well as patients suffering from mood and anxiety disorders, including posttraumatic stress disorder (PTSD) and chronic pain disorder.

Dr. Gouws served almost 17 years in the South African Air Force and his master and doctoral degrees' research contributed extensively to the understanding of the stressors to which soldiers are exposed in military service. The clinical assessment and treatment models he developed laid the foundation for other clinicians working in the South African military and law enforcement professions at that time.

Dr. Gouws is the president and CEO of Human and System Interface Consulting, a company providing professional services to industry in areas such as leadership, management functions, personnel development, work transition/change management, and stress management.

Dr. Gouws and three other medical specialists established the Stress and Trauma Research and Education Institute (STREI) a collaborative effort to collect, collate, process and disseminate data from clinical practice in order to identify continuing education and training needs for mental health and health care providers in the assessment, diagnosis and treatment of adult-onset PTSD, in particular as it relates to military service PTSD and stress reactions.

Dr. Gouws is a member of several professional associations and holds military merit decorations from South Africa and Portugal, the latter where he had served as Assistant Military, Air and Naval attaché. You may learn more about Dr. Gouws and his work at www.humansysteminterface.ca or www.strei.ca.

Linda Speer Graham

Linda Speer Graham, Ed.S., is a nationally-certified school psychologist. She has worked in Northeast Arkansas schools as a teacher, counselor and school psychology specialist. Linda served as crisis counseling center coordinator in the aftermath of the 1998 Westside Middle School shooting which left four students and a teacher dead and ten others wounded. After the 2001 World Trade Center terrorist attacks, Linda worked with victims and family members at the New York and New Jersey Family Assistance Center. She has received advanced crisis response training through the National Organization for Victim Assistance (NOVA) and is a certified crisis responder. As a member of the Craighead County and Arkansas Crisis Response Teams, Linda has worked with law enforcement officers and other first responders as well as families, children and community members who have been impacted by crisis situations. She is a member of the Local Emergency Planning Committee, Citizens Corps Council and is coordinator of the Craighead County Crisis Response Team. Over the last five years, Linda has worked with school districts in developing crisis response plans. Linda and her husband Dennis reside in Jonesboro, Arkansas.

Bernie Homme

Bernie Homme served 17 years as a police officer in Southern California working his way through the ranks and retiring as a chief of police. For 15 years, he worked as a law enforcement consultant for the California Commission on Peace Officer Standards and Training (POST) where he served as the POST consultant for the Los Angeles Police Department and LASO. Currently he coordinates training courses for Professional Public Safety Seminars (P2S2).

Jordan Hughes

Jordan Hughes is currently assigned as the Assistant Chief of Staff, U.S. Army Special Forces Command, Fort Bragg, North Carolina. He has been on active duty in this position since 1 March 2002. The command consists of five active and two reserve component Special Forces groups, just short of 10,000 soldiers, with a global responsibility in all of the primary Special Forces missions.

Colonel Hughes has served as the Commander, 19th Special Forces Group, with headquarters in Salt Lake City, Utah. Jordan was assigned to the 19th Group for 27 years, and worked in all areas of administration and logistics, plus operations and training. Jordan has traveled and served throughout many parts of Asia, plus assignments in Germany and Bosnia.

Jordan is a 25-year veteran with the Salt Lake City Police Department. Assignments there have included uniformed field operations, detectives, training, and planning and research. He is on military leave while completing his current duties at Fort Bragg because of 9/11.

Jordan was born and raised in Salt Lake City, Utah, where he graduated from the University of Utah. He is married to the former Darlene Wagstaff and they have seven children.

Totti "Mike" Karpela

Totti Karpela has been a law enforcement professional for 17 years and is currently a sergeant and shift supervisor for the National Police of Finland. Mike is the founder of the Helsinki Police Department's Threat Management Services and Training Unit and is a hostage negotiator. He teaches conflict management at the police academy. He is an instructor/trainer in defensive tactics and firearms, holds a black belt in jujitsu and is a certified instructor in krav maga. During his years of service on the streets as a tactical officer Mike has gathered experience from over 30,000 violent encounters.

As a nationally recognized expert in Finland in work place violence prevention, threat management and violent behavior, Mike has authored four books on the subject. Mike is the regional representative in Europe for two American training companies. www.verbaljudoeurope.com and www.mielenrauha.com.

Gary Klugiewicz

Gary T. Klugiewicz is the Director of Training for the Tactical Training Division at Fox Valley Technical College in Appleton, Wisconsin. In this capacity, he supervises a national tactical training initiative. Mr. Klugiewicz retired from the Milwaukee County Sheriff's Department as a captain after 25 years' of service. He has a martial arts background and championships in knockdown karate. Mr. Klugiewicz was a Street Survival Seminar instructor and is a nationally known defensive tactics instructor. Gary is the developer of the Active Countermeasures System of Unarmed Blocking and Striking Techniques that is the cornerstone of High Level Control Tactics. Gary's team tactics training for special weapons and tactics (SWAT), Correctional Emergency Response Team (CERT®), and crowd management teams are among the best in the world. His instructor training programs stress adult learning, sub-skill development, guided discovery, decision making simulation scenarios, and positive group debriefing techniques. More importantly, as a righteous police use-of-force defense expert, Gary has defended scores of officers in legal proceedings. www.fvtcttd.com.

Lynne McClure

Lynn McClure, Ph.D., is nationally recognized as a leading expert in managing high-risk behavior before it escalates to violence.

Consultant and author, Dr. McClure's most recent books are *Angry Men: Managing Anger in an Unforgiving World* and *Angry Women: Stop Letting Anger Control Your Life!* Dr. McClure also wrote two books used extensively by corporations—*Risky Business: Managing Employee Violence in the Workplace* which *EAP Digest* called "the best book" on violence-prevention—and *Anger & Conflict in the Workplace: Spot the Signs, Avoid the Trauma.* By invitation, Dr. McClure wrote a chapter in the National Mental Health Association's book *Violence in Homes and Communities.*

Popular with the media, Dr. McClure has been featured by CNN *News Stand*, CBS *This Morning*, Fox News Channel's *The O'Reilly Factor* and Y*our*

World, U.S. News & World Report, USA Today, Newsday, the *Los Angeles Times, Fortune, Harvard Management Update, Risk Management,* and other prominent media. www.McClureAssociates.com.

George H. "Hal" McNair

Lieutenant Colonel George H. "Hal" McNair, U.S. Army (ret.), has more than 18 years of increasing experience and responsibility in special operations forces (SOF). Since joining the Joint Special Operations University (JSOU), he has served as the primary instructor in all matters related to Special Operations Command and Control. He lectures in numerous courses and with the mobile education team preparing SOF for deployment. He is also the JSOU representative to USSOCOM for joint doctrine review. Colonel McNair's Army service included assignments as the Deputy J3 Special Operations Command Atlantic, responsible for conceptualizing, coordinating and conducting SO training exercises in multiple sites within the eastern United States; Senior Military Advisor, CARICOM Battalion, directed over 300 personnel from eight nations in providing humanitarian and security assistance for the Haitian government during its return to democratic rule by guiding the daily interaction of this multi-national task force with leaders from the Haitian government, Department of State, U.S. Military, and Caribbean political leaders. Colonel McNair commanded a Special Forces Operational Detachment 'A,' a Special Forces Company and was a Special Forces Battalion Executive Officer and S3.

Ken Murray

Ken Murray is the Director of Training for the Armiger Police Training Institute. He is the co-founder of Simunition and the developer of the original Simunition Instructor Training Program. He has been active in law enforcement and military training since 1985. He has lectured nationally and internationally as well as written numerous articles on officer survival and reality based training. He is the co-author with Lieutenant Colonel Dave Grossman of the "Behavioral Psychology" entry in the *Encyclopedia of Violence, Peace and Conflict* and author of the book *Training At The Speed Of Life*, a training manual for reality based training. www.armiger.net.

Ed Nowicki

Ed Nowicki is the Executive Director of the prestigious International Law Enforcement Educators and Trainers Association (ILEETA). He is a nationally known law enforcement trainer having received the "Award of Excellence in Law Enforcement Training for Individual Achievement" from the U.S. Treasury and personally presented by Secretary Lloyd Bentsen. In 1998, he received the "Integrity Pioneer Award" from the National Institute of Ethics. Mr. Nowicki has been a sworn law enforcement officer since 1968 and presently serves as a part-time officer for the Police Department of Twin Lakes, Wisconsin. He began his law enforcement career with the Chicago Police Department and has held the ranks of patrolman, detective, lieutenant, and chief of police with four law enforcement agencies. Mr. Nowicki recently retired as a Police Training Specialist with Milwaukee Area Technical College, but continues to train officers across the nation in various use of force topics. The U.S. Marine Corps and the U.S. Navy have utilized his expertise in Europe and he has trained police constabulary instructors from England, Scotland and Wales.

Mr. Nowicki is a survivor of many lethal encounters, is recognized as an expert witness on police training, standards and procedures, OC spray, self-defense and the use of force, and is in national demand as a speaker and presenter. Nowicki compiled and edited the highly acclaimed law enforcement training texts, "Total Survival and Supervisory Survival." He is a widely published author and is on the advisory board for *Police* and *The Police Marksman* magazines and writes a monthly "training" column for *Law and Order* magazine. Nowicki is a former municipal judge and holds a bachelor of science degree in Criminal Justice and a master of arts degree in management. He is the co-developer of the nationally known OCAT (Oleoresin Capsicum Aerosol Training) Program. www.ileeta.org.

Steel Parsons

Chief Warrant Officer Five (CW5) Steel Parsons is an active duty U.S. Army Aviator who has more than 6,200 hours of rotary wing flight time with 3,000 of those hours using night vision goggles (NVGs). He holds a commercial pilot (instrument) certification for rotor craft and single engine/multi-engine fixed wing aircraft. He is assigned to D Company, 1st Battalion, 160th Special Operations Aviation Regiment (Airborne). He has held various jobs ranging from assault pilot to Flight Lead to Regiment Standardization Instructor Pilot. He was awarded the U.S. Army Aviation Association of America Trainer of the Year in 1999.

Parsons flew combat operations in the Persian Gulf area in 1987, 1988, 1989. He participated in Operation Just Cause, Operation Desert Shield, Operation Desert Storm, Operation Uphold Democracy, Operation Enduring Freedom and Operation Iraqi Freedom. He has 27 years' of active duty service and 26 years as a rated Army Aviator. He has associate and bachelor degrees in professional aeronautical studies from Embry Riddle Aeronautical University and a master of science degree in management of technology from Murray State University.

Mr. Parsons is a PPCT/Warrior Science Group Staff Instructor since 1988. He trained various law enforcement organizations in defensive tactics including the Drug Enforcement Agency (DEA) agents who participated in Operation Snow Cap.

Chris Pascoe

Sergeant Chris Pascoe started his career with the Michigan State Police in 1986. He trooped at three different posts before being assigned to the Training Division in Lansing. His current mission is running supervisor and leadership development programs, as well as publishing the training bulletin known as *Tuebor* (Latin for "We Will Protect'). Sergeant Pascoe is also a veteran of the United States Coast Guard Reserve. *Tuebor* and other law enforcement materials can be found at www.michigan.gov.

John M. Peterson

John Peterson is a firearms and tactics instructor and former member of the U.S. Army Special Forces. Mr. Peterson was called to active duty during the Global War on Terrorism and has completed a tour of duty in Operation Enduring Freedom as a U.S. Army Special Forces Weapons Sergeant assigned to a Special Forces "A" team.

Mr. Peterson is Director of the Personal Security Institute where he teaches concealed carry pistol and carbine/rifle. He serves as an adjunct/contract instructor for two training companies to include being a patrol rifle instructor/trainer and sniper/observer instructor for the Centermass Training Institute (www.centermassinc.com). He is the former Senior Instructor of the SigArms Academy and he has served on the staff of the Smith & Wesson Academy.

Mr. Peterson sits on the advisory boards of many profession-related organizations and is on the executive board of the American Sniper Association (www.americansniper.org). He is also a member or life-time member of many profession-related organizations.

Chris Pollack

Chris Pollack served 29 years and 27 days as a police officer, supervisor and firearms instructor with the Police Department of Phoenix, Arizona. The author of numerous articles on police firearms and training, he is currently a contributing editor for *Law & Order* magazine and was elected to membership in the Outdoor Writers Association of America. He served 15 years on the Board of Directors and remains a member of the International Association of Law Enforcement Firearms Instructors (IALEFI). Since retirement, he has continued to serve as a reserve police officer and now works as a writer and consultant on law enforcement training and firearms. He has a bachelor of arts degree in journalism from Arizona State University and a masters of education from Northern Arizona University.

O. Frank Repass

O. Frank Repass is a nationally recognized and court-certified firearms expert. Mr. Repass served as the Orlando Police Department's range master and as a member of the special weapons and tactic (SWAT) team for 21 years. He was selected the Fraternal Order of Police's 1999 Officer of the year. During his time on the SWAT team he was involved in more than 500 operations. He retired from active duty after 25 years' of distinguished service and currently teaches local, state and federal law enforcement in the areas of firearms operations, tactical firearms and SWAT. He has been a member of the International Association of Law Enforcement Firearms Instructors (IALEFI) since 1984 and he has served on the board of directors since 1986. Frank is the first vice-president of IALEFI and is chairman of the ATC program. Mr. Repass serves as a sport director of the Florida Law Enforcement Games (FLEG) and he coordinates FLEG's practical handgun, practical shotgun and three-gun match. He is director of training for the Streamlight Academy.

David Rose

David Rose is currently a lieutenant with the Sheriff's Department of Placer County, California. He has been with the department since 1978. He is the department's lead physical skills instructor and SWAT commander. Lieutenant Rose has co-authored with Sergeant Rocky Warren numerous articles for various law enforcement periodicals. In affiliation with Don Cameron, they updated the *Weaponless Defense Instructor* written manual and the *Impact Weapons Instructor* written manual.

Lieutenant Rose has been training in martial arts since the age of 10 and was instrumental in the development of the law enforcement martial art, USA Aiki Jujitsu. He has received numerous awards, medals and honors for his distinguished service to community and country.

Bruce Siddle

Bruce Siddle is a 30 year (plus) law enforcement veteran with a background which specializes in use of force training. He is the founder of PPCT Management Systems, Inc., a research-based use of force training organization.

Mr. Siddle began his career as a police officer in 1977 in Southern Illinois. In 1984 he left the Monroe County Sheriff's Department as a patrol sergeant and a tactical team leader to become the Special Programs Coordinator for the Greater St. Louis Police Academy. In 1987 he left the academy to manage PPCT Management Systems, Inc. full time.

Mr. Siddle has been an active consultant for hundreds of criminal justice agencies, including the U.S. Department of Navy, U.S. Department of Army, U.S. Air Force, U.S. Department of State, U.S. Department of Defense, the FBI's Hostage Rescue Unit, 22nd SAS, a large number of U. S. military special operation/warfare units, the Queen of England's personal protection unit (Royal Protection Group), and as a contract instructor to the intelligence community from 1988 to the spring of 2000. He has provided multiple training contracts to the Hong Kong government.

Currently, Mr. Siddle is a Senior Partner in Warrior Science Group with Col. Dave Grossmann and Dr. Steve Stahle. He is also a Senior Partner in Detonics Defense Technologies, LLC.

Michael L. Sparks

Mike Sparks is a co-author with General David L. Grange of the book *Air-Mech-Strike: Asymmetric Maneuver Warfare for the 21st Century.* He leads a non-profit think-tank, the 1st Tactical Studies Group (Airborne) originally based out of Fort Bragg, North Carolina, that has field-tested and proven equipment, offering them for no charge to the U.S. Army www.combatreform.com. He has been involved in amphibious infantry, combat engineer, logistics, airborne civil affairs, airborne combat camera, Special Forces, and mechanized infantry units throughout his 23-year career. A prior service marine NCO and officer, his numerous articles on military excellence have been published in *U.S. Army Infantry, Armor, Air Defense Artillery Online, Special Warfare, Army Logistician,* the *Rucksack, Armed Forces Journal International, National Guard, Marine Corps Gazette, Behind the Lines, U.S. Naval Institute Proceedings, Behind the Lines, Soldier of Fortune, Mountain Bike, Fort Bragg POST, Fort Benning Bayonet, PS Magazine and Military Review.*

Rocky Warren

Rocky Warren retired as a police sergeant after 28 years in the law enforcement profession. During his career he received two Bronze Medals of Valor for Police Service. He is a U.S. Army veteran, former SWAT officer and an active use-of-force instructor. Rocky is on staff for two community college districts and works as a consultant and expert witness on use-of-force issues. He wrote *Behind the Badge,* and has co-written with Dave Rose "Police Use of Force Case Law," and the soon to be released *Paradigm of the Moral Warrior.* He has authored numerous training and tactical articles for law enforcement trade publications. www.rockywarren.com.

Steven R. (Randy) Watt

Assistant Chief Steven R. (Randy) Watt is a 23-year veteran of the Police Department of Ogden, Utah, currently assigned as the Commander of the Uniform Division. He is a nationally recognized expert in the field of law enforcement special operations and use of force and has taught hostage rescue tactics and techniques to foreign military and police units. Chief Watt is a major in the Utah Army National Guard's 19th Special Forces Group with 21 years' of experience. As a result of the 9/11 terrorist attack, he was activated as part of a combined task force sent to Afghanistan to locate and destroy Al Qaida terrorists and conducted operations directly against enemy forces.

"Major Randy" who was featured in the ABC special, "Profiles from the Front Line," has received the Medal of Valor, Medal of Merit and numerous commendations and medals for his service with the Ogden Police Department and the Bronze Star Medal with "V" device for valor in direct engagement with the enemy, the Bronze Star Medal for Meritorious Service in Combat, and numerous other honors for his service to country. He holds an MBA from the University of Phoenix and a B.Sc. degree from Weber State University and is a graduate of Session 191 of the FBI National Academy.

Aaron J. Westrick

Dr. Aaron J. Westrick earned a bachelor of arts degree in social science and criminal justice from Michigan State University, masters of science degree in criminal justice and a doctorate of philosophy degree in sociology (studying police shootings) from Wayne State University. Dr. Westrick has 21 years' of law enforcement experience in various areas, i.e., assault team member, hostage negotiator, and detective. Early in his career Aaron became a "save" when his vest/ armor stopped a .357 mag. bullet over his heart, fired by a paroled robber.

Currently, Dr. Westrick is a director of research, a law enforcement consultant, and a deputy sheriff in Michigan. He is an adjunct faculty member at Lake Superior State University and North Central Michigan College and has taught at numerous universities, colleges, police academies and organizations such as the ASLET/ IACP. Dr. Westrick is widely recognized by officers as an advocate for police causes/rights creating the study of "police phenomenology." He is a highly decorated police officer. Dr. Westrick teaches seminars regarding crisis management and intervention. He has published numerous articles regarding police action and body armor applications and is a columnist for recognized police/correction journals and serves as an expert witness. www.westrickphd.com.

Paul Whitesell

Paul Whitesell, Ph.D., is presently a police psychotherapist. He has been a police officer for some 30 years with distinguished service at the local, county, and state level. He is a long standing police and military trainer and serves as a staff instructor for H & K, Thunder Ranch, and PPCT/Warrior Science Group. Dr. Whitesell is a high ranking martial artist and he was inducted into the Black

Belt Hall of Fame in 2002. Whitesell is a Vietnam veteran with enlisted service in the U.S. Marine Corps and he was an armor officer in the U.S. Army.

Duane Wolfe

Duane Wolfe has served as a law enforcement officer since 1988 in the capacities of patrolman, sergeant, firearms instructor, defensive tactics instructor, special response team (SRT) leader-member and trainer. As a martial artist with almost 30 years' experience, he holds a 6th degree black belt in Matsumura Kenpo karate and is regional director for the Shorin Ryu Matsumura Kenpo Karate and Kobudo Association.

Since 1994, Mr. Wolfe has been an instructor at Alexandria Technical College in the Law Enforcement Program, teaching courses in firearms, officer survival, and patrol response tactics. He holds a B.S. degree in criminal justice from Bemidji State University with minors in psychology and sociology, and an M.S. degree in education from Southwest State University in Minnesota. Dr. Wolfe's research projects on officer safety and the effects of stress on firearms performance have been published by Calibre Press and the International Association of Law Enforcement Firearm Instructor's magazine. He also serves as the editor of the Minnesota Association of Law Enforcement Firearms Instructors Association quarterly publication.

And finally I must recognize Sandy Siddle and Tracy Donnelly at PPCT/Warrior Science Group, who is the Operations Manager for the Siddles; my wonderful wife, Jeanne; my operations assistant, Chris McCorkle; my research assistant, Aubrey Grossman; and *special* thanks to my extraordinarily competent administrative assistant, Susan Tacker.

To *all* these dear friends and all the others who helped, I say, "Thank you."

Think where man's glory most begins and ends
And say my glory was I had such friends.

Yeats

Bibliography

Book

Acosta, J., and J. Prager. 2002. *The worst is over: what to say when every moment counts.* San Diego: Jodere.

American Psychiatric Association. 2000. *Diagnostic and Statistical Manual of Mental Disorders,* 4th Ed., Text Rev. Washington, D.C.

Allen, T. 1995. *Offerings at the wall: artifacts from the Vietnam Veterans Memorial collection.* Turner Publishing.

Ardant du Picq, C. 1946. *Battle studies.* Harrisburg, PA: Telegraph Press.

Artwohl, A., and L. Christensen. 1997. *Deadly force encounters: what cops need to know to mentally and physically prepare for and survive a gunfight.* Boulder: Paladin Press.

de Becker, G. (2002). *Fear less: real truth about risk, safety and security in a time of terrorism.* Boston: Little, Brown.

de Becker, G. (1997). *The gift of fear: and other survival signals that protect us from violence.* New York: Dell.

Burkett, B.G. 1998. *Stolen valor: how the Vietnam generation was robbed of its heroes and its history.* Verity Press.

Christensen, L. 2002. *Crazy crooks.* Adventure Book Publishers.

Christensen, L. 1998. *Far beyond defensive tactics: advanced concepts, techniques, drills and tricks for cops on the street.* Boulder: Paladin Press.

Christensen, L. 1999. *The mental edge.* Revised. Desert Publications.

Clagett, R. 2003. *After the echo.* Varro Press.

Clausewitz, C. M. von. 1976. *On war.* Ed. 2nd trans. M. Howard and P. Paret. Princeton, NJ: Princeton University Press.

Dolan, J. P. 1964. *The essential Erasmus: intellectual titan of the renaissance.* Dutton/Plume.

Dyer, G. 1985. *War.* Crown Publishers.

Gabriel, R. A. 1988. *No more heroes: madness and psychiatry in war.* New York: Hill and Wang.

Gilmartin, K. 2002. *Emotional survival for law enforcement: A guide for officers and their families.* E-S Press.

Gray, J. G. 1977. *The warriors: reflections of men in battle.* Harper-Collins.

Griffith, P. 1989. *Battle tactics of the civil war.* New Haven, CT: Yale University Press.

Griffith, P. 1990. *Forward into battle.* Presidio Press.

Grossman, D. 1996. *On killing: the psychological cost of learning to kill in war and society.* Little, Brown.

Grossman, D., and DeGaetano, G. 1999. *Stop teaching our kids to kill: a call to action against television, movie and video game violence.* Crown Books.

Grossman, D., and Frankowski, L. 2004. *The two-space war.* Baen Books.

Holmes, R. 1985. *Acts of war: the behavior of men in battle.* The Free Press.

Keegan, J. 1994. *A history of warfare.* Knopf.

Keegan, J. 1997. *Fields of battle.* New York: First Vintage Books.

Keegan, J. 1976. *The face of battle.* Chaucer Press.

Keegan, J., and R. Holmes. 1985. *Soldiers.* Guild Publishing.

Kelly, C.E., and P. Martin. 1944. *One man's war.* Knopf.

Kosslyn, S., and O. Koenig. 1995. *Wet mind: new cognitive neuroscience.* Free Press.

Klinger, D. 2004. *Into the kill zone: a cop's eye view of deadly force.* San Francisco: Josey-Bass.

Marshal, S.L.A. 1978. *Men against fire: the problem of battle command in future war.* Gloucester, MA: Peter Smith.

McDonough, J.R. 1985. *Platoon leader.* Novato, CA: Presidio Press.

Medved, M. 1993. *Hollywood vs. America.* Perennial.

Murray, K. In development. *Training at the speed of life.*

Pressfield, S. 1999. *Gates of fire.* New York: Bantam.

Remsberg, C. 1985. *The tactical edge: surviving high-risk patrol.* Calibre Press

Shay, J. 1995. *Achilles in Vietnam: combat trauma and the undoing of character.* Touchstone Books

Shephard, B. 2001. *A war of nerves: soldiers and psychiatrists in the twentieth century.* Cambridge, MA: Harvard University Press.

Siddle, B. 1996. *Sharpening the warrior's edge.* Millstadt, IL:
      Warrior Science Publications.

Siddle, B. In development. *Warrior science.* Millstadt, IL:
      Warrior Science Publications.

Spick, M. 1998. *The ace factor: air combat and the role of situational
      awareness.* United States Naval Institution.

Strauss, W., and N. Howe. 1998. *The fourth turning: an American prophecy.*
      Broadway Books.

Stouffer, S. 1949. *The American soldier: combat and its aftermath.* Princeton
      University Press.

Tarani, S., & D. Fay. 2004. *Contact weapons: lethality and defense.*
      Wolfe Pub Co.

Vila, B. 2000. *Tired cops: the importance of managing police fatigue.*
      Police Executive Research Forum.

Watson, P. 1978. *War on the mind: the military uses and abuses of psychology.*
      Basic Books.

Wavell, A.P. 1986. *Other men's flowers: an anthology of poetry compiled
      by A. P. Wavell.* London: Jonathan Cape, Ltd.

Woodward, B. 2002. *Bush at war.* Simon and Schuster.

Yeager, C. 1986. *Yeager, an autobiography.* Bantam Books.

Book Chapters

Davis, R. C., & L. N. Friedman. 1985. The emotional aftermath of crime and
      violence. C. R. Figley. ed. *Trauma and its wake: the study and treatment
      of posttraumatic stress disorder.* New York: Brunner/Mazel, Inc.

Grossman, D. 2000. Evolution of weaponry. *Encyclopedia of Violence,
      Peace and Conflict.* Academic Press

Grossman, D., and B.K. Siddle. 2000. Psychological effects of combat.
      Encyclopedia of Violence, Peace and Conflict. Academic Press.

Articles

Artwohl, A. Oct. 2002. Perceptual and memory distortions in officer involved
     shootings. *FBI Law Enforcement Bulletin.* Washington, D.C.:
     Federal Bureau of Investigation.
Dreher, R. March 10, 2003. Ministers of war: the amazing chaplaincy of the
     U.S. military. *National Review.*
Gouws, J. October 11, 2000. Combat stress inoculation, PTSD recognition,
     and early intervention. Operational Trauma & Stress Support Center
     (Western Area).
Grossman, D., and B. K. Siddle. Aug. 2001. Critical incident amnesia: the
     physiological basis and implications of memory loss during extreme
     survival situations. *The Firearms Instructor: The Official Journal of the
     International Association of Law Enforcement Firearms Instructors.*
Kolata, G. March 30, 2003. New battlefield techniques. *New York Times.*
Lyons, P. July 1998. Think fast! *Popular Science.*
Maass, P. January 11, 2004. Professor Nagl's war. *New York Times Magazine.*
Owens, C.H. Winter 1999. Uncle Joe. *Southern Humanities Review.*
Pashley, G. July 2003. Huffy: cop, friend and hero. *The Rap Sheet.*
Phillips. M.M. April 11, 2003. Life flowed right out. *Wall Street Journal.*
Siddle, B.K. 1999. The impact of the sympathetic nervous system on use of
     force investigations. *Research Abstract.*
Weddle, D. July 22, 2001. Secrets at the bottom of the drawer.
     Los Angeles Times.

Poems

"A Purple Heart for You," used with the kind permission of the author,
     Fred Grossman.
"The Thin Blue Line," used with the kind permission of the author,
     Joseph "Lil Joe" Ferrera.
"The Freedom Of A Soldier," used with the kind permission of the author,
     James Adam Holland.

Web sites

Hackworth, D. May 22, 2002. Where do we find such remarkable
    men? http://sftt.org/dw05222002.html.
Hane, T. 9th Infantry Division - Riverine. Retrieved September
    19, 2003 from: www.grunt.space.swri.edu/tjhain.htm.
    Permission granted by his wife Alice.
Veith, G.E. Sentimentality has replaced both martial virtues and clear thinking.
    Archived Nov. 29, 2003. Vol. 18, Number 46. Worldmag.com

Videos

Avery, R. Secrets of a professional shooter. www.praticalshootingacad.com.
Phillips, J. 1988. Surviving edged weapons. Calibre Press.

The authors are grateful for permission from Virginia Kelly Newland, as representative of the heirs of Charles "Commando" Kelly, to include material from One Man's War.

Index

Author Biographies

Lt. Col. Dave Grossman
U.S. Army (Ret.)
Director, Warrior Science Group
(870) 931-5172 (voice)/3077 (fax)
www.warriorscience.com

Lieutenant Colonel Dave Grossman is an internationally recognized scholar, author, soldier, and speaker who is one of the world's foremost experts in the field of human aggression and the roots of violence and violent crime.

Colonel Grossman is a West Point psychology professor, Professor of Military Science, and an Army Ranger who has combined his experiences to become the founder of a new field of scientific endeavor, which he has termed "killology." In this new field Colonel Grossman has made revolutionary new contributions to our understanding of killing in war, the psychological costs of war, the root causes of the current "virus" of violent crime that is raging around the world, and the process of healing the victims of violence, in war and peace.

He is the author of *On Killing: The Psychological Cost of Learning to Kill in War and Society*, which was nominated for a Pulitzer Prize and is required reading in classes at West Point, the U.S. Air Force Academy, police academies worldwide, and "peace studies" programs in numerous universities and colleges. *Stop Teaching Our Kids to Kill: A Call to Action Against TV, Movie and Video Game Violence*, co-authored with Gloria DeGaetano, has received international acclaim. Colonel Grossman's book *On Combat: The Psychology and Physiology of Deadly Conflict in War and in Peace*, now in its third edition, is on the USMC Commandant's required reading list and is required reading at the DEA Academy.

Colonel Grossman has been called upon to write the entry on "Aggression and Violence" in the Oxford Companion to American Military History, three entries in the Academic Press Encyclopedia of Violence, Peace and Conflict and numerous entries in scholarly journals, to include the *Harvard Journal of Law and Public Policy*.

He has presented papers before the national conventions of the American Medical Association, the American Psychiatric Association, the American Psychological Association, and the American Academy of Pediatrics.

He has presented to over 40 different colleges and universities world-wide.

He has served as an expert witness and consultant in state and Federal courts, to include United States vs. Timothy McVeigh.

He helped train mental health professionals after the Jonesboro school shootings, and he was also involved in counseling, training, or court cases in the aftermath of the school shootings at Paducah, Springfield, Littleton, Nickel Mines Amish School, and Virginia Tech.

He has testified before U.S. Senate and Congressional committees and numerous state legislatures, and he and his research have been cited in a national address by the President of the United States.

Col. Grossman is an Airborne Ranger infantry officer, and a prior-service sergeant and paratrooper, with a total of over 23 years experience in leading U.S. soldiers worldwide. He retired from the Army in February 1998 and has devoted himself full-time to teaching, writing, speaking, and research. Today he is the director of the Warrior Science Group, and in the wake of the 9/11 terrorist attacks he is on the road almost 300 days a year, training elite military and law enforcement organizations worldwide about the reality of combat.

Loren W. Christensen

Loren W. Christensen is a recognized expert in self-defense, street gangs, white supremacy crimes, police officer survival, and the psychological implications of police-involved deadly force encounters.

Christensen retired from the Portland (Oregon) Police Bureau in 1997 after 29 years in law enforcement, which includes three years in the U.S. Army military police with service in Vietnam.

He has testified in state and federal court cases as an expert on police use of physical force and deadly force.

Christensen has authored 40 books, dozens of articles, edited a police newspaper for seven years, and starred in six instructional martial arts DVDs. In 1997, he co-wrote *Deadly Force Encounters: What Cops Need to Know to Mentally and Physically Prepare for and Survive a Gunfight*. The co-author of that book, Dr. Alexis Artwohl, is a recognized police psychologist specializing in posttraumatic stress disorder. Most recently, he wrote *Warriors: On Living With Courage, Discipline and Honor*, published by Paladin Press, and coauthored *Warrior Mindset* with Dr. Mike Asken and Lt. Col. Dave Grossman, published by Warrior Science Group.

Christensen brings to *On Combat* an insider's knowledge of the nature of police work, the police mind-set, the experience of having been in three police-involved shootings, the experience of serving in the army and in Vietnam, and an ability to write in a manner that is highly readable.

Loren W. Christensen can be contacted through his site LWC Books www.lwcbooks.com